Richardson and Clark: Sexual Offences

A Practitioner's Guide

To Mary and Ruth

Richardson and Clark: Sexual Offences

A Practitioner's Guide

Nigel Richardson
Partner, Hodge, Jones & Allen

Peter Clark
Barrister, 187 Fleet Street

Bloomsbury Professional

Bloomsbury Professional Ltd, Maxwelton House, 41–43 Boltro Road, Haywards Heath, West Sussex, RH16 1BJ

Bloomsbury Professional, an imprint of Bloomsbury Publishing Plc

A CIP Catalogue record for this book is available from the British Library.

ISBN: 978 1 78043 327 1

Typeset by Phoenix Photosetting, Chatham, Kent

Foreword

It is perhaps stating the obvious to say that serious sexual offences form a substantial portion of the workloads of the courts. In the Crown Court centre in which I sit, it is not unusual for three of the five courts to be trying sex cases. The legal system has recognised that such cases are in a category of their own. Judges are trained to try such cases and to deal with vulnerable witnesses. The Crown Prosecution Service have a rape panel and will only instruct advocates from it. Steps are being considered to have accreditation for defence lawyers in such cases.

It is absolutely right that such steps are taken. History has shown that vulnerable complainants have been let down in the past. Those who have the courage to complain of sexual abuse upon them are entitled to know that they will be treated sympathetically, but more, that when their case comes into the hands of the lawyers it will be dealt with competently; it will be dealt with by lawyers who don't simply know the law but know how to deal with cases, how to achieve best evidence, how to deal with disclosure, how to handle case presentation and how to cross-examine defendants.

Complainants are vulnerable and need to be handled with care, but they are not the only ones. In sexual offences often the defendant is equally vulnerable. Of course, for some defendants, when the knock on the door comes, it is what has been expected for some time, but that is far from typical. Often a defendant accused of a sexual offence is in contact with the criminal justice system because, in their mind, they have misread what has occurred in a sexual situation or because they have been caught up in an historic enquiry into institutional abuse.

It is often said to juries that it is understandable and appropriate to have sympathy for victims of sexual abuse and it is equally understandable and appropriate to have sympathy for those who are wrongly accused of sexual abuse, and the task of the jury, putting emotion to one side, is to determine the facts so that we might see where their sympathy should lie. How they fully and properly assess those facts depends upon the skills of the practitioners before them, both prosecution and defence.

It is not easy to do sex cases well. A good practitioner realises the particular skill sets required and develops them. A good practitioner makes proper use of the tools at their disposal. Those tools include the various books written on the subject, and there are some very good books around.

This book, combining the skills of a very experienced solicitor in this field, and a barrister who specialises in this work, is an important addition to the library. It deliberately sets out, as the title suggests, to be a practitioner's guide, and a practitioner's guide from a very early stage, whether instructed on behalf of the Crown or the defence. A prosecutor using this book will be guided from the earliest stages of case preparation through the drafting of the indictment to the trial and sentencing process. The defence team obtain guidance from the point of the first telephone call from a distressed accused in a police station to their trial and potential acquittal.

The text is straightforward, easy to understand and logically ordered. It is easy to find the relevant point upon which assistance is needed. The guidance from the text is clear. That does not mean that this is in any way a dumbed down recital of law and practice. It is not. Where something is contentious the authors set out the issues, with authority for their propositions. The authors are not afraid to highlight what appear to be unusual consequences of some of the offences contained within the Sexual Offences Act 2003. The end result is a tool which should be available to all practitioners in this field. It should be in every solicitor's library, in the robe bag of every advocate, and I would say, without hesitation, in the judges' library of every Crown Court, and ideally on each judicial bookshelf.

HHJ John Lodge
Resident Judge
Basildon Crown Court

Preface

In August 2012 an email from Nigel reached Peter courtesy of the wi-fi signal in a coffee bar in France. The subject heading was 'modest proposal'. It canvassed working together to produce a sexual offences guide. The aim would be to create a highly practical resource for practitioners. The response to the email was an expression of eager agreement.

Although we warned ourselves that we were undertaking a huge task, the true enormity of it only fully dawned over the following months. Fortunately we had enjoyed relaxing family holidays that summer, because thereafter it was a case of 'all leave cancelled'. We were determined to cover the full breadth of offences, current and 'historic', plus a comprehensive range of associated topics. Eventual release of the new Sentencing Guidelines necessarily added considerably to our task.

Our collaboration was founded on warm professional friendship and the experience of working very closely together on sex cases in recent years. As a team we have drawn on the separate perspectives afforded by our contrasting experience encompassing defence, prosecution, legal education and judicial service. Few individual lawyers will, for example, have given midnight advice at police stations, drafted indictments, cross-examined alleged rapists and passed custodial sentences: collectively we do all these things on a regular basis.

Essentially, we have set out to write the book that we wished we could buy. Indeed, since completing the draft we have found ourselves regularly using it in practice. We hope that colleagues will similarly find it a valuable resource.

Legislation covering all current sexual offences is included, with analysis of the essential legal ingredients of each. All 'historic' offences likely still to be encountered are similarly set out. Before detailing the separate offences, we scrutinise key concepts such as consent and the meaning of 'sexual'.

Later we cover topics including forensic science, computer interrogation and the laws of evidence, including the crucial area of previous sexual history. We discuss the legal and tactical considerations relating to advice at the police station and we offer general case preparation checklists, separately for prosecution and defence.

An individual chapter reviews practical considerations for 'historic' sex cases, including potential abuse of process submissions.

Our colleague Alison Lambert has kindly supplied a chapter on her specialist area, third party disclosure.

In addition to the particular sentencing parameters and guidelines included throughout the substantive offence chapters, a complete section of the book is given over to general sentencing matters.

Material provided in appendix form includes specimen indictments for each indictable offence, plus a draft Sexual Offences Prevention Order.

We express our gratitude for the support and contributions of friends and colleagues, especially the following:

Richard Christie QC momentously introduced us to each other in March 2010 and, a year later, led us in the Court of Appeal, achieving the quashing of convictions in a complex marital rape case.

Alison Lambert, barrister at 187 Fleet Street, contributed the whole of the chapter on third party disclosure. From the same chambers, Marc Brown utilised his computer expertise to help us with chapter 38.

His Honour Judge John Lodge has been throughout a highly-valued sounding board and provides the generous Foreword to the book.

Gregory Dearman BSc, MSc, MIBMS, a biomedical scientist at Southend University Hospital, aided our exposition of DNA evidence.

Law student Rebecca Christie undertook extensive legal research, as did pupil barristers (as they then were) Charlotte Brewer, Susannah Brooke and Daisy Monahan.

Hanna Llewellyn-Waters of 2 Bedford Row brought to our attention the case of *R v RD* (discussed at **40.14**) in which she appeared.

Paul and Sarah Vella of Evidence Matters assisted extensively with the indecent images sections, as indeed they have in many previous cases.

Samira Noor-Khan, partner at Hodge Jones & Allen, turned her considerable expertise representing suspects at police stations into the basis for chapter 30. From the same firm, Myles Jackman, expert in obscenity law, contributed generously on his specialist subject. Indeed we are grateful to the entire Hodge Jones & Allen criminal team for advice, shared experience and for their patient understanding that book-writing occasionally had to take priority over court attendance.

Finally we thank the friends and family who had far too little of our time during the book's gestation, especially our patient wives, Mary and Ruth, to whom we dedicate our work.

Nigel Richardson
Peter Clark
May 2014

Contents

Part C Other statutory and common law offences

Table of Statutes

[*All references are to paragraph numbers and appendices*]

S

Table of Statutory Instruments

[All references are to paragraph number]

Table of Cases

[*All references are to paragraph number*]

Part A
Concepts

Chapter 1

Consent

INTRODUCTION

1.1 Absence of consent features as an ingredient of a number of sexual offences, current and historic. The Sexual Offences Act 2003 has now provided, for the first time, a statutory definition of consent, along with some statutory presumptions as to consent.

The statutory definition is not expressed to be retrospective. Therefore, in a trial that features only pre-2004 offences, the old direction might appear to be required. What about trials covering old and new non-consensual offences? Does the judge have to give two different directions to cover the respective statutory regimes? We would suggest that such a course would be unhelpful and potentially confusing. Parliament has now defined consent, no doubt in terms considered to be sensible and fair. We would submit that the carefully worded definition is bound to assist a jury seeking to divine the 'ordinary meaning' of consent. Therefore, we suggest at the end of this chapter a form of words that might form the basis for directing the jury in trials including historic (pre-2004) allegations. Before that, we summarise the separate positions, 'old' and 'new'.

CONSENT – SEXUAL OFFENCES ACT 1956

1.2 Consent under the 1956 Act was not defined. In 1981 the Court of Appeal considered in *Olugboja*[1] what judicial assistance should be given to juries. It was observed that consent is a word in common usage, adding:

> 'it covers a wide range of states of mind … ranging from actual desire on the one hand to reluctant acquiescence on the other. We do not think that the issue of consent should be left to a jury without some further direction. What this should be will depend on the circumstances of each case. The jury … should be directed that consent, or the absence of it, is to be given its ordinary meaning and if need be, by way of example, that there is a

1 73 Cr App R 344.

> difference between consent and submission … the dividing line … may not be easy to draw. Where it is to be drawn in a given case is for the jury to decide, applying their combined good sense, experience and knowledge of human nature and modern behaviour to all the relevant facts of that case.'

In 1998, in *R v Malone*,[2] the Court of Appeal clarified that the prosecution does not have to show that the complainant communicated to the defendant the lack of consent.

CONSENT – SEXUAL OFFENCES ACT 2003

1.3 Consent is now defined by the Sexual Offences Act 2003 (SOA 2003), s 74:

> '…a person consents if he agrees by choice and has the freedom and capacity to make that choice.'

In relation to capacity where the complainant may have been affected by drink or drugs, see 'Intoxication' (**4.3**).

Under the 2003 Act, whenever the elements of offence include absence of consent, absence of the defendant's reasonable belief in consent arises too.

These issues should be approached sequentially:

- Did A believe that B was consenting? (factual)
- If so, was such belief reasonable? (objective – jury standard)

In summary, the prosecution have to prove that:

- B did not consent

  [either because there was no 'ostensible' consent or because B did not have the capacity or freedom to choose]

  and either

- A did not believe that B was consenting

  or

- any belief by A that B was consenting was not a reasonable belief.

Presumptions

1.4 The 2003 Act provides for presumptions concerning consent, some conclusive and others rebuttable. These aroused interest when proposed, but in the decade since enactment they have proved quite ineffectual. As the

2 [1998] 2 Cr App R 447, at 457.

Court of Appeal has observed:[3] 'in most cases, the absence of consent, and the appropriate state of the defendant's mind, will be proved without reference to evidential or conclusive presumptions'.

The CPS website realistically advises: 'prosecutors should note that in practice the evidential presumptions very rarely apply'.

Conclusive presumptions

1.5 Section 76 provides two conclusive presumptions that B was not consenting to the activity and A did not believe that B was consenting:

> '(2) The circumstances are that—
>
> (a) the defendant intentionally deceived the complainant as to the nature or purpose of the relevant act;
>
> (b) the defendant intentionally induced the complainant to consent to the relevant act by impersonating a person known personally to the complainant.'

The Court of Appeal upheld the judge's application of the first presumption in *R v Devonald*,[4] a case under SOA 2003, s 4. In order to cause embarrassment to a young man who had slighted his daughter, the defendant tricked him into masturbating to a webcam by posing as a young woman.

In contrast in *R v Jheeta*,[5] where the defendant had constructed an elaborate fictitious scenario to draw the complainant into having sex with him over a long period of time, the Court of Appeal held that the conclusive presumption did not apply because, while there had been abundant deception, there had been no deception as to the nature or purpose of the sexual intercourse:

> 'In our judgment the ambit of s 76 is limited to the "act" to which it is said to apply. In rape cases the "act" is vaginal, anal or oral intercourse … s 76(2)(a) is relevant only to the comparatively rare cases where the defendant deliberately deceives the complainant about the *nature or purpose* of one or other form of intercourse. No conclusive presumptions arise merely because the complainant was deceived in some way or other by disingenuous blandishments of or common or garden lies by the defendant. These may well be deceptive and persuasive, but they will rarely go to the nature or purpose of intercourse.'

---

3 *R v Jheeta* [2007] EWCA Crim 1699, at [23].
4 [2008] EWCA Crim 527.
5 [2007] EWCA Crim 1699.

Rebuttable presumptions

1.6 Section 75 sets out circumstances in which a rebuttable presumption arises in relation to consent, when the defendant is aware of the circumstances and nonetheless does the 'relevant act'. The circumstances are listed in s 75(2):

> 'The circumstances are that—
>
> (a) any person was, at the time of the relevant act or immediately before it began, using violence against the complainant or causing the complainant to fear that immediate violence would be used against him;
>
> (b) any person was, at the time of the relevant act or immediately before it began, causing the complainant to fear that violence was being used, or that immediate violence would be used, against another person;
>
> (c) the complainant was, and the defendant was not, unlawfully detained at the time of the relevant act;
>
> (d) the complainant was asleep or otherwise unconscious at the time of the relevant act;
>
> (e) because of the complainant's physical disability, the complainant would not have been able at the time of the relevant act to communicate to the defendant whether the complainant consented;
>
> (f) any person had administered to or caused to be taken by the complainant, without the complainant's consent, a substance which, having regard to when it was administered or taken, was capable of causing or enabling the complainant to be stupefied or overpowered at the time of the relevant act.'

These presumptions are not conclusive, merely evidential, and are defeated where sufficient evidence is adduced to 'raise an issue'. The question of such sufficiency is one for the judge.

SUGGESTED JUDICIAL DIRECTION FOR CASES INCLUDING NON-CONSENSUAL OFFENCES UNDER SOA 1956:

1.7 There was no definition of consent in the 1956 Sexual Offences Act. The approach taken was that 'consent' was an ordinary word that jurors would understand. So the interpretation of consent was left to you.

When Parliament introduced the 2003 Sexual Offences Act, it took a different approach. It wanted to provide everyone with a clear definition of consent.

The purpose was not to *change* what consent meant, but to make its meaning clearer to everyone.

Parliament defined consent as follows:

> 'a person consents if (s)he agrees by choice and has the freedom and capacity to make that choice.'

So consent means agreement by choice by someone with the freedom and capacity to make that choice.

That is the definition of consent that must be applied to allegations under the 2003 Act.

It is a matter for you, but you may think it appropriate to use that same clear and concise definition when considering consent under the 1956 Act.

It would, you might think, be consistent and helpful to use the same definition (for each count): *a person consents if (s)he agrees by choice and has the freedom and capacity to make that choice.*

There is a difference however when you come to consider the question of belief in consent.

For offences contrary to the 1956 Act, if the defendant honestly believed at the time of the sexual act that the complainant was consenting to it, then the prosecution would have failed to establish a vital ingredient and you would find him not guilty. That would still be so even if you felt that his belief, although genuine, was wholly unreasonable. The reasonableness or otherwise of his belief in the complainant's consent would only be relevant if it helped you to decide the question of whether he did genuinely believe that she was consenting.

For offences contrary to the 2003 Act, there is an important difference. Here, the prosecution must prove that the complainant did not consent and that the defendant did not *reasonably* believe at the time that she was consenting. So the question has three parts:

(1) Are we sure that the complainant did not consent? If no – not guilty, if yes:

(2) May the defendant have believed that she was consenting? If no – guilty, if yes:

(3) Was any such belief by the defendant reasonable? If you are sure that it was not reasonable – guilty, but if you are not sure – not guilty.

Chapter 2

Sexual

Sexual Offences Act 2003, s 78

INTRODUCTION

2.1 The adjective 'sexual' occurs throughout the 2003 Act and is a crucial concept for many of the offences created under it. Older offences did not rely on this concept. Of course, the word sexual contributed to the important phrase 'sexual intercourse', but there it formed part of a convenient label, rather than denoting a separate ingredient of offence: sexual intercourse was penetration of the vagina (and latterly the anus) with the penis, it could not fail to be sexual in nature.

For pre-2004 offences the corresponding concept was indecency, as can be seen by comparing the 'new' sexual assault to the 'old' indecent assault:

- Sexual Offences Act 1956, s 14(1):

  'It is an offence…for a person to make an *indecent* assault on a woman.'[1]

- Sexual Offences Act 2003, s 3(1):

  A person (A) commits an offence if—

  (a) he intentionally touches another person (B),

  (b) the touching is *sexual*

The 2003 Act provides a statutory definition of 'sexual' which mirrors the interpretation of indecency under the previous legislation.[2]

DEFINITION

2.2 Section 78 of the 2003 Act:

---

1 Section 15, in like terms, covered indecent assault on a man.

2 See *R v* Court [1989] AC 28, HL.

'For the purposes of this Part[3] (except section 71[4]), penetration, touching or any other activity is sexual if a reasonable person would consider that—

(a) whatever its circumstances or any person's purpose in relation to it, it is because of its nature sexual, or

(b) because of its nature it may be sexual and because of its circumstances or the purpose of any person in relation to it (or both) it is sexual.'

DISCUSSION

2.3 The s 78 definition presents a staged test. The use of the words 'reasonable person' clearly indicates the objective nature of these considerations. In a Crown Court trial, these will be questions for the jury, unless the judge withdraws the count from them on the basis that no jury properly directed could answer the staged questions against the defendant.

- s 78(a)

  The first limb requires the tribunal to consider the touching, penetration or other activity *of itself*, and decide whether it is sexual by its very nature. The intention or purpose of 'any person' – normally the defendant – is irrelevant to this consideration. This limb is satisfied where the behaviour alleged is unambiguously sexual. By way of example, the Explanatory Notes to the Act suggest 'where the activity is, for example, oral sex, it seems likely that the reasonable person would only need to consider the nature of the activity to determine that it is sexual'.

- s 78(b)

  If the s 78(a) test is not made out, consideration moves on to the second limb, which itself presents a two-staged test[5]:

  – would a reasonable person consider[6] that the penetration, touching or other activity *might* be sexual? If yes,

  – would a reasonable person consider that the circumstances or the purpose of any person (usually the defendant) in relation to it – or both – render(s) the behaviour sexual?

  In *R v H (Karl Anthony)* the appellant had approached the complainant late at night and asked 'do you fancy a shag?' before grabbing the side

---

3 Part One of the SOA 2003, comprising ss 1 to 79.

4 Section 71, dealing with sexual activity in a public lavatory, has its own specific definition of 'sexual' – see 20.45.

5 *R v H (Karl Anthony)* [2005] EWCA Crim 732, [2005] 2 Cr App R 9.

6 For a jury, the question can be phrased '*would you, as reasonable people, consider …*'.

of her tracksuit bottoms.[7] The trial judge had erred in not directing the jury properly in relation to the two-stage s 78(b) test for 'sexual', instead taking matters as a whole, so that there was no discrete initial step of asking whether the touching, in isolation from its attendant circumstances, *may* be sexual. Although emphasising that the judge's approach had been inappropriate, the Court dismissed the appeal on the basis that the safety of the conviction had not been compromised, adding 'in the great majority of cases the answer will be the same whether the two-stage approach is adopted or the position is looked at as a whole'.

There is arguably artificiality about the two-stage test under s 78(b). Consideration at the first stage is meant to be detached from the circumstances of the touching or other activity. However, as an example, we may take the facts of the famous old case of *R v George*[8] in which it was held that the repeated removal of the complainant's shoe from her foot was incapable of being regarded as indecent, despite the appellant's later admission of having done this for his sexual gratification. If those facts came before a court today as an allegation of sexual assault contrary to SOA 2003, s 3, the staged process might be as follows:

Q1 (s 78(a)):	Is the behaviour (shoe removal) *inherently* sexual?
A:	No.
Q2 (s 78(b)(i)):	Putting aside what you know about the defendant's actual motivation, would you (as reasonable people) consider that his behaviour *might* be sexual?
A:	Well, whether or not we'd have thought that before this trial, having heard the defendant's explanation, we now fully understand that some people do 'get off' on this behaviour – so obviously it *can* be sexual, yes.
Q3 (s 78(b)(ii)):	Because of the defendant's (stated) purpose, do you consider that his behaviour *was* sexual?
A:	Of course it was – he says so.

It might be observed that in addressing the middle question above, the direction to put aside the attendant circumstances has not been obeyed, but is it asking too much to expect jurors in this context to forget what they have learned in the trial?

In fact, the Court of Appeal in *R v H* suggested that the *George* scenario might be decided differently under the 2003 law: it would depend on the jury's answers to those staged questions.

7 The Court of Appeal agreed that this constituted 'touching' – see **9.16**.
8 [1956] Crim LR 52.

The Explanatory Notes to the Act suggest that 'obscure fetishes do not fall within the definition of sexual activity'. However, thanks to the internet and more risqué television programmes than were broadcast in the mid-1950s, there is greater public awareness of the breadth of sexual proclivity. As Professor Ormerod comments:[9] 'Fetishism knows no bounds…it will only be the most unusual fetishes where A derives sexual gratification from the most innocuous conduct that will definitely fall outside the scope …'

Cases can arise in respect of intimate medical procedures. The touching of breasts and external genitalia and the digital penetration of body orifices are capable equally of being sexual acts or proper acts of medical care. The courts have considered cases involving such actions. In *R v Kumar*,[10] although a physical breast examination was a genuinely necessary medical procedure, the doctor had undertaken it in an entirely inappropriate way (making contact between his head and the patient's body and prolonging the physical contact far beyond the duration necessary for the examination) so that this fell outside the 'secret intent' cases. The appeal was dismissed. The Court of Appeal added:

> 'In so far as *Court* is binding authority for the proposition that a doctor who obtains sexual satisfaction from a necessary medical examination properly conducted is not guilty of indecent assault, that was not the issue in the present case. It is we would add something that would only be likely to occur in the most unusual circumstances'.[11]

COMMENT

2.4 Other than simply following the pre-existing legal framework, the rationale for the first part of s 78(b) is not clear. Would anything valuable be lost if the first nine words of the subsection were repealed? The second limb would then simply read: '… because of its circumstances or the purpose of any person in relation to it (or both) it is sexual'. For now though, we are stuck with the multiple stages.

Nor is it clear why secretly obtained sexual gratification from contact with patients by doctors, nurses, osteopaths, etc should not be prohibited by the criminal law so long as the professional procedures are carried out in accordance with normal practice. The person touched is violated whether or not they receive their correct treatment and regardless of whether they become aware of the sexual pleasure of the person touching them. The voyeur is guilty

9 [2005] Crim LR 737.
10 [2006] EWCA Crim 1946.
11 See Commentary below (at **2.4**).

irrespective of whether the person observed or filmed is aware of the crime,[12] why should the medical professional, in whom intimate trust is reposed, escape such liability?

12 See **20.18**.

Chapter 3

Penetration

3.1 'Penetration' is a required element of a number of offences within the Sexual Offences Act 2003:

- Rape (ss 1 and 5) requires penile penetration of the vagina, anus or mouth
- Assault by penetration (ss 2 and 6) requires penetration of the vagina or anus with a part of the defendant's body or anything else
- Sex with an adult relative (ss 64 and 65) requires penetration of the vagina or anus with a part of the defendant's body or anything else; or penile penetration of the mouth
- Intercourse with an animal (s 69) requires penile penetration of the vagina or anus
- Sexual penetration of a corpse (s 70) requires penetration of 'part of the body' with part of the defendant's body or anything else

Additionally, in relation to certain other offences (for example s 4 or 9) penetration is a statutory feature determining classification and maximum sentence (as well, of course, as a relevant factor within the Sentencing Guidelines).

Penetration is defined at s 79(2) as 'a continuing act from entry to withdrawal'. Thus, where a defendant entered the victim with consent (or reasonably believing that he had consent), and such consent was thereafter withdrawn (or he came to realise that the victim was not consenting) the offence of rape or assault by penetration is made out from that point.

NON-PENILE PENETRATION

3.2 The Act does not limit which parts of the defendant's body may be used to penetrate for an offence under s 2, 6, 64, 65 or 70 to be made out. While digital penetration is likely to be the most common allegation, penetration by the fist, tongue or even toe will suffice. Similarly, there is no limitation upon what other object apart from a part of the defendant's body ('anything else') may be used in the commission of the offence.

3.2 *Penetration*

Where non-penile penetration is alleged, it is a requirement that the penetration must be 'sexual'.[1] Since the penetration must be of the vagina or anus, it will be rare that circumstances arise where non-sexual penetration is an issue, limited perhaps to genuine medical examinations, intimate searches and occasions when the defendant may claim that the purpose of the act was violent or for the purpose of intimidation, rather than being sexual (see **Chapter 2**).

NATURE OF THE PENETRATION

3.3 The slightest penetration will be sufficient to found the offence. In respect of vaginal penetration 'vagina includes vulva' (s 79(9)), comprising the external genital organs, the *labia majora*, *labia minora* and the vaginal vestibule. Where there has been penile or vaginal reconstruction, 'references to a part of the body include references to part surgically constructed (in particular, through gender reassignment surgery)' (s 79(3)).

It is no bar to a conviction if the complainant cannot be certain whether she was penetrated in the vagina or anus, so long as the jury is sure that penetration of one of those orifices took place.[2] Consequently, a count may be drafted in the alternative in this respect, without being bad.

---

1 Strictly, the prosecution also have to prove the sexual element where penile penetration is alleged for an offence under ss 64 and 65, although that is not conceivably problematic.

2 *R v K (Robert)* [2008] EWCA Crim 1923, [2009] 1 Cr App R 24.

Chapter 4

Intoxication

4.1 This topic falls to be considered under two headings:

- Intoxication of defendant – potentially affecting *mens rea*; and
- Intoxication (voluntary or otherwise) of a complainant – going to the issue of consent.

INTOXICATION OF DEFENDANT

4.2 The subject of whether a defendant's voluntary intoxication (from knowingly consuming alcohol or mind-altering drugs) affords him a defence to various categories of criminal allegation has been the subject of extensive historic debate and case law (including *DPP v Majewski*[1] and *R v Caldwell*[2]). The leading case on intoxication of the defendant in sexual offences is now *R v Heard.*[3]

Heard concerned an allegation of sexual assault contrary to s 3 of the Sexual Offences Act 2003. The Court of Appeal concluded: 'We are wholly satisfied that there is no basis for construing the new Sexual Offences Act as having altered the law so as to make voluntary intoxication available to the allegation that the defendant intentionally touched the complainant.'

This decision was reached (with the observation that 'there is a great deal of policy in the decision whether voluntary intoxication can or cannot be relied upon') notwithstanding the use of the word 'intentionally' throughout the 2003 Act.

The same, policy-driven, reasoning would surely be applicable to other sexual offences, including rape and assault by penetration.

As reflected in the 2010 Crown Court Bench Book, the requisite touching or penetration in each case 'must be the consequence of a deliberate (as opposed

---

1 [1977] AC 443, HL.
2 [1982] AC 341, HL.
3 [2007] 1 Cr App R 37.

to an accidental) act, drunken or not. It is not necessary that the defendant should have 'intended" penetration'.

The jury questions are stated sequentially:

(i) whether B was in fact consenting;

(ii) whether A genuinely believed that B was consenting (subjective – taking A as he was, drunk or sober); and

(iii) whether A's belief was reasonable in the circumstances (objective – applying the standard of a sober person).

If A was mistaken as to the circumstances, and the jury is sure that the defendant's mistake was made because he was drunk, he will not be able to rely on the consequences of his mistake.

Nevertheless, if the defendant's belief was reasonable, although drunken, it remains reasonable.

INTOXICATION OF COMPLAINANT

4.3 In *R v Bree*,[4] the Court of Appeal explored the issue of capacity and consent, stating that if, through drink or for any other reason, a complainant had temporarily lost her capacity to choose whether to have sexual intercourse, she was not consenting. Therefore, subject to the defendant's state of mind, if intercourse took place, this would be rape. However, where a complainant had voluntarily consumed substantial quantities of alcohol, but nevertheless remained capable of choosing whether to have intercourse, and agreed to do so, that would not be rape. Further, the Court identified that capacity to consent may evaporate well before a complainant becomes unconscious. Whether this is so or not, however, depends on the facts of the case.

4 [2007] EWCA Crim 804.

Chapter 5

Position of trust

SEXUAL OFFENCES ACT 2003, SS 21–24

5.1 Sections 16 to 19 create offences where a defendant aged at least 18 (A) is in a 'position of trust' over another person (B) who is under 18. The purpose of the provisions is to prevent adults from abusing their professional relationships with young people who consent to sexual activity, but from a position of inequality. The term 'position of trust' is intricately defined by s 21 and the interpretations contained in s 22.

CIRCUMSTANCES IN WHICH A 'POSITION OF TRUST' ARISES

5.2 Section 21 contains an exhaustive list of circumstances in which a position of trust arises.[1]

'A' is in a position of trust if:

- he looks after persons under 18 who are detained in an institution by virtue of a court order or under an enactment, and B is detained in that institution (s 21(2)).
  - This applies if the victim (B) is detained in a secure training centre or a young offender institution following conviction or bail having been refused.
- he looks after persons under 18 who are resident in a home or other place in which accommodation and maintenance are provided by a local authority under s 23(2) of the Children Act 1989 or by a voluntary organisation under s 59(1) of that Act, and B is resident and provided with accommodation and maintenance in that place (s 21(3)).

---

1 Section 21(1)(b) provides that further circumstances may be added by order of the Secretary of State, although none has yet been added.

- This covers foster care, residential care (whether local authority, private or voluntary, including secure accommodation) and semi-independent accommodation.

- he looks after persons under 18 who are accommodated and cared for in:

  (a) a hospital;

  (b) in Wales, an independent clinic;

  (c) a care home;

  (d) a community home, voluntary home or children's home; or

  (e) a home provided under s 82(5) of the Children Act 1989 (relating to children with special needs),

  and B is accommodated and cared for in that institution (s 21(4)).

  - This covers places where young people with medical conditions, physical or learning disabilities, mental illness or behavioural problems might be accommodated and includes NHS, private and voluntary accommodation.

- he looks after persons under 18 who are receiving education at an educational institution and B is receiving, and A is not receiving, education at that institution (s 21(5))

  - B receives education at an educational institution if she/he is registered or enrolled as a student or pupil at an institution, or he receives education at the institution under arrangements with another educational institution at which he is so registered or otherwise enrolled (s 22(4)).
  - It does not matter if the student is full time or part time.
  - If A is also receiving education at the institution then he or she cannot be in a position of trust, so a prefect would not be in a position of trust over a junior pupil.

- he is engaged in the provision of services under, or pursuant to anything done under:

  (a) sections 8 to 10 of the Employment and Training Act 1973, or

  (b) sections 68, 70(1)(b) or 74 of the Education and Skills Act 2008.

  and, in that capacity, looks after B on an individual basis (s 21(7)).

  - This covers Connexions Personal Advisors who provide an advice and guidance service to 13 to 19 year olds and under 25 year olds with learning difficulties.

- he regularly has unsupervised contact with B (whether face to face or by any other means) in the exercise of functions of a local authority under s 20 or 21 of the Children Act 1989 (s 21(8)).

- This includes people who arrange accommodation for children who are not being looked after by those who have parental responsibility for them, and check that their welfare is being looked after once such accommodation has been found. They include local authority staff such as social workers and family centre staff who visit the accommodation in which a child has been placed in order to oversee the child's welfare.

- he, as a person who is to report to the court under s 7 of the Children Act 1989 on matters relating to the welfare of B, regularly has unsupervised contact with B (whether face to face or by any other means) (s 21(9)).
  - This includes those appointed by courts to provide reports on the welfare of children under their capacity as children and family reporters.

- he is a personal adviser appointed for B under s 23B(2) of, or para 19C of Sch 2 to, the Children Act 1989, and, in that capacity, looks after B on an individual basis (s 21(10)).
  - Personal advisers generally provide help and support to children aged 16–17 who have been in local authority care.

- B is subject to a care order, a supervision order or an education supervision order, and, in the exercise of functions conferred by virtue of the order on an authorised person or the authority designated by the order, A looks after B on an individual basis (s 21(11)).
  - This includes persons who supervise children pursuant to a care order, supervision order or educational supervision order under various provisions in the Children Act 1989.

- he is an officer of the Children and Family Court Advisory Service or Welsh family proceedings officer appointed for B under s 41(1) of the Children Act 1989 or is appointed a children's guardian of B under r 6 or 18 of the Adoption Rules 1984 or to be the guardian ad litem of B under r 9.5 of the Family Proceedings Rules 1991 and, in that capacity regularly has unsupervised contact with B (whether face to face or by any other means) (s 21(12)).
  - This covers those appointed by courts in a variety of proceedings to be children's guardians.

- B is subject to requirements imposed by or under an enactment on his release from detention for a criminal offence, or is subject to requirements imposed by a court order made in criminal proceedings, and A looks after B on an individual basis in pursuance of the requirements (s 21(13)).

5.3 *Position of trust*

- This includes those such as members of Youth Offending Teams (YOTs) who are supervising young people under bail supervision, or in connection with community sentences or following a young person's release on license from a sentence of detention.

INTERPRETATIONS

5.3 A number of situations cited above (subsections 2, 3, 4 and 5) require that A '*looks after*' persons under 18. This is defined at s 22(2):

> 'a person looks after persons under 18 if he is regularly involved in caring for, training, supervising or being in sole charge of such persons.'

Note that nothing in this definition or in the subsections themselves requires that A regularly cares for B, as long as he is regularly caring for 'such persons' as those under 18. Thus, a teacher at a school may be guilty of an offence involving a sexual relationship with a pupil he or she does not teach and with whom there has been no professional contact, so long as the teacher knows or could reasonably be expected to know that the pupil is a student at the same school.

The statute provides no definition of 'regularly'.

A number of situations cited above (subsections 7, 10, 11, and 13) require that A '*looks after B on an individual basis*'. This is defined by s 22(3) as:

(a) A is regularly involved in caring for, training or supervising B; and

(b) in the course of his involvement, A regularly has unsupervised contact with B (whether face to face or by any other means).

The contact must be both regular and unsupervised, but does not need to be face to face, so this covers situations where an adviser may be contacting and establishing a relationship with a young person by telephone, email or social media.

It is not a requirement that A be in paid employment in his dealings with B or under 18s, but the nature of the situations cited at s 21 all imply some form of professional relationship.

STATUTORY DEFENCES

5.4 Although these do not affect the existence of a position of trust, it should be noted that there are statutory defences concerning spouses and civil partners (s 23) and sexual relationships which pre-date the position of trust (s 24).

Chapter 6

Brothel and prostitution

BROTHEL

6.1 There is no statutory definition of a brothel. The commonly accepted definition is derived from *Gorman v Standon*:[1]

> 'A house resorted to or used by more than one woman for the purposes of fornication'

Section 6 of the Sexual Offences Act 1967 widens the ambit to include premises used 'for the purpose of lewd homosexual practices'. However, two or more men offering heterosexual prostitution would appear not to be caught either by the case law definition or by s 6.

More than one woman must use the premises, although it is not necessary that they be present or use the premises at the same time[2].

What constitutes 'a house' has been the subject of somewhat contradictory and now rather old case law. As might be expected, however, it is likely that rooms in a building let out to different women, will constitute a house and therefore a brothel.[3] Each case will turn on its specific facts, and a court deciding the issue will want to look at the layout of the building and the domestic arrangements of its inhabitants.

'For the purposes of fornication'. Strictly, it is not necessary that prostitution takes place within premises for a brothel to be established, merely acts of fornication. This both blunt and euphemistic term is difficult to define accurately. In *Winter v Woolfe*[4] the Divisional Court held that a brothel existed where people of opposite sexes frequented a dancehall for 'illicit intercourse', despite the fact that prostitution did not take place there. Such activity apparently amounted to 'fornication'. In a modern setting, sado-masochistic

---

1 [1964] 1 QB 294.

2 *Stevens v Christy* (1987) 85 Cr App R 249.

3 *Donovan v Gavin* [1965] 2 QB 648 – a case in which the somewhat unfortunate term 'a nest of prostitutes' was coined.

4 [1931] 1 KB 549.

sex venues, hardcore gay clubs and group sex parties could be caught by the definition even though the sex is of a non-commercial nature.

Relationship between Sexual Offences Act 1956, s 33 and Sexual Offences Act, s 33A

6.2 Under SOA 1956, s 33, it is an offence:

> 'to keep, manage or act in or assist in the management of a brothel.'

The Sexual Offences Act 2003 introduced a new offence (s 33A) narrower in scope than the original s33. It is thus an offence:

> 'to keep, manage or act in or assist in the management of a brothel to which people resort for practices involving prostitution.'

The essential difference therefore is that prostitution is not required for the offence under s 33, merely 'fornication' (see above).

While there is a modest difference between the legal definitions of the two offences, it is suggested that the significant distinction lies in the different charging options available to the CPS. Section 33 is summary only while s 33A (in line with other controlling prostitution offences under the 2003 Act) is an either way offence, with a maximum penalty of 7 years imprisonment in the Crown Court. The retention of the s 33 offence allows the prosecuting authorities the option of charging a summary only offence in circumstances where they may consider the brothel is a less serious commercial operation, despite the fact that full prostitution is taking place on the premises. The defendant will, of course, be denied the option of electing a Crown Court trial while the prosecution will be unable to bring proceedings under the Proceeds of Crime Act against a convicted defendant.

Note that under ss 34 and 35 (letting or permitting premises to be used as a brothel) there is no additional requirement that prostitution takes place.

PROSTITUTION

6.3 As provided under SOA 2003, s 51(2) and (3), for the purposes of ss 48 to 50 of the 2003 Act and s 33A:

> '"Prostitute" means a person (A) who, on at least one occasion and whether or not compelled to do so, offers or provides sexual services to another person in return for payment or a promise of payment to A or a third person; and "prostitution" is to be interpreted accordingly.
>
> "Payment" means 'any financial advantage, including the discharge of an obligation to pay or the provision of goods or services (including sexual services) gratuitously or at a discount.'

There is no need for full sexual intercourse to take place. Since there is no definition of 'sexual services' within the Act, it would arguably encompass circumstances where the parties are not even in physical contact, such as phone or webcam sex, although those providing such services would no doubt be surprised to find that the law considered them prostitutes and their premises potentially brothels.[5]

Note that, in relation to the street-based offences of loitering and soliciting, the Street Offences Act 1959 which creates these offences contains no statutory definition of prostitution. However, the body of case law which defines 'common prostitute' is not dissimilar in total to the statutory definition under the 2003 Act – that there needs to be an exchange of sexual services for reward and that the sexual activity which takes place need not include intercourse. We would suggest that the definition in the 2003 Act should be persuasive were this issue to arise in relation to an allegation of loitering or soliciting.

---

5 The case of *Armhouse Lee Ltd v Chappell* (The Independent, 26 July, 1996, DC) would suggest the contrary – that there must be some form of physical contact between the prostitute and her client. However, this case pre-dates the statutory definition in the 2003 Act and concerned the enforcement of a debt under an alleged immoral contract rather than a criminal allegation.

Chapter 7

Age

INTRODUCTION

7.1 Many of the statutory sections considered in this book have provisions relating to various age limits. Also to be considered are important age constraints regarding the criminal capacity of a defendant.

GENERAL

7.2 A person attains any given age at the start of the corresponding birthday. For example, a person becomes 16 as soon as the 16th birthday arrives, at 00:00 hours that day. The time of day at which the person had been born is immaterial. This technical detail could be of vital significance in a case where, for example, allegations arise from events at a birthday party.

PROOF

7.3 If not proved by admission, age may conveniently be established by a certified 'birth certificate' or a copy entry from the Adoption Register.

Age can also be proved by evidence from the child's mother or other relative who has known the child throughout its life.

In case of unusual difficulty (for example with an orphan refugee), the age of the child may be presumed 'as it appears to the court to have been' at the material time.[1]

Likewise, in relation to indecent photographs, a person is to be taken as having been a child at any material time if it appears from the evidence as a whole that he was then under the age of 18.[2]

---

1 Children & Young Persons Act 1933, s 99(2) and Sch 1, as amended by SOA 2003, s 139 and Sch 6.

2 Protection of Children Act 1978, s 2(3) and Criminal Justice Act 1988, s 160(4) (both as amended by Sexual Offences Act 2003, s 45(2)).

AGE AND CRIMINAL CAPACITY

7.4 The age of criminal responsibility in English law has been set at 10 years since 1 February 1964.[3] For three decades before then it had been just eight.[4] Below the minimum age, there was (as now) a conclusive presumption that the child was *doli incapax* (incapable of crime).

Usually of greater significance is the further *rebuttable* presumption that a child from the age of 10 until 14 was incapable of crime. That presumption was only displaced if the prosecution proved to the criminal standard that the child knew his action was seriously wrong. Otherwise, the child had to be acquitted, however strong the evidence might be in other respects.

This common law rule remained in force until its abolition on 30 September 1998.[5] It will continue to apply to historic cases from before that date.

Another important presumption was that at common law a boy under the age of 14 was deemed incapable of sexual intercourse. This remained a conclusive presumption until its abolition on 20 September 1993 by Sexual Offences Act 1993, s 1. Evidence of penetration might remain admissible in support of a lesser charge of indecent assault, or potentially as 'bad character' evidence.

DEFENDANTS UNDER 18

7.5 Throughout the substantive offence chapters (Parts B, C and D) reference is made to certain offences being 'triable on indictment only'. Although not laboriously stated on each occasion, all such references should be read as applying to adult defendants only. All sexual offences, whatever their classification in respect of defendants aged 18 or over, are capable of being tried in the Youth Court.

---

3 Children & Young Persons Act 1963, s 16(1), commencement date.
4 Children & Young Persons Act 1933.
5 By Crime and Disorder Act 1998, s 34.

Part B
Sexual Offences Act 2003 offences

Chapter 8

Non-consensual penile penetration

Rape
Sexual Offences Act 2003, s 1

DEFINITION

8.1 Section 1(1):

A person (A) commits an offence if—

(a) he intentionally penetrates the vagina, anus or mouth of another person (B) with his penis;

(b) B does not consent to the penetration; and

A does not reasonably believe that B consents.

SUMMARY

8.2 This section expanded the definition of the physical act of rape to include penile penetration of the mouth.

It also introduced the mental element of absence of *reasonable* belief in consent, replacing the former *mens rea* (see 28.2) whereby a genuine belief in consent amounted to a complete defence, whether that belief was reasonable or not.

ELEMENTS

8.3

- Intentional *penetration* with the penis – see **Chapter 3**
- of *vagina, anus* or *mouth* – see **Chapter 3**
- *Absence of consent* – see **Chapter 1**
- *Absence of reasonable belief in consent* – see **Chapter 1**

PARTIES

8.4 This offence can only be committed as principal by a male (but a female might aid and abet). Defendants can be of any age.[1]

The complainant can be male or female and of any age (although if under 13 the allegation should be charged under s 5).

There is no marital exception.[2]

PRACTITIONER POINTER
PROS – where the complainant is unable to exclude the possibility that the penetration was with a finger or an inanimate object, rather than with the defendant's penis, 'assault by penetration' contrary to s 2 should be considered.

CLASSIFICATION

8.5 Offence is triable on indictment only (for adult defendants – see **7.5** regarding youths).

SENTENCING AND OTHER ORDERS

Maximum sentence

8.6 Life imprisonment

Sentencing guidelines

Determining the category

8.7 Offences may be of such severity, for example involving a campaign of rape, that sentences of 20 years and above may be appropriate.

1 See Chapter 7 for considerations re defendant's age.
2 *R v R* [1991] UKHL 12, [1992] 1 AC 599 and see discussion in 28.2 (historic rape).

Cat	Harm	Cat	Culpability
1	The extreme nature of one or more category 2 factors or the extreme impact caused by a combination of category 2 factors may elevate to category 1	A	• Significant degree of planning
2	• Severe psychological or physical harm • Pregnancy or STI as a consequence of offence • Additional degradation/ humiliation • Abduction • Prolonged detention/ sustained incident • Violence or threats of violence (beyond that which is inherent in the offence) • Forced/uninvited entry into victim's home • Victim is particularly vulnerable due to personal circumstances* * *for victims under 13 please refer to the guideline in ch 10, s 5*		• Offender acts together with others to commit the offence • Use of alcohol/drugs on victim to facilitate the offence • Abuse of trust • Offence committed in course of burglary • Recording of the offence • Commercial exploitation and/or motivation • Offence racially or religiously aggravated • Offence motivated by, or demonstrating, hostility to the victim based on his or her sexual orientation (or presumed sexual orientation) or transgender identity (or presumed transgender identity) • Offence motivated by, or demonstrating, hostility to the victim based on his or her disability (or presumed disability)
3	Factor(s) in categories 1 & 2 not present	B	Factor(s) in category A not present

8.8 *Non-consensual penile penetration*

Starting point and category range

8.8

	A	**B**
Category 1	Starting point: 15 yrs custody Range: 13–19 yrs custody	Starting point: 12 yrs custody Range: 10–15 yrs custody
Category 2	Starting point: 10 yrs custody Range: 9–13 yrs custody	Starting point: 8 yrs custody Range: 7–9 yrs custody
Category 3	Starting point: 7 yrs custody Range: 6–9 yrs custody	Starting point: 5 yrs custody Range: 4–7 yrs custody

Additional factual elements

8.9

Aggravating factors
Statutory aggravating factors
• Previous convictions, having regard to: (a) the nature of the offence to which the conviction relates and its relevance to the current offence; and (b) the time that has elapsed since the conviction
Other aggravating factors
• Offence committed whilst on bail
• Timing of offence
• Use of weapon or other item to frighten or injure
• Victim compelled to leave their home (including victims of domestic violence)
• Failure to comply with current court orders
• Offence committed whilst on licence
• Exploiting contact arrangements with a child to commit an offence
• Presence of others, especially children
• Any steps taken to prevent the victim reporting an incident, obtaining assistance and/or from assisting or supporting the prosecution
• Attempts to dispose of or conceal evidence
• Commission of offence whilst under the influence of alcohol or drugs

- Specific targeting of a particularly vulnerable victim
- Ejaculation (where not taken into account at step one)
- Blackmail or other threats made (where not taken into account at step one)

Mitigating factors

- No previous convictions or no relevant/recent convictions
- Remorse
- Previous good character and/or exemplary conduct*
- Age and/or lack of maturity where it affects the responsibility of the offender
- Mental disorder or learning disability, particularly where linked to the commission of the offence

* Previous good character/exemplary conduct is different from having no previous convictions. The more serious the offence, the less the weight which should normally be attributed to this factor. Where previous good character/exemplary conduct has been used to facilitate the offence, this mitigation should not normally be allowed and such conduct may constitute an aggravating factor.

In the context of this offence, previous good character/exemplary conduct should not normally be given any significant weight and will not normally justify a reduction in what would otherwise be the appropriate sentence

Other orders

8.10

Relevant factors	
Extended and life sentence availability (CJA 2003)	Sch 15 (specified offence): yes Sch 15B (life sentence for second listed offence): yes
Trigger offence for:	SOPO: yes FTO: yes, where but only where v *was under 18*
Inclusion in barred lists	Children: automatic if victim is a child (subject to representations if victim is an adult) Vulnerable adult: subject to representations if victim is a child[1]
Notification	Yes

1 It seems a curious anomaly that there is no provision for a rapist of an adult to be included in the adults' barred list, whether automatically or subject to representations.

Chapter 9

Other non-consensual sexual offences

Assault by penetration
Sexual Offences Act 2003, s 2

DEFINITION

9.1 Section 2(1):

A person (A) commits an offence if—

(a) he intentionally penetrates the vagina or anus of another person (B) with a part of his body or anything else;

(b) the penetration is sexual;

(c) B does not consent to the penetration; and

(d) A does not reasonably believe that B consents.

SUMMARY

9.2 The primary focus of this section is non-consensual penetration of the vagina or anus other than by the penis. The section can also be used where there is doubt as to whether or not the penetration was penile.

ELEMENTS

9.3

- Intentional *penetration* – see Chapter 3
- *Sexual* – see Chapter 2
- *Vagina* or *anus* – see Chapter 3
- *Absence of consent* – see Chapter 1
- *Absence of reasonable belief in consent* – see **Chapter 1**

PARTIES

9.4 This offence can be committed by males or females, of any age. Complainants may be male or female, of any age. (although if under 13 the allegation should be charged under s 6).

There is no marital exception.

DISCUSSION

9.5 It is not necessary under this section for a complainant to identify the item with which they were penetrated. The offence can be used where, for example, the alleged penetration was in the dark or the complainant was blindfolded at the time and unable to be specific about the penetrating object or body part. A defendant's penis would readily fall within the definition 'a part of his body or anything else', so the section would be equally applicable where the evidence was any of the following:

(i) 'He forced the vibrator up my bum';

(ii) 'I think it was his penis, but I can't be certain';

(iii) 'I've no idea what it was, but he put something up me'

Notably, penetration of the mouth is excluded, so a potential oral rape with uncertainty as to the object would have to be dealt with as a sexual assault (s 3).

CLASSIFICATION

9.6 Offence is triable on indictment only.

SENTENCING AND OTHER ORDERS

Maximum sentence

9.7 Life imprisonment

Sentencing guidelines

Determining the category

9.8

Cat	Harm	Cat	Culpability
1	As 'Rape' (see **8.7**), s 1	A	As 'Rape' (see **8.7**), s 1
2	As 'Rape' (see **8.7**), s 1 But additional factor: • Penetration using large or dangerous object(s) Omit factor: • 'Pregnancy or STI as a consequence of offence'		
3	Factor(s) in categories 1 & 2 not present	B	Factor(s) in categories A not present

Staring point and category range

9.9

	A	**B**
Category 1	Starting point: 15 yrs custody Range: 13–19 yrs custody	Starting point: 12 yrs custody Range: 10–15 yrs custody
Category 2	Starting point: 8 yrs custody Range: 5–13 yrs custody	Starting point: 6 yrs custody Range: 4–9 yrs custody
Category 3	Starting point: 4 yrs custody Range: 2–6 yrs custody	Starting point: 2 yrs custody Range: High level community order–4 yrs custody

Additional factual elements

9.10

Aggravating factors
As 'Rape' (see **8.9**), s 1 omitting aggravating factor of 'ejaculation'

Mitigating factors
As 'Rape' (see **8.9**), s 1

Other orders

9.11

Extended and life sentence availability (CJA 2003)	Sch 15 (specified offence): yes Sch 15B (life sentence for second listed offence): yes
Trigger offence for:	SOPO: yes FTO: yes, but only where v *was under 18*
Inclusion in barred lists	Children: automatic if victim is a child (subject to representations if victim is an adult) Vulnerable adult: subject to representations
Notification	Yes

Sexual assault
Sexual Offences Act 2003 s 3

DEFINITION

9.12 Section 3(1)

A person (A) commits an offence if—

(a) he intentionally touches another person (B),

(b) the touching is sexual,

(c) B does not consent to the touching, and

(d) A does not reasonably believe that B consents.

SUMMARY

9.13 This section can be viewed as a non-gender-specific replacement for the offences of indecent assault on a woman (SOA 1956, s 14) and indecent assault on a man (SOA 1956, s 15), but the offences are not identical. In particular, this section covers only touching.

ELEMENTS

9.14

- *Intentional touching*
  Section 79(8) provides that:

  Touching includes touching:

  (a) with any part of the body,

  (b) with anything else,

  (c) through anything,

  and in particular includes touching amounting to penetration.

  See discussion at **9.16**.
- *Sexual* – see **Chapter 2**
- *Absence of consent* – see **Chapter 1**
- *Absence of reasonable belief in consent* – see **Chapter 1**

PARTIES

9.15 This offence can be committed by males or females, of any age.

Complainants may be male or female, of any age (although if under 13 the allegation should be charged under s 7).

There is no marital exception.

> PRACTITIONER POINTER
>
> PROS – in order to circumvent any difficulty regarding consent, consider whether the following alternative charges are appropriate:
>
> where A is at least 18 and B is 13–15, consider an allegation under s 9 (see **11.1**)
>
> where A is at least 18 and in a position of trust re B aged 16–17, consider s 16 (see **12.1**)

DISCUSSION

9.16 Given the reference in s 79(8) to penetration, there is potential overlap with the s 1 and s 2 offences.

The Court of Appeal has held[1] that merely touching the clothing worn by B (as contrasted with touching B through that clothing) can suffice.

B need not be aware of the touching.

The touching by A must be intentional – in other words, deliberate and not accidental.[2]

A need not intend his touching of B to be sexual, nor need he derive or seek sexual gratification. Any touching of B which was obviously sexual because of its nature (for example thrusting a hand inside underwear to touch the outside of the vagina) could amount to a sexual assault even if A's sole purpose was to cause distress to B.

In contrast to the replaced offences of indecent assault under SOA 1956 (see **28.25** and **28.33**), sexual touching must actually occur (for the completed offence) – the mere apprehension of such touching is insufficient (but might indicate an attempt or an offence contrary to s 62[3]).

Home Office Guidance: 'Touching' covers all physical contact, including touching with any part of the body, with anything else and through anything, for example, through clothing. This could include for example, where a person rubs up against someone's private parts through the person's clothes for sexual gratification. It also includes penetration. However, where there is sufficient evidence, forced penile penetration of the vagina, anus or mouth would normally be charged as rape and forced penetration of the vagina or anus with any other part of a person's body or another object would normally be charged as assault by penetration.

CLASSIFICATION

9.17 Offence is triable either way.

SENTENCING AND OTHER ORDERS

Maximum sentence

9.18 On indictment: 10 years

Summarily: 6 months imprisonment or a fine not exceeding the statutory maximum (currently £5000)

---

1 *R v H (Karl Anthony)* [2005] EWCA Crim 732, [2005] 2 Cr App R 9.
2 *R v Heard* [2007] EWCA Crim 125.
3 Raised *per curiam* in *R v H (Karl Anthony)* [2005] EWCA Crim 732, [2005] 2 Cr App R 9, per Lord Woolf CJ at [15].

Sentencing guidelines

Determining the category

9.19

Cat	**Harm**	**Cat**	**Culpability**
1	• Severe psychological or physical harm • Abduction • Violence or threats of violence • Forced/uninvited entry into victim's home	A	As 'Rape' (see **8.7**), s 1
2	• Touching of naked genitalia or naked breasts • Prolonged detention/ sustained incident • Additional degradation/ humiliation • Victim is particularly vulnerable due to personal circumstances* **for victims under 13 refer to guideline at* ***10.30–10.32***		
3	Factor(s) in categories 1 & 2 not present	B	Factor(s) in category A not present

Starting point and category range

9.20

	A	**B**
Category 1	Starting point: 4 yrs custody Range: 3–7 yrs custody	Starting point: 2 yrs 6 months custody Range: 2–4 yrs custody
Category 2	Starting point: 2 yrs custody Range: 1–4 yrs custody	Starting point: 18 months custody Range: High level community order–2 yrs custody

Category 3	Starting point: 26 wks custody Range: High level community order–1 yr custody	Starting point: High level community order Range: Medium level community order–26 wks custody

Additional factual elements

9.21

Aggravating factors
As 'Rape' (see **8.9**), s 1, omitting aggravating factor of 'ejaculation'
Mitigating factors
As 'Rape' (see **8.9**), s 1, but additional factor: • Demonstration of steps taken to address offending behaviour

Other orders

9.22

Extended and life sentence availability (CJA 2003)	Sch 15 (specified offence): yes Sch 15B (life sentence for second listed offence): no
Trigger offence for:	SOPO: yes FTO: yes, but only where V *was under 18*, and D under 18 and sentenced to at least 12 months imprisonment; D over 18 and sentenced to prison or detention in hospital or community sentence of at least 12 months
Inclusion in barred lists	Children: subject to representations Vulnerable adult: subject to representations
Notification	Yes, if: D under 18 and sentenced to at least 12 months imprisonment; D over 18 and • V under 18, *or* • D sentenced to prison or detention in hospital or community sentence of at least 12 months

Causing a person to engage in sexual activity without consent
Sexual Offences Act 2003 s 4

DEFINITION

9.23 Section 4:

(1) A person (A) commits an offence if—

(a) he intentionally causes another person (B) to engage in an activity,

(b) the activity is sexual,

(c) B does not consent to engaging in the activity, and

(d) A does not reasonably believe that B consents.

...

(4) A person guilty of an offence under this section, if the activity caused or incited involved—

(a) penetration of B's anus or vagina,

(b) penetration of B's mouth with a person's penis,

(c) penetration of a person's anus or vagina with a part of B's body or by B with anything else, or

(d) penetration of a person's mouth with B's penis,

is liable, on conviction on indictment, to imprisonment for life.

SUMMARY

9.24 This section makes it an offence for a person (A) intentionally to cause another person (B) to engage in sexual activity without that person's consent, if he does not reasonably believe that B consents.

Subsection 4(4) creates an aggravated version of the offence, relating to penetration.

ELEMENTS

9.25

- *Intentionally*

'*Intentionally*' relates to the causing of the activity. In theory, it is not necessary that A intends the resulting activity to be sexual, but this distinction is unlikely to arise in practice. It must likewise be rare that someone accidentally or recklessly causes another person to engage in a sexual activity, but this would not suffice.

- *Causes*

  '*Causes*' is not defined by the Act and should be given its natural meaning of bringing about or making happen. 'Causing' requires something more than merely 'allowing'.

  It may be achieved by words, action or both.

- B to engage in an *activity*

  'Activity' is not defined, but notably is not limited to touching or penetration.[4]

  For example, it can include B exposing himself either directly or over the internet.

  It seems that engaging in a conversation on sexual matters can suffice.[5]

- *Sexual* – see **Chapter 2**.

  The relevant activity which must be sexual is that engaged in by person B at A's behest, rather than anything done by A without B's participation.

- *Absence of consent* – see **Chapter 1**
- *Absence of reasonable belief in consent* – see **Chapter 1**
- (where alleged – see **9.26**) specific type of penetration (to be specified in the Indictment).

AGGRAVATED FORM OF THE OFFENCE (PENETRATION)

9.26 By virtue of subs 4(4), which provides for different maximum penalties where the sexual activity caused involves particular forms of penetration, there are two subsets of this offence, penetrative and non-penetrative. Because of the differing penalties and modes of trial (see below), it is essential that the indictment specifies which version is alleged (see Specimen Indictments, **Appendix 1**).

---

4 Note that s 78, which defines 'sexual', refers to 'penetration, touching or *any other activity*'.

5 *R v Grout* [2011] EWCA Crim 299 at [29], discussed at **10.36**.

9.26 *Other non-consensual sexual offences*

The aggravated version of the offence involves:

(a) penetration of B's anus or vagina,

(b) penetration of B's mouth with a person's penis,

(c) penetration of a person's anus or vagina with a part of B's body or by B with anything else, or

(d) penetration of a person's mouth with B's penis.

In (a) the penetration can be by anything (although if by A's penis it would constitute rape and if by any other part of A's body it would amount to a s 2 offence).

In (b) the envisaged penetration is by the penis of a person other than A (or else it would be rape).

In (c) the person whose anus or vagina is penetrated can be any person, including A (and, it would appear, B himself).

In (d) the person whose mouth is penetrated can be any person, including A (and, if achievable, B himself).

PRACTITIONER POINTERS

PROS – in order to circumvent any difficulty regarding consent, consider whether the following alternative charges are appropriate:

Where A is at least 18 and B is 13–15, consider an allegation under s 10 (see **11.14**). In addition to removing the consent issue, s 10 can cover incitement – potentially useful where performance of the sexual activity is disputed but there is strong evidence of encouragement (for example text messages);

Where A is at least 18 and in a position of trust re B aged 16–17, consider s 17 (see **12.17**)

DEF – Consider whether s 4(4) applies (specific penetration/higher maximum penalty/indictable only) – are the particulars of offence clear in this regard? (see **9.26**)

PARTIES

9.27 This offence can be committed by males or females, of any age.

Complainants may be male or female, of any age (although if under 13 the allegation should be charged under s 8).

There is no marital exception.

DISCUSSION

9.28 Person A may himself participate in the sexual activity with B, but need not. The activity may involve B alone, but equally there could be other persons, animals or objects involved.

EXAMPLES

9.29

- A causes B to engage in sexual activity with A (for example, a woman compels a man to penetrate her);
- A causes B to engage in solo sexual activity (for example, a woman forces a man to masturbate himself);
- A causes B to engage in sexual activity with C (for example, one person makes someone else masturbate a third person, whether that third party is a willing participant or another victim);
- A forces B to expose herself over a webcam (for viewing perhaps by A and/or others);
- A makes B take a naked photograph of herself and send it via a mobile phone (to A or C).[6]

CLASSIFICATION

9.30 Where specific penetration contrary to s 4(4) is alleged (see **9.26**), the offence is indictable only, otherwise it is triable either way.

SENTENCING AND OTHER ORDERS

Maximum sentence

9.31 In aggravated form: Life imprisonment

In non-aggravated form:

- On indictment: 10 years
- Summarily: 6 months imprisonment or a fine not exceeding the statutory maximum (currently £5000)

---

6 *Broughton* [2007] EWCA Crim 566 – a case under s 8, arguably the taking of the photograph, even before its onward transmission, constitutes sexual activity.

9.32 *Other non-consensual sexual offences*

Sentencing guidelines

Determining the category

9.32

Cat	Harm	Cat	Culpability
1	As 'Rape' (see **8.7**), s 1	A	As 'Rape' (see **8.7**), s 1
2	As 'Rape' (see **8.7**), s 1 But additional factor: • Penetration using large or dangerous object(s)		
3	Factor(s) in categories 1 & 2 not present	B	Factor(s) in category A not present

Starting point and category range

9.33 Where offence involved penetration:

	A	B
Category 1	Starting point: 15 yrs custody Range: 13–19 yrs custody	Starting point: 12 yrs custody Range: 10–15 yrs custody
Category 2	Starting point: 8 yrs custody Range: 5–13 yrs custody	Starting point: 6 yrs custody Range: 4–9 yrs custody
Category 3	Starting point: 4 yrs custody Range: 2–6 yrs custody	Starting point: 2 yrs custody Range: High level community order–4 yrs custody

Where offence did not involve penetration:

	A	B
Category 1	Starting point: 4 yrs custody Range: 3–7 yrs custody	Starting point: 2 yrs 6 mths custody Range: 2–4 yrs custody
Category 2	Starting point: 2 yrs custody Range: 1–4 yrs custody	Starting point: 1 yr custody Range: High level community order–2 yrs custody

Category 3	Starting point: 26 wks custody Range: High level community order–1 yr custody	Starting point: High level community order Range: Medium level community order–26 wks custody

Additional factual elements

9.34

Aggravating factors
As 'Rape' (see **8.9**), s 1
Mitigating factors
As 'Rape' (see **8.9**), s 1

Other orders

9.35

Extended and life sentence availability (CJA 2003)	Sch 15 (specified offence): yes Sch 15B (life sentence for second listed offence): yes, if the offence is in aggravated form
Trigger offence for:	SOPO: yes FTO: yes, but only where v *was under 18*
Inclusion in barred lists	Children: subject to representations Vulnerable adult: subject to representations
Notification	Yes

Chapter 10

Child sex offences (under 13)

Rape of a child under 13
Sexual Offences Act 2003 s 5

DEFINITION

10.1 Section 5:

(1) A person commits an offence if—

(a) he intentionally penetrates the vagina, anus or mouth of another person with his penis; and

(b) the other person is under 13.

SUMMARY

10.2 This offence is the 'victim under 13' version of rape. Two crucial features stand out:

Consent is irrelevant – a child under 13 does not, under any circumstances, have the legal capacity to consent to any form of sexual activity – whether or not the child ostensibly consented to this act is immaterial;

There is *strict liability as to the age of the child*[1] – it is no defence that a defendant genuinely and reasonably believed that the child was 13 or older.

ELEMENTS

10.3

- Intentional *penetration* – see **Chapter 3**
- of *vagina*, *anus* or *mouth* – see **Chapter 3**

---

1 *R v G* [2008] UKHL 37.

- *B was under 13*[2]

  This must be specified in the indictment.
- Consent is irrelevant.

PARTIES

10.4 This offence can only be committed (as principal) by a male (although a female might aid and abet). Defendants may be of any age.[3]

The complainant can be male or female, subject to being under 13.

CLASSIFICATION

10.5 Offence is triable on indictment only.

SENTENCING AND OTHER ORDERS

10.6

Maximum sentence

10.7 Life imprisonment

Sentencing guidelines

Determining the category

10.8 Offences may be of such severity, for example involving a campaign of rape, that sentences of 20 years and above may be appropriate.

When dealing with the statutory offence of rape of a child under 13, the court may be faced with a wide range of offending behaviour.

Sentencers should have particular regard to the fact that these offences are not only committed through force or fear of force but may include exploitative behaviour towards a child which should be considered to indicate high culpability.

This guideline is designed to deal with the majority of offending behaviour which deserves a significant custodial sentence; the starting points and ranges

---

2 See **Chapter 7**.
3 See **Chapter 7** for considerations re defendant's age.

reflect the fact that such offending merits such an approach. There may also be exceptional cases, where a lengthy community order with a requirement to participate in a sex offender treatment programme may be the best way of changing the offender's behaviour and of protecting the public by preventing any repetition of the offence. This guideline may not be appropriate where the sentencer is satisfied that on the available evidence, and in the absence of exploitation, a young or particularly immature defendant genuinely believed, on reasonable grounds, that the victim was aged 16 or over and that they were engaging in lawful sexual activity.

Cat	Harm	Cat	Culpability
1	The extreme nature of one or more category 2 factors or the extreme impact caused by a combination of category 2 factors may elevate to category 1	A	• Significant degree of planning
2	• Severe psychological or physical harm		• Offender acts together with others to commit the offence
	• Pregnancy or STI as a consequence of offence		• Use of alcohol/drugs on victim to facilitate the offence
	• Additional degradation/ humiliation		• Grooming behaviour used against victim
	• Abduction		• Abuse of trust
	• Prolonged detention/ sustained incident		• Previous violence against victim
	• Violence or threats of violence		• Offence committed in course of burglary
	• Forced/uninvited entry into victim's home		• Sexual images of victim recorded, retained, solicited or shared
	• Child is particularly vulnerable due to extreme youth and/or personal circumstances		• Deliberate isolation of victim
			• Commercial exploitation and/or motivation
			• Offence racially or religiously aggravated

Cat	Harm	Cat	Culpability
			• Offence motivated by, or demonstrating, hostility to the victim based on his or her sexual orientation (or presumed sexual orientation) or transgender identity (or presumed transgender identity) • Offence motivated by, or demonstrating, hostility to the victim based on his or her disability (or presumed disability)
3	Factor(s) in categories 1 & 2 not present	B	Factor(s) in category A not present

Starting point and category range

10.9

	A	B
Category 1	Starting point: 16 yrs custody Range: 13–19 yrs custody	Starting point: 13 yrs custody Range: 11–17 yrs custody
Category 2	Starting point: 13 yrs custody Range: 11–17 yrs custody	Starting point: 10 yrs custody Range: 8–13 yrs custody
Category 3	Starting point: 10 yrs custody Range: 8–13 yrs custody	Starting point: 8 yrs custody Range: 6–11 yrs custody

Additional factual elements

10.10

Aggravating factors
Statutory aggravating factors
• Previous convictions, having regard to a) the nature of the offence to which the conviction relates and its relevance to the current offence; and b) the time that has elapsed since the conviction
• Offence committed whilst on bail

• Victim compelled to leave their home, school, etc
• Failure to comply with current court orders
• Offence committed whilst on licence
• Exploiting contact arrangements with a child to commit an offence
• Presence of others, especially other children
• Any steps taken to prevent the victim reporting an incident, obtaining assistance and/or from assisting or supporting the prosecution
• Attempts to dispose of or conceal evidence
• Commission of offence whilst under the influence of alcohol or drugs
• Victim encouraged to recruit others
Other aggravating factors
• Specific targeting of a particularly vulnerable child
• Ejaculation (where not taken into account at step one)
• Blackmail or other threats made (where not taken into account at step one)
• Location of offence
• Timing of offence
• Use of weapon or other item to frighten or injure
Mitigating factors
• No previous convictions or no relevant/recent convictions
• Remorse
• Previous good character and/or exemplary conduct*
• Age and/or lack of maturity where it affects the responsibility of the offender

* Previous good character/exemplary conduct is different from having no previous convictions. The more serious the offence, the less the weight which should normally be attributed to this factor. Where previous good character/exemplary conduct has been used to facilitate the offence, this mitigation should not normally be allowed and such conduct may constitute an aggravating factor.

In the context of this offence, previous good character/exemplary conduct should not normally be given any significant weight and will not normally justify a reduction in what would otherwise be the appropriate sentence

Other orders

10.11

Extended and life sentence availability (CJA 2003)	Sch 15 (specified offence): yes Sch 15B (life sentence for second listed offence): yes
Trigger offence for:	SOPO: yes FTO: yes
Inclusion in barred lists	Children: automatic Vulnerable adult: subject to representations
Notification	Yes

Assault of a child under s 13 by penetration Sexual Offences Act 2003, s 6

DEFINITION

10.12 Section 6:

(1) A person commits an offence if—

(a) he intentionally penetrates the vagina or anus of another person with a part of his body or anything else;

(b) the penetration is sexual; and

(c) the other person is under 13.

EXPLANATION

10.13 This is the 'victim under 13' version of s 2. This section makes it an offence for a person intentionally to penetrate sexually the vagina or anus of a child under the age of 13 with a part of his body (such as a finger) or with anything else (such as a vibrator). Two crucial features stand out:

Consent is irrelevant – a child under 13 does not, under any circumstances, have the legal capacity to consent to any form of sexual activity – whether or not the child ostensibly consented to this act is immaterial.

There is *strict liability as to the age of the child*[4] – it is no defence that a defendant genuinely and reasonably believed that the child was 13 or older.

4 *R v G* [2008] UKHL 37.

10.14 *Child sex offences (under 13)*

ELEMENTS

10.14

- Intentional *penetration* – see **Chapter 3**
- of *vagina* or *anus* – see **Chapter 3**
- *Sexual* – see **Chapter 2**
- *B was under 13*[5] – this must be specified in the indictment
- Consent is irrelevant

PARTIES

10.15 This offence can be committed by males or females, of any age.

The complainant may be male or female, subject to being under 13.

DISCUSSION

10.16 It is not necessary under this section for a complainant to identify what they were penetrated with. The offence can be used where, for example, the alleged penetration was in the dark or the child for any other reason is unable to be specific about the penetrating object or body part. Of course, a defendant's penis would readily fall within the definition 'a part of his body or anything else', so the section would be equally applicable where the evidence were any of the following:

(i) 'He stuck his finger in my minny';

(ii) 'I think it was his willy, but I'm not too sure';

(iii) 'I don't know what it was, but he put something up my bum'

Notably, penetration of the mouth is excluded, so a potential oral rape with uncertainty as to the penetrating object would have to be dealt with as a sexual assault (s 7).

CLASSIFICATION

10.17 Offence is triable on indictment only.

5 See **Chapter 7**.

SENTENCING AND OTHER ORDERS

Maximum sentence

10.18 Life imprisonment

Sentencing guidelines

Determining the category

10.19

Cat	Harm	Cat	Culpability
1	As 'Rape of a child under 13' (see **10.8**), s 5	A	As 'Rape of a child under 13' (see **10.8**), s 5
2	As 'Rape of a child under 13' (see **10.8**), s 5 But additional factor: ● Penetration using large or dangerous object(s) Omit factor: ● 'Pregnancy or STI as a consequence of offence'		
3	Factor(s) in categories 1 & 2 not present	B	Factor(s) in category A not present

Starting point and category range

10.20

	A	B
Category 1	Starting point: 16 yrs custody Range: 13–19 yrs custody	Starting point: 13 yrs custody Range: 11–17 yrs custody
Category 2	Starting point: 11 yrs custody Range: 7–15 yrs custody	Starting point: 8 yrs custody Range: 5–13 yrs custody
Category 3	Starting point: 6 yrs custody Range: 4–9 yrs custody	Starting point: 4 yrs custody Range: 2–6 yrs custody

10.21 *Child sex offences (under 13)*

Additional factual elements

10.21

Aggravating factors
As 'Rape of a child under 13' (see **10.10**), s 5, omitting aggravating factor of 'ejaculation'
Mitigating factors
As 'Rape of a child under 13' (see **10.10**), s 5

Other orders

10.22

Maximum	Life imprisonment
Extended and life sentence availability (CJA 2003)	Sch 15 (specified offence): yes Sch 15B (life sentence for second listed offence): yes
Trigger offence for:	SOPO: yes FTO: yes
Inclusion in barred lists	Children: automatic Vulnerable adult: subject to representations
Notification	Yes

Sexual assault of a child under 13 Sexual Offences Act 2003, s 7

DEFINITION

10.23 Section 7

(1) A person commits an offence if—

(a) he intentionally touches another person;

(b) the touching is sexual; and

(c) the other person is under 13.

EXPLANATION

10.24 This offence is the 'victim under 13' version of s 3. Two crucial features stand out:

Consent is irrelevant – a child under 13 does not, under any circumstances, have the legal capacity to consent to any form of sexual activity – whether or not the child ostensibly consented to this act is immaterial;

There is *strict liability as to the age of the child*[6] – it is no defence that a defendant genuinely and reasonably believed that the child was 13 or older.

ELEMENTS

10.25

- *Intentional touching*

  Section 79(8) provides that:

  Touching includes touching–

  (a) with any part of the body;

  (b) with anything else;

  (c) through anything;

  and in particular includes touching amounting to penetration.

  See further **10.27**.

- *Sexual* – see **Chapter 2**
- *B was under 13*[7]

  This must be specified in the indictment.

- Consent is irrelevant.

PARTIES

10.26 This offence can be committed by males or females, of any age.

The complainant may be male or female, subject to being under 13.

6 *R v G* [2008] UKHL 37.
7 See **Chapter 7**.

DISCUSSION

10.27 Given the reference in s 79(8) to penetration, there is potential overlap with the s 1 and s 2 offences.

The Court of Appeal has held[8] that merely touching the clothing worn by B (as contrasted with touching B through that clothing) can suffice.

B need not be aware of the touching.

The touching by A must be intentional – in other words, deliberate and not accidental.[9]

A need not intend his touching of B to be sexual, nor need he derive or seek sexual gratification. Any touching of B which was obviously sexual because of its nature (for example thrusting a hand inside underwear to touch the outside of the vagina) could amount to a sexual assault even if A's sole purpose was to cause distress to B.

In contrast to the repealed offences of indecent assault under SOA 1956 (see **28.25** and **28.33**), sexual touching must actually occur (for the completed offence) – the mere apprehension of such touching is insufficient (but may indicate an attempt).

Home Office Guidance: This could include for example, where a person rubs up against the child's private parts through the child's clothes for sexual gratification. It also includes penetration. However, where there is sufficient evidence, forced penile penetration of the vagina, anus or mouth would normally be charged as 'rape of a child under 13' (s 5) and forced penetration of the vagina or anus with any other part of a person's body or another object would normally be charged as 'assault of a child under 13 by penetration' (s 6).

CLASSIFICATION

10.28 Offence is triable either way.

SENTENCING AND OTHER ORDERS

Maximum sentence

10.29

- On indictment: 14 years

---

8 *R v H (Karl Anthony)* [2005] EWCA Crim 732, [2005] 2 Cr App R 9.
9 *R v Heard* [2007] EWCA Crim 125.

- Summarily: 6 months imprisonment or a fine not exceeding the statutory maximum (currently £5000)

Sentencing guidelines

Determining the category

10.30

Cat	Harm	Cat	Culpability
1	• Severe psychological or physical harm • Abduction • Violence or threats of violence • Forced/uninvited entry into victim's home	A	As 'Rape of a child under 13' (see **10.8**), s 5
2	• Touching of naked genitalia or breast area • Prolonged detention/ sustained incident • Additional degredation/ humiliation • Child is particularly vulnerable due to extreme youth and/or personal circumstances		
3	Factor(s) in categories 1 & 2 not present	B	Factor(s) in category A not present

Starting point and category range

10.31

	A	B
Category 1	Starting point: 6 yrs custody Range: 4–9 yrs custody	Starting point: 4 yrs custody Range: 3–7 yrs custody

10.31 *Child sex offences (under 13)*

Category 2	Starting point: 4 yrs custody Range: 3–7 yrs custody	Starting point: 2 yrs custody Range: 1–4 yrs custody
Category 3	Starting point: 1 yr custody Range: 26 wks–2 yrs custody	Starting point: 26 wks custody Range: High level community order–1 yr custody

Additional factual elements

10.32

Aggravating factors
As 'Rape of a child under 13' (see **10.10**), s 5
Mitigating factors
As 'Rape of a child under 13' (see **10.10**), s 5

Other orders

10.33

Extended and life sentence availability (CJA 2003)	Sch 15 (specified offence): yes Sch 15B (life sentence for second listed offence): yes
Trigger offence for:	SOPO: yes FTO: yes, if: D is over 18, *or* Is sentenced to at least 12 months imprisonment
Inclusion in barred lists	Children: automatic Vulnerable adult: subject to representations
Notification	Yes, if: D is over 18, *or* Is sentenced to at least 12 months imprisonment

Causing or inciting a child under 13 to engage in sexual activity
Sexual Offences Act 2003, s 8

DEFINITION

10.34 Section 8:

(1) A person commits an offence if—

(a) he intentionally causes or incites another person (B) to engage in an activity;

(b) the activity is sexual; and

(c) B is under 13.

(2) A person guilty of an offence under this section, if the activity caused or incited involved—

(a) penetration of B's anus or vagina;

(b) penetration of B's mouth with a person's penis;

(c) penetration of a person's anus or vagina with a part of B's body or by B with anything else; or

(d) penetration of a person's mouth with B's penis;

is liable, on conviction on indictment, to imprisonment for life.

SUMMARY

10.35 This offence is the 'victim under 13' version of s 4, with the significant addition of specifically criminalising incitement in this context. Two crucial features stand out:

Consent is irrelevant – a child under 13 does not, under any circumstances, have the legal capacity to consent to any form of sexual activity – whether or not the child ostensibly consented to this act is immaterial;

There is *strict liability as to the age of the child*[10] – it is no defence that a defendant genuinely and reasonably believed that the child was 13 or older.

Subsection 8(2) creates an aggravated version of the offence, relating to penetration.

---

10 *R v G* [2008] UKHL 37.

ELEMENTS

10.36

- Intentionally

  'Intentionally' relates to causing/inciting the activity.

  In theory, it is not necessary that A intends the activity to be sexual, but this distinction is unlikely to arise in practice. It must likewise be rare that someone accidentally or recklessly causes another person to engage in a sexual activity, but this would not suffice.

- causes *or* incites

  The section creates two separate offences (see Specimen Indictments, **Appendix 1**).

- '*Causes*' is not defined by the Act and should be given its natural meaning of bringing about or making happen.

  'Causing' requires something more than merely 'allowing'.

  It may be achieved by words, action or both.

- '*Incites*' is not defined by the Act and should be given its natural meaning of urges or provokes.

  The incited activity need not actually place.

- B to engage in an *activity*

  'Activity' is not defined, but notably is not limited to touching or penetration.[11]

  For example, it can include B exposing himself either directly or over the internet or other electronic link.

  It seems that engaging in a conversation on sexual matters can suffice. In *R v Grout*[12] the Court of Appeal said:

  > 'There is no definition of "activity" in the Sexual Offences Act. We are prepared to accept, for the purposes of this appeal, that "activity" on the part of the child could embrace "the activity" of conversation or sending text or MSN messages, depending on the circumstances. Whether a child sending a text or MSN message could amount to being engaged in "sexual" activity would depend on whether that "activity" came within the definition of "sexual" set out in s 78 of the Sexual Offences Act.'

---

11 Note that s 78, which defines 'sexual', refers to 'penetration, touching or *any other activity*'.
12 [2011] EWCA Crim 299.

- *Sexual* – see **Chapter 2**.

  Relates to the activity in which B is caused or incited to engage rather than anything done by A without B's participation.

- (where the aggravated offence is alleged) specific type of penetration (to be specified in the Indictment).
- *B was under 13*[13] (to be specified in the Indictment).
- Consent is irrelevant.

AGGRAVATED FORM OF THE OFFENCE (PENETRATION)

10.37 By virtue of subs 8(2), which provides for different maximum penalties where the sexual activity caused involves particular forms of penetration, there are two subsets of this offence, penetrative and non-penetrative. Because of the differing penalties and modes of trial (see below), it is essential to specify which version is alleged (see Specimen Indictments, **Appendix 1**).

The aggravated version of the offence involves:

(a) penetration of B's anus or vagina;

(b) penetration of B's mouth with a person's penis;

(c) penetration of a person's anus or vagina with a part of B's body or by B with anything else; or

(d) penetration of a person's mouth with B's penis.

In (a) the penetration can be by anything (although if by A's penis it would constitute rape and if by any other part of A's body it would amount to a s 2 offence).

In (b) the envisaged penetration is by the penis of a person other than A (or else it would be rape).

In (c) the person whose anus or vagina is penetrated can be any person, including A (and, it would appear, B himself).

In (d) the person whose mouth is penetrated can be any person, including A (and, if achievable, B himself).

13 See **Chapter 7**.

PARTIES

10.38 This offence may be committed by males or females of any age – contrast with the s 10 offence (causing or inciting a child to engage in sexual activity) where the defendant must be at least 18.

The complainant may be male or female, subject to being under 13.

DISCUSSION

10.39 Person A may himself participate in the sexual activity with B, but need not. The activity may involve B alone, but equally there could be other persons, animals or objects involved.

EXAMPLES

10.40

- A causes B to engage in sexual activity with A (for example, a woman compels a boy to penetrate her);
- A causes B to engage in solo sexual activity (for example, a man forces a girl to masturbate herself);
- A causes B to engage in sexual activity with C (for example, an adult makes a girl masturbate a boy);
- A forces B expose himself over a webcam (for viewing perhaps by A and/or others);
- A makes B take a naked photograph of herself and send it via a mobile phone (to A or C)[14]

Home Office Guidance (which consistently refers to the offender as 'the adult', despite there being no age parameter in the statute): The offence covers cases where the adult makes the child engage in sexual activity, for example sexual intercourse, with the adult himself and where he makes the child engage in such activity with a third party, whether that third party is a willing participant or another victim. The offence also covers cases where the adult makes the child carry out a sexual act, such as masturbation or stripping.

Examples of an adult causing or inciting a child to engage in sexual activity could be promising a reward, persuading the child that it is perfectly acceptable behaviour that other children engage in all the time and he/she would be

14 *Broughton* [2007] EWCA Crim 566 – arguably the taking of the photograph, even before its onward transmission, constitutes sexual activity.

abnormal not to agree, or saying that it was necessary to check the child's body for – bruises/lice etc, or to try on clothes.

The offence can be charged where the adult incites the child to take part in sexual activity, even where the activity itself does not take place, for example because a parent intervenes.

CLASSIFICATION

10.41 Where specific penetration contrary to s 8(2) is alleged (see **10.37**), the offence is indictable only, otherwise it is triable either way.

SENTENCING AND OTHER ORDERS

Maximum sentence

10.42 In aggravated form: life imprisonment

In non-aggravated form:

- On indictment: 14 years
- Summarily: 6 months imprisonment or a fine not exceeding the statutory maximum (currently £5000)

Sentencing guidelines

Determining the category

10.43

Cat	Harm	Cat	Culpability
1	The extreme nature of one or more category 2 factors or the extreme impact caused by a combination of category 2 factors may elevate to category 1	A	As 'Rape of a child under 13' (see **10.8**), s 5
2	• Severe psychological or physical harm • Penetration of vagina or anus (using body or object) by, or of, the victim • Penile penetration of mouth by, or of, the victim		

10.43 *Child sex offences (under 13)*

Cat	Harm	Cat	Culpability
	• Additional degradation/ humiliation • Abduction • Prolonged detention/ sustained incident • Violence or threats of violence • Forced/uninvited entry into victim's home • Child is particularly vulnerable due to extreme youth and/or personal circumstances		
3	Factor(s) in categories 1 & 2 not present	B	Factor(s) in category A not present

Starting point and category range

10.44

	A	B
Category 1	Starting point: 13 yrs custody Range: 11–17 yrs custody	Starting point: 11 yrs custody Range: 10–15 yrs custody
Category 2	Starting point: 8 yrs custody Range: 5–10 yrs custody	Starting point: 6 yrs custody Range: 3–9 yrs custody
Category 3	Starting point: 5 yrs custody Range: 3–8 yrs custody	Starting point: 2 yrs custody Range: 1–4 yrs custody

Additional factual elements

10.45

Aggravating factors
As 'Rape of a child under 13' (see **10.10**), s 5, but additional factor: • Pregnancy or STI as a consequence of offence

Mitigating factors
As 'Rape of a child under 13' (see **10.10**), s 5, but additional factor: ● Sexual activity was incited but no activity took place because the offender voluntarily desisted or intervened to prevent it

Other orders

10.46

Extended and life sentence availability (CJA 2003)	Sch 15 (specified offence): yes Sch 15B (life sentence for second listed offence): yes
Trigger offence for:	SOPO: yes FTO: yes
Inclusion in barred lists	Children: automatic Vulnerable adult: subject to representations
Notification	Yes

Chapter 11

Child sex offences (under 16)

Sexual activity with a child
Sexual Offences Act 2003, s 9

DEFINITION

11.1 Section 9:

(1) A person aged 18 or over (A) commits an offence if—

(a) he intentionally touches another person (B);

(b) the touching is sexual; and

(c) either—

(i) B is under 16 and A does not reasonably believe that B is 16 or over; or

(ii) B is under 13.

(2) A person guilty of an offence under this section, if the touching involved—

(a) penetration of B's anus or vagina with a part of A's body or anything else,

(b) penetration of B's mouth with A's penis,

(c) penetration of A's anus or vagina with a part of B's body, or

(d) penetration of A's mouth with B's penis,

is liable, on conviction on indictment, to imprisonment for a term not exceeding 14 years.

SUMMARY

11.2 This section makes it an offence for a person aged 18 or over intentionally to engage in sexual touching of a child under 16.

Despite the headnote reading 'sexual activity', only *touching* is caught by s 9 (contrast ss 10 and 11).

Subsection 9(2) creates an aggravated version of the offence, relating to penetration.

ELEMENTS

11.3

- *Intentional touching*

  Section 79(8) provides that:

  Touching includes touching:

  (a) with any part of the body;

  (b) with anything else;

  (c) through anything;

  and in particular includes touching amounting to penetration.

  The touching by A must be intentional – in other words, deliberate and not accidental.[1]

- *Sexual* – see Chapter 2
- Age of B

  either

  B is under 16 and A does not reasonably believe that B is 16 or over

  or

  B is under 13

  Applicable age element must be pleaded in the indictment.

- Consent is irrelevant.

PARTIES

11.4 This offence may be committed by males and females, subject to being at least 18 (if younger, s 13 applies).

The complainant may be male or female, subject to being below the relevant age (13 or 16).

Section 9 relates particularly to complainants aged 13 to 15. In order to close a loophole, those under 13 are included, but sexual contact offences against children as young as that would usually be charged under s 5, 6, or 7.

DISCUSSION

11.5 The Court of Appeal has held[2] that merely touching the clothing worn by B (as contrasted with touching B through that clothing) can suffice for this offence.

B need not be aware of the touching.

---

1 *R v Heard* [2007] EWCA Crim 125.

2 *R v H (Karl Anthony)* [2005] EWCA Crim 732, [2005] 2 Cr App R 9.

A need not intend his touching of B to be sexual, nor need he derive or seek sexual gratification. Any touching of B which was obviously sexual because of its nature (for example thrusting a hand inside underwear to touch the outside of the vagina) could amount to a sexual assault even if A's sole purpose was to cause distress to B.

In notable contrast between this offence and the SOA 1956 offences of indecent assault (see **28.25** and **28.33**) sexual touching must actually occur (for the completed offence) – the mere apprehension of such touching is insufficient (but may indicate an attempt).

EXAMPLES

11.6 Examples of this offence would include where an adult rubs up against a child's private parts through clothes for sexual gratification. It also includes penetration, so penile/digital penetration where absence of consent could not be proved, would be covered by this section.

DEFENCES

11.7 Where B was aged 13 to 15, reasonable belief that B was 16 or over.

Section 73 provides that a person will not be guilty of aiding, abetting or counselling an offence contrary to s 9 if acting to protect the child's physical safety, protect them from sexually transmitted infection or pregnancy, or to promote their well-being by the giving of advice. This defence is unlikely to have frequent application, but might conceivably arise if a health professional provided contraceptive advice to a girl who said she was having sex with an older man.

CLASSIFICATION

11.8 Where specific penetration contrary to s 9(2) is alleged, the offence is indictable only, otherwise it is triable either way.

SENTENCING AND OTHER ORDERS

Maximum sentence

11.9 In aggravated form: 14 years

In non-aggravated form:

- On indictment: 14 years

- Summarily: 6 months imprisonment or a fine not exceeding the statutory maximum (currently £5000)

Sentencing guidelines

Determining the category

11.10

Cat	Harm	Cat	Culpability
1	• Penetration of vagina or anus (using body or object) • Penile penetration of mouth In either case by, or of, the victim	A	• Significant degree of planning • Offender acts together with others to commit the offence • Use of alcohol/drugs on victim to facilitate the offence • Grooming behaviour used against victim • Abuse of trust • Use of threats (including blackmail) • Sexual images of victim recorded, retained, solicited or shared • Specific targeting of a particularly vulnerable child • Offender lied about age • Significant disparity in age • Commercial exploitation and/or motivation • Offence racially or religiously aggravated • Offence motivated by, or demonstrating, hostility to the victim based on his or her sexual orientation (or presumed sexual orientation) or transgender identity (or presumed transgender identity)
2	Touching, or exposure, of naked genitalia or naked breasts by, or of, the victim		

11.10 *Child sex offences (under 16)*

Cat	Harm	Cat	Culpability
			• Offence motivated by, or demonstrating, hostility to the victim based on his or her disability (or presumed disability)
3	Other sexual activity	B	Factor(s) in category A not present

Starting point and category range

11.11

	A	B
Category 1	Starting point: 5 yrs custody Range: 4–10 yrs custody	Starting point: 1 yr custody Range: High level community order–2 yrs custody
Category 2	Starting point: 3 yrs custody Range: 2–6 yrs custody	Starting point: 26 wks custody Range: High level community order–1 yr custody
Category 3	Starting point: 26 wks custody Range: High level community order–3 yrs custody	Starting point: Medium level community order Range: Low level community order–High level community order

Additional factual elements

11.12

Aggravating factors
Statutory aggravating factors
• Previous convictions, having regard to: (a) the nature of the offence to which the conviction relates and its relevance to the current offence; and (b) the time that has elapsed since the conviction

Other aggravating factors
• Offence committed whilst on bail • Severe psychological or physical harm • Ejaculation • Pregnancy or STI as a consequence of offence • Location of offence • Timing of offence • Victim compelled to leave their home, school, etc • Failure to comply with current court orders • Offence committed whilst on licence • Exploiting contact arrangements with a child to commit an offence • Presence of others, especially other children • Any steps taken to prevent the victim reporting an incident, obtaining assistance and/or from assisting or supporting the prosecution • Attempts to dispose of or conceal evidence • Failure of offender to respond to previous warnings • Commission of offence whilst under the influence of alcohol or drugs
• Victim encouraged to recruit others • Period over which offence committed
Mitigating factors
• No previous convictions or no relevant/recent convictions • Remorse • Previous good character and/or exemplary conduct* • Age and/or lack of maturity where it affects the responsibility of the offender • Mental disorder or learning disability, particularly where linked to the commission of the offence • Sexual activity was incited but no activity took place because the offender voluntarily desisted or intervened to prevent it

* Previous good character/exemplary conduct is different from having no previous convictions. The more serious the offence, the less the weight which should normally be attributed to this factor. Where previous good character/exemplary conduct has been used to facilitate the offence, this

mitigation should not normally be allowed and such conduct may constitute an aggravating factor.

In the context of this offence, previous good character/exemplary conduct should not normally be given any significant weight and will not normally justify a reduction in what would otherwise be the appropriate sentence

Other orders

11.13

Extended and life sentence availability (CJA 2003)	Sch 15 (specified offence): yes Sch 15B (life sentence for second listed offence): yes
Trigger offence for:	SOPO: yes FTO: yes
Inclusion in barred lists	Children: subject to representations Vulnerable adult: subject to representations
Notification	Yes

Causing or inciting a child to engage in sexual activity
Sexual Offences Act 2003, s 10

DEFINITION

11.14 Section 10(1):

A person aged 18 or over (A) commits an offence if—

(a) he intentionally causes or incites another person (B) to engage in an activity,

(b) the activity is sexual, and

(c) either—

(i) B is under 16 and A does not reasonably believe that B is 16 or over, or

(ii) B is under 13.

SUMMARY

11.15 This section makes it an offence for a person aged 18 or over intentionally to cause or incite a child under 16 to engage in sexual activity.

ELEMENTS

11.16

- *Intentionally*

  'Intentionally' relates to causing/inciting the activity.

  In theory, it is not necessary that A intends the activity to be sexual, but this distinction is unlikely to arise in practice.

  It must likewise be rare that someone accidentally or recklessly causes another person to engage in a sexual activity, but this would not suffice.

- causes *or* incites

  The section creates two separate offences (see Specimen Indictments, **Appendix 1**).

- '*Causes*' is not defined by the Act and should be given its natural meaning of bringing about or making happen.

  'Causing' requires something more than merely 'allowing'.

  It may be achieved by words, action or both.

- '*Incites*' is not defined by the Act and should be given its natural meaning of urges or provokes.

  The incited activity need not actually place.

- B to engage in an *activity*.

  'Activity' is not defined, but notably is not limited to touching or penetration.[3]

  For example, it can include B exposing himself either directly or over the internet.

  It seems that engaging in a conversation on sexual matters can suffice.[4]

- *Sexual* – see Chapter 2.

  Relates to the activity in which B is caused or incited to engage rather than anything done by A without B's participation.

---

3 Note that s 78, which defines 'sexual', refers to 'penetration, touching or *any other activity*'.

4 *R v Grout* [2011] EWCA Crim 299 at [29], discussed at **10.36**.

- (where the aggravated offence is alleged) specific type of penetration (to be specified in the Indictment).
- Age of B:[5]

  either

  B is under 16 and A does not reasonably believe that B is 16 or over

  or

  B is under 13

  Applicable age element must be pleaded in the indictment.
- Consent is irrelevant.

PARTIES

11.17 The offence may be committed by males or females, subject to being aged at least 18 (if younger, s 13 applies).

The complainant may be male or female, subject to being below the relevant age (13 or 16).

Section 10 relates particularly to complainants aged 13 to 15. In order to close a loophole, those under 13 are included, but sexual contact offences against children as young as that would usually be charged under s 8.

DISCUSSION

11.18 Person A may himself participate in the sexual activity with B, but need not. The activity may involve B alone, but equally there could be other persons, animals or objects involved.

Unlike s 8, although s 10(2) provides an aggravated version of the offence where the sexual activity involves penetration,[6] it does not affect the maximum penalty. It does, however, change the mode of trial classification (see below).

EXAMPLES

11.19 Home Office Guidance: The offence covers cases where the adult makes the child engage in sexual activity, for example sexual intercourse, with

---

5 See **Chapter 7**.

6 The wording of subsection 10(2) is identical to that of s 8(2), except for the penalty – 14 years instead of life imprisonment.

the adult himself and where he makes the child engage in such activity with a third party, whether that third party is a willing participant or another victim. The offence also covers cases where the adult makes the child carry out a sexual act, such as masturbation or stripping.

Examples of an adult causing or inciting a child to engage in sexual activity could be promising a reward, persuading the child that it is perfectly acceptable behaviour that other children engage in all the time and he/she would be abnormal not to agree, or saying that it was necessary to check the child's body for bruises/lice etc, or to try on clothes. It is not intended to cover health professionals, or anyone else providing sex education, advice or contraception to children.

The offence can be charged where the adult incites the child to take part in sexual activity, even where the activity itself does not take place, for example because a parent intervenes.

Explanatory Notes to the Act: The sexual activity which is caused or incited may be activity with A (for example, where A causes or incites the child to have sexual intercourse with him), on the child himself (for example, where A causes or incites the child to strip for A's sexual gratification) or with a third person (for example, where A causes or incites the child to have sexual intercourse with A's friend). The incitement constitutes an offence whether or not the activity incited actually takes place.

DEFENCE

11.20 Where B was aged 13 to 15, reasonable belief that B was 16 or over.

CLASSIFICATION

11.21 Where specific penetration contrary to s 10(2) is alleged (see 11.18), the offence is indictable only, otherwise it is triable either way.

SENTENCING AND OTHER ORDERS

Maximum sentence

11.22 In aggravated form: 14 years

In non-aggravated form:

- On indictment: 14 years
- Summarily: 6 months imprisonment or a fine not exceeding the statutory maximum (currently £5000)

Sentencing guidelines

11.23 Identical to 'Sexual Activity with a Child; see 11.10–11.12.

Other orders

11.24

Extended and life sentence availability (CJA 2003)	Sch 15 (specified offence): yes Sch 15B (life sentence for second listed offence): yes
Trigger offence for:	SOPO: yes FTO: yes
Inclusion in barred lists	Children: subject to representations Vulnerable adult: subject to representations
Notification	Yes

Engaging in sexual activity in the presence of a child
Sexual Offences Act 2003, s 11

DEFINITION

11.25 Section 11(1):

A person aged 18 or over (A) commits an offence if—

(a) he intentionally engages in an activity;

(b) the activity is sexual;

(c) for the purpose of obtaining sexual gratification, he engages in it—

(i) when another person (B) is present or is in a place from which A can be observed; and

(ii) knowing or believing that B is aware, or intending that B should be aware, that he is engaging in it, and

(d) either—

(i) B is under 16 and A does not reasonably believe that B is 16 or over; or

(ii) B is under 13.

SUMMARY

11.26 This section makes it an offence for a person aged 18 or over, for the purpose of obtaining sexual gratification, intentionally to engage in sexual activity when a child under 16 is present or in a vantage point. The offender must know, believe or intend that the child is aware of the sexual activity.

ELEMENTS

11.27

- *Age of A* – must be at least 18
- Intentionally *engages*
- *Activity*

  'Activity' is not defined, but notably is not limited to touching or penetration.[7]

  For example, it can include A exposing himself either directly or over the internet or other electronic link.

  The activity may involve A alone, but equally there could be other persons, animals or objects involved.

  The activity may take place in the physical presence of B and be seen by B, but neither of these conditions is necessary – see under 'Examples' below.
- *Sexual* – see **Chapter 2**
- For the purpose of A obtaining *sexual gratification* A engages in the activity when:
  - *B present or* in a place from which *A can be observed*
  - A knowing/believing/intending that B should be aware

    The offence is committed if A knows or believes that B is aware that he is engaging in the activity, or A intends that B should be aware that he is engaging in it, *and* A carries out the activity for the purposes of obtaining sexual gratification from B's awareness.
- *Age of B*:

  either

  B is under 16 and A does not reasonably believe that B is 16 or over

---

7 Note that s 78, which defines 'sexual', refers to 'penetration, touching or *any other activity*'.

or

B is under 13

Applicable age element must be pleaded in the indictment.[8]

- Consent is irrelevant.

PARTIES

11.28 The offence may be committed by males or females, subject to being aged at least 18 (if younger, s 13 applies).

The complainant may be male or female, subject to being below the relevant age (13 or 16).

DISCUSSION

11.29 The offence is intended to cover the situation where someone seeks sexual gratification not from the sexual act itself but rather from the fact that he is performing that act in the presence or intended presence of a child. Home Office Guidance says: 'the motive of sexual gratification is a necessary safeguard intended to avoid capturing those who engage in sexual activity in front of a child for a legitimate reason. For example, a teacher who sexually kisses his partner just outside the school gates, could be deemed to be engaging in sexual activity intentionally in front of a child and might otherwise be caught by the offence.' Of course, if the teacher were motivated by being 'turned on' by the observation by pupils, this section would apply, unless pupils aged 16 to 17 and no younger were involved, in which case s 18 would be engaged (the 'position of trust' version of this offence – see **12.30**).

EXAMPLES

11.30 The offence covers situations such as A masturbating himself in B's presence but without being seen by B (perhaps because the lights are off, or B is covering his face), so long as A knows, believes or intends that B is aware of what A is doing.

Equally, B need not be physically present. A might perform a sexual act in a place where he knows that he can be seen by B, for example via a webcam, but again it is not necessary for B actually to observe the activity.

---

8 See generally 'Age', **Chapter 7**.

DEFENCES

11.31 Where B was aged 13 to 15, reasonable belief that B was 16 or over.

Despite A obtaining sexual gratification from the activity, none was sought from the observation or potential observation by B.

CLASSIFICATION

11.32 Offence is triable either-way.

SENTENCING AND OTHER ORDERS

Maximum sentence

11.33 On indictment: 10 years

Summarily: 6 months imprisonment or a fine not exceeding the statutory maximum (currently £5000)

Determining the category

11.34

Cat	Harm	Cat	Culpability
1	• Causing victim to view extreme pornography • Causing victim to view indecent/prohibited images of children • Engaging in, or causing victim to view live sexual activity involving sadism/violence/sexual activity with an animal/a child	A	• Significant degree of planning • Offender acts together with others to commit the offence • Use of alcohol/drugs on victim to facilitate the offence
2	Engaging in, or causing victim to view images of, or view live, sexual activity involving: • penetration of vagina or anus (using body or object) • penile penetration of mouth		• Grooming behaviour used against victim • Abuse of trust • Use of threats (including blackmail)

11.34 *Child sex offences (under 16)*

Cat	Harm	Cat	Culpability
	• masturbation		• Specific targeting of a particularly vulnerable child • Commercial exploitation and/or motivation • Offence racially or religiously aggravated • Offence motivated by, or demonstrating, hostility to the victim based on his or her sexual orientation (or presumed sexual orientation) or transgender identity (or presumed transgender identity) • Offence motivated by, or demonstrating, hostility to the victim based on his or her disability (or presumed disability)
3	Factor(s) in categories 1 & 2 not present	B	Factor(s) in category A not present

Starting point and category range

11.35

	A	**B**
Category 1	Starting point: 4 yrs custody Range: 3–6 yrs custody	Starting point: 2 yrs custody Range: 1–3 yrs custody
Category 2	Starting point: 2 yrs custody Range: 1–3 yrs custody	Starting point: 1 yr custody Range: High level community order –18 mths custody
Category 3	Starting point: 26 wks custody Range: High level community order–1 yr custody	Starting point: Medium level community order Range: Low level community order–Medium level community order

Additional factual elements

11.36

Aggravating factors
Statutory aggravating factors
• Previous convictions, having regard to a) the nature of the offence to which the conviction relates and its relevance to the current offence; and b) the time that has elapsed since the conviction
• Offence committed whilst on bail
Other aggravating factors
• Location of offence
• Timing of offence
• Victim compelled to leave their home, school, etc
• Failure to comply with current court orders
• Offence committed whilst on licence
• Exploiting contact arrangements with a child to commit an offence
• Presence of others, especially other children
• Any steps taken to prevent the victim reporting an incident, obtaining assistance and/or from assisting or supporting the prosecution
• Attempts to dispose of or conceal evidence
• Failure of offender to respond to previous warnings
• Commission of offence whilst under the influence of alcohol or drugs
• Victim encouraged to recruit others
Mitigating factors
• No previous convictions or no relevant/recent convictions
• Remorse
• Previous good character and/or exemplary conduct*
• Age and/or lack of maturity where it affects the responsibility of the offender
• Mental disorder or learning disability, particularly where linked to the commission of the offence
• Demonstration of steps taken to address offending behaviour

* Previous good character/exemplary conduct is different from having no previous convictions. The more serious the offence, the less the weight which should normally

be attributed to this factor. Where previous good character/exemplary conduct has been used to facilitate the offence, this mitigation should not normally be allowed and such conduct may constitute an aggravating factor.

11.37

Extended and life sentence availability (CJA 2003)	Sch 15 (specified offence): yes Sch 15B (life sentence for second listed offence): yes
Trigger offence for:	SOPO: yes FTO: yes
Inclusion in barred lists	Children: subject to representations Vulnerable adult: subject to representations
Notification	Yes

Causing a child to watch a sexual act Sexual Offences Act 2003, s 12

DEFINITION

11.38 Section 12(1):

A person aged 18 or over (A) commits an offence if—

(a) for the purpose of obtaining sexual gratification, he intentionally causes another person (B) to watch a third person engaging in an activity, or to look at an image of any person engaging in an activity;

(b) the activity is sexual; and

(c) either—

(i) B is under 16 and A does not reasonably believe that B is 16 or over; or

(ii) B is under 13.

SUMMARY

11.39 This section makes it an offence for a person aged 18 or over, for sexual gratification, intentionally to cause a child under 16 either to watch a third person engaging in a sexual act, or to look at an image of any person engaging in a sexual act.

Where the sexual activity is watched 'live' and direct (rather than, for example, via a webcam or recording) only activity involving a 'third person' is covered – if the activity involved A himself, s 11 would apply.

ELEMENTS

11.40

- *Age of A* – must be at least 18.
- Intentionally *causes*.

  'Causes' is not defined by the Act and should be given its natural meaning of bringing about or making happen. 'Causing' requires something more than merely 'allowing'.

  It may be achieved by words, action or both.

  either:

  – B to *watch* a third person (*not* A) engaging in a sexual activity; *or*

  – B to look at an *image* of any person (could be A) engaging in a sexual activity.
- *Sexual activity* – see discussion of 'sexual' at **Chapter 2**.

  'Activity' is not defined, but notably is not limited to touching or penetration[9].
- Image (where it applies) – defined in the Act:

  Section 79(4): 'Image' means a moving or still image and includes an image produced by any means and, where the context permits, a three-dimensional image.

  Section 79(5): References to an image of a person include references to an image of an imaginary person.
- For the purpose of obtaining *sexual gratification* – the gratification may be immediate (A being 'turned on' by the child's observation of the sexual activity) or future gratification (getting the child 'in the mood' to provide A with sexual gratification).[10]
- Age[11] of B:

  either

  B is under 16 and A does not reasonably believe that B is 16 or over

---

9 Note that s 78, which defines 'sexual', refers to 'penetration, touching or *any other activity*'.
10 *R v Abdullahi* [2006] EWCA Crim 2060 – and see remarks about 'grooming' at **11.42**.
11 See **Chapter 7**.

11.40 *Child sex offences (under 16)*

or

B is under 13

Applicable age element must be pleaded in the indictment.

- Consent is irrelevant.

PARTIES

11.41 The offence may be committed by males or females, subject to being aged at least 18 (if younger, s.13 applies).

The complainant may be male or female, subject to being below the relevant age (13 or 16).

DISCUSSION

11.42 As the Home Office Guidance observes, this offence does not require any element of coercion, though it may be a factor in some cases.

In order for an offence to be committed, the adult must act for his own sexual gratification. This ensures that, adults showing children sex education material, either in a school or other setting, will not be liable for this offence.

This provision appears to have been created in response to general concerns about the exposure of children to pornography and in particular its use in the sexual 'grooming' of children.

EXAMPLES

11.43 Home Office Guidance: Examples of this offence would be where a person, for the purposes of his own sexual gratification, enables a child to watch two people have sex, either in the physical presence of the activity or remotely, for instance via a webcam; or where someone invites a child to watch a pornographic film or sends a child indecent images over the internet.

DEFENCES

11.44 Where B was aged 13 to 15, reasonable belief that B was 16 or over.

A merely allowed, rather than caused, B to observe the sexual act.

Whether or not intending that B should obtain sexual gratification, A sought to derive no gratification for himself.

CLASSIFICATION

11.45 Offence is triable either-way.

SENTENCING AND OTHER ORDERS

Maximum sentence

11.46 On indictment: 10 years

Summarily: 6 months imprisonment or a fine not exceeding the statutory maximum (currently £5000)

Sentencing guidelines

11.47 Identical to guidelines for 'Engaging in sexual activity in the presence of a child' (see 11.34–11.36).

Other orders

11.48

Extended and life sentence availability (CJA 2003)	Sch 15 (specified offence): yes Sch 15B (life sentence for second listed offence): yes
Trigger offence for:	SOPO: yes FTO: yes
Inclusion in barred lists	Children: subject to representations Vulnerable adult: subject to representations
Notification	Yes

Child sex offences committed by children or young persons
Sexual Offences Act 2003, s 13

DEFINITION

11.49 Section 13(1):

> A person under 18 commits an offence if he does anything which would be an offence under any of sections 9 to 12 if he were aged 18.

SUMMARY

11.50 This section makes youths (aged 10 to 17) subject to the adult offences in ss 9 to 12 of the Act, but with a lower maximum penalty (five years).

The indictment will allege 'sexual activity with a child', 'causing or inciting a child to engage in sexual activity', 'engaging in sexual activity in the presence of a child' or 'causing a child to watch a sexual act', but contrary to s 13. The particulars should state that the defendant was aged under 18 at the time of the offence.

ELEMENTS

11.51 The elements of the s 13 offence are the same elements, save for those relating to the age of the offender, as for the respective adult offence under ss 9–12. Reference should be made to 11.3, 11.16, 11.27 or 11.40 as appropriate.

As with all the child sex offences, consent remains irrelevant.

PARTIES

11.52 The offence may be committed by males or females, subject to being aged 10–17 (if older, s 9, 10, 11 or 12 applies).

The complainant may be male or female, subject to being below the relevant age (13 or 16).

DISCUSSION

11.53 For notes and examples, reference should be made to the appropriate adult section: 11.5–11.6, 11.18–11.19, 11.29–11.30 or 11.42–11.43.

Explanatory Notes to the Act: In practice (although there is no provision about this in the Act) decisions on whether persons under 18 should be charged with child sex offences will be made by Crown Prosecutors in accordance with the principles set out in the Code for Crown Prosecutors. In deciding whether it is in the public interest to prosecute these offences, where there is enough evidence to provide a realistic prospect of conviction, prosecutors may take into consideration factors such as the ages of the parties; the emotional maturity of the parties; whether they entered into a sexual relationship willingly; any coercion or corruption by a person; and the relationship between the parties and whether there was any existence of a duty of care or breach of trust.

Home Office Guidance: It is not intended that young people should be prosecuted or issued with a reprimand or final warning where the sexual activity was entirely mutually agreed and non-exploitative. The way in which the law will be interpreted applies equally to males and females, whatever their sexual orientation.

In deciding whether it is in the public interest to prosecute these offences, where there is enough evidence to provide a realistic prospect of conviction, prosecutors may take into consideration factors which include the age and emotional maturity of the parties, whether they entered into the sexual relationship willingly, any coercion or corruption by a person, the relationship between the parties and whether there was any existence of a duty of care or breach of trust.

Where the two parties are close in age, and the sexual activity is mutually agreed a prosecution may be less likely to be in the public interest than if one party is much older than the other. Where both parties are particularly young, for example, under 13, it may be more appropriate to draw the children to the attention of the Social Services rather than to pursue a prosecution. However, such decisions are a matter for the CPS, and need to be considered on a case-by-case basis.

Reprimand and final warning guidance is being amended to make clear that neither is to be given unless it is clearly in the public interest, and that they will no longer automatically trigger sex offender notification requirements.

DEFENCES

11.54 Refer to 11.7, 11.20, 11.31 or 11.44 as appropriate.

Section 73 provides that a person will not be guilty of aiding, abetting or counselling an offence contrary to s 13 (in relation to a s 9 offence) if acting to protect the child's physical safety, protect them from sexually transmitted infection or pregnancy, or to promote their well-being by the giving of advice. This defence is unlikely to have frequent application, but might conceivably arise if a health professional provided contraceptive advice to a girl under 16 who said she was having sex with an unnamed boy.

CLASSIFICATION

11.55 Offence is triable either-way.

SENTENCING AND OTHER ORDERS

Maximum sentence

11.56 On indictment: 5 years

Summarily: 6 months imprisonment or a fine not exceeding the statutory maximum (currently £5,000).

Sentencing factors

11.56A There are no guidelines for this offence within the Sexual Offences Definitive Guideline 2014.

When sentencing offenders under 18, a court must in particular:

Follow the definitive guideline Overarching Principles – Sentencing Youths;

and have regard to:

- the principal aim of the youth justice system (to prevent offending by children and young people); and
- the welfare of the young offender

This is a 'grave crime' for the purposes of section 91 of the Powers of Criminal Courts (Sentencing) Act 2000.

Other orders

11.57

Extended and life sentence availability (CJA 2003)	Sch 15 (specified offence): no Sch 15B (life sentence for second listed offence): no
Trigger offence for:	SOPO: yes FTO: yes, if d is sentenced to at least 12 months imprisonment
Inclusion in barred lists	Children: no Vulnerable adult: no
Notification	Yes, if D is sentenced to at least 12 months imprisonment

Arranging or facilitating the commission of a child sex offence
Sexual Offences Act 2003, s 14

DEFINITION

11.58 Section 14(1):

A person commits an offence if—

(a) he intentionally arranges or facilitates something that he intends to do, intends another person to do, or believes that another person will do, in any part of the world, and

(b) doing it will involve the commission of an offence under any of sections 9 to 13.

SUMMARY

11.59 This section makes it an offence for a person intentionally to arrange or facilitate a child sex offence anywhere in the world, by himself or another.

ELEMENTS

11.60

- *intentionally* – see discussion of mental element at **11.62**.
- *arranges or facilitates*

  neither verb is defined in the Act, so should be given its natural meanings:

  - arrange – organise/set up
  - facilitate – make easier/assist
- something A:
  - *intends* to do;
  - *intends another* person to do; or
  - *believes another* person will do
- anywhere:

  The arrangement or facilitation must take place in the UK (if not, a s 72 offence is likely to arise – see **Chapter 31**), but the contemplated child sex offence may be located in the UK or in any other part of the world.

- doing it will involve an offence under ss 9 to 13 – see **11.62**.
- Consent is irrelevant.

PARTIES

11.61 The offence may be committed by males or females. Although offences under ss 9 to 12 can only be committed by persons aged 18 or over, the inclusion of s 13 within the offences listed under s 14(1)(b) means that the person whose anticipated offence is arranged or facilitated may be under 18.

The child against whom the ultimate offence is contemplated may be male or female, subject to being under 16.

DISCUSSION

11.62 The mental element of this offence requires *intentional* arrangement or facilitation of the activity with, it is submitted, sufficient awareness of its nature. For example, the friend who arranges or pays for a foreign holiday believing that the traveller will engage in some form of sexual activity does not commit this offence unless he believes that a child will be involved.

If such a traveller sexually touches a 12 year old in the genuine belief that the child is 16 (thereby committing an offence contrary to s 9 by virtue of the strict liability imposed by s 9(1)(c)(ii) regarding age), would the friend by guilty of a s 14 offence? We would suggest not.

The specific reference within s 14(1)(b) to ss 9 to 13 only, with the notable omission of ss 5 to 8, is inexplicable. Parliament cannot have intended to exempt from this provision those who arrange or facilitate offences such as the rape of a child under 13. However, because ss 9 to 13 protect all children under the age of 16 (not just those aged 13–15), the arrangement or facilitation of child abuse covered by ss 5 to 8 can still be caught. For example, someone arranging the rape of a 12 year old commits a s 14 offence on the basis that the rape contrary to s 5 would also amount to a s 9 offence of sexual activity with a child. The apparent legislative oversight does mean, though, that the 14 years maximum penalty under this section, which matches or exceeds the maxima for the specified sections, falls short of the life imprisonment available for ss 5, 6 and 8 offences.

The contemplated child sex offence need not actually take place. For example, if police foil a planned sexual encounter with a child, a person who had intentionally facilitated the encounter would have committed a *completed* s 14 offence.

An attempt to commit a s 14 offence (contrary to Criminal Attempts Act 1981, s 1) is also possible, notwithstanding the preparatory nature of the s 14 offence itself.[12]

There is considerable overlap with offences contrary to ss 44 to 46 of the Serious Crime Act 2007 (intentionally encouraging or assisting the commission of an offence) and other inchoate offences such as conspiracy and aiding and abetting. However, s 14 captures relevant preparatory behaviour more widely.

EXAMPLES

11.63 An example of the first two limbs of the offence is where an adult approaches an agency requesting the agency to procure a child for the purpose of sexual activity with either himself or a friend. Arrangements might be made over the internet or by telephone but can also result from personal contact between one person who wants to find a child to abuse and another person who is in contact with a child or children.

An example of the third limb of the offence is where the adult (A) intentionally drives another person (B) to meet a child with whom he knows B is going to engage in sexual activity. A may not intend B to have sexual activity with the child, but he believes that he will do so if he meets that child. Another example might be where one person offers a bedroom in his house to friends or associates for the purposes of having sex with a particular child or children.

The offence is committed whether or not the offence takes place. For example, a prosecution could still be pursued where the police, acting on intelligence in order to safeguard a child, apprehend the offender before a substantive sexual offence has been committed. Similarly, a prosecution could be pursued where a person had arranged the procuring of a child, but where the child was not delivered, or where a person had given permission for his premises to be used for sexual activity with a child, but circumstances prevented the activity from taking place. Where the police set up a 'sting' operation and an offender contacts them believing they are offenders who can procure him a child for sexual abuse, but no real child is actually involved, an attempt at the s 14 offence might be charged.

DEFENCES

11.64 Subsections (2) and (3) afford a statutory defence to those whose actions are intended to protect the child, providing as follows:

(2) A person does not commit an offence under this section if—

---

12 *R v Robson* [2008] 2 Cr App R 38; [2008] EWCA Crim 619.

(a) he arranges or facilitates something that he believes another person will do, but that he does not intend to do or intend another person to do; and

(b) any offence within subsection (1)(b) would be an offence against a child for whose protection he acts.

(3) For the purposes of subsection (2), a person acts for the protection of a child if he acts for the purpose of—

(a) protecting the child from sexually transmitted infection;

(b) protecting the physical safety of the child;

(c) preventing the child from becoming pregnant; or

(d) promoting the child's emotional well-being by the giving of advice;

and not for the purpose of obtaining sexual gratification or for the purpose of causing or encouraging the activity constituting the offence within subsection (1)(b) or the child's participation in it.

An example of the operation of the statutory defence would be where a health worker (A) believes that a person (B) is having sex with a child under 16. A advises B that it is unlawful to have sex with children under 16 but supplies B with condoms because A believes that B will otherwise have sex with the child without protection.

The exception does not apply only to health workers, but to anyone who acts for the purposes of protecting a child, for example teachers, social workers, carers, youth workers whether professionals or volunteers.

The use of the expression 'a child for whose protection he acts' does not mean that any formal or prior care relationship needs to exist between A and the child. The phrase is a term of art with the particular meaning defined by s 14(3).

The statutory defence applies only where A does not act to cause or encourage the sexual activity to take place or for the purpose of sexual gratification.

Lack of intention would also be a defence – see discussion of mental element at **11.62**.

CLASSIFICATION

11.65 Offence is triable either way.

SENTENCING AND OTHER ORDERS

Maximum sentence

11.66 On indictment: 14 years

Summarily: 6 months imprisonment or a fine not exceeding the statutory maximum (currently £5000)

Sentencing guidelines

11.67 There is no specific sentencing guideline for this offence. Reference should be made to the guideline for the applicable substantive offence.

The level of harm should be determined by reference to the type of activity arranged or facilitated. Sentences commensurate with the applicable starting point and range will ordinarily be appropriate. For offences involving significant commercial exploitation and/or an international element, it may, in the interests of justice, be appropriate to increase a sentence to a point above the category range. In exceptional cases, such as where a vulnerable offender performed a limited role, having been coerced or exploited by others, sentences below the starting point and range may be appropriate.

Other orders

11.68

Extended and life sentence availability (CJA 2003)	Sch 15 (specified offence): yes Sch 15B (life sentence for second listed offence): yes
Trigger offence for:	SOPO: yes FTO: yes, if D is over 18, *or* Is sentenced to at least 12 months imprisonment
Inclusion in barred lists	Children: subject to representations Vulnerable adult: subject to representations
Notification	Yes, if: D is over 18, *or* Is sentenced to at least 12 months imprisonment
Confiscation	This is a lifestyle offence within Proceeds of Crime Act 2002, Sch 2

Meeting a child following sexual grooming etc Sexual Offences Act 2003, s 15

DEFINITION

11.69 Section 15(1):

A person aged 18 or over (A) commits an offence if—

(a) A has met or communicated with another person (B) on at least two occasions and subsequently—

(i) A intentionally meets B;

(ii) A travels with the intention of meeting B in any part of the world; or arranges to meet B in any part of the world; or

(iii) B travels with the intention of meeting A in any part of the world;

(b) A intends to do anything to or in respect of B, during or after the meeting mentioned in paragraph (a)(i) to (iii) and in any part of the world, which if done will involve the commission by A of a relevant offence;

(c) B is under 16; and

(d) A does not reasonably believe that B is 16 or over.

SUMMARY

11.70 This section deals with sexual 'grooming' of children by adults.

Its aim is to protect children from adults who communicate with them and then meet them, or intend to meet them, intending to commit a sexual offence against them, during that meeting or subsequently.

Following amendment of this section,[13] the offence is committed when the adult meets the child, travels with the intention of meeting the child, arranges to meet the child, or when the child travels with the intention of meeting the adult.

---

13 By Criminal Justice & Immigration Act 2008, s 73, in force from 14 July 2008.

ELEMENTS

11.71

- *Age of A* – must be at least 18.
- A has *met or communicated* with B *at least twice.*

A minimum of two prior interactions must have occurred (one is insufficient however much 'grooming' takes place during it) but there is no limitation on timing (even pre-commencement of SOA 2003) or location. Communication can be 'by any means'[14] so includes Facebook, email, texting and all current and future technologies.

- subsequently:
  - A intentionally *meets* B; or
  - *A travels* with the intention of meeting B (anywhere); or
  - A *arranges* to meet B (anywhere); or
  - B *travels* with the intention of meeting A (anywhere).

As to location, see **11.73**.

- A *intends* to do (at any time – 'during or after the meeting') something re B which would amount to a *relevant offence*:
  - a 'relevant offence' is any offence contrary to ss 1–79 of SOA 2003;[15] or
  - anything which would be such offence if done in England and Wales.[16]
- Consent is irrelevant.

PARTIES

11.72 The offence may be committed by males or females, subject to them being at least 18 at the time of the ultimate activity (although the requisite prior meeting/communications can have occurred before A attained this age).

The complainant may be male or female, subject to being under 16.

14 Section 15(2)(a).
15 Section 15(2)(b)(i).
16 Section 15(2)(b)(iii).

JURISDICTION

11.73 For prosecution under this section, one of the following must occur in England or Wales: the ultimate meeting between A and B, the arrangement by A, or any part of A or B's journey to an intended meeting. Otherwise s 72 (offences outside the UK) might apply – see **Chapter 31**.

DISCUSSION

11.74 Although s 15 is expressly aimed at grooming, it is noticeable that the two requisite prior interactions ('met or communicated') may have been entirely innocent. It is only necessary for A to hold the sexual intention at the key time (meeting/travelling/arranging) thereafter.

As was observed by the Court of Appeal in *Gaviria*:[17] 'There is absolutely no requirement that either communication be sexual in nature…the aim of the statute is to penalise those who use a relationship which they have developed (whether innocently or otherwise) as a platform from which to launch sexual offending.'

If A's sexual intention were formed only during the meeting with B, s 15 would not be engaged – see examples, below.

EXAMPLES

11.75 However disturbing, the following would reveal a complete defence: 'Having communicated twice with B, I arranged an innocent meeting between us. It was only at that meeting that I formed a firm intention to have sex with her despite knowing that she was aged 10. Before I could act on that intention, the police intervened.'

Conversely, imagine A (aged 18) said: 'I know she is 15 and that her birthday is in three months' time. We'd exchanged two emails about our shared interest in Egyptology and she suggested meeting at the British Museum tomorrow. Nothing would happen at the museum, but I planned to see her again next week when I intended to snog her. However, I saw a photo of her yesterday and I changed my mind.' In fact, A had already committed a full offence contrary to s 15 when their museum meeting was arranged.

DEFENCES

11.76 Reasonable belief that B was 16 or over.

---

17 [2010] EWCA Crim 1693 at [16].

PRACTITIONER POINTER

Where the prior interactions have not been face to face, the apparent age of B in any shared photograph or any representation made by B as to age will be significant.

Is there evidence of B exaggerating his or her age, whether to A or generally? How old does B appear on Facebook? Are there indicative references to school or parents implying a particular age range, or reports of 'adult' activities?

Intention only formed during the meeting with B, not in advance (see **11.74** and **11.75**).

CLASSIFICATION

11.77 Offence is triable either-way.

SENTENCING AND OTHER ORDERS

Maximum sentence

11.78 On indictment: 10 years

Summarily: 6 months imprisonment or a fine not exceeding the statutory maximum (currently £5000)

Sentencing guidelines

Determining the category

11.79 The court should determine the offence category using the table below.

Category 1	Raised harm **and** raised culpability
Category 2	Raised harm **or** raised culpability
Category 3	Grooming **without** raised harm or culpability factors present

The court should determine culpability and harm caused or intended, by reference **only** to the factors below, which comprise the principal factual elements of the offence. Where an offence does not fall squarely into a category, individual factors may require a degree of weighting before making an overall assessment and determining the appropriate offence category.

11.79 *Child sex offences (under 16)*

Factors indicating raised harm	**Factors indicating raised culpability**
• Continued contact despite victim's attempts to terminate contact	• Offender acts together with others to commit the offence
• Sexual images exchanged	• Communication indicates penetrative sexual activity is intended
• Victim exposed to extreme sexual content (for example, extreme pornography)	• Offender lied about age/persona
• Child is particularly vulnerable due to personal circumstances	• Use of threats (including blackmail), gifts or bribes
	• Abuse of trust
	• Specific targeting of a particularly vulnerable child
	• Abduction/detention
	• Commercial exploitation and/or motivation
	• Offence racially or religiously aggravated
	• Offence motivated by, or demonstrating, hostility to the victim based on his or her sexual orientation (or presumed sexual orientation) or transgender identity (or presumed transgender identity)
	Offence motivated by, or demonstrating, hostility to the victim based on his or her disability (or presumed disability)

Starting point and category range

11.80

Category 1	Starting point: 4 yrs custody Range: 3–7 yrs custody
Category 2	Starting point: 2 yrs custody Range: 1–4 yrs custody

Category 3	Starting point: 18 mths custody Range: 1 yr–2 yrs 6 mths custody

Additional factual elements

11.81

Aggravating factors
Statutory aggravating factors
• Previous convictions, having regard to a) the nature of the offence to which the conviction relates and its relevance to the current offence; and b) the time that has elapsed since the conviction
• Offence committed whilst on bail
Other aggravating factors
• Failure to comply with current court orders
• Offence committed whilst on licence
• Any steps taken to prevent the victim reporting an incident, obtaining assistance and/or from assisting or supporting the prosecution
• Attempts to dispose of or conceal evidence
• Victim encouraged to recruit others
Mitigating factors
• No previous convictions or no relevant/recent convictions
• Remorse
• Previous good character and/or exemplary conduct*
• Age and/or lack of maturity where it affects the responsibility of the offender
• Mental disorder or learning disability, particularly where linked to the commission of the offence
• Demonstration of steps taken to address offending behaviour

* Previous good character/exemplary conduct is different from having no previous convictions. The more serious the offence, the less the weight which should normally be attributed to this factor. Where previous good character/exemplary conduct has been used to facilitate the offence, this mitigation should not normally be allowed and such conduct may constitute an aggravating factor.

11.82 *Child sex offences (under 16)*

11.82

Extended and life sentence availability (CJA 2003)	Sch 15 (specified offence): yes Sch 15B (life sentence for second listed offence): yes
Trigger offence for:	SOPO: yes FTO: yes
Inclusion in barred lists	Children: subject to representations Vulnerable adult: subject to representations
Notification	Yes

Chapter 12

Child sex offences: abuse of position of trust

Abuse of position of trust: sexual activity with a child
Sexual Offences Act 2003, s 16

DEFINITION

12.1 Section 16(1):

A person aged 18 or over (A) commits an offence if—

(a) he intentionally touches another person (B);

(b) the touching is sexual;

(c) A is in a position of trust in relation to B;

(d) where subsection (2) applies, A knows or could reasonably be expected to know of the circumstances by virtue of which he is in a position of trust in relation to B; and

(e) either—

(i) B is under 18 and A does not reasonably believe that B is 18 or over; or

(ii) B is under 13.

Section 16(2):

This subsection applies where A—

(a) is in a position of trust by virtue of circumstances within section 21(2), (3), (4) or (5); and

(b) is not in such a position of trust by virtue of other circumstances.

[For the full circumstances within s 21(2) to 21(5) see **Chapter 5**: positions of trust arising through schools, hospitals, care homes and custody institutions are included.]

SUMMARY

12.2 This section makes it an offence for an adult to touch sexually someone under 18 over whom they are in 'a position of trust'.

Although children of all ages are covered by the section, its primary focus is complainants aged 16 or 17. As with all the child sex offences, consent is irrelevant, indeed most cases under this section will feature ostensible consent, otherwise an offence under ss 1–4 would apply.

Despite the section's heading reading 'sexual activity', only touching (which includes penetration) is caught.

ELEMENTS

12.3

- *Age of A* – must be at least 18.
- *Intentional touching:*

  Section 79(8) provides that:

  Touching includes touching:

  (a) with any part of the body;

  (b) with anything else;

  (c) through anything;

  and in particular includes touching amounting to penetration.

  The touching by A must be *intentional* – in other words, deliberate and not accidental.[1]
- *Sexual* – see **Chapter 2**
- A is in a *position of trust* in relation to B – see **Chapter 5**
- Where subs 16(2) applies (including positions of trust arising through schools, hospitals, care homes and custody institutions), A knows or could reasonably be expected to *know of the circumstances* creating A's position of trust over B.
- *Age of B*

  either

  B is under 18 and A does not reasonably believe that B is 18 or over

1 *R v Heard* [2007] EWCA Crim 125.

or

B is under 13

Applicable age element must be pleaded in the indictment.

- Consent is irrelevant.

PARTIES

12.4 This offence may be committed by males or females, subject to being aged at least 18.

B may be male or female, and must be under 18.

Most complainants will be aged 16 or 17, because s 9 protects those aged 13–15 while younger children are covered by ss 5 to 7. However, s 16 might be preferred when there is a trust relationship and A claims a reasonable belief that (for example) a 15-year-old complainant was older – it will be easier for the prosecution to disprove a reasonable belief that B was 18 rather than merely 16.

EVIDENTIAL PRESUMPTIONS

12.5 Once it is proved that B was under 18, it is taken that A did not reasonably believe that B was 18 or over unless sufficient evidence is adduced to raise the issue (s 16(3)).

Likewise, where s 16(2) applies (because the position of trust exists only by virtue of circumstances within s 21(2), (3), (4) or (5)), it is taken that the defendant knew or could reasonably have been expected to know of those circumstances unless sufficient evidence is adduced to raise the issue (s 16(4)).

Note that in both instances the Act simply refers to sufficient evidence being 'adduced', without specifying by which party. Therefore the presumptions could be displaced not only by a defendant giving evidence at trial, but equally by evidence adduced during the prosecution case such as comments on arrest and answers in interview. The 'sufficient evidence' might even be drawn from other sources (for example a colleague who says 'students don't normally come to our college until they are eighteen' or 'a science lecturer wouldn't have any dealings with students taking art courses: they're in a separate annex'). It is a question of law for the judge whether there has been sufficient evidence to displace the relevant statutory presumption, the test being 'some foundation in the evidence, not merely speculative or fanciful'.[2]

2 *R v Gavin White* [2010] EWCA Crim 1929 at [10], a case dealing with the similarly worded evidential presumptions about consent (SOA 2013, s 75).

DISCUSSION

12.6 The most obvious 'position of trust' will be that between a pupil and a teacher, but the offence covers much wider circumstances.

Given that the defining borderline is set at 18 years, an offence is possible between two people who are very close in age. For instance, a nurse who turned 18 last week could commit the offence by responding to the advances of a professional footballer aged just one month younger who is having overnight treatment for an injury. There is considerable reliance on prosecutorial discretion.

The offence covers all children under 18, however it is principally designed to protect young people aged 16 and 17 who, even though they are over the age of consent for sexual activity, are considered to be vulnerable to sexual abuse and exploitation from particular classes of persons who hold a position of trust or authority in relation to them.

Where the child is aged between 13 and 15, it would normally be more appropriate for the offence of 'sexual activity with a child' (s 9) to be charged, as this carries a heavier maximum penalty of 14 years in recognition of the fact that the child is below the legal age of consent. Where the child is under 13, it would be expected to proceed under one of the specific 'under 13' offences.

The s 16 offence, rather than 'sexual activity with a child' might be charged would be where it is considered plausible that the person in a position of trust reasonably believed a 15-year-old child to be 16 or over, but less tenable that he or she reasonably believed the child to be 18 or over.

EXAMPLES

12.7 A typical example of this offence would be where a teacher responds to a 'crush' by a pupil aged 16 or 17 and a personal relationship develops which eventually includes consensual sexual touching. The touching could be limited to 'playing footsie' under the dining table, a slow dance at the school prom (so long as these were deemed sexual) or a kiss behind the bike sheds, although the offence would also cover full intercourse.

Home Office guidance provides an example where the evidential presumption under s 16(4) might be defeated: where a teacher meets in a bar, and subsequently has sex with, a sixth-form student who he is not aware attends the school at which he teaches.

An example of the defence under s 24 (see below) would be where a male aged 17 goes to stay in the hospital where his 18 year old girlfriend works as a nurse and she masturbates him behind the screens (either when she is on duty or when she visits him after her shift).

12.8

Statutory Defences
Section 23 provides a defence where A and B were lawfully married or civil partners at the material time (s 23(2) places the burden on the defendant to prove this) on condition that B was aged 16 or over.
Section 24 provides a defence where A and B were in a sexual relationship immediately before the position of trust arose (s 24(3) places the burden on the defendant to prove this). However, s 24(2) removes from the scope of this defence any relationship in which sexual intercourse between the parties would have been unlawful. This rules out a sexual relationship with a child under 16.
Section 73 provides that a person will not be guilty of aiding, abetting or counselling an offence contrary to s 16 if acting to protect the child's physical safety, protect them from sexually transmitted infection or pregnancy, or to promote their well-being by the giving of advice. This defence, which is not available for the other 'position of trust' offences, is unlikely to have frequent application, but might conceivably arise if a health professional provided contraceptive advice to a pupil who said she was having sex with an unnamed teacher.

OTHER DEFENCES

12.9 Lack of knowledge of the circumstances giving rise to the position of trust.

Where B was aged 13–17, reasonable belief that B was 18 or over.

CLASSIFICATION

12.10 Offence is triable either way.

SENTENCING AND OTHER ORDERS

Maximum sentence

12.11 On indictment: 5 years

Summarily: 6 months imprisonment or a fine not exceeding the statutory maximum (currently £5000)

Sentencing guidelines

12.12 This guideline also applies to offences committed remotely/online (only applicable to s 17 offences).

12.13 *Child sex offences: abuse of position of trust*

Determining the category

12.13

Cat	Harm	Cat	Culpability
1	• Penetration of vagina or anus (using body or object) • Penile penetration of mouth In either case by, or of, the victim	A	• Significant degree of planning • Offender acts together with others to commit the offence • Use of alcohol/drugs on victim to facilitate the offence • Grooming behaviour used against victim • Use of threats (including blackmail) • Sexual images of victim recorded, retained, solicited or shared • Commercial exploitation and/or motivation • Offence racially or religiously aggravated • Offence motivated by, or demonstrating, hostility to the victim based on his or her sexual orientation (or presumed sexual orientation) or transgender identity (or presumed transgender identity) • Offence motivated by, or demonstrating, hostility to the victim based on his or her disability (or presumed disability)
2	Touching, or exposure, of naked genitalia or naked breasts by, or of, the victim		
3	Factor(s) in categories 1 & 2 not present	B	Factor(s) in category A not present

Starting point and category range

12.14

	A	B
Category 1	Starting point: 18 mths custody Range: 1–2 yrs custody	Starting point: 1 yr custody Range: 26 wks–18 mths custody
Category 2	Starting point: 1 yr custody Range: 26 wks–18 mths custody	Starting point: 26 wks custody Range: High level community order–1 yr custody
Category 3	Starting point: 26 wks custody Range: High level community order–1 yr custody	Starting point: Medium level community order Range: Low level community order–High level community order

Additional factual elements

12.15

Aggravating factors
Statutory aggravating factors
• Previous convictions, having regard to a) the nature of the offence to which the conviction relates and its relevance to the current offence; and b) the time that has elapsed since the conviction • Offence committed whilst on bail
Other aggravating factors
• Ejaculation • Pregnancy or STI as a consequence of offence • Location of offence • Timing of offence • Victim compelled to leave their home, school, etc • Failure to comply with current court orders • Offence committed whilst on licence • Presence of others, especially other children

• Any steps taken to prevent the victim reporting an incident, obtaining assistance and/or from assisting or supporting the prosecution
• Attempts to dispose of or conceal evidence
• Failure of offender to respond to previous warnings
• Commission of offence whilst under the influence of alcohol or drugs
• Victim encouraged to recruit others
Mitigating factors
• No previous convictions or no relevant/recent convictions
• Remorse
• Previous good character and/or exemplary conduct*
• Age and/or lack of maturity where it affects the responsibility of the offender
• Mental disorder or learning disability, particularly where linked to the commission of the offence
• Sexual activity was incited but no activity took place because the offender voluntarily desisted or intervened to prevent it
• Demonstration of steps taken to address offending behaviour

* Previous good character/exemplary conduct is different from having no previous convictions. The more serious the offence, the less the weight which should normally be attributed to this factor. Where previous good character/exemplary conduct has been used to facilitate the offence, this mitigation should not normally be allowed and such conduct may constitute an aggravating factor.

Other orders

12.16

Extended and life sentence availability (CJA 2003)	Sch 15 (specified offence): yes Sch 15B (life sentence for second listed offence): no
Trigger offence for:	SOPO: yes FTO: yes, if D sentenced to prison or detention in hospital or community sentence of at least 12 months
Inclusion in barred lists	Children: subject to representations Vulnerable adult: subject to representations
Notification	Yes, if D sentenced to prison or detention in hospital or community sentence of at least 12 months

Abuse of position of trust: causing or inciting a child to engage in sexual activity Sexual Offences Act 2003, s 17

DEFINITION

12.17 Section 17(1):

A person aged 18 or over (A) commits an offence if—

(a) he intentionally causes or incites another person (B) to engage in an activity;

(b) the activity is sexual;

(c) A is in a position of trust in relation to B;

(d) where subsection (2) applies, A knows or could reasonably be expected to know of the circumstances by virtue of which he is in a position of trust in relation to B; and

(e) either—

(i) B is under 18 and A does not reasonably believe that B is 18 or over; or

(ii) B is under 13.

Section 17(2):

This subsection applies where A—

(a) is in a position of trust by virtue of circumstances within section 21(2), (3), (4) or (5); and

(b) is not in such a position of trust by virtue of other circumstances.

[For the full circumstances within s 21(2) to 21(5) see **Chapter 5**: positions of trust arising through schools, hospitals, care homes and custody institutions are included]

SUMMARY

12.18 This section makes it an offence for an adult to cause or incite someone under 18, over whom they are in 'a position of trust', to engage in sexual activity.

Although children of all ages are covered by the section, its primary focus is complainants aged 16 or 17. As with all the child sex offences, consent is irrelevant.

ELEMENTS

12.19

- *Age of A* – must be at least 18
- *'Intentionally'* relates to causing/inciting the activity.

  In theory, it is not necessary that A intends the activity to be sexual, but this distinction is unlikely to arise in practice.

  It must likewise be rare that someone accidentally or recklessly causes another person to engage in a sexual activity, but this would not suffice.
- Causes *or* incite

  The section creates two separate offences.
- '*Causes*' is not defined by the Act and should be given its natural meaning of bringing about or making happen.

  'Causing' requires something more than merely 'allowing'.

  It may be achieved by words, action or both.
- *'Incites'* is not defined by the Act and should be given its natural meaning of urges or provokes.

  The incited activity need not actually take place.
- B to engage in *activity*

  '*Activity*' is not defined, but notably is not limited to touching or penetration.[3]

  For example, it can include B exposing himself either directly or over the internet or other electronic link.

  It seems that engaging in a conversation on sexual matters can suffice.[4]
- *Sexual* – see **Chapter 2**.

  Relates to the activity in which B is caused or incited to engage rather than anything done by A without B's participation.
- A is in a *position of trust* in relation to B – see **Chapter 5**.
- Where subsection 2 applies (including positions of trust arising through schools, hospitals, care homes and custody institutions), A knows or could reasonably be expected to *know of the circumstances* creating A's position of trust over B.

---

3 Note that s.78, which defines 'sexual', refers to 'penetration, touching or *any other activity*'.

4 *R v Grout* [2011] EWCA Crim 299 at [29], discussed at **10.36**.

- *Age*[5] *of B*

  either

  B is under 18 and A does not reasonably believe that B is 18 or over

  or

  B is under 13

  Applicable age element must be pleaded in the indictment.
- Consent is irrelevant.

PARTIES

12.20 This offence may be committed by males or females, subject to being aged at least 18.

B may be male or female, and must be under 18.

Most complainants will be aged 16 or 17, because s 10 protects those aged 13–15 while younger children are covered by s 8. However, s 17 might be preferred when there is a trust relationship and A claims (for example) a reasonable belief that a 15-year-old complainant was older – it will be easier for the prosecution to disprove a reasonable belief that B was 18 rather than merely 16.

EVIDENTIAL PRESUMPTIONS

12.21 Once it is proved that B was under 18, it is taken that A did not reasonably believe that B was 18 or over unless sufficient evidence is adduced to raise the issue (s 17(3)).

Likewise, where subs 17(2) applies (because the position of trust exists only by virtue of circumstances within s 21(2), (3), (4) or (5)), it is taken that the defendant knew or could reasonably have been expected to know of those circumstances unless sufficient evidence is adduced to raise the issue (s 17(4)).

Note that in both instances the Act simply refers to sufficient evidence being 'adduced', without specifying by which party. Therefore the presumptions could be displaced not only by a defendant giving evidence at trial, but equally by evidence adduced during the prosecution case such as comments on arrest and answers in interview. The 'sufficient evidence' might even be drawn from other sources (for example a colleague who says 'students don't normally come to our college until they are eighteen' or 'a science lecturer wouldn't have any

---

5 See **Chapter 7**.

dealings with students taking art courses: they're in a separate annex'). It is a question of law for the judge whether there has been sufficient evidence to displace the relevant statutory presumption, the test being 'some foundation in the evidence, not merely speculative or fanciful'.[6]

DISCUSSION

12.22 The activity which is caused or incited may involve B alone, but equally other persons (including person A), animals or objects might be involved, or contemplated to be included.

See the general discussion of '*position of trust*' in **12.6**.

EXAMPLES

12.23 An example of this offence can be found in the sentencing appeal case of *Howell*[7] in which the Court of Appeal upheld an immediate custodial sentence (albeit reducing its length) on a teacher who sent sexually explicit text messages to a sixth form student.

Had the teacher been unaware that the girl was a student at his particular establishment, an essential element of the offence would have been missing, but a defendant would have to adduce sufficient evidence to raise that issue in order to displace the evidential presumption under subs 17(4).

As discussed in relation to s 16, 'position of trust' offences can arise where the parties are very close in age. A s 17 offence could arise, for example, where an 18-year-old hospital worker communicates on Facebook with a current patient aged 17 and suggests how the patient might relieve sexual tension.

12.24

Statutory defences

Section 23 provides a defence where A and B were lawfully married or civil partners at the material time (subs 23(2) places the burden on the defendant to prove this) on condition that B was aged 16 or over.

Section 24 provides a defence where A and B were in a sexual relationship immediately before the position of trust arose (s 24(3) places the burden on the defendant to prove this). However, s 24(2) removes from the scope of this defence any relationship in which sexual intercourse between the parties would have been unlawful. This rules out a sexual relationship with a child under 16.

6 *R v Gavin White* [2010] EWCA Crim 1929 at [10], a case dealing with the similarly worded evidential presumptions about consent (SOA 2013, s 75).
7 [2007] EWCA Crim 1863.

OTHER DEFENCES

12.25 Lack of knowledge of the circumstances giving rise to the position of trust.

Where B was aged 13–17, reasonable belief that B was 18 or over.

CLASSIFICATION

12.26 Offence is triable either way.[8]

SENTENCING AND OTHER ORDERS

Maximum sentence

12.27 On indictment: 5 years

Summarily: 6 months imprisonment or a fine not exceeding the statutory maximum (currently £5000)

Sentencing guidelines

12.28 Identical to guidelines for 'Abuse of position of trust: sexual activity with a child' (see **12.12–12.15**).

Other orders

12.29

Extended and life sentence availability (CJA 2003)	Sch 15 (specified offence): yes Sch 15B (life sentence for second listed offence): no
Trigger offence for:	SOPO: yes FTO: yes, if D sentenced to prison or detention in hospital or community sentence of at least 12 months
Inclusion in barred lists	Children: subject to representations Vulnerable adult: subject to representations
Notification	Yes, if D sentenced to prison or detention in hospital or community sentence of at least 12 months

8 In contrast to ss 8 and 10, there is no 'aggravated' version of this offence relating to penetration.

Abuse of position of trust: sexual activity in the presence of a child
Sexual Offences Act 2003, s 18

DEFINITION

12.30 Section 18(1):

A person aged 18 or over (A) commits an offence if—

(a) he intentionally engages in an activity;

(b) the activity is sexual;

(c) for the purpose of obtaining sexual gratification, he engages in it—

(i) when another person (B) is present or is in a place from which A can be observed; and

(ii) knowing or believing that B is aware, or intending that B should be aware, that he is engaging in it;

(d) A is in a position of trust in relation to B,

(e) where subsection (2) applies, A knows or could reasonably be expected to know of the circumstances by virtue of which he is in a position of trust in relation to B; and

(f) either—

(i) B is under 18 and A does not reasonably believe that B is 18 or over; or

(ii) B is under 13.

Section 18(2):

This subsection applies where A—

(a) is in a position of trust by virtue of circumstances within section 21(2), (3), (4) or (5); and

(b) is not in such a position of trust by virtue of other circumstances.

[For the full circumstances within s 21(2) to 21(5) see **Chapter 5**: positions of trust arising through schools, hospitals, care homes and custody institutions are included]

SUMMARY

12.31 This section is the 'position of trust' version of s 11. It makes it an offence for a person aged 18 or over, for the purpose of obtaining sexual gratification, intentionally to engage in sexual activity when a child under 16, in respect of whom he is in a position of trust, is present or in a vantage point. The offender must know, believe or intend that the child is aware of the sexual activity.

Although children of all ages are covered by the section, its primary focus is complainants aged 16 or 17 (see 'Parties' at **12.33** below).

ELEMENTS

12.32

- *Age of A* – must be at least 18.
- Intentionally *engages*
- *Activity*

'*Activity*' is not defined, but notably is not limited to touching or penetration.[9]

For example, it can include A exposing himself either directly or over the internet or other electronic link.

It seems that engaging in a conversation on sexual matters can suffice.[10]

The activity may involve A alone, but equally there could be other persons, animals or objects involved.

- *Sexual* – see **Chapter 2**
- For the purpose of A obtaining *sexual gratification*:
  - B present or in a place from which A can be observed
  - A knowing/believing/intending that B should be aware

  The offence is committed if A knows or believes that B is aware that he is engaging in the activity, or A intends that B should be aware that he is engaging in it, *and* A carries out the activity for the purposes of obtaining sexual gratification from B's awareness.
- A is in a *position of trust* in relation to B – see **Chapter 5**
- Where s 18(2) applies (including positions of trust arising through schools, hospitals, care homes and custody institutions), A knows or could reasonably be expected to *know of the circumstances* creating A's position of trust over B.
- *Age of B*

9 Note that s 78, which defines 'sexual', refers to 'penetration, touching or *any other activity*'.
10 *R v Grout* [2011] EWCA Crim 299 at [29], discussed at **10.36**.

either

B is under 18 and A does not reasonably believe that B is 18 or over

or

B is under 13

Applicable age element must be pleaded in the indictment.

- Consent is irrelevant.

PARTIES

12.33 This offence may be committed by males or females, subject to being aged at least 18.

B may be male or female, and must be under 18.

Most complainants will be aged 16 or 17, because s 11 protects those aged under 16. However, s 18 might be preferred when there is a trust relationship and A claims (for example) a reasonable belief that a 15 year old complainant was older – it will be easier for the prosecution to disprove a reasonable belief that B was 18 rather than merely 16.

EVIDENTIAL PRESUMPTIONS

12.34 Once it is proved that B was under 18, it is taken that A did not reasonably believe that B was 18 or over unless sufficient evidence is adduced to raise the issue (s 18(3)).

Likewise, where s 18(2) applies (because the position of trust exists only by virtue of circumstances within s 21(2), (3), (4) or (5)), it is taken that the defendant knew or could reasonably have been expected to know of those circumstances unless sufficient evidence is adduced to raise the issue (s 18(4)).

Note that in both instances the Act simply refers to sufficient evidence being 'adduced', without specifying by which party. Therefore the presumptions could be displaced not only by a defendant giving evidence at trial, but equally by evidence adduced during the prosecution case such as comments on arrest and answers in interview. The 'sufficient evidence' could be obtained through cross-examination of the complainant or drawn from other sources (for example a colleague who says 'students don't normally come to our college until they are eighteen' or 'a science lecturer wouldn't have any dealings with students taking art courses: they're in a separate annex'). It is a question of law for the judge whether there has been sufficient evidence to displace the relevant statutory presumption, the test being 'some foundation in the evidence, not merely speculative or fanciful'.[11]

DISCUSSION

12.35 See the general discussion of '*position of trust*' in **12.6**.

The activity may take place in the physical presence of B and be seen by B, but neither of these conditions is necessary – see examples below.

The offence is intended to cover the situation where someone seeks sexual gratification not from the sexual act itself but rather from the fact that he is performing that act in the presence or intended presence of a child. Home Office Guidance[12] says: 'the motive of sexual gratification is a necessary safeguard intended to avoid capturing those who engage in sexual activity in front of a child for a legitimate reason. For example, a teacher who sexually kisses his partner just outside the school gates, could be deemed to be engaging in sexual activity intentionally in front of a child and might otherwise be caught by the offence.' Of course, if the teacher were motivated by being 'turned on' by the observation by pupils, this section would apply.

EXAMPLES

12.36 The offence covers situations such as A masturbating himself in B's presence but without being seen by B (perhaps because the lights are off, or B is covering his face), so long as A knows, believes or intends that B is aware of what A is doing.

Equally, B need not be physically present. A might perform a sexual act in a place where he knows that he can be seen by B, for example via a webcam, but again it is not necessary for B actually to observe the activity.

12.37

Statutory defences

Section 23 provides a defence where A and B were lawfully married or civil partners at the material time (s 23(2) places the burden on the defendant to prove this) on condition that B was aged 16 or over.

---

11 *R v Gavin White* [2010] EWCA Crim 1929 at [10], a case dealing with the similarly worded evidential presumptions about consent (SOA 2013, s 75).

12 At [62], referring actually to s 11.

> Section 24 provides a defence where A and B were in a sexual relationship immediately before the position of trust arose (s 24(3) places the burden on the defendant to prove this). However, s 24(2) removes from the scope of this defence any relationship in which sexual intercourse between the parties would have been unlawful. This rules out a sexual relationship with a child under 16.

OTHER DEFENCES

12.38 Lack of knowledge of the circumstances giving rise to the position of trust.

Where B was aged 13–17, reasonable belief that B was 18 or over.

Despite A obtaining sexual gratification from the activity, none was sought from the observation or potential observation by B.

CLASSIFICATION

12.39 Offence is triable either way.

SENTENCING AND OTHER ORDERS

Maximum sentence

12.40 On indictment: 5 years

Summarily: 6 months imprisonment or a fine not exceeding the statutory maximum (currently £5000)

Sentencing guidelines

Determining the category

12.41

Cat	Harm	Cat	Culpability
1	• Causing victim to view extreme pornography • Causing victim to view indecent/prohibited images of children	A	As 'Abuse of position of trust – sexual activity with a child' (s 16 (see **12.13**)) But omit factor:

Cat	Harm	Cat	Culpability
	• Engaging in, or causing victim to view live sexual activity involving sadism/violence/sexual activity with an animal/a child		• Sexual images of victim recorded, retained, solicited or shared
2	Engaging in, or causing victim to view images of, or view live, sexual activity involving: • penetration of vagina or anus (using body or object) • penile penetration of mouth • masturbation		
3	Factor(s) in categories 1 & 2 not present	B	Factor(s) in category A not present

Starting point and category range

12.42

	A	B
Category 1	Starting point: 18 mths custody Range: 1–2 yrs custody	Starting point: 1 yr custody Range: 26 wks–18 mths custody
Category 2	Starting point: 1 yr custody Range: 26 wks–18 mths custody	Starting point: 26 wks custody Range: High level community order–1 yr custody
Category 3	Starting point: 26 wks custody Range: High level community order–1 yr custody	Starting point: Medium level community order Range: Low level community order–High level community order

12.43 *Child sex offences: abuse of position of trust*

Additional factual elements

12.43

Aggravating factors
As 'Abuse of position of trust – sexual activity with a child' (s 16 (see 12.15))
But omit factors:
• Ejaculation
• Pregnancy or STI as a consequence of offence
Mitigating factors
As 'Abuse of position of trust – sexual activity with a child' (s 16 (see **12.15**))
But omit factors:
• Sexual activity was incited but no activity took place because the offender voluntarily desisted or intervened to prevent it

Other orders

12.44

Extended and life sentence availability (CJA 2003)	Sch 15 (specified offence): yes Sch 15B (life sentence for second listed offence): no
Trigger offence for:	SOPO: yes FTO: yes, if D sentenced to prison or detention in hospital or community sentence of at least 12 months
Inclusion in barred lists	Children: subject to representations Vulnerable adult: subject to representations
Notification	Yes, if D sentenced to prison or detention in hospital or community sentence of at least 12 months

Abuse of position of trust: causing a child to watch a sexual act Sexual Offences Act 2003, s 19

DEFINITION

12.45 Section 19(1):

A person aged 18 or over (A) commits an offence if—

(a) for the purpose of obtaining sexual gratification, he intentionally causes another person (B) to watch a third person engaging in an activity, or to look at an image of any person engaging in an activity,

(b) the activity is sexual,

(c) A is in a position of trust in relation to B,

(d) where subsection (2) applies, A knows or could reasonably be expected to know of the circumstances by virtue of which he is in a position of trust in relation to B, and

(e) either—

(i) B is under 18 and A does not reasonably believe that B is 18 or over, or

(ii) B is under 13.

Section 19(2):

This subsection applies where A—

(a) is in a position of trust by virtue of circumstances within section 21(2), (3), (4) or (5), and

(b) is not in such a position of trust by virtue of other circumstances.

[For the full circumstances within s 21(2) to 21(5) see **Chapter 5**: positions of trust arising through schools, hospitals, care homes and custody institutions are included]

SUMMARY

12.46 This section is the 'position of trust' version of s 12. It makes it an offence for a person aged 18 or over, for the purpose of obtaining sexual gratification, intentionally to cause a child under 16, in respect of whom he is in a position of trust, either to watch a third person engaging in a sexual act, or to look at an image of any person engaging in a sexual act.

Where the sexual activity is watched 'live' and direct (rather than, for example, via a webcam or recording) only activity involving a 'third person' is covered – if the act involved A himself, s 18 would apply.

Although children of all ages are covered by the section, its primary focus is complainants aged 16 or 17 (see 'Parties' at **12.48**).

ELEMENTS

12.47

- *Age of A* – must be at least 18.

- Intentionally *causes* – contrast 'allows' which would not suffice.
- *either:*
  - B to *watch* a third person (*not* A) engaging in a sexual activity; *or*
  - B to look at an *image* of any person (could be A) engaging in a sexual activity.
- *Sexual* activity – see discussion of 'sexual' at **Chapter 2**
- '*Activity*' is not defined, but notably is not limited to touching or penetration.[13]
- Image (where it applies) – defined in the Act:

Section 79(4): 'Image' means a moving or still image and includes an image produced by any means and, where the context permits, a three-dimensional image.

Section 79(5): References to an image of a person include references to an image of an imaginary person.

- For the purpose of obtaining sexual gratification – the gratification may be immediate (A being 'turned on' by the child's observation of the sexual activity) or future gratification (getting the child 'in the mood' to provide A with sexual gratification).[14]
- A is in a *position of trust* in relation to B – see **Chapter 5**
- Where s 19(2) applies (including positions of trust arising through schools, hospitals, care homes and custody institutions), A knows or could reasonably be expected to *know of the circumstances* creating A's position of trust over B.
- *Age of B*

  either

  B is under 18 and A does not reasonably believe that B is 18 or over

  or

  B is under 13

  Applicable age element must be pleaded in the indictment.
- Consent is irrelevant.

---

13 Note that s 78, which defines 'sexual', refers to 'penetration, touching or *any other activity*'.
14 *R v Abdullahi* [2006] EWCA Crim 2060.

PARTIES

12.48 This offence may be committed by males or females, subject to being aged at least 18.

B may be male or female, and must be under 18.

Most complainants will be aged 16 or 17, because s 12 protects those aged under 16. However, s 19 might be preferred when there is a trust relationship and A claims (for example) a reasonable belief that a 15-year-old complainant was older – it will be easier for the prosecution to disprove a reasonable belief that B was 18 rather than merely 16.

EVIDENTIAL PRESUMPTIONS

12.49 Once it is proved that B was under 18, it is taken that A did not reasonably believe that B was 18 or over unless sufficient evidence is adduced to raise the issue (s 19(3)).

Likewise, where s 19(2) applies (because the position of trust exists only by virtue of circumstances within s 21(2), (3), (4) or (5)), it is taken that the defendant knew or could reasonably have been expected to know of those circumstances unless sufficient evidence is adduced to raise the issue (s 19(4)).

Note that in both instances the Act simply refers to sufficient evidence being 'adduced', without specifying by which party. Therefore the presumptions could be displaced not only by a defendant giving evidence at trial, but equally by evidence adduced during the prosecution case such as comments on arrest and answers in interview. The 'sufficient evidence' could be obtained through cross-examination of the complainant or drawn from other sources (for example a colleague who says 'students don't normally come to our college until they are eighteen' or 'a science lecturer wouldn't have any dealings with students taking art courses: they're in a separate annex'). It is a question of law for the judge whether there has been sufficient evidence to displace the relevant statutory presumption, the test being 'some foundation in the evidence, not merely speculative or fanciful'.[15]

DISCUSSION

12.50 See the general discussion of '*position of trust*' at **12.6**.

As the Home Office Guidance observes: The offence does not require any element of coercion, though it may be a factor in some cases.

15 *R v Gavin White* [2010] EWCA Crim 1929 at [10], a case dealing with the similarly worded evidential presumptions about consent (SOA 2013, s 75).

12.50 *Child sex offences: abuse of position of trust*

In order for an offence to be committed, the adult must act for his own sexual gratification. This ensures that, adults showing children sex education material, either in a school or other setting, will not be liable for this offence.

EXAMPLES

12.51 Home Office Guidance: Examples of this offence would be where a person, for the purposes of his own sexual gratification, enables a child to watch two people have sex, either in the physical presence of the activity or remotely, for instance via a webcam; or where someone invites a child to watch a pornographic film or sends a child indecent images over the internet.

12.52

Statutory defences
Section 23 provides a defence where A and B were lawfully married or civil partners at the material time (subs 23(2) places the burden on the defendant to prove this) on condition that B was aged 16 or over.
Section 24 provides a defence where A and B were in a sexual relationship immediately before the position of trust arose (subs 24(3) places the burden on the defendant to prove this). However, s 24(2) removes from the scope of this defence any relationship in which sexual intercourse between the parties would have been unlawful. This rules out a sexual relationship with a child under 16.

OTHER DEFENCES

12.53 Lack of knowledge of the circumstances giving rise to the position of trust.

Where B was aged 13–17, reasonable belief that B was 18 or over.

Despite A obtaining sexual gratification from the activity, none was sought from the observation or potential observation by B.

CLASSIFICATION

12.54 Offence is triable either way.

SENTENCING AND OTHER ORDERS

Maximum sentence

12.55 On indictment: 5 years

Summarily: 6 months imprisonment or a fine not exceeding the statutory maximum (currently £5000)

Sentencing guidelines

12.56 Identical to guidelines for 'Abuse of position of trust: sexual activity in the presence of a child' (see s 18 (at **12.41–12.43**).

Other orders

12.57

Extended and life sentence availability (CJA 2003)	Sch 15 (specified offence): yes Sch 15B (life sentence for second listed offence): no
Trigger offence for:	SOPO: yes FTO: yes, if D sentenced to prison or detention in hospital or community sentence of at least 12 months
Inclusion in barred lists	Children: subject to representations Vulnerable adult: subject to representations
Notification	Yes, if D sentenced to prison or detention in hospital or community sentence of at least 12 months

Chapter 13

Familial child sex offences

Sexual activity with a child family member Sexual Offences Act 2003, s 25

DEFINITION

13.1 Section 25(1):

A person (A) commits an offence if—

(a) he intentionally touches another person (B);

(b) the touching is sexual;

(c) the relation of A to B is within section 27;

(d) A knows or could reasonably be expected to know that his relation to B is of a description falling within that section; and

(e) either—

(i) B is under 18 and A does not reasonably believe that B is 18 or over; or

(ii) B is under 13.

SUMMARY

13.2 This section makes it an offence for a person to sexually touch anyone under the age of 18 with whom they are in a familial relationship. The scope of offence is very broad, encompassing a variety of cohabiting circumstances which would not normally be expressed as 'family relationships'.

Subsections 25(4) to (6) create an aggravated version of the offence, relating to penetration – see 'Classification' at **13.7** and Specimen Indictments (**Appendix 1**).

ELEMENTS

13.3

- *Intentional touching*

  Section 79(8) provides that:

  Touching includes touching:

  (a) with any part of the body;

  (b) with anything else;

  (c) through anything;

  and in particular includes touching amounting to penetration.

  The touching by A must be *intentional* – in other words, deliberate and not accidental.[1]

- *Sexual* – see **Chapter 2**

- *Age*[2] *of B*

  either

  B is under 18 and A does not reasonably believe that B is 18 or over

  or

  B is under 13

  Applicable age element must be pleaded in the indictment.

- Consent is irrelevant. This is so even when B is 16 or 17 years old.

- *Familial relationships*

  Section 27 defines which family relationships are prohibited for the purposes of s 25:

  – Blood relationships (s 27(2)): parents, grandparents, brothers, sisters, half-brothers, half-sisters, aunts and uncles.[3]

  – Foster parents (s 27(2)): where A is or has been B's foster parent.[4] Thus, the relationship is still prohibited where A has ceased to be B's foster parent, until B reaches the age of 18.

---

1 *R v Heard* [2007] EWCA Crim 125.
2 See Chapter 7.
3 Defined at s 27(5)(a) to exclude aunts and uncles by marriage.
4 Foster parent defined at s 27(5)(c) by reference to the Children Act 1989.

- Where A and B live or have lived in the same household, or A is or has been regularly involved in caring for, training, supervising or being in sole charge of B, and
  - (a) one of them is or has been the other's step-parent,[5]
  - (b) A and B are cousins,[6]
  - (c) one of them is or has been the other's stepbrother or stepsister, or
  - (d) the parent or present or former foster parent of one of them is or has been the other's foster parent (s 27(3)).

Note here that the prohibition still applies if A and B cease living together or if A stops caring for B.

- Where A and B live in the same household, and A is regularly involved in caring for, training, supervising or being in sole charge of B (s 27(4)). The ambit of this section is very wide and could include au pairs, nannies or lodgers. Note here that the prohibition ceases to apply if A and B stop living together or A stops caring for B.
- Adoptive relationships (s 27(1)(b)): when a child is formally adopted, they become the child of their adoptive parents. Section 27(1)(b) preserves the prohibition in relation to the child's biological relatives even after the adoption.

13.4

Statutory defences

Section 28 provides a defence where A and B are lawfully married, or in a civil partnership. The burden is on the defendant to prove this on the balance of probabilities

Section 29 provides a defence where A and B were in a lawful sexual relationship which immediately predated the familial relationship. This defence does not apply to relationships prohibited by s 27(2) ('blood relationships'). Examples of this defence in operation would be two young couple having a sexual relationship whose parents meet and marry, thereby making them step-siblings whose relationship would fall within s 27(3); or cousins having a relationship and then moving in together. It is a requirement that the pre-existing relationship is 'lawful', thus both parties must be over 16 years of age. The burden is on the defendant to prove all elements of the defence, on the balance of probabilities.

---

5 Defined at s 27(5)(e) to include a parent's partner (persons of different or the same sex living together in enduring family relationships). 'stepbrother' and 'stepsister' include the children of a parent's partner.

6 Defined at s 27(5)(b) as the child of an aunt or uncle.

Section 73 provides that a person will not be guilty of aiding, abetting or counselling an offence contrary to s 25 if acting to protect the child's physical safety, protect them from sexually transmitted infection or pregnancy, or to promote their well-being by the giving of advice. This defence is unlikely to have frequent application, but might conceivably arise if a health professional provided contraceptive advice to a girl who said she was having sex with a family member.

OTHER DEFENCES

13.5 No knowledge that B was a family member.

No knowledge that B was under 18.

To be guilty of the offence A must know, or be in a position where he could reasonably be expected to know, that the child is his family member (within the definition of s 27). Where the relationship is proved by the Crown, there is a presumption that A knew this and an evidential burden on A to displace the presumption should he choose to dispute it (s 25(3)).

To be guilty of the offence A must not reasonably believe that B is 18 or over. Where the age is proved by the Crown, there is a presumption that the defendant did not reasonably believe B to be 18 or over and an evidential burden on A to displace the presumption should he choose to dispute it (s 25(2)). The defence is not available where the child is aged under 13 years.

PARTIES

13.6 The offence may be committed by males or females and may be committed by those under 18 years old.

CLASSIFICATION

13.7

A. Where the defendant was 18 or over at the time of the offence, it is triable as follows:

 1. Where the touching involved:

 - penetration of B's anus or vagina with a part of A's body or anything else;
 - penetration of B's mouth with A's penis;
 - penetration of A's anus or vagina with a part of B's body; or
 - penetration of A's mouth with B's penis;

the offence is indictable only.

2. In all other circumstances, the offence is triable either way.

B. Where the defendant was under 18 at the time of the offence, it is triable either way.

SENTENCING AND OTHER ORDERS

Maximum sentence

13.8 In category A(1) above: 14 years imprisonment

In category A(2) above:

- On indictment: 14 years imprisonment
- Summarily: 6 months imprisonment or a fine not exceeding the statutory maximum (currently £5,000).

In category B above:

- On indictment: 5 years imprisonment
- Summarily: 6 months imprisonment or a fine not exceeding the statutory maximum (currently £5,000) or both.

Sentencing guidelines

Determining the category

13.9

Cat	Harm	Cat	Culpability
1	• Penetration of vagina or anus (using body or object) • Penile penetration of mouth In either case by, or of, the victim	A	• Significant degree of planning • Offender acts together with others to commit the offence • Use of alcohol/drugs on victim to facilitate the offence
2	Touching, or exposure, of naked genitalia or naked breasts by, or of, the victim		• Grooming behaviour used against victim • Use of threats (incl blackmail)

Cat	**Harm**	**Cat**	**Culpability**
			• Sexual images of victim recorded, retained, solicited or shared • Specific targeting of a particularly vulnerable child • Significant disparity in age • Commercial exploitation and/or motivation • Offence racially or religiously aggravated • Offence motivated by, or demonstrating, hostility to the victim based on his or her sexual orientation (or presumed sexual orientation) or transgender identity (or presumed transgender identity) • Offence motivated by, or demonstrating, hostility to the victim based on his or her disability (or presumed disability)
3	Other sexual activity	B	Factor(s) in category A not present

Starting point and category range

13.10

	A	**B**
Category 1	Starting point: 6 yrs custody Range: 4–10 yrs custody	Starting point: 3 yrs 6 mths custody Range: 2 yrs 6 mths–5 yrs custody

13.10 *Familial child sex offences*

Category 2	Starting point: 2–6 yrs custody Range: 9–13 yrs custody	Starting point: 26 wks–2 yrs 6 mths custody Range: 7–9 yrs custody
Category 3	Starting point: 1 yr custody Range: High level community order–3 yrs custody	Starting point: Medium level custody Range: Low level community order–High level community order

Additional factual elements

13.11

Aggravating factors
Statutory aggravating factors
• Previous convictions, having regard to: (a) the nature of the offence to which the conviction relates and its relevance to the current offence; and (b) the time that has elapsed since the conviction • Offence committed whilst on bail
Other aggravating factors
• Severe psychological or physical harm • Ejaculation • Pregnancy or STI as a consequence of offence • Location of offence • Timing of offence • Victim compelled to leave their home, school, etc • Failure to comply with current court orders • Offence committed whilst on licence • Exploiting contact arrangements with a child to commit an offence • Presence of others, especially other children • Any steps taken to prevent the victim reporting an incident, obtaining assistance and/or from assisting or supporting the prosecution • Attempts to dispose of or conceal evidence • Failure of offender to respond to previous warnings

• Commission of offence whilst under the influence of alcohol or drugs • Victim encouraged to recruit others • Period over which offence committed
Mitigating factors
• No previous convictions or no relevant/recent convictions • Remorse • Previous good character and/or exemplary conduct • Age and/or lack of maturity where it affects the responsibility of the offender • Mental disorder or learning disability, particularly where linked to the commission of the offence • Sexual activity was incited but no activity took place because the offender voluntarily desisted or intervened to prevent it

* Previous good character/exemplary conduct is different from having no previous convictions. The more serious the offence, the less the weight which should normally be attributed to this factor. Where previous good character/exemplary conduct has been used to facilitate the offence, this mitigation should not normally be allowed and such conduct may constitute an aggravating factor.

In the context of this offence, previous good character/exemplary conduct should not normally be given any significant weight and will not normally justify a reduction in what would otherwise be the appropriate sentence.

Sentencing factors (category B above, defendant under 18)

13.12 There are no guidelines for this offence, committed by a defendant under 18, within the Sexual Offences Definitive Guideline 2014.

When sentencing offenders under 18, a court must in particular:

- Follow the definitive guideline Overarching Principles – Sentencing Youths;

  and have regard to:

- the principal aim of the youth justice system (to prevent offending by children and young people); and
- the welfare of the young offender

This is a 'grave crime' for the purposes of section 91 of the Powers of Criminal Courts (Sentencing) Act 2000.

Other orders

13.13

Extended and life sentence availability (CJA 2003)	Sch 15 (specified offence): yes Sch 15B (life sentence for second listed offence): yes, if the offender is aged 18 or over at the time of the offence
Trigger offence for:	SOPO: yes FTO: yes, if: D is over 18, *or* Is sentenced to at least 12 months imprisonment
Inclusion in barred lists	Children: subject to representations Vulnerable adult: subject to representations
Notification	Yes, if: D is over 18, *or* Is sentenced to at least 12 months imprisonment

Inciting a child family member to engage in sexual activity
Sexual Offences Act 2003, s 26

DEFINITION

13.14 Section 26(1):

A person (A) commits an offence if—

(a) he intentionally incites another person (B) to touch, or allow himself to be touched by, A

(b) the touching is sexual,

(c) the relation of A to B is within section 27,

(d) A knows or could reasonably be expected to know that his relation to B is of a description falling within that section, and

(e) either—

(i) B is under 18 and A does not reasonably believe that B is 18 or over, or

(ii) B is under 13.

SUMMARY

13.15 This section makes it an offence for a person to incite someone under the age of 18 to touch him, or to allow touching by him, where a familial relationship exists between them. The offence encompasses a broad range of cohabiting circumstances which would not normally be expressed as 'family relationships'. However, s 26 has narrower application than other sections, because its scope is limited to incitement of touching only (not sexual activity generally) – and only touching between A and B (excluding solo activity or touching of, or by, a third party).

The offence is committed by virtue of the incitement, whether or not the incited sexual touching actually results.

ELEMENTS

13.16

- *Intentionally*

  '*Intentionally*' relates to the incitement.

  It seems highly unlikely that someone would accidentally or recklessly incite someone to engage in sexual touching, but this would not suffice.

- *Incites*

  '*Incites*' is not defined by the Act and should be given its natural meaning of urges or provokes.

  The incited touching need not actually take place.

- *B to touch or allow* himself to be touched

  Section 79(8) provides that:

  Touching includes touching:

  (a) with any part of the body,

  (b) with anything else,

  (c) through anything,

  and in particular includes touching amounting to penetration.

  See further consideration of 'touching' at **9.16**

- *Sexual* – see **Chapter 2**
- *Age*[7] *of B*

---

7 See **Chapter 7**.

13.16 *Familial child sex offences*

either

B is under 18 and A does not reasonably believe that B is 18 or over

or

B is under 13

Applicable age element must be pleaded in the Indictment.

- A and B in a *familial relationship* – defined by s 27 – see **13.3**
- Consent is irrelevant. This is so even when B is 16 or 17 years old.

13.17

Statutory defences
Provided by ss 28 and 29 – see **13.4**.

OTHER DEFENCES

13.18 No knowledge that B was family member: see s 26(3) at **13.5**.

No knowledge that B was under 18: see s 26(2) at **13.5**.

PARTIES

13.19 The offence may be committed by males or females, including those aged under 18.

DISCUSSION

13.20 It is important to remember the limitations of this offence. It covers incitement only, touching only, and touching only of B by A or vice versa.

EXAMPLES

13.21 Home Office Guidance cites two examples: A encourages B to masturbate A; and A cajoles B into agreeing to have sex with him.

CLASSIFICATION

13.22

A. Where the defendant was 18 or over at the time of the offence, it is triable as follows:

1. Where the touching involved:
   - penetration of B's anus or vagina with a part of A's body or anything else;
   - penetration of B's mouth with A's penis;
   - penetration of A's anus or vagina with a part of B's body; or
   - penetration of A's mouth with B's penis;

   the offence is indictable only.

2. In all other circumstances, the offence is triable either way.

B. Where the defendant was under 18 at the time of the offence, it is triable either way.

SENTENCING AND OTHER ORDERS

Maximum sentence

13.23 In category A(1) above: 14 years imprisonment

In category A(2) above:

- On indictment: 14 years imprisonment
- Summarily: 6 months imprisonment or a fine not exceeding the statutory maximum (currently £5000).

In category B above:

- On indictment: 5 years imprisonment
- Summarily: 6 months imprisonment or a fine not exceeding the statutory maximum (currently £5000) or both.

Sentencing guidelines and factors

13.24 Identical to guidelines for 'Sexual activity with a child family member' (see s 26, **13.9–13.11**).

Other orders

13.25

Extended and life sentence availability (CJA 2003)	Sch 15 (specified offence): yes Sch 15B (life sentence for second listed offence): yes, if offender is aged 18 or over at the time of the offence
Trigger offence for:	SOPO: yes FTO: yes, if: D is over 18, *or* Is sentenced to at least 12 months imprisonment
Inclusion in barred lists	Children: subject to representations Vulnerable adult: subject to representations
Notification	Yes, if: D is over 18, *or* Is sentenced to at least 12 months imprisonment

Chapter 14

Offences against persons with mental disorder impeding choice

Sexual activity with a person with a mental disorder impeding choice
Sexual Offences Act 2003, s 30

DEFINITION

14.1 Section 30(1):

A person (A) commits an offence if—

(a) he intentionally touches another person (B);

(b) the touching is sexual;

(c) B is unable to refuse because of or for a reason related to a mental disorder; and

(d) A knows or could reasonably be expected to know that B has a mental disorder and that because of it or for a reason related to it B is likely to be unable to refuse.

SUMMARY

14.2 This section makes it an offence to touch someone sexually where the victim is unable to agree to the sexual activity because of a mental disorder which impedes their choice. Despite the headnote reading 'sexual activity', only *touching* is caught by s 9, although touching includes penetration.

ELEMENTS

14.3

- *Intentional touching*

  Section 79(8) provides that:

Touching includes touching:

(a) with any part of the body,

(b) with anything else,

(c) through anything,

and in particular includes touching amounting to penetration.

The touching by A must be intentional – in other words, deliberate and not accidental.[1]

- *Sexual* – see **Chapter 2**
- B has a *mental disorder*

  Section 79(6) defines this as having the same meaning as s 1 of the Mental Health Act 1983,[2] namely 'any disorder or disability of the mind'. This wide-ranging definition will include such diverse conditions as personality disorder, learning disability, autistic spectrum disorder, dementia, depressive illnesses and brain damage (if leading to a disorder or disability of the mind). However, the disorder must give rise to, or be related to, an inability to refuse.
- B is 'unable to refuse'

  defined by s 30(2) as:

  (a) he lacks the capacity to choose whether to agree to the touching (whether because he lacks sufficient understanding of the nature or reasonably foreseeable consequences of what is being done, or for any other reason), or

  (b) he is unable to communicate such a choice to A.
- *For a reason related to* – it is not necessary that the mental disorder is the direct cause of the inability to refuse. Taking medication for a psychiatric disorder – the effect of which is to impair a patient's free choice – could be a situation related to (although not specifically caused by) mental disorder.
- Mental element – in addition to intentional touching, the prosecution must show that:

  – the defendant knew or could reasonably be expected to know that B had a mental disorder, and

---

1 *R v Heard* [2007] EWCA Crim 125.

2 Now amended and simplified from its original definition by s 1(2) of the Mental Health Act 2007.

– the defendant knew or could reasonably be expected to know that because of the mental disorder, or because of a reason related to it, B was likely to be unable to refuse the touching.

DISCUSSION

Touching

14.4 See discussion of touching at **9.16**.

Capacity

14.5 Subsection 30(2) postulates four circumstances in which a person (B) may be unable to refuse the touching:

- where B lacks capacity due to insufficient understanding of the nature of what is being done;
- where B lacks capacity due to insufficient understanding of the reasonably foreseeable consequences of what is being done;
- where B lacks capacity for any other reason;
- where B is unable to communicate his or her choice.

Insufficient understanding of the nature of the act might arise from an inability to understand the difference between sexual behaviour and washing or personal care.

Sufficient understanding of the consequences would be a realisation that there is a risk to sexual health or a risk of pregnancy by some activities.

In *R v Cooper*,[3] the House of Lords considered the words 'for any other reason' in particular as they related to an irrational fear or phobia. While a complainant might well understand the nature of the act and its consequences, a fear or phobia derived from mental disorder might deprive them of the ability to make an autonomous choice (just as an anorexic might irrationally refuse food, while understanding the nature of what they were doing and its dangers).

The question was not whether the complainant had a general capacity to consent, but whether they had the capacity to consent to this specific sexual act, with this person at this time. A mentally disordered person might be quite capable of exercising choice in one situation but not in another.[4] This fits with the overall purpose of this part of the Act, namely to prevent the sexual

3 [2009] UKHL 42.
4 *ibid*, per Baroness Hale, at [26].

exploitation of those with mental disorders or impairments, while allowing them the right to an independent and autonomous sex life.

The fourth situation in which a person is deemed to be unable to refuse sexual touching is where they are unable to communicate their choice (and presumably, in this circumstance, they have the mental capacity to choose, and have chosen not to consent). The inability must be because of or related to a mental, rather than purely a physical, disorder.[5]

The prosecution must prove both mental disorder and an inability to refuse. In severe cases this may be obvious and the connection clear. Where the impairment is less severe or fluctuates, this may be a significant issue, requiring evidence from the complainant themselves, from their families or those treating them or from expert psychiatric evidence. Expert evidence, while usual, is not necessary to prove the disorder or its extent.[6]

Given that many versions of this offence involve the absence of capacity to refuse, there can be overlap with the mainstream non-consensual offences under ss 1 to 4. The topic is discussed in *Cooper*.[7] Consideration must be given in each case as to which is the appropriate charge.

DEFENCES

14.6 Defendant did not know, and could not reasonably be expected to know, of B's mental disorder.

Section 73 provides that a person will not be guilty of aiding, abetting or counselling an offence contrary to s 30 if acting to protect the child's physical safety, protect them from sexually transmitted infection or pregnancy, or to promote their well-being by the giving of advice. This defence, which is not available for other offences against those with mental disorders impeding choice, is unlikely to have frequent application, but might conceivably arise if a health professional provided contraceptive advice to a young patient who said she was having sex in the circumstances envisaged in s 30. Note that the defence only applies if the person being protected is under 16.

CLASSIFICATION

14.7 Offences under s30 are triable as follows:

1. Where the touching involved:

---

5 *ibid*, per Lord Rodger at [5] to [7].

6 See *R v Hall* (1987) 86 Cr App R 159: in relation to the question of whether a victim was 'defective' in accordance with SOA 1956, a doctor's opinion as to whether there was severe impairment was not regarded as being preferable to the observation of the jury.

7 [2009] UKHL 42, per Baroness Hale, at [32].

- penetration of B's anus or vagina with a part of A's body or anything else;
- penetration of B's mouth with A's penis;
- penetration of A's anus or vagina with a part of B's body; or
- penetration of A's mouth with B's penis;

the offence is indictable only.

2. In all other circumstances, the offence is triable either way.

SENTENCING AND OTHER ORDERS

Maximum sentence

14.8 In aggravated form: Life imprisonment

In non-aggravated form:

- On indictment: 14 years
- Summarily: 6 months imprisonment or a fine not exceeding the statutory maximum (currently £5000)

Sentencing guidelines

Determining the category

14.9

Cat	Harm	Cat	Culpability
1	The extreme nature of one or more category 2 factors or the extreme impact caused by a combination of category 2 factors may elevate to category 1	A	• Significant degree of planning
2	• Severe psychological or physical harm • Pregnancy or STI as a consequence of offence • Additional degradation/ humiliation • Abduction		• Offender acts together with others to commit the offence • Use of alcohol/drugs on victim to facilitate the offence • Grooming behaviour used against victim • Abuse of trust

14.9 *Offences against persons with mental disorder impeding choice*

Cat	Harm	Cat	Culpability
	• Prolonged detention/ sustained incident • Violence or threats of violence • Forced/uninvited entry into victim's home or residence		• Previous violence against victim • Offence committed in course of burglary • Sexual images of victim recorded, retained, solicited or shared • Deliberate isolation of victim • Commercial exploitation and/or motivation • Offence racially or religiously aggravated • Offence motivated by, or demonstrating, hostility to the victim based on his or her sexual orientation (or presumed sexual orientation) or transgender identity (or presumed transgender identity) • Offence motivated by, or demonstrating, hostility to the victim based on his or her disability (or presumed disability)
3	Factor(s) in categories 1 & 2 not present	B	Factor(s) in category A not present

Starting point and category range

14.10

Where offence involved penetration:		
	A	**B**
Category 1	Starting point: 16 yrs custody Range: 13–19 yrs custody	Starting point: 13 yrs custody Range: 11–17 yrs custody

Category 2	Starting point: 13 yrs custody Range: 11–17 yrs custody	Starting point: 10 yrs custody Range: 8–13 yrs custody
Category 3	Starting point: 10 yrs custody Range: 8–13 yrs custody	Starting point: 8yrs custody Range: 6–11 yrs custody

Where offence did not involve penetration:		
	A	**B**
Category 1	Starting point: 6 yrs custody Range: 4–9 yrs custody	Starting point: 4 yrs custody Range: 3–7 yrs custody
Category 2	Starting point: 4 yrs custody Range: 3–7 yrs custody	Starting point: 2 yrs custody Range: 1–4 yrs custody
Category 3	Starting point: 1 yr custody Range: 26 wks–2 yrs custody	Starting point: 26 wks custody Range: High level community order–1 yr custody

Additional factual elements

14.11

Aggravating factors
Statutory aggravating factors
• Previous convictions, having regard to a) the nature of the offence to which the conviction relates and its relevance to the current offence; and b) the time that has elapsed since the conviction • Offence committed whilst on bail
Other aggravating factors
• Ejaculation (where not taken into account at step one) • Blackmail or other threats made (where not taken into account at step one) • Location of offence • Timing of offence • Use of weapon or other item to frighten or injure • Victim compelled to leave their home or institution (including victims of domestic violence)

• Failure to comply with current court orders • Offence committed whilst on licence • Presence of others, especially children • Any steps taken to prevent the victim reporting an incident, obtaining assistance and/or from assisting or supporting the prosecution • Attempts to dispose of or conceal evidence • Commission of offence whilst under the influence of alcohol or drugs
Mitigating factors
• No previous convictions or no relevant/recent convictions • Remorse • Previous good character and/or exemplary conduct* • Age and/or lack of maturity where it affects the responsibility of the offender • Mental disorder or learning disability, particularly where linked to the commission of the offence • Sexual activity was incited but no activity took place because the offender voluntarily desisted or intervened to prevent it

* Previous good character/exemplary conduct is different from having no previous convictions. The more serious the offence, the less the weight which should normally be attributed to this factor. Where previous good character/exemplary conduct has been used to facilitate the offence, this mitigation should not normally be allowed and such conduct may constitute an aggravating factor.

In the context of this offence, previous good character/exemplary conduct should not normally be given any significant weight and will not normally justify a reduction in what would otherwise be the appropriate sentence.

Other offences

14.12

Extended and life sentence availability (CJA 2003)	Sch 15 (specified offence): yes Sch 15B (life sentence for second listed offence): yes,if offence is in aggravated form
Trigger offence for:	SOPO: yes FTO: yes, but only where V *was under 18*

Inclusion in barred lists	Children: automatic if V is a child subject to representations if V is an adult Vulnerable adult: automatic
Notification	Yes

Causing or inciting a person, with a mental disorder impeding choice, to engage in sexual activity
Sexual Offences Act 2003, s 31

DEFINITION

14.13 Section 31(1):

A person (A) commits an offence if—

(a) he intentionally causes or incites another person (B) to engage in an activity,

(b) the activity is sexual,

(c) B is unable to refuse because of or for a reason related to a mental disorder, and

(d) A knows or could reasonably be expected to know that B has a mental disorder and that because of it or for a reason related to it B is likely to be unable to refuse.

SUMMARY

14.14 This section makes it an offence to cause or incite someone to engage in a sexual activity where the victim is unable to agree to the activity because of a mental disorder which impedes their choice.

ELEMENTS

14.15

- *Intentionally*

  '*Intentionally*' relates to causing/inciting the activity.

  In theory, it is not necessary that A intends the activity to be sexual, but this distinction is unlikely to arise in practice.

It must likewise be rare that someone accidentally or recklessly causes another person to engage in a sexual activity, but this would not suffice.

- causes *or* incites

  The section creates two separate offences (see Specimen Indictments, **Appendix 1**).

- '*Causes*' is not defined by the Act and should be given its natural meaning of bringing about or making happen.

  'Causing' requires something more than merely 'allowing'.

  It may be achieved by words, action or both.

- '*Incites*' is not defined by the Act and should be given its natural meaning of urges or provokes.

  The incited activity need not actually place.

- B to engage in an *activity*.

  '*Activity*' is not defined, but notably is not limited to touching or penetration[8].

- *Sexual* – see **Chapter 2**

- B has a *mental disorder*

  Section 79(6) defines this as having the same meaning as s 1 of the Mental Health Act 1983,[9] namely 'any disorder or disability of the mind'. This wide-ranging definition will include such diverse conditions as personality disorder, learning disability, autistic spectrum disorder, dementia, depressive illnesses and brain damage (if leading to a disorder or disability of the mind). However, the disorder must give rise to, or be related to, an inability to refuse.

- B is '*unable to refuse*'

  defined by s 31(2) as:

  (a) he lacks the capacity to choose whether to agree to engaging in the activity caused or incited (whether because he lacks sufficient understanding of the nature or reasonably foreseeable consequences of the activity, or for any other reason), or

  (b) he is unable to communicate such a choice to A.

- F*or a reason related to* – it is not necessary that the mental disorder is the direct cause of the inability to refuse. Taking medication for a psychiatric

---

8 Note that s 78, which defines 'sexual', refers to 'penetration, touching or *any other activity*'.

9 Now amended and simplified from its original definition by s 1(2) of the Mental Health Act 2007.

disorder – the effect of which is to impair a patient's free choice – could be a situation related to (although not specifically caused by) mental disorder.

- Mental element – in addition to intentionally causing or inciting B to engage in sexual activity, the prosecution must show that:
  - the defendant knew or could reasonably be expected to know that B had a mental disorder, and
  - the defendant knew or could reasonably be expected to know that because of the mental disorder, or because of a reason related to it, B was likely to be unable to refuse to engage in the activity.

DISCUSSION

14.16 See **14.5** for discussion on inability to refuse and consent in relation to almost identical provisions under s 30.

A may himself participate in the sexual activity with B, but need not. The activity may involve B alone, but equally there could be other persons, animals or objects involved.

EXAMPLES

14.17 The offence could involve A getting B to touch A's genitalia.

It could be committed by A urging B to have sexual intercourse with A's friend C, or inciting him to do so, even if the incitement does not actually result in B engaging in any sexual activity.

DEFENCE

14.18 Defendant did not know and could not reasonably be expected to know of B's mental disorder.

CLASSIFICATION

14.19 Offences under s 31 are triable as follows:

1. Where the sexual activity caused or incited involved:
   - penetration of B's anus or vagina with a part of A's body or anything else,
   - penetration of B's mouth with A's penis,

- penetration of A's anus or vagina with a part of B's body, or
- penetration of A's mouth with B's penis,

the offence is indictable only.

2. In all other circumstances, the offence is triable either way.

SENTENCING AND OTHER ORDERS

Maximum sentence

14.20 In aggravated form: Life imprisonment

In non-aggravated form:

- On indictment: 14 years
- Summarily: 6 months imprisonment or a fine not exceeding the statutory maximum (currently £5000)

Sentencing guidelines

14.21 Identical to guidelines for 'Sexual activity with a person with a mental disorder impeding choice' (see **14.9–14.11**).

Other orders

14.22

Extended and life sentence availability (CJA 2003)	Sch 15 (specified offence): yes Sch 15B (life sentence for second listed offence): yes, if offence is in aggravated form
Trigger offence for:	SOPO: yes FTO: yes, but only where V *was under 18*
Inclusion in barred lists	Children: automatic if V is a child subject to representations if V is an adult Vulnerable adult: automatic
Notification	Yes

Engaging in sexual activity in the presence of a person with a mental disorder impeding choice Sexual Offences Act 2003, s 32

DEFINITION

14.23 Section 32(1):

A person (A) commits an offence if—

(a) he intentionally engages in an activity,

(b) the activity is sexual,

(c) for the purpose of obtaining sexual gratification, he engages in it—

  (i) when another person (B) is present or is in a place from which A can be observed, and

  (ii) knowing or believing that B is aware, or intending that B should be aware, that he is engaging in it,

(d) B is unable to refuse because of or for a reason related to a mental disorder, and

(e) A knows or could reasonably be expected to know that B has a mental disorder and that because of it or for a reason related to it B is likely to be unable to refuse.

SUMMARY

14.24 This section makes it an offence for a person (A), for the purpose of obtaining sexual gratification, intentionally to engage in sexual activity when a person (B) is present or in a vantage point. B must be unable, because of a mental disorder which impedes his or her choice, to agree to being present. The offender must know, believe or intend that B is aware of the sexual activity.

ELEMENTS

14.25

- *Intentionally engages*
- *Activity*

  '*Activity*' is not defined, but notably is not limited to touching or penetration.[10]

---

10 Note that s 78, which defines 'sexual', refers to '*penetration, touching or any other activity*'.

For example, it can include A exposing himself.

It seems that engaging in a conversation on sexual matters can suffice.[11]

The activity may involve A alone, but equally there could be other persons, animals or objects involved.

- *Sexual* – see **Chapter 2**
- For the purpose of A obtaining *sexual gratification*:
  - B present or in a place from which A can be observed
  - A knowing/believing/intending that B should be aware

  The offence is committed if A knows or believes that B is aware that he is engaging in the activity, or A intends that B should be aware that he is engaging in it, and A carries out the activity for the purposes of obtaining sexual gratification from B's awareness.
- B has a mental disorder

  Section 79(6) defines this as having the same meaning as s 1 of the Mental Health Act 1983,[12] namely 'any disorder or disability of the mind'. This wide-ranging definition will include such diverse conditions as personality disorder, learning disability, autistic spectrum disorder, dementia, depressive illnesses and brain damage (if leading to a disorder or disability of the mind). However, the disorder must give rise to, or be related to, an inability to refuse.
- B is '*unable to refuse*'

  defined by s 32(2) as:

  (a) he lacks the capacity to choose whether to agree to being present (whether because he lacks sufficient understanding of the nature of the activity, or for any other reason), or

  (b) he is unable to communicate such a choice to A.
- *For a reason related to* – it is not necessary that the mental disorder is the direct cause of the inability to refuse. Taking medication for a psychiatric disorder – the effect of which is to impair a patient's free choice – could be a situation related to (although not specifically caused by) mental disorder.
- Mental element – in addition to intentionally engaging in an activity, the prosecution must show that:

---

11 *R v Grout* [2011] EWCA Crim 299 at [29], discussed at **10.36**.

12 Now amended and simplified from its original definition by s 1(2) of the Mental Health Act 2007.

- the defendant did so in order to obtain sexual gratification, and
- the defendant knew or could reasonably be expected to know that B had a mental disorder, and
- the defendant knew or could reasonably be expected to know that because of the mental disorder, or because of a reason related to it, B was likely to be unable to refuse to be present or to watch.

DISCUSSION

14.26 See **14.5** for discussion on inability to refuse and consent in relation to almost identical provisions under s 30.

Note that lacking 'sufficient understanding of the consequences of the activity' as an instance in which B is deemed unable to refuse, is omitted from this section.

EXAMPLES

14.27 The offence covers situations such as A masturbating himself in B's presence but without being seen by B (perhaps because the lights are off, or B is covering his face), so long as A knows, believes or intends that B is aware of what A is doing.

Equally, B need not be physically present. A might perform a sexual act in a place where he knows that he can be seen by B, for example via a CCTV system, but again it is not necessary for B actually to observe the activity.

DEFENCES

14.28 Defendant did not know and could not reasonably be expected to know of B's mental disorder.

Despite A obtaining sexual gratification from the activity, none was sought from the observation or potential observation by B.

CLASSIFICATION

14.29 Offence is triable either way.

SENTENCING AND OTHER ORDERS

Maximum Sentence

14.30 On indictment: 10 years

Summarily: 6 months imprisonment or a fine not exceeding the statutory maximum (currently £5000)

Sentencing guidelines

Determining the category

14.31

Cat	Harm	Cat	Culpability
1	• Causing victim to view extreme pornography • Causing victim to view indecent/prohibited images of children • Engaging in, or causing victim to view live sexual activity involving sadism/ violence/sexual activity with an animal/a child	A	• Significant degree of planning • Offender acts together with others to commit the offence • Use of alcohol/drugs on victim to facilitate the offence
2	Engaging in, or causing victim to view images of, or view live, sexual activity involving: • penetration of vagina or anus (using body or object) • penile penetration of mouth • masturbation		• Grooming behaviour used against victim • Use of threats (including blackmail) • Commercial exploitation and/or motivation • Offence racially or religiously aggravated • Offence motivated by, or demonstrating, hostility to the victim based on his or her sexual orientation (or presumed sexual orientation) or transgender identity (or presumed transgender identity)

Cat	Harm	Cat	Culpability
			Offence motivated by, or demonstrating, hostility to the victim based on his or her disability (or presumed disability)
3	Factor(s) in categories 1 & 2 not present	B	Factor(s) in category A not present

Starting point and category range

14.32

	A	B
Category 1	Starting point: 4 yrs custody Range: 3–6 yrs custody	Starting point: 2 yrs custody Range: 1–3 yrs custody
Category 2	Starting point: 2 yrs custody Range: 1–3 yrs custody	Starting point: 1 yr custody Range: High level community order–18 mths custody
Category 3	Starting point: 26 wks custody Range: High level community order–1 yr custody	Starting point: Medium level community order Range: Low level community order–Medium level community order

Additional factual elements

14.33

Aggravating factors
Statutory aggravating factors
• Previous convictions, having regard to: (a) the nature of the offence to which the conviction relates and its relevance to the current offence; and (b) the time that has elapsed since the conviction • Offence committed whilst on bail
Other aggravating factors
• Location of offence • Timing of offence

• Failure to comply with current court orders • Offence committed whilst on licence • Any steps taken to prevent the victim reporting an incident, obtaining assistance and/or from assisting or supporting the prosecution • Attempts to dispose of or conceal evidence • Commission of offence whilst under the influence of alcohol or drugs
Mitigating factors
• No previous convictions or no relevant/recent convictions • Remorse • Previous good character and/or exemplary conduct* • Age and/or lack of maturity where it affects the responsibility of the offender • Mental disorder or learning disability, particularly where linked to the commission of the offence • Demonstration of steps taken to address offending behaviour

* Previous good character/exemplary conduct is different from having no previous convictions. The more serious the offence, the less the weight which should normally be attributed to this factor. Where previous good character/exemplary conduct has been used to facilitate the offence, this mitigation should not normally be allowed and such conduct may constitute an aggravating factor.

Other orders

14.34

Extended and life sentence availability (CJA 2003)	Sch 15 (specified offence): yes Sch 15B (life sentence for second listed offence): no
Trigger offence for:	SOPO: yes FTO: yes, but only where V *was under 18*
Inclusion in barred lists	Children: automatic if V is a child subject to representations if V is an adult Vulnerable adult: automatic
Notification	Yes

Causing a person, with a mental disorder impeding choice, to watch a sexual act Sexual Offences Act 2003, s 33

DEFINITION

14.35 Section 33(1):

A person (A) commits an offence if—

(a) for the purpose of obtaining sexual gratification, he intentionally causes another person (B) to watch a third person engaging in an activity, or to look at an image of any person engaging in an activity,

(b) the activity is sexual,

(c) B is unable to refuse because of or for a reason related to a mental disorder, and

(d) A knows or could reasonably be expected to know that B has a mental disorder and that because of it or for a reason related to it B is likely to be unable to refuse.

SUMMARY

14.36 This section makes it an offence for a person (A), for sexual gratification, intentionally to cause a person (B) either to watch a third person engaging in a sexual act, or to look at an image of any person engaging in a sexual act, where B is unable to refuse to watch because of a mental disorder which impedes his or her choice.

ELEMENTS

14.37

- *Intentionally causes* – contrast 'allows' which would not suffice.
- *either:*
  - B to *watch* a third person (*not* A) engaging in a sexual activity

  or

  - B to look at an *image* of any person (could be A) engaging in a sexual activity.
- *Sexual* – see discussion of 'sexual' at **Chapter 2**

- *Activity*

  'Activity' is not defined, but notably is not limited to touching or penetration.[13]

- *Image* (where it applies) – defined in the Act:

  – s 79(4): 'Image' means a moving or still image and includes an image produced by any means and, where the context permits, a three-dimensional image.

  – s 79(5): References to an image of a person include references to an image of an imaginary person.

- For the purpose of obtaining *sexual gratification* – the gratification may be immediate (A being 'turned on' by B's observation of the sexual act) or future gratification (getting B 'in the mood' to provide A with sexual gratification)[14]

- B has a *mental disorder*

  Section 79(6) defines this as having the same meaning as s 1 of the Mental Health Act 1983,[15] namely 'any disorder or disability of the mind'. This wide-ranging definition will include such diverse conditions as personality disorder, learning disability, autistic spectrum disorder, dementia, depressive illnesses and brain damage (if leading to a disorder or disability of the mind). However, the disorder must give rise to, or be related to, an inability to refuse.

- B is '*unable to refuse*'

  defined by s 33(2) as:

  (a) he lacks the capacity to choose whether to agree to watching or looking (whether because he lacks sufficient understanding of the nature of the activity, or for any other reason), or

  (b) he is unable to communicate such a choice to A.

- '*For a reason related to*' – it is not necessary that the mental disorder is the direct cause of the inability to refuse. Taking medication for a psychiatric disorder – the effect of which is to impair a patient's free choice – could be a situation related to (although not specifically caused by) mental disorder.

---

13 Note that s 78, which defines 'sexual', refers to '"*penetration, touching or any other activity'*.

14 *R v Abdullahi* [2006] EWCA Crim 2060 – in relation to sexual gratification and s 12 – causing a child to watch a sexual act.

15 Now amended and simplified from its original definition by s 1(2) of the Mental Health Act 2007.

- Mental element – in addition to intentionally causing B to watch an activity, the prosecution must show that:
  - The defendant did so in order to obtain sexual gratification, and
  - The defendant knew or could reasonably be expected to know that B had a mental disorder, and
  - The defendant knew or could reasonably be expected to know that because of the mental disorder, or because of a reason related to it, B was likely to be unable to refuse to watch.

DISCUSSION

14.38 See **14.5** for discussion on inability to refuse and consent in relation to almost identical provisions under s 30.

Note that lacking 'sufficient understanding of the consequences of the activity' as an instance in which B is deemed unable to refuse, is omitted from this section.

Where a sexual act is watched 'live' and direct (rather than, for example, via a webcam or recording) only acts involving a 'third person' are covered. If the act involved A himself, s 32 would apply.

The requirement that the defendant obtain sexual gratification protects those who might, for instance, show a mentally disabled person sexually explicit material for educational purposes.

EXAMPLES

14.39 Examples of this offence would be where someone gets a mentally disordered person to watch two people having sex, or shows them a pornographic film.

DEFENCES

14.40 Defendant did not know and could not reasonably be expected to know of B's mental disorder.

Defendant merely allowed, rather than caused, B to observe the sexual act.

Whether or not intending that B should obtain sexual gratification, defendant sought to derive no gratification for himself.

CLASSIFICATION

14.41 Offence is triable either way.

SENTENCING AND OTHER ORDERS

Maximum sentence

14.42 On indictment: 10 years

Summarily: 6 months imprisonment or a fine not exceeding the statutory maximum (currently £5000)

Sentencing guidelines

14.43 Identical to guidelines for 'Engaging in sexual activity in the presence of a person with a mental disorder impeding choice' (see **14.31–14.33**).

Other orders

14.44

Extended and life sentence availability (CJA 2003)	Sch 15 (specified offence): yes Sch 15B (life sentence for second listed offence): no
Trigger offence for:	SOPO: yes FTO: yes, but only where V *was under 18*
Inclusion in barred lists	Children: automatic if V is a child subject to representations if V is an adult Vulnerable adult: automatic
Notification	Yes

Chapter 15

Sexual offences involving inducements, threats or deception to person with a mental disorder

Inducement, threat or deception to procure sexual activity with a person with a mental disorder Sexual Offences Act 2003, s 34

DEFINITION

15.1 Section 34(1):

A person (A) commits an offence if—

(a) with the agreement of another person (B) he intentionally touches that person,

(b) the touching is sexual,

(c) A obtains B's agreement by means of an inducement offered or given, a threat made or a deception practised by A for that purpose,

(d) B has a mental disorder, and

(e) A knows or could reasonably be expected to know that B has a mental disorder.

SUMMARY

15.2 This section makes it an offence to touch someone (B) sexually, with his or her agreement, but where that agreement has been improperly obtained by an inducement, threat or deception. B must have a mental disorder and A must know this, but there is no need to establish a link between the mental disorder and B's agreement.

Despite the headnote reading 'sexual activity', only *touching* is caught by s 34, although touching includes penetration.

ELEMENTS

15.3

- *Intentional touching.*

  Section 79(8) provides that:

  Touching includes touching –

  (a) with any part of the body,

  (b) with anything else,

  (c) through anything,

  and in particular includes touching amounting to penetration.

  The touching by A must be intentional – in other words, deliberate and not accidental.[1]

- *Sexual* – see **Chapter 2**.
- B has a *mental disorder.*

  Section 79(6) defines this as having the same meaning as s 1 of the Mental Health Act 1983,[2] namely 'any disorder or disability of the mind'. This wide-ranging definition will include such diverse conditions as personality disorder, learning disability, autistic spectrum disorder, dementia, depressive illnesses and brain damage (if leading to a disorder or disability of the mind).

- B's agreement – without this a different charge would have to be considered.
- There is *no need to establish a link between B's mental disorder and B's agreement* to the touching.
- *Inducement, threat or deception* – these terms are not defined in the Act, but would appear to be wide – see **15.6**.
- Mental element – in addition to intentionally touching B, the prosecution must show that A knew or could reasonably be expected to know that B had a mental disorder.

---

1 *R v Heard* [2007] EWCA Crim 125.

2 Now amended and simplified from its original definition by s 1(2) of the Mental Health Act 2007.

DISCUSSION

Presence of mental disorder

15.4 For the offences contrary to ss 34 to 37, there is no need to prove that B was 'unable to refuse'. There is no need to establish any causative link between B's mental disorder and B's agreement to the activity in question.

Under this section, therefore, it is not necessary for the prosecution to prove that B was duped or responded to threats because of his or her mental condition, only that B's agreement was obtained by inducement, threat or deception and (quite separately) that B had a mental disorder.

Touching

15.5 The Court of Appeal has held[3] that merely touching the clothing worn by B (as contrasted with touching B through that clothing) can suffice. B need not be aware of the touching.

EXAMPLES

15.6 Deceptions caught by this section would include those about the nature of the activity – for instance, where B agreed because A misrepresented that the touching was for a medical reason. A promise of payment for sex would amount to an inducement, whether or not payment was eventually made.

Home Office Guidance: An inducement might be A promising B presents of anything from sweets to a holiday; a threat might be A stating that he will hurt a member of B's family; and a deception might be A stating that B will get into trouble if he does not engage in sexual activity, or persuading him that it is expected that friends should engage in sexual activity.

DEFENCES

15.7 Defendant did not know and could not reasonably be expected to know of B's mental disorder.

Section 73 provides that a person will not be guilty of aiding, abetting or counselling an offence contrary to s 34 if acting to protect the child's physical safety, protect them from sexually transmitted infection or pregnancy, or to promote their well-being by the giving of advice. This defence, which is not available for the other 'inducement' offences, is unlikely to have frequent

---

3 *R v H (Karl Anthony)*; [2005] EWCA Crim 732, [2005] 2 Cr App R 9.

application, but might conceivably arise if a health professional provided contraceptive advice to a young patient who said she was having sex in the circumstances envisaged in s 34. Note that the defence only applies if the person being protected is under 16 years old.

CLASSIFICATION

15.8 Offences under s 34 are triable as follows:

1. Where the touching involved:
   - penetration of B's anus or vagina with a part of A's body or anything else,
   - penetration of B's mouth with A's penis,
   - penetration of A's anus or vagina with a part of B's body, or
   - penetration of A's mouth with B's penis,

   the offence is indictable only.
2. In all other circumstances, the offence is triable either way.

SENTENCING AND OTHER ORDERS

Maximum sentence

15.9 In aggravated form: Life imprisonment

In non-aggravated form:

- On indictment: 14 years
- Summarily: 6 months imprisonment or a fine not exceeding the statutory maximum (currently £5000)

Sentencing guidelines

15.10 This guideline also applies to offences committed remotely/online.

Determining the category

15.11

Cat	Harm	Cat	Culpability
1	• Penetration of vagina or anus (using body or object)	A	• Significant degree of planning

Cat	**Harm**	**Cat**	**Culpability**
	• Penile penetration of mouth In either case by, or of, the victim		• Offender acts together with others to commit the offence • Use of alcohol/drugs on victim to facilitate the offence
2	Touching, or exposure, of naked genitalia or naked breasts by, or of, the victim		• Abuse of trust • Sexual images of victim recorded, retained, solicited or shared • Commercial exploitation and/or motivation • Offence racially or religiously aggravated • Offence motivated by, or demonstrating, hostility to the victim based on his or her sexual orientation (or presumed sexual orientation) or transgender identity (or presumed transgender identity) • Offence motivated by, or demonstrating, hostility to the victim based on his or her disability (or presumed disability)
3	Other sexual activity	B	Factor(s) in category A not present

Starting point and category range

15.12

	A	**B**
Category 1	Starting point: 5 yrs custody Range: 4–10 yrs custody	Starting point: 1 yr custody Range: High level community order–2 yrs custody

15.12 *Sexual offences involving inducements, threats or deception*

Category 2	Starting point: 3 yrs custody Range: 2–6 yrs custody	Starting point: 26 wks custody Range: High level community order–1 yr custody
Category 3	Starting point: 26 wks custody Range: High level community order–3 yrs custody	Starting point: Medium level community order Range: Low level community order–High level community order

Additional factual elements

15.13

Aggravating factors
Statutory aggravating factors
• Previous convictions, having regard to: (a) the nature of the offence to which the conviction relates and its relevance to the current offence; and (b) the time that has elapsed since the conviction • Offence committed whilst on bail
Other aggravating factors
• Severe psychological or physical harm • Ejaculation • Pregnancy or STI as a consequence of offence • Location of offence • Timing of offence • Victim compelled to leave their home or institution (including victims of domestic violence) • Failure to comply with current court orders • Offence committed whilst on licence • Any steps taken to prevent the victim reporting an incident, obtaining assistance and/or from assisting or supporting the prosecution • Attempts to dispose of or conceal evidence • Commission of offence whilst under the influence of alcohol or drugs
Mitigating factors
• No previous convictions or no relevant/recent convictions

- Remorse
- Previous good character and/or exemplary conduct*
- Age and/or lack of maturity where it affects the responsibility of the offender
- Mental disorder or learning disability, particularly where linked to the commission of the offence

* Previous good character/exemplary conduct is different from having no previous convictions. The more serious the offence, the less the weight which should normally be attributed to this factor. Where previous good character/exemplary conduct has been used to facilitate the offence, this mitigation should not normally be allowed and such conduct may constitute an aggravating factor.

In the context of this offence, previous good character/exemplary conduct should not normally be given any significant weight and will not normally justify a reduction in what would otherwise be the appropriate sentence.

Other orders

15.14

Extended and life sentence availability (CJA 2003)	Sch 15 (specified offence): yes Sch 15B (life sentence for second listed offence): yes, if offence is in aggravated form
Trigger offence for:	SOPO: yes FTO: yes, but only where V *was under 18*
Inclusion in barred lists	Children: automatic if V is a child Subject to representations if V is an adult Vulnerable adult: automatic
Notification	Yes

Causing a person with a mental disorder to engage in, or agree to engage in, sexual activity by inducement, threat or deception Sexual Offences Act 2003, s 35

DEFINITION

15.15 Section 35(1):

A person (A) commits an offence if—

(a) by means of an inducement offered or given, a threat made or a deception practised by him for this purpose, he intentionally causes another person (B) to engage in, or to agree to engage in, an activity,

(b) the activity is sexual,

(c) B has a mental disorder, and

(d) A knows or could reasonably be expected to know that B has a mental disorder.

SUMMARY

15.16 This section makes it an offence to cause someone (B) to engage in a sexual activity or to agree to do so, by means of an inducement, threat or deception. B must have a mental disorder and A must know this, but there is no need to establish a link between the mental disorder and B's participation in, or agreement to, the sexual activity.

The offence might be committed, for example, where A causes B to have sexual intercourse with A's friend. An offence is complete when B agrees to engage in sexual activity, even if it does not subsequently take place.

ELEMENTS

15.17

- *Intentionally causes* B – contrast 'allows' which would not suffice.

  'Causes' is not defined by the Act and should be given its natural meaning of bringing about or making happen. It may be achieved by words, action or both.

  or

- *Intentionally causes* B *to agree* – note this alternative way of committing the offence – by 'causing to agree'.

  This contrasts with 'incites' used elsewhere in the Act (ss 8, 10, 17, 26, 31, 39, 48 and 52). An offence under this limb is completed at the point when B agrees, even if the contemplated activity never takes place. If A is unsuccessful in obtaining B's agreement, an attempted offence might be made out.

- to engage in an *activity*.

  'Activity' is not defined, but notably is not limited to touching or penetration.[4]

---

4 Note that s 78, which defines 'sexual', refers to 'penetration, touching *or any other activity*'.

For example, it can include B exposing himself either directly or over the internet or other electronic link. It seems that engaging in a conversation on sexual matters can suffice.[5]

Person A may participate in the sexual activity with B, but need not. The activity may involve B alone, but equally there could be other persons, animals or objects involved.

- *Sexual* – see **Chapter 2**.
- B has a mental disorder.

  Section 79(6) defines this as having the same meaning as s 1 of the Mental Health Act 1983[6], namely 'any disorder or disability of the mind'. This wide-ranging definition will include such diverse conditions as personality disorder, learning disability, autistic spectrum disorder, dementia, depressive illnesses and brain damage (if leading to a disorder or disability of the mind).
- There is no need to establish a link between B's mental disorder and B's agreement to engage in sexual activity.
- Inducement, threat or deception – these terms are not defined in the Act, but would appear to be wide – see **15.18** and **15.19**.
- Mental element – in addition to intentionally causing B to engage in a sexual activity, or causing B to agree to engage in it, the prosecution must show that A knew or could reasonably be expected to know that B had a mental disorder.

DISCUSSION

15.18 For the offences contrary to ss 34 to 37, there is no need to prove that B was 'unable to refuse'. There is no need to establish any causative link between B's mental disorder and B's agreement to engage in sexual activity.

Under this section, therefore, it is not necessary for the prosecution to prove that B was duped or responded to threats because of his or her mental condition, only that B's agreement was obtained by inducement, threat or deception and (quite separately) that B had a mental disorder.

---

5 *R v Grout* [2011] EWCA Crim 299 at [29], discussed at **10.36**.

6 Now amended and simplified from its original definition by s 1(2) of the Mental Health Act 2007.

EXAMPLES

15.19 An example of the offence would be where B agrees to meet A for sex because A threatened that otherwise to distribute naked photos of B. The offence could still be made out even if B's carer found out about the situation and intervened to stop B meeting A.

Home Office Guidance: An inducement might be A promising B presents of anything from sweets to a holiday; a threat might be A stating that he will hurt a member of B's family; and a deception might be A stating that B will get into trouble if he does not engage in sexual activity, or persuading him that it is expected that friends should engage in sexual activity.

DEFENCE

15.20 Defendant did not know and could not reasonably be expected to know of B's mental disorder.

CLASSIFICATION

15.21 Offences under s 35 are triable as follows:

1. Where the sexual activity involved:
   - penetration of B's anus or vagina with a part of A's body or anything else,
   - penetration of B's mouth with A's penis,
   - penetration of A's anus or vagina with a part of B's body, or
   - penetration of A's mouth with B's penis,

   the offence is indictable only.
2. In all other circumstances, the offence is triable either way.

SENTENCING AND OTHER ORDERS

Maximum sentence

15.22 In aggravated form: Life imprisonment

In non-aggravated form:

- On indictment: 14 years
- Summarily: 6 months imprisonment or a fine not exceeding the statutory maximum (currently £5000)

Sentencing guidelines

15.23 Identical to guidelines for s 34; see **15.10–15.13**.

Other orders

15.24

Extended and life sentence availability (CJA 2003)	Sch 15 (specified offence): yes Sch 15B (life sentence for second listed offence): yes, if offence is in aggravated form
Trigger offence for:	SOPO: yes FTO: yes, but only where V *was under 18*
Inclusion in barred lists	Children: automatic if V is a child Subject to representations if V is an adult Vulnerable adult: automatic
Notification	Yes

Engaging in sexual activity in the presence, procured by inducement, threat or deception, of a person with a mental disorder Sexual Offences Act 2003, s 36

DEFINITION

15.25 Section 36(1):

A person (A) commits an offence if—

(a) he intentionally engages in an activity,

(b) the activity is sexual,

(c) for the purpose of obtaining sexual gratification, he engages in it—

(i) when another person (B) is present or is in a place from which A can be observed, and

(ii) knowing or believing that B is aware, or intending that B should be aware, that he is engaging in it,

(d) B agrees to be present or in the place referred to in paragraph (c) (i) because of an inducement offered or given, a threat made or a deception practised by A for the purpose of obtaining that agreement,

(e) B has a mental disorder, and

(f) A knows or could reasonably be expected to know that B has a mental disorder.

SUMMARY

15.26 This section makes it an offence for a person (A), for the purpose of obtaining sexual gratification, intentionally to engage in sexual activity when a person (B) is present or in a vantage point and B's agreement to being present has been improperly obtained by an inducement, threat or deception. B must have a mental disorder and A must know, or reasonably be expected to know, of this.

ELEMENTS

15.27

- *Intentionally engages.*
- *Activity.*

  'Activity' is not defined, but notably is not limited to touching or penetration.[7]

  For example, it can include A exposing himself.

  It seems that engaging in a conversation on sexual matters can suffice[8]

  The activity may involve A alone, but equally there could be other persons, animals or objects involved.
- *Sexual* – see **Chapter 2.**
- For the purpose of A obtaining *sexual gratification*:
  - B present or in a place from which A can be observed
  - A knowing/believing/intending that B should be aware

  The offence is committed if A knows or believes that B is aware that he is engaging in the activity, or A intends that B should be aware that he is engaging in it, *and* A carries out the activity for the purposes of obtaining sexual gratification from B's awareness.
- B has a mental disorder.

---

7 Note that s 78, which defines 'sexual', refers to '*penetration, touching or any other activity*'.

8 *R v Grout* [2011] EWCA Crim 299 at [29], discussed at **10.36**.

Section 79(6) defines this as having the same meaning as s 1 of the Mental Health Act 1983,[9] namely 'any disorder or disability of the mind'. This wide-ranging definition will include such diverse conditions as personality disorder, learning disability, autistic spectrum disorder, dementia, depressive illnesses and brain damage (if leading to a disorder or disability of the mind).

- There is no need to establish a link between B's mental disorder and B's agreement to be present at the relevant location.
- *Inducement, threat or deception* – these terms are not defined in the Act, but would appear to be wide – see **15.28** and **15.29**.
- Mental element – the prosecution must show that, in addition to intentionally engaging in the sexual activity:
  - the defendant did so in order to obtain sexual gratification from B's presence or observation; and
  - the defendant knew or could reasonably be expected to know that B had a mental disorder.

DISCUSSION

15.28 For the offences contrary to ss 34 to 37, there is no need to prove that B was 'unable to refuse'. There is no need to establish any causative link between B's mental disorder and B's agreement to be present at the relevant location.

Under this section, therefore, it is not necessary for the prosecution to prove that B was duped or responded to threats because of his or her mental condition, only that B's agreement to be present was obtained by inducement, threat or deception and (quite separately) that B had a mental disorder.

EXAMPLES

15.29 The offence covers situations such as A masturbating himself in B's presence but without being seen by B (perhaps because the lights are off, or B is covering his face), so long as A knows, believes or intends that B is aware of what A is doing.

Equally, B need not be physically present. A might perform a sexual act in a place where he knows that he can be seen by B, for example via a CCTV monitor, but again it is not necessary for B actually to observe the activity.

---

9 Now amended and simplified from its original definition by s 1(2) of the Mental Health Act 2007.

15.29 *Sexual offences involving inducements, threats or deception*

An inducement might be A promising B presents of anything from sweets to a holiday; a threat might be A stating that he will hurt a member of B's family; and a deception might be A persuading B that people expect their friends to watch them engaging in sexual activity.

DEFENCE

15.30 Defendant did not know and could not reasonably be expected to know of B's mental disorder.

Despite A obtaining sexual gratification from the activity, none was sought from the observation or potential observation by B.

CLASSIFICATION

15.31 The offence is triable either way.

SENTENCING AND OTHER ORDERS

Maximum sentence

15.32 On indictment: 10 years

Summarily: 6 months imprisonment or a fine not exceeding the statutory maximum (currently £5000)

Sentencing guidelines

Determining the category

15.33

Cat	Harm	Cat	Culpability
1	• Causing victim to view extreme pornography • Causing victim to view indecent/prohibited images of children • Engaging in, or causing victim to view live sexual activity involving sadism/ violence/sexual activity with an animal/a child	A	• Significant degree of planning • Offender acts together with others to commit the offence • Use of alcohol/drugs on victim to facilitate the offence

Cat	Harm	Cat	Culpability
2	Engaging in, or causing victim to view images of, or view live, sexual activity involving: • penetration of vagina or anus (using body or object) • penile penetration of mouth • masturbation		• Abuse of trust • Commercial exploitation and/or motivation • Offence racially or religiously aggravated • Offence motivated by, or demonstrating, hostility to the victim based on his or her sexual orientation (or presumed sexual orientation) or transgender identity (or presumed transgender identity) • Offence motivated by, or demonstrating, hostility to the victim based on his or her disability (or presumed disability)
3	Factor(s) in categories 1 & 2 not present	B	Factor(s) in category A not present

Starting point and category range

15.34

	A	B
Category 1	Starting point: 4 yrs custody Range: 3–6 yrs custody	Starting point: 2 yrs custody Range: 1–3 yrs custody
Category 2	Starting point: 2 yrs custody Range: 1–3 yrs custody	Starting point: 1 yr custody Range: High level community order–18 mths custody
Category 3	Starting point: 26 wks custody Range: High level community order–1 yr custody	Starting point: Medium level community order Range: Low level community order–Medium level community order

15.35 *Sexual offences involving inducements, threats or deception*

Additional factual elements

15.35

Aggravating factors
Statutory aggravating factors
• Previous convictions, having regard to: (a) the nature of the offence to which the conviction relates and its relevance to the current offence; and (b) the time that has elapsed since the conviction • Offence committed whilst on bail
Other aggravating factors
• Location of offence • Timing of offence • Failure to comply with current court orders • Offence committed whilst on licence • Any steps taken to prevent the victim reporting an incident, obtaining assistance and/or from assisting or supporting the prosecution • Attempts to dispose of or conceal evidence • Commission of offence whilst under the influence of alcohol or drugs
Mitigating factors
• No previous convictions or no relevant/recent convictions • Remorse • Previous good character and/or exemplary conduct* • Mental disorder or learning disability, particularly where linked to the commission of the offence • Demonstration of steps taken to address offending behaviour

* Previous good character/exemplary conduct is different from having no previous convictions. The more serious the offence, the less the weight which should normally be attributed to this factor. Where previous good character/exemplary conduct has been used to facilitate the offence, this mitigation should not normally be allowed and such conduct may constitute an aggravating factor.

Other orders

15.36

Extended and life sentence availability (CJA 2003)	Sch 15 (specified offence): yes Sch 15B (life sentence for second listed offence): no
Trigger offence for:	SOPO: yes FTO: yes, but only where V *was under 18*
Inclusion in barred lists	Children: automatic if V is a child Subject to representations if V is an adult Vulnerable adult: automatic
Notification	Yes

Causing a person with a mental disorder to watch a sexual act by inducement, threat or deception Sexual Offences Act 2003, s 37

DEFINITION

15.37 Section 37(1):

A person (A) commits an offence if –

(a) for the purpose of obtaining sexual gratification, he intentionally causes another person (B) to watch a third person engaging in an activity, or to look at an image of any person engaging in an activity,

(b) the activity is sexual,

(c) B agrees to watch or look because of an inducement offered or given, a threat made or a deception practised by A for the purpose of obtaining that agreement,

(d) B has a mental disorder, and

(e) A knows or could reasonably be expected to know that B has a mental disorder.

SUMMARY

15.38 This section makes it an offence for a person (A), for the purpose of obtaining sexual gratification, intentionally to cause a person (B) either to watch a third person engaging in a sexual activity, or to look at an image of any person engaging in a sexual activity, where B's agreement to viewing these things has been improperly obtained by an inducement, threat or deception. B must have a mental disorder and A must know this.

Where the sexual act is watched 'live' and direct (rather than, for example, via a webcam or recording) only acts involving a 'third person' are covered – if the act involved A himself, s 36 would apply.

ELEMENTS

15.39

- *Intentionally causes* – contrast 'allows' which would not suffice.

  either:

  – B to *watch* a third person (*not* A) engaging in a sexual activity; *or*

  – B to look at an *image* of any person (could be A) engaging in a sexual activity.

- *Sexual* – see **Chapter 2**.
- Activity

  'Activity' is not defined, but notably is not limited to touching or penetration.[10]

- *Image* (where it applies) – defined in the Act:

  – s 79(4): 'Image' means a moving or still image and includes an image produced by any means and, where the context permits, a three-dimensional image.

  – s 79(5): References to an image of a person include references to an image of an imaginary person.

- For the purpose of obtaining *sexual gratification* – the gratification may be immediate (A being 'turned on' by B's observation of the sexual act) or future gratification (getting B 'in the mood' to provide A with sexual gratification).[11]
- B has a mental disorder.

  Section 79(6) defines this as having the same meaning as s 1 of the Mental Health Act 1983,[12] namely 'any disorder or disability of the

10 Note that s 78, which defines 'sexual', refers to '*penetration, touching or any other activity*'.

11 *R v Abdullahi* [2006] EWCA Crim 2060 – in relation to sexual gratification and s 12 – causing a child to watch a sexual act.

12 Now amended and simplified from its original definition by s 1(2) of the Mental Health Act 2007.

mind'. This wide-ranging definition will include such diverse conditions as personality disorder, learning disability, autistic spectrum disorder, dementia, depressive illnesses and brain damage (if leading to a disorder or disability of the mind).

- There is no need to establish a link between B's mental disorder and B's agreement to watch or look.
- Inducement, threat or deception – these terms are not defined in the Act, but would appear to be wide – see **15.40** and **15.41**.
- Mental element – in addition to intentionally causing B to watch the activity or to look at the image, the prosecution must show that:
  - the defendant did so in order to obtain sexual gratification; and
  - the defendant knew or could reasonably be expected to know that B had a mental disorder.

DISCUSSION

15.40 For the offences contrary to ss 34 to 37, there is no need to prove that B was 'unable to refuse'. There is no need to establish any causative link between B's mental disorder and B's agreement to watch sexual activity or to look at an image.

Under this section, therefore, it is not necessary for the prosecution to prove that B was duped or responded to threats because of his or her mental condition, only that B's agreement to watch or look was obtained by inducement, threat or deception and (quite separately) that B had a mental disorder.

EXAMPLES

15.41 Examples of this offence would be where someone gets a mentally disordered person to watch two people having sex, or shows him or her a pornographic film.

An inducement might be A promising B gifts; a threat might be A stating that he will hurt a member of B's family; and a deception might be A persuading B that people expect their friends to watch them engaging in sexual activity.

DEFENCES

15.42 Defendant did not know and could not reasonably be expected to know of B's mental disorder.

Defendant merely allowed, rather than caused, B to look at an image.

15.42 *Sexual offences involving inducements, threats or deception*

Whether or not intending that B should obtain sexual gratification, defendant sought to derive no gratification for himself.

CLASSIFICATION

15.43 The offence is triable either way.

SENTENCING AND OTHER ORDERS

Maximum sentence

15.44 On indictment: 10 years

Summarily: 6 months imprisonment or a fine not exceeding the statutory maximum (currently £5000)

Sentencing guidelines

15.45 Identical to guidelines for s 36; see **15.33–15.35**.

Other orders

15.46

Extended and life sentence availability (CJA 2003)	Sch 15 (specified offence): yes Sch 15B (life sentence for second listed offence): no
Trigger offence for:	SOPO: yes FTO: yes, but only where V *was under 18*
Inclusion in barred lists	Children: automatic if V is a child Subject to representations if V is an adult Vulnerable adult: automatic
Notification	Yes

Chapter 16

Sexual offences by care workers against persons with a mental disorder

Care workers: sexual activity with a person with a mental disorder
Sexual Offences Act 2003, s 38

DEFINITION

16.1 Section 38(1):

A person (A) commits an offence if—

(a) he intentionally touches another person (B);

(b) the touching is sexual;

(c) B has a mental disorder;

(d) A knows or could reasonably be expected to know that B has a mental disorder; and

(e) A is involved in B's care in a way which falls within section 42.

SUMMARY

16.2 This section makes it an offence for a care worker (and many others involved in care environments[1]) to touch sexually someone in whose care they are involved when that person has a mental disorder. Despite the headnote reading 'sexual activity', only touching is caught by s 38, although touching includes penetration.

The offence is committed (with certain statutory exceptions) whether or not B consents. Therefore B's capacity to consent is immaterial.

---

1 See **16.5**.

ELEMENTS

16.3 *Intentional touching.*

Section 79(8) provides that:

- Touching includes touching:

  (a) with any part of the body;

  (b) with anything else;

  (c) through anything;

  and in particular includes touching amounting to penetration.

  The touching by A must be intentional – in other words, deliberate and not accidental.[2]

- *Sexual* – see **Chapter 2**.

- B has a mental disorder.

  Section 79(6) defines this as having the same meaning as s 1 of the Mental Health Act 1983,[3] namely 'any disorder or disability of the mind'. This wide-ranging definition will include such diverse conditions as personality disorder, learning disability, autistic spectrum disorder, dementia, depressive illnesses and brain damage (if leading to a disorder or disability of the mind).

- Involved in B's care

  This concept is defined at s 42 of the Act and includes:

  – where B is in a care, community, voluntary or children's home;

  – where B is a patient of the NHS or an independent agency or hospital;

  in each case, A must be in employment with that body which bring him, or is likely to bring him, into regular face-to-face contact with B;

  – where A provides care, assistance or services to B in connection with B's mental disorder.

In this latter case, A may be an employed or voluntary carer, but must have, or be likely to have, regular face-to-face contact with B.[4]

- Mental element

---

2 *R v Heard* [2007] EWCA Crim 125.

3 Now amended and simplified from its original definition by s 1(2) of the Mental Health Act 2007.

4 Children's home, care home, employment etc are further defined at s 42(5) and (6).

In addition to intentionally touching B, the prosecution must show that A knew or could reasonably be expected to know that B had a mental disorder.

PARTIES

16.4 The offence may be committed by a person of either gender, who must be a care worker, as defined.

B can be male or female, of any age.

DISCUSSION

16.5 It is an offence contrary to ss 38 to 41 for a care worker to have sexual interaction with someone in their care, even if that person has capacity to consent and does so. The rationale for this is that the potential for imbalance of power and abusive relationships is so great, that all such activity should be unlawful.

Pre-existing sexual relationships which then become 'care' relationships are accounted for by the statutory defences of ss 43 and 44 and, in circumstances where a carer and 'patient' wish to have a consensual sexual relationship, there is no bar on this occurring after the carer has left that position.

There is a requirement that the care worker comes into, or is likely to come into, 'regular face-to-face contact' with B. In fact, the term 'care worker' is inaccurate, since the offence is not limited to those who provide medical or nursing services, but encompasses those who have 'functions to perform' in the home or hospital, including secretarial staff, cleaners or porters who will frequently have 'regular face-to-face contact'.

EXAMPLES

16.6 Home Office guidance:

An example of a relationship covered by s 42(2) would be where the care worker is a member of staff in a care home and the person with a mental disorder is resident there.

An example of a relationship covered by s 42(3) would be where the care worker is a receptionist at a clinic attended regularly by the person with a mental disorder.

An example of a relationship covered by s 42(4) would be where the care worker takes the person with a mental disorder on outings every week or visits him at home to provide complementary therapy.

16.7

> **Statutory defences**
>
> Section 43 provides a defence where A and B were lawfully married or civil partners at the material time.
>
> Section 44 provides a defence where A and B were in a lawful sexual relationship immediately before A became involved in B's care.
>
> In both cases, the burden is on the defendant to prove the facts of the applicable defence, on the balance of probabilities.
>
> Section 73 provides that a person will not be guilty of aiding, abetting or counselling an offence contrary to s 38 if acting to protect the child's physical safety, protect them from sexually transmitted infection or pregnancy, or to promote their well-being by the giving of advice. This defence, which is not available for the other 'care worker' offences, is unlikely to have frequent application, but might conceivably arise if a health professional provided contraceptive advice to a young person who said she was having sex in the circumstances envisaged in s 34. Note that the defence only applies if the person being protected is under 16 years old.

OTHER DEFENCES

16.8 Defendant did not know and could not reasonably be expected to know of B's mental disorder. But note, where B is proved to have had a mental disorder, s 38(2) imposes a rebuttable presumption that the defendant knew or could reasonably be expected to know this. If sufficient evidence is adduced to raise the issue, the prosecution then have to prove that A knew, or could reasonably be expected to know, of B's mental disorder.

CLASSIFICATION

16.9 Offences under s 38 are triable as follows:

1. Where the touching involved:
   - penetration of B's anus or vagina with a part of A's body or anything else;
   - penetration of B's mouth with A's penis;
   - penetration of A's anus or vagina with a part of B's body; or
   - penetration of A's mouth with B's penis;

   the offence is indictable only.
2. In all other circumstances, the offence is triable either way.

SENTENCING AND OTHER ORDERS

Maximum sentence

16.10 In aggravated form: 14 years imprisonment

In non-aggravated form:

- On indictment: 10 years imprisonment
- Summarily: 6 months imprisonment or a fine not exceeding the statutory maximum (currently £5000)

Sentencing guidelines

Determining the category

16.11

Cat	Harm	Cat	Culpability
1	• Penetration of vagina or anus (using body or object) • Penile penetration of mouth In either case by, or of, the victim	A	• Significant degree of planning • Offender acts together with others to commit the offence • Use of alcohol/drugs on victim to facilitate the offence
2	Touching, or exposure, of naked genitalia or naked breasts by, or of, the victim		• Grooming behaviour used against victim • Use of threats (including blackmail) • Sexual images of victim recorded, retained, solicited or shared • Commercial exploitation and/or motivation • Offence racially or religiously aggravated

16.11 *Sexual offences by care workers*

Cat	Harm	Cat	Culpability
			• Offence motivated by, or demonstrating, hostility to the victim based on his or her sexual orientation (or presumed sexual orientation) or transgender identity (or presumed transgender identity) • Offence motivated by, or demonstrating, hostility to the victim based on his or her disability (or presumed disability)
3	Other sexual activity	B	Factor(s) in category A not present

Starting point and category range

16.12

	A	B
Category 1	Starting point: 5 yrs custody Range: 4–10 yrs custody	Starting point: 18 mths custody Range: 1–2 yrs custody
Category 2	Starting point: 3 yrs custody Range: 2–6 yrs custody	Starting point: 26 wks custody Range: Medium level community order–1 yr custody
Category 3	Starting point: 26 wks custody Range: High level community order–3 yrs custody	Starting point: Medium level community order Range: Low level community order—High level community order

Additional factual elements

16.13

Aggravating factors
Statutory aggravating factors
• Previous convictions, having regard to a) the nature of the offence to which the conviction relates and its relevance to the current offence; and b) the time that has elapsed since the conviction • Offence committed whilst on bail
Other aggravating factors
• Ejaculation • Pregnancy or STI as a consequence of offence • Location of offence • Timing of offence • Victim compelled to leave their home or institution (including victims of domestic violence) • Failure to comply with current court orders • Offence committed whilst on licence • Any steps taken to prevent the victim reporting an incident, obtaining assistance and/or from assisting or supporting the prosecution • Attempts to dispose of or conceal evidence • Failure of offender to respond to previous warnings • Commission of offence whilst under the influence of alcohol or drugs
Mitigating factors
• No previous convictions or no relevant/recent convictions • Remorse • Previous good character and/or exemplary conduct* • Age and/or lack of maturity where it affects the responsibility of the offender • Mental disorder or learning disability, particularly where linked to the commission of the offence • Sexual activity was incited but no activity took place because the offender voluntarily desisted or intervened to prevent it

16.31 *Sexual offences by care workers*

* Previous good character/exemplary conduct is different from having no previous convictions. The more serious the offence, the less the weight which should normally be attributed to this factor. Where previous good character/exemplary conduct has been used to facilitate the offence, this mitigation should not normally be allowed and such conduct may constitute an aggravating factor.

In the context of this offence, previous good character/exemplary conduct should not normally be given any significant weight and will not normally justify a reduction in what would otherwise be the appropriate sentence.

Other orders

16.14

Extended and life sentence availability (CJA 2003)	Sch 15 (specified offence): yes Sch 15B (life sentence for second listed offence): no
Trigger offence for:	SOPO: yes FTO: yes, but only where V *was under 18*, and D under 18 and sentenced to at least 12 months imprisonment; D over 18 and sentenced to prison or detention in hospital or community sentence of at least 12 months
Inclusion in barred lists	Children: automatic if V is a child Subject to representations if V is an adult Vulnerable adult: automatic
Notification	Yes, if: D under 18 and sentenced to at least 12 months imprisonment; D over 18 and sentenced to prison or detention in hospital or community sentence of at least 12 months

Care workers: causing/inciting to engage in sexual activity
Sexual Offences Act 2003, s 39

DEFINITION

16.15 Section 39(1):

A person (A) commits an offence if—

(a) he intentionally causes or incites another person (B) to engage in an activity,

(b) the activity is sexual,

(c) B has a mental disorder,

(d) A knows or could reasonably be expected to know that B has a mental disorder, and

(e) A is involved in B's care in a way which falls within section 42.

SUMMARY

16.16 This section makes it an offence for a care worker to cause or incite someone in their care to engage in a sexual activity when that person has a mental disorder.

The offence could be committed where A persuades B to have sexual intercourse with A's friend, or encourages B to do so, even if the encouragement does not result in B engaging in sexual activity.

The offence is committed (with certain statutory exceptions) whether or not B consents. Therefore B's capacity to consent is immaterial.

ELEMENTS

16.17

- *Intentionally*

  'Intentionally' relates to causing/inciting the activity.

- Causes *or* incites

  The section creates two separate offences (see Specimen Indictments, **Appendix 1**).

- '*Causes*' is not defined by the Act and should be given its natural meaning of bringing about or making happen.

  'Causing' requires something more than merely 'allowing'.

  It may be achieved by words, action or both.

- '*Incites*' is not defined by the Act and should be given its natural meaning of urges or provokes.

  The incited activity need not actually take place.

- B to engage in activity

'*Activity*' is not defined, but notably is not limited to touching or penetration.[5]

For example, it can include B exposing himself either directly or over the internet or other electronic link.

It seems that engaging in a conversation on sexual matters can suffice.[6]

- *Sexual* – see **Chapter 2**.

  This relates to the activity in which B is caused or incited to engage rather than anything done by A without B's participation.

- (where the aggravated offence is alleged) specific type of penetration (to be specified in the indictment).

- B has a *mental disorder*.

  Section 79(6) defines this as having the same meaning as s 1 of the Mental Health Act 1983,[7] namely 'any disorder or disability of the mind'. This wide-ranging definition will include such diverse conditions as personality disorder, learning disability, autistic spectrum disorder, dementia, depressive illnesses and brain damage (if leading to a disorder or disability of the mind).

- *Involved in B's care* – this concept is defined at s 42 of the Act and includes:

  - where B is in a care, community, voluntary or children's home;
  - where B is a patient of the NHS or an independent agency or hospital;

  in each case, A must be in employment with that body which bring him, or is likely to bring him, into regular face-to-face contact with B;

  - where A provides care, assistance or services to B in connection with B's mental disorder.

  In this latter case, A may be an employed or voluntary carer, but must have, or be likely to have, regular face-to-face contact with B.[8]

- *Mental element*

  In addition to intentionally causing or inciting, the prosecution must show that A knew or could reasonably be expected to know that B had a mental disorder.

---

5 Note that s 78, which defines 'sexual', refers to '*penetration, touching or any other activity*'.
6 *R v Grout* [2011] EWCA Crim 299 at [29], discussed at **10.36**.
7 Now amended and simplified from its original definition by s 1(2) of the Mental Health Act 2007.
8 Children's home, care home, employment etc are further defined at s 42(5) and (6).

PARTIES

16.18 The offence may be committed by a person of either gender, who must be a care worker, as defined.

B can be male or female, of any age.

DISCUSSION

16.19 It is an offence contrary to ss 38 to 41 for a care worker to have sexual interaction with someone in their care, even if that person has capacity to consent and does so. The rationale for this is that the potential for imbalance of power and abusive relationships is so great, that all such activity should be unlawful.

Pre-existing sexual relationships which then become 'care' relationships are accounted for by the statutory defences of ss 43 and 44 and, in circumstances where a carer and 'patient' wish to have a consensual sexual relationship, there is no bar on this occurring after the carer has left that position.

There is a requirement that the care worker comes into, or is likely to come into, 'regular face-to-face contact' with B. In fact, the term 'care worker' is inaccurate, since the offence is not limited to those who provide medical or nursing services, but encompasses those who have 'functions to perform' in the home or hospital, including secretarial staff, cleaners or porters who will frequently have 'regular face-to-face contact'.

EXAMPLES

16.20 Home Office guidance:

An example of a relationship covered by s 42(2) would be where the care worker is a member of staff in a care home and the person with a mental disorder is resident there.

An example of a relationship covered by s 42(3) would be where the care worker is a receptionist at a clinic attended regularly by the person with a mental disorder.

An example of a relationship covered by s 42(4) would be where the care worker takes the person with a mental disorder on outings every week or visits him at home to provide complementary therapy.

16.21

Statutory defences
Section 43 provides a defence where A and B were lawfully married or civil partners at the material time.
Section 44 provides a defence where A and B were in a lawful sexual relationship immediately before A became involved in B's care.
In both cases, the burden is on the defendant to prove the facts of the applicable defence, on the balance of probabilities.

OTHER DEFENCES

16.22 Defendant did not know and could not reasonably be expected to know of B's mental disorder. But note, where B is proved to have had a mental disorder, s 38(2) imposes a rebuttable presumption that the defendant knew or could reasonably be expected to know this. If sufficient evidence is adduced to raise the issue, the prosecution then have to prove that A knew, or could reasonably be expected to know, of B's mental disorder.

CLASSIFICATION

16.23 Offences under s 39 are triable as follows:

1. Where the touching involved:
   - penetration of B's anus or vagina with a part of A's body or anything else;
   - penetration of B's mouth with A's penis;
   - penetration of A's anus or vagina with a part of B's body; or
   - penetration of A's mouth with B's penis;

   the offence is indictable only.
2. In all other circumstances, the offence is triable either way.

SENTENCING AND OTHER ORDERS

Maximum sentence

16.24 In aggravated form: 14 years imprisonment

In non-aggravated form:

- On indictment: 10 years imprisonment

- Summarily: 6 months imprisonment or a fine not exceeding the statutory maximum (currently £5000)

Sentencing guidelines

16.25 Identical to guidelines s 39; see **16.11–16.13**.

Other orders

16.26

Extended and life sentence availability (CJA 2003)	Sch 15 (specified offence): yes Sch 15B (life sentence for second listed offence): no
Trigger offence for:	SOPO: yes FTO: yes, but only where V *was under 18*, and D under 18 and sentenced to at least 12 months imprisonment; D over 18 and sentenced to prison or detention in hospital or community sentence of at least 12 months
Inclusion in barred lists	Children: automatic if V is a child Subject to representations if V is an adult Vulnerable adult: automatic
Notification	Yes, if: D under 18 and sentenced to at least 12 months imprisonment; D over 18 and sentenced to prison or detention in hospital or community sentence of at least 12 months

Care workers: sexual activity in the presence of a person with a mental disorder
Sexual Offences Act 2003, s 40

DEFINITION

16.27 Section 40(1):

A person (A) commits an offence if—

(a) he intentionally engages in an activity,

(b) the activity is sexual,

(c) for the purpose of obtaining sexual gratification, he engages in it—

(i) when another person (B) is present or is in a place from which A can be observed, and

(ii) knowing or believing that B is aware, or intending that B should be aware, that he is engaging in it,

(d) B has a mental disorder,

(e) A knows or could reasonably be expected to know that B has a mental disorder, and

(f) A is involved in B's care in a way which falls within section 42.

SUMMARY

16.28 This section makes it an offence for a care worker, for the purpose of obtaining sexual gratification, intentionally to engage in sexual activity when a person, in whose care they are involved and who has a mental disorder, is present or in a vantage point. The offender must know, believe or intend that B is aware of the sexual activity.

The offence is committed (with certain statutory exceptions) whether or not B consents. Therefore B's capacity to consent is immaterial.

ELEMENTS

16.29

- *Intentionally engages*
- *Activity*

  'Activity' is not defined, but notably is not limited to touching or penetration.[9]

  For example, it can include A exposing himself.

  It seems that engaging in a conversation on sexual matters can suffice.[10]

  The activity may involve A alone, but equally there could be other persons, animals or objects involved.
- *Sexual* – see **Chapter 2**.
- For the purpose of A obtaining *sexual gratification*:

9 Note that s 78, which defines 'sexual', refers to '*penetration, touching or any other activity*'.
10 *R v Grout* [2011] EWCA Crim 299 at [29], discussed at **10.36**.

- B present or in a place from which A can be observed;
- A knowing/believing/intending that B should be aware.

The offence is committed if A knows or believes that B is aware that he is engaging in the activity, or A intends that B should be aware that he is engaging in it, *and* A carries out the activity for the purposes of obtaining sexual gratification from B's awareness.

- B has a mental disorder.

  Section 79(6) defines this as having the same meaning as s 1 of the Mental Health Act 1983[11], namely 'any disorder or disability of the mind'. This wide-ranging definition will include such diverse conditions as personality disorder, learning disability, autistic spectrum disorder, dementia, depressive illnesses and brain damage (if leading to a disorder or disability of the mind).

- *Involved in B's care* – this concept is defined at s 42 of the Act and includes:
  - where B is in a care, community, voluntary or children's home;
  - where B is a patient of the NHS or an independent agency or hospital;

  (in each case, A must be in employment with that body which brings him, or is likely to bring him, into regular face-to-face contact with B);
  - where A provides care, assistance or services to B in connection with B's mental disorder.

  In this latter case, A may be an employed or voluntary carer, but must have, or be likely to have, regular face-to-face contact with B.[12]

- Mental element

  In addition to intentionally engaging in the activity for sexual gratification, the prosecution must show that A knew or could reasonably be expected to know that B had a mental disorder.

PARTIES

16.30 The offence may be committed by a person of either gender, who must be a care worker, as defined.

B can be male or female, of any age.

---

11 Now amended and simplified from its original definition by s 1(2) of the Mental Health Act 2007.

12 Children's home, care home, employment etc are further defined at s 42(5) and (6).

DISCUSSION

16.31 It is an offence contrary to ss 38 to 41 for a care worker to have sexual interaction with someone in their care, even if that person has capacity to consent and does so. The rationale for this is that the potential for imbalance of power and abusive relationships is so great, that all such activity should be unlawful.

Pre-existing sexual relationships which then become 'care' relationships are accounted for by the statutory defences of ss 43 and 44 and, in circumstances where a carer and 'patient' wish to have a consensual sexual relationship, there is no bar on this occurring after the carer has left that position.

There is a requirement that the care worker comes into, or is likely to come into, 'regular face-to-face contact' with B. In fact, the term 'care worker' is inaccurate, since the offence is not limited to those who provide medical or nursing services, but encompasses those who have 'functions to perform' in the home or hospital, including secretarial staff, cleaners or porters who will frequently have 'regular face-to-face contact'.

EXAMPLES

16.32 The offence covers situations such as A masturbating himself in B's presence but without being seen by B (perhaps because the lights are off, or B is covering his face), so long as A knows, believes or intends that B is aware of what A is doing.

Equally, B need not be physically present. A might perform a sexual act in a place where he knows that he can be seen by B, for example via a CCTV monitor, but again it is not necessary for B actually to observe the activity.

Home Office guidance:

An example of a relationship covered by s 42(2) would be where the care worker is a member of staff in a care home and the person with a mental disorder is resident there.

An example of a relationship covered by s 42(3) would be where the care worker is a receptionist at a clinic attended regularly by the person with a mental disorder.

An example of a relationship covered by s 42(4) would be where the care worker takes the person with a mental disorder on outings every week or visits him at home to provide complementary therapy.

16.33

Statutory defences
Section 43 provides a defence where A and B were lawfully married or civil partners at the material time.
Section 44 provides a defence where A and B were in a lawful sexual relationship immediately before A became involved in B's care.
In both cases, the burden is on the defendant to prove the facts of the applicable defence, on the balance of probabilities.

OTHER DEFENCES

16.34 Despite A obtaining sexual gratification from the activity, none was sought from the observation or potential observation by B.

Defendant did not know and could not reasonably be expected to know of B's mental disorder. But note, where B is proved to have had a mental disorder, s 38(2) imposes a rebuttable presumption that the defendant knew or could reasonably be expected to know this. If sufficient evidence is adduced to raise the issue, the prosecution then have to prove that A knew, or could reasonably be expected to know, of B's mental disorder.

CLASSIFICATION

16.35 Offence is triable either way.

SENTENCING AND OTHER ORDERS

Maximum sentence

16.36 On indictment: 7 years

Summarily: 6 months imprisonment or a fine not exceeding the statutory maximum (currently £5000)

Sentencing guidelines

Determining the category

16.37

Cat	Harm	Cat	Culpability
1	• Causing victim to view extreme pornography • Causing victim to view indecent/prohibited images of children • Engaging in, or causing victim to view live sexual activity involving sadism/ violence/sexual activity with an animal/a child	A	• Significant degree of planning • Offender acts together with others to commit the offence • Use of alcohol/drugs on victim to facilitate the offence • Grooming behaviour used against victim • Use of threats (including blackmail) • Commercial exploitation and/or motivation • Offence racially or religiously aggravated • Offence motivated by, or demonstrating, hostility to the victim based on his or her sexual orientation (or presumed sexual orientation) or transgender identity (or presumed transgender identity) • Offence motivated by, or demonstrating, hostility to the victim based on his or her disability (or presumed disability)
2	Engaging in, or causing victim to view images of, or view live, sexual activity involving: • penetration of vagina or anus (using body or object) • penile penetration of mouth • masturbation		
3	Factor(s) in categories 1 & 2 not present	B	Factor(s) in category A not present

Starting point and category range

16.38

	A	B
Category 1	Starting point: 18 mths custody Range: 1–2 yrs custody	Starting point: 1 yr custody Range: 26 wks–18 mths custody
Category 2	Starting point: 1 yr custody Range: 26 wks–18 mths custody	Starting point: 26 wks custody Range: High level community order–1 yr custody
Category 3	Starting point: 26 wks custody Range: High level community order–1 yr custody	Starting point: Medium level community order Range: Low level community order–High level community order

Additional factual elements

16.39

Aggravating factors
Statutory aggravating factors
• Previous convictions, having regard to: (a) the nature of the offence to which the conviction relates and its relevance to the current offence; and (b) the time that has elapsed since the conviction • Offence committed whilst on bail
Other aggravating factors
• Location of offence • Timing of offence • Failure to comply with current court orders • Offence committed whilst on licence • Any steps taken to prevent the victim reporting an incident, obtaining assistance and/or from assisting or supporting the prosecution • Attempts to dispose of or conceal evidence • Failure of offender to respond to previous warnings • Commission of offence whilst under the influence of alcohol or drugs

Mitigating factors
• No previous convictions or no relevant/recent convictions
• Remorse
• Previous good character and/or exemplary conduct*
• Age and/or lack of maturity where it affects the responsibility of the offender
• Mental disorder or learning disability, particularly where linked to the commission of the offence
• Demonstration of steps taken to address offending behaviour

* Previous good character/exemplary conduct is different from having no previous convictions. The more serious the offence, the less the weight which should normally be attributed to this factor. Where previous good character/exemplary conduct has been used to facilitate the offence, this mitigation should not normally be allowed and such conduct may constitute an aggravating factor.

Other orders

16.40

Extended and life sentence availability (CJA 2003)	Sch 15 (specified offence): yes Sch 15B (life sentence for second listed offence): no
Trigger offence for:	SOPO: yes FTO: yes, but only where V *was under 18*, and D under 18 and sentenced to at least 12 months imprisonment; D over 18 and sentenced to prison or detention in hospital or community sentence of at least 12 months
Inclusion in barred lists	Children: automatic if V is a child subject to representations if V is an adult Vulnerable adult: automatic
Notification	Yes, if: D under 18 and sentenced to at least 12 months imprisonment; D over 18 and sentenced to prison or detention in hospital or community sentence of at least 12 months

Care workers: causing a person with a mental disorder to watch a sexual activity Sexual Offences Act 2003, s 41

DEFINITION

16.41 Section 41(1):

A person (A) commits an offence if—

(a) for the purpose of obtaining sexual gratification, he intentionally causes another person (B) to watch a third person engaging in an activity, or to look at an image of any person engaging in an activity,

(b) the activity is sexual,

(c) B has a mental disorder,

(d) A knows or could reasonably be expected to know that B has a mental disorder, and

(e) A is involved in B's care in a way which falls within section 42.

SUMMARY

16.42 This section makes it an offence for a care worker, for sexual gratification, intentionally to cause a person in their care who has a mental disorder either to watch a third person engaging in a sexual act, or to look at an image of any person engaging in a sexual act.

Where the sexual act is watched 'live' and direct (rather than, for example, via a webcam or recording) only acts involving a 'third person' are covered – if the act involved A himself, s 40 would apply.

The offence is committed (with certain statutory exceptions) whether or not B consents. Therefore B's capacity to consent is immaterial.

ELEMENTS

16.43

- *Intentionally causes* – contrast 'allows' which would not suffice.
- *either:*
  - B to *watch* a third person (*not* A) engaging in a sexual activity; *or*
  - B to look at an *image* of any person (could be A) engaging in a sexual activity.

- *Sexual* – see Chapter 2.
- *Activity*

  'Activity' is not defined, but notably is not limited to touching or penetration.[13]
- *Image* (where it applies) – defined in the Act:
  - s 79(4): 'Image' means a moving or still image and includes an image produced by any means and, where the context permits, a three-dimensional image.
  - s 79(5): References to an image of a person include references to an image of an imaginary person.
- For the purpose of obtaining *sexual gratification* – the gratification may be immediate (A being 'turned on' by B's observation of the sexual act) or future gratification (getting B 'in the mood' to provide A with sexual gratification).[14]
- B has a mental disorder.

  Section 79(6) defines this as having the same meaning as s 1 of the Mental Health Act 1983,[15] namely 'any disorder or disability of the mind'. This wide-ranging definition will include such diverse conditions as personality disorder, learning disability, autistic spectrum disorder, dementia, depressive illnesses and brain damage (if leading to a disorder or disability of the mind).
- *Involved in B's care* – this concept is defined at s 42 of the Act and includes:
  - where B is in a care, community, voluntary or children's home;
  - where B is a patient of the NHS or an independent agency or hospital.

  In each case, A must be in employment with that body which bring him, or is likely to bring him, into regular face-to-face contact with B.
  - where A provides care, assistance or services to B in connection with B's mental disorder

  In this latter case, A may be an employed or voluntary carer, but must have, or be likely to have, regular face-to-face contact with B.[16]

---

13 Note that s 78, which defines 'sexual', refers to '*penetration, touching or any other activity*'.

14 *R v Abdullahi* [2006] EWCA Crim 2060 – in relation to sexual gratification and s 12 – causing a child to watch a sexual act.

15 Now amended and simplified from its original definition by s 1(2) of the Mental Health Act 2007.

16 Children's home, care home, employment etc are further defined at s 42(5) and (6).

- *Mental element* – in addition to intentionally causing B to watch the activity or to look at the image, the prosecution must show that:
  - the defendant did so in order to obtain sexual gratification; and
  - the defendant knew or could reasonably be expected to know that B had a mental disorder.

PARTIES

16.44 The offence may be committed by a person of either gender, who must be a care worker, as defined.

B can be male or female, of any age.

DISCUSSION

16.45 It is an offence contrary to ss 38 to 41 for a care worker to have sexual interaction with someone in their care, even if that person has capacity to consent and does so. The rationale for this is that the potential for imbalance of power and abusive relationships is so great, that all such activity should be unlawful.

Pre-existing sexual relationships which then become 'care' relationships are accounted for by the statutory defences of ss 43 and 44 and, in circumstances where a carer and 'patient' wish to have a consensual sexual relationship, there is no bar on this occurring after the carer has left that position.

There is a requirement that the care worker comes into, or is likely to come into, 'regular face-to-face contact' with B. In fact, the term 'care worker' is inaccurate, since the offence is not limited to those who provide medical or nursing services, but encompasses those who have 'functions to perform' in the home or hospital, including secretarial staff, cleaners or porters who will frequently have 'regular face-to-face contact'.

EXAMPLES

16.46 Examples of this offence would be where someone gets a mentally disordered person to watch two people having sex, or shows him or her a pornographic film.

Home Office guidance:

An example of a relationship covered by s 42(2) would be where the care worker is a member of staff in a care home and the person with a mental disorder is resident there.

16.46 *Sexual offences by care workers*

An example of a relationship covered by s 42(3) would be where the care worker is a receptionist at a clinic attended regularly by the person with a mental disorder.

An example of a relationship covered by s 42(4) would be where the care worker takes the person with a mental disorder on outings every week or visits him at home to provide complementary therapy.

16.47

Statutory defences
Section 43 provides a defence where A and B were lawfully married or civil partners at the material time.
Section 44 provides a defence where A and B were in a lawful sexual relationship immediately before A became involved in B's care.
In both cases, the burden is on the defendant to prove the facts of the applicable defence, on the balance of probabilities.

OTHER DEFENCES

16.48 Defendant merely allowed, rather than caused, B to observe the sexual act.

Whether or not intending that B should obtain sexual gratification, defendant sought to derive no gratification for himself.

Defendant did not know and could not reasonably be expected to know of B's mental disorder. But note, where B is proved to have had a mental disorder, s 38(2) imposes a rebuttable presumption that the defendant knew or could reasonably be expected to know this. If sufficient evidence is adduced to raise the issue, the prosecution then have to prove that A knew, or could reasonably be expected to know, of B's mental disorder.

CLASSIFICATION

16.49 Offence is triable either way.

SENTENCING AND OTHER ORDERS

Maximum sentence

16.50 On indictment: 7 years

Summarily: 6 months imprisonment or a fine not exceeding the statutory maximum (currently £5000)

Sentencing guidelines

16.51 Identical to guidelines for s 40, see **16.37–16.39**.

Other orders

16.52

Extended and life sentence availability (CJA 2003)	Sch 15 (specified offence): yes Sch 15B (life sentence for second listed offence): no
Trigger offence for:	SOPO: yes FTO: yes, but only where V *was under 18*, and D under 18 and sentenced to at least 12 months imprisonment; D over 18 and sentenced to prison or detention in hospital or community sentence of at least 12 months
Inclusion in barred lists	Children: automatic if V is a child Subject to representations if V is an adult Vulnerable adult: automatic
Notification	Yes, if: D under 18 and sentenced to at least 12 months imprisonment; D over 18 and sentenced to prison or detention in hospital or community sentence of at least 12 months

Chapter 17

Exploitation and trafficking

Paying for sexual services of a child Sexual Offences Act 2003, s 47

DEFINITION

17.1 Section 47(1):

A person (A) commits an offence if—

(a) he intentionally obtains for himself the sexual services of another person (B);

(b) before obtaining those services, he has made or promised payment for those services to B or a third person, or knows that another person has made or promised such a payment; and

(c) either—

(i) B is under 18, and A does not reasonably believe that B is 18 or over, or

(ii) B is under 13.

SUMMARY

17.2 This section creates an offence where a person intentionally obtains the sexual services of a person under 18, having previously paid or promised payment for those services. The consent of the young person is irrelevant, even where he or she is over 16 years old.

ELEMENTS

17.3

- *Sexual services*: 'sexual' is defined at s 78 (see **Chapter 2**). 'Services' is undefined and is potentially very broad in scope, possibly extending to stripping and posing nude.

- *Payment* includes not only monetary payment, but also 'the discharge of an obligation to pay' and the free or discounted 'provision of goods or services (including sexual services)' (s 47(2)). Thus, a man supplying drugs or alcohol to a young girl in exchange for sex would be caught by this provision. The inclusion of 'sexual services' as a method of payment would cover a situation where, for instance, B's boyfriend is offered sex with another person if he arranges for A to have sex with his underage girlfriend. Payment may be made to a third party (ie a pimp or manager), and another party may make the payment on behalf of A, although he must himself obtain the sexual services.
- *Mental element*: The defendant must intentionally obtain sexual services. In the case of a young person (B) aged between 13 and 18 years the offence is not committed where the defendant has a reasonable belief that B is in fact over 18 years old. However, where B is under 13, the defendant's belief in age is irrelevant. In the case of payment being made by a third party, the defendant must know that such payment or promise has taken place.

PARTIES

17.4 The offence may be committed by males and females. The young person may be either male or female. It is the clear intention of this section to protect young people from exploitation, so prosecution of B as some form of accessory would be entirely inappropriate.

DISCUSSION

17.5 The offence is aimed at customers, thus a pimp who procures the child or the other person envisaged in s 47(1)(b) who pays for, but does not himself use, the services is not caught by this section.

Note the requirement that payment or a promise of payment be made before the sexual services are obtained. While this sounds straightforward, matters are sometimes not so simple. Relationships between older and younger people sometimes have a financial element to them, even if the parties feel themselves to be in a 'sugar daddy' relationship which they do not regard as being in any way commercial. Clearly it is a matter of fact and degree.

Inter-relationship with other offences

17.6 Where child is under 13, offences under ss 5 to 8 are likely to have been committed and these do not require the additional proof of payment. Where the young person is under 16 an offence under s 9 is likely to have been committed.

If the sexual activity involves posing for photographs, offences under the Protection of Children Act 1978, s 1 may have been committed (see **22.1**).

CLASSIFICATION

17.7 Offences under s.47 are triable as follows:

1. Where B was under 13 at the material time and the offence involved:
   - penetration of B's anus or vagina with a part of A's body or anything else;
   - penetration of B's mouth with A's penis;
   - penetration of A's anus or vagina with a part of B's body or by B with anything else; or
   - penetration of A's mouth with B's penis;

   the offence is indictable only.
2. Where B was 13, 14 or 15 at the material time and the offence involved penetration as set out above, the offence is indictable only.
3. Where B was 15 or younger at the material time and no penetration was involved, the offence is triable either way.
4. Where B was 16 or 17 at the material time, then whether or not penetration was involved the offence is triable either way.

SENTENCING AND OTHER ORDERS

Maximum sentence

17.8 In category 1. above: life imprisonment

In category 2. above: 14 years

In category 3. above:

- On indictment: 14 years
- Summarily: 6 months imprisonment or a fine not exceeding the statutory maximum (currently £5000), or both.

In category 4. above:

- On indictment: 7 years
- Summarily: 6 months imprisonment or a fine not exceeding the statutory maximum (currently £5000) or both.

Sentencing guidelines

17.9 This guideline should only be used where the victim is aged 16 or 17 years old.

If the victim is under 13 refer to the guidelines for rape of a child under 13 (see s 5, **10.8–10.10**), assault by penetration of a child under 13 (s 6, **10.19–10.21**), sexual assault of a child under 13 (s 7, **10.30–10.32**) or causing or inciting a child under 13 to engage in sexual activity (s 8, **10.43–10.45**), depending on the activity involved in the offence.

If the victim is aged 13–15 refer to the guideline for sexual activity with a child guideline (s 9, **11.10–11.12**).

Determining the category

17.10

Cat	Harm	Cat	Culpability
1	• Penetration of vagina or anus (using body or object) by, or of, the victim • Penile penetration of mouth by, or of, the victim • Violence or threats of violence • Victim subject to unsafe/degrading sexual activity (beyond that which is inherent in the offence)	A	• Abduction/detention • Sexual images of victim recorded, retained, solicited or shared • Offender acts together with others to commit the offence • Use of alcohol/drugs on victim • Abuse of trust • Previous violence against victim • Blackmail or other threats made (including to expose victim to the authorities, family/friends or others) • Offender aware that he has a sexually transmitted disease • Offender aware that victim has been trafficked
2	Touching, or exposure, of naked genitalia or naked breasts by, or of, the victim		

17.10 *Exploitation and trafficking*

Cat	Harm	Cat	Culpability
3	Other sexual activity	B	Factor(s) in category A not present

Starting point and category range

17.11

	A	B
Category 1	Starting point: 4 yrs custody Range: 2–5 yrs custody	Starting point: 2 yrs custody Range: 1–4 yrs custody
Category 2	Starting point: 3 yrs custody Range: 1–4 yrs custody	Starting point: 1 yr custody Range: 26 wks–2 yrs custody
Category 3	Starting point: 1 yr custody Range: 26 wks–2 yrs custody	Starting point: 26 wks custody Range: High level community order–1 yr custody

Additional factual elements

17.12

Aggravating factors
Statutory aggravating factors
• Previous convictions, having regard to: (a) the nature of the offence to which the conviction relates and its relevance to the current offence; and (b) the time that has elapsed since the conviction • Offence committed whilst on bail
Other aggravating factors
• Ejaculation • Failure to comply with current court orders • Offence committed whilst on licence • Any steps taken to prevent the victim reporting an incident, obtaining assistance and/or from assisting or supporting the prosecution • Attempts to dispose of or conceal evidence

Mitigating factors
• No previous convictions or no relevant/recent convictions
• Remorse
• Previous good character and/or exemplary conduct*
• Age and/or lack of maturity where it affects the responsibility of the offender
• Mental disorder or learning disability, particularly where linked to the commission of the offence
• Demonstration of steps taken to address offending behaviour

* Previous good character/exemplary conduct is different from having no previous convictions. The more serious the offence, the less the weight which should normally be attributed to this factor. Where previous good character/exemplary conduct has been used to facilitate the offence, this mitigation should not normally be allowed and such conduct may constitute an aggravating factor.

Other orders

17.13

Extended and life sentence availability (CJA 2003)	Sch 15 (specified offence): yes Sch 15B (life sentence for second listed offence): yes, if victim (or other party) was under 16
Trigger offence for:	SOPO: yes FTO: yes, where victim was under 16 *and* D is over 18, *or* Is sentenced to at least 12 months imprisonment
Inclusion in barred lists	Children: subject to representations Vulnerable adult: subject to representations
Notification	Yes, where victim was under 16 *and* D is over 18, *or* Is sentenced to at least 12 months imprisonment

Causing or inciting child prostitution or pornography
Sexual Offences Act 2003, s 48

DEFINITION

17.14 Section 48(1):

A person (A) commits an offence if—

(a) he intentionally causes or incites another person (B) to become a prostitute, or to be involved in pornography, in any part of the world, and

(b) either—

(i) B is under 18, and A does not reasonably believe that B is 18 or over, or

(ii) B is under 13.

SUMMARY

17.15 This section is aimed at preventing the recruitment of young people into prostitution and pornography

ELEMENTS

17.16

- Causes *or* incites.

  The section creates two separate offences (see Specimen Indictments, **Appendix 1**).

- '*Causes*' is not defined by the Act and should be given its natural meaning of bringing about or making happen. There is no necessity that force be used. The 'causing' limb requires that the young person actually becomes a prostitute, etc.

  'Causing' requires something more than merely 'allowing'.

  It may be achieved by words, action or both.

- '*Incites*' is not defined by the Act and should be given its natural meaning of urges or provokes.

  The incited activity need not actually place.

- *Prostitute*: see definition at **Chapter 6** and s 51(2).

  The offence requires that A cause or incite B to '*become*' a prostitute and it would appear that if a young person was already working as a prostitute, further encouragement to do so would not be an offence under s 48.

- 'A person is "*involved in pornography*" if an indecent image of that person is recorded' (s 51(1)).

- *In any part of the world*: the offence is committed if the causing or inciting takes place in the UK, albeit that the prostitution or recording of pornography takes place outside the jurisdiction.

  There is no requirement that the causing or inciting be done for gain by the defendant, thus including within the ambit of the offence paedophiles who act with no financial motive.

- *Mental element*: The defendant must intentionally cause or incite a young person to become a prostitute or be involved in pornography. Arguably, if A believes B already to be a prostitute, he commits no offence.

  In the case of a young person (B) aged between 13 and 18 years the offence is not committed where the defendant has a reasonable belief that B is in fact over 18 years old.

  Where B is under 13, the defendant's belief in age is irrelevant.

PARTIES

17.17 The offence may be committed by males and females. The young person may be either male or female. It is the clear intention of this section to protect young people from exploitation, so prosecution of B as some form of accessory would be entirely inappropriate.

DISCUSSION

17.18 Section 48 provides protection from sexual exploitation for young people who have reached the age of consent. For abuse of children under that age it may be equally appropriate for charges to be brought for causing or inciting a child (aged under 13 or under 16) to engage in sexual activity (ss 9 or 11).

Where the prosecution cannot show that the defendant believes that a person aged 13 to 17 was actually 18, nevertheless an offence may have been committed under ss 52 or 53 in relation to causing, inciting or controlling adult prostitution (here 'gain' is required).

CLASSIFICATION

17.19 Offence is triable either way.

SENTENCING AND OTHER ORDERS

Maximum sentence

17.20 On indictment: 14 years

Summarily: 6 months imprisonment or a fine not exceeding the statutory maximum (currently £5000)

Sentencing guidelines

17.21 For offences that involve wide scale commercial and/or international activity sentences above the category range may be appropriate.

Determining the category

17.22

Cat	Harm	Cat	Culpability
1	• Victims involved in penetrative sexual activity • Abduction/detention • Violence or threats of violence • Sustained and systematic psychological abuse • Victim(s) participated in unsafe/ degrading sexual activity beyond that which is inherent in the offence • Victim(s) passed around by the offender to other 'customers' and/or moved to other brothels	A	• Directing or organising child prostitution or pornography on significant commercial basis • Expectation of significant financial or other gain • Abuse of trust • Exploitation of victim(s) known to be trafficked • Significant involvement in limiting the freedom of the victim(s) • Grooming of a victim to enter prostitution or pornography including through cultivation of a dependency on drugs or alcohol

Cat	Harm	Cat	Culpability
		B	Close involvement with inciting, controlling, arranging or facilitating child prostitution or pornography (where offender's involvement is not as a result of coercion)
2	Factor(s) in category 1 not present	C	• Performs limited function under direction • Close involvement but engaged by coercion/ intimidation/exploitation

Starting point and category range

17.23

Cat	Age	A	B	C
1	U13	Starting point: 10 yrs custody Range : 8–13 yrs custody	Starting point: 8 yrs custody Range: 6–11 yrs custody	Starting point: 5 yrs custody Range: 2 – 6 yrs custody
	13–15	Starting point: 8 yrs custody Range : 6–11 yrs custody	Starting point: 5 yrs custody Range: 4–8 yrs custody	Starting point: 2 yrs 6 mths custody Range : 1–4 yrs custody
	16–17	Starting point: 4 yrs custody Range: 3–7 yrs custody	Starting point: 2 yrs custody Range: 1–4 yrs custody	Starting point: 1 yr custody Range: 26 wks–2 yrs custody

17.23 *Exploitation and trafficking*

Cat	Age	A	B	C
2	U13	Starting point: 8 yrs custody Range: 6–11 yrs custody	Starting point: 6 yrs custody Range: 4–9 yrs custody	Starting point: 2 yrs custody Range: 1–4 yrs custody
	13–15	Starting point: 6 yrs custody Range: 4–9 yrs custody	Starting point: 3 yrs custody Range: 2–5 yrs custody	Starting point: 1 yr custody Range: 26 wks–2 yrs custody
	16–17	Starting point: 3 yrs custody Range: 2–5 yrs custody	Starting point: 1 yr custody Range: 26 wks–2 yrs custody	Starting point: 26 wks custody Range: High level community order–1yr custody

Additional factual elements

17.24

Aggravating factors
Statutory aggravating factors
• Previous convictions, having regard to a) the nature of the offence to which the conviction relates and its relevance to the current offence; and b) the time that has elapsed since the conviction • Offence committed whilst on bail
Other aggravating factors
• Failure to comply with current court orders • Offence committed whilst on licence • Deliberate isolation of victim(s) • Vulnerability of victim(s) • Threats made to expose victim(s) to the authorities (for example, immigration or police), family/friends or others • Harm threatened against the family/friends of victim(s) • Passport/identity documents removed • Victim(s) prevented from seeking medical treatment • Victim(s) prevented from attending school • Food withheld

• Earnings withheld/kept by offender or evidence of excessive wage reduction or debt bondage, inflated travel or living expenses or unreasonable interest rates
• Any steps taken to prevent the victim reporting an incident, obtaining assistance and/or from assisting or supporting the prosecution
• Attempts to dispose of or conceal evidence
• Timescale over which the operation has been run
Mitigating factors
• No previous convictions or no relevant/recent convictions
• Remorse
• Previous good character and/or exemplary conduct*
• Age and/or lack of maturity where it affects the responsibility of the offender
• Mental disorder or learning disability, particularly where linked to the commission of the offence

* Previous good character/exemplary conduct is different from having no previous convictions. The more serious the offence, the less the weight which should normally be attributed to this factor. Where previous good character/exemplary conduct has been used to facilitate the offence, this mitigation should not normally be allowed and such conduct may constitute an aggravating factor.

In the context of this offence, previous good character/exemplary conduct should not normally be given any significant weight and will not normally justify a reduction in what would otherwise be the appropriate sentence.

Other orders

17.25

Extended and life sentence availability (CJA 2003)	Sch 15 (specified offence): yes Sch 15B (life sentence for second listed offence): yes
Trigger offence for:	SOPO: yes FTO: yes, if: D is over 18, *or* Is sentenced to at least 12 months imprisonment
Inclusion in barred lists	Children: subject to representations Vulnerable adult: subject to representations

Notification	Yes, if: D is over 18, *or* Is sentenced to at least 12 months imprisonment
Confiscation	This is a lifestyle offence within Proceeds of Crime Act 2002, Sch 2

Controlling a child prostitute or a child involved in pornography
Sexual Offences Act 2003, s 49

DEFINITION

17.26 Section 49(1):

A person (A) commits an offence if—

(a) he intentionally controls any of the activities of another person (B) relating to B's prostitution or involvement in pornography in any part of the world, and

(b) either—

(i) B is under 18, and A does not reasonably believe that B is 18 or over, or

(ii) B is under 13.

ELEMENTS

17.27

- *Controls any of the activities*: the offence is committed even where a person other than A controls some or most of B's time or activities. Control may be through a third party, but must be exercised in some form – merely, for instance, profiting from the proceeds of pornography would be insufficient. 'Control' includes, but is not limited to, one who forces another to carry out the relevant activity. It is not necessary to show that B acts under compulsion or coercion from A.[1]
- *Prostitution*: see definition at **Chapter 6** and s 51(2).
- 'A person is "*involved in pornography*" if an indecent image of that person is recorded' (s 51(1)).

---

1 *R v Massey* [2007] EWCA Crim 2664.

- *In any part of the world*: the offence is committed if the control takes place in the UK, albeit that the prostitution or recording of pornography takes place outside the jurisdiction.

  There is no requirement that the control be done for gain by the defendant, thus including within the ambit of the offence paedophiles who act with no financial motive.

- *Mental element*: The defendant must intentionally control the activities of a young person relating to prostitution or involvement in pornography.

  In the case of a young person (B) aged between 13 and 18 years the offence is not committed where the defendant has a reasonable belief that B is in fact over 18 years old.

  Where B is under 13, the defendant's belief in age is irrelevant.

PARTIES

17.28 The offence may be committed by males and females. The young person may be either male or female. It is the clear intention of this section to protect young people for exploitation, so prosecution of B as some form of accessory would be entirely inappropriate.

DISCUSSION

17.29 See discussion on s 48 at **17.18**.

CLASSIFICATION

17.30 Offence is triable either way.

SENTENCING AND OTHER ORDERS

Maximum sentence

17.31 On indictment: 14 years

Summarily: 6 months imprisonment or a fine not exceeding the statutory maximum (currently £5000)

Sentencing guidelines

17.32 Identical to guidelines for s 48; see **17.21–17.24**.

Other orders

17.33

Extended and life sentence availability (CJA 2003)	Sch 15 (specified offence): yes Sch 15B (life sentence for second listed offence): yes
Trigger offence for:	SOPO: yes FTO: yes, if: D is over 18, *or* Is sentenced to at least 12 months imprisonment
Inclusion in barred lists	Children: subject to representations Vulnerable adult: subject to representations
Notification	Yes, if: D is over 18, *or* Is sentenced to at least 12 months imprisonment
Confiscation	This is a lifestyle offence within Proceeds of Crime Act 2002, Sch 2

Arranging or facilitating child prostitution or pornography Sexual Offences Act 2003, s 50

DEFINITION

17.34 Section 50(1):

A person (A) commits an offence if—

(a) he intentionally arranges or facilitates the prostitution or involvement in pornography in any part of the world of another person (B), and

(b) either—

(i) B is under 18, and A does not reasonably believe that B is 18 or over, or

(ii) B is under 13.

SUMMARY

17.35 This section makes culpable those who, while not controlling a young person's prostitution or involvement in pornography, make it easier or possible to happen.

ELEMENTS

17.36

- Arranges or facilitates:

  neither verb is defined in the Act, so should be given its natural meaning:

  - arrange – organise/set up
  - facilitate – make easier/assist

- '*Prostitution*': see definition at **Chapter 6** and s 51(2).
- 'A person is "*involved in pornography*" if an indecent image of that person is recorded' (s 51(1)).
- *In any part of the world*: the offence is committed if the control takes place in the UK, albeit that the prostitution or recording of pornography takes place outside the jurisdiction.

  There is no requirement that the control be done for gain by the defendant.

- *Mental element*: The defendant must intentionally arrange or facilitate the prostitution or involvement in pornography of a young person.

  In the case of a young person (B) aged between 13 and 18 years the offence is not committed where the defendant has a reasonable belief that B is in fact over 18 years old.

  Where B is under 13, the defendant's belief in age is irrelevant.

PARTIES

17.37 The offence may be committed by males and females. The young person may be either male or female. It is the clear intention of this section to protect young people from exploitation, so prosecution of B as some form of accessory would be entirely inappropriate.

EXAMPLES

17.38 Since gain is not required for the commission of this offence, a wide variety of behaviour may be culpable, eg:

- Driving a young person to an appointment
- Booking a hotel room, or lending a room or house
- Introducing a client

CLASSIFICATION

17.39 Offence is triable either way.

SENTENCING AND OTHER ORDERS

Maximum sentence

17.40 On indictment: 14 years

Summarily: 6 months imprisonment or a fine not exceeding the statutory maximum (currently £5000)

Sentencing guidelines

17.41 Identical to guidelines for s 48; see **17.21–17.24**).

Other orders

17.42

Extended and life sentence availability (CJA 2003)	Sch 15 (specified offence): yes Sch 15B (life sentence for second listed offence): yes
Trigger offence for:	SOPO: yes FTO: yes, if: D is over 18, *or* Is sentenced to at least 12 months imprisonment
Inclusion in barred lists	Children: subject to representations Vulnerable adult: subject to representations
Notification	Yes, if: D is over 18, *or* Is sentenced to at least 12 months imprisonment
Confiscation	This is a lifestyle offence within Proceeds of Crime Act 2002, Sch 2

Soliciting
Sexual Offences Act 2003, s 51A

(inserted by Policing and Crime Act 2009, s 19)

DEFINITION

17.43 Section 51A:

(1) It is an offence for a person in a street or public place to solicit another (B) for the purpose of obtaining B's sexual services as a prostitute.

(2) The reference to a person in a street or public place includes a person in a vehicle in a street or public place.

SUMMARY

17.44 This offence is aimed at those who solicit the services of a prostitute, rather than the prostitute herself.

ELEMENTS

17.45

- *Soliciting* involves asking or requesting, but the request need not be in words. See discussion in **Chapter 24**.
- By sub-section (4), *street* has the meaning given by the Street Offences Act 1959, s 1(4) – including any 'bridge, road, lane, footway, subway, square, court, alley, passage … which is open to the public and the doorways and entrances of premises abutting on the street and any ground adjoining and open to a street'. This is not necessarily an exhaustive list. In the case of a person in a vehicle, the vehicle must be on a street or public place.
- *Public place* carries no statutory definition. It is likely to include both places where the public are admitted only on certain occasions (ie a business car park) or places the public actually frequent even when they have no right of entry.
- *Sexual services*: 'sexual' is defined at s 78 (see **Chapter 2**). 'Services' is undefined and is potentially very broad in scope. Soliciting a prostitute in the street for some purpose other than sex would not be covered by this offence.
- *Prostitute*: see definition at **Chapter 6** and s 51(2). It does not matter that the person solicited is not a prostitute.

PARTIES

17.46 The offence may be committed by males and females. The person being solicited may be either male or female.

DISCUSSION

17.47 This offence replaces the earlier offences of kerb crawling and persistent soliciting in a street or public place contrary to ss 1 and 2 of the Sexual Offences Act 1985 (now repealed). These offences required an element of persistency or behaviour likely to cause nuisance or annoyance to the person solicited or nuisance to others in the neighbourhood. There are no such requirements contained in s 51A and the offence may be committed by a single act towards a willing recipient with no nuisance caused to others.

The ambit of the offence includes those who proposition women who in fact are not working as prostitutes in the belief that they are. Such behaviour, if unwonted, might also be an offence of using insulting or abusive words or behaviour with intent to cause harassment, alarm or distress, contrary to s 4A of the Public Order Act 1986.

CLASSIFICATION

17.48 Offence is summary only.

SENTENCING AND OTHER ORDERS

Maximum sentence

17.49 A fine not exceeding level 3 on the standard scale (currently £1000)

Sentencing guidelines

17.50 There are no sentencing guidelines for this offence.

Other orders

17.51

Extended and life sentence availability (CJA 2003)	Sch 15 (specified offence): no Sch 15B (life sentence for second listed offence): no

Trigger offence for:	SOPO: no FTO: no
Inclusion in barred lists	Children: no Vulnerable adult: no
Notification	No

Causing or inciting prostitution for gain Sexual Offences Act 2003, s 52

DEFINITION

17.52 Section 52(1):

A person commits an offence if—

(a) he intentionally causes or incites another person to become a prostitute in any part of the world, and

(b) he does so for or in the expectation of gain for himself or a third person.

SUMMARY

17.53 This offence is intended to criminalise those who profit by recruiting others into prostitution

ELEMENTS

17.54

- Causes or incites:

  The section creates two separate offences (see Specimen Indictments, **Appendix 1**).

- '*Causes*' is not defined by the Act and should be given its natural meaning of bringing about or making happen. There is no necessity that force be used. The 'causing' limb requires that the person actually becomes a prostitute.

  'Causing' requires something more than merely 'allowing'.

  It may be achieved by words, action or both.

- '*Incites*' is not defined by the Act and should be given its natural meaning of urges or provokes.

  The incited activity need not actually place.

- *Prostitute*: see definition at **Chapter 6** and s 51(2).

  The offence requires that the offender cause another person to *become* a prostitute and it would appear that if a person was already working as a prostitute, further encouragement to do so would not be an offence under s 52. However, where a woman who has previously been involved was 're-recruited' back into prostitution, the offence could be made out.

- *In any part of the world*: the offence is committed if the control takes place in the UK, albeit that the prostitution takes place outside the jurisdiction.

- *Gain* is defined at s 54(1) as including not only monetary payment but also 'the discharge of an obligation to pay or the provision of goods or services (including sexual services) gratuitously or at a discount'. The inclusion of 'sexual services' covers the situation where a pimp might receive only sexual favours for his involvement in the prostitute's activities. Further and somewhat amorphously, it includes 'the goodwill of any person which is or appears likely, in time, to bring financial advantage'.

- *Mental element*: the defendant must intentionally cause or incite a person to become a prostitute. Arguably, if he believes she is already a prostitute, he commits no offence.

PARTIES

17.55 The offence may be committed by males and females. The 'target' may be either male or female.

DISCUSSION

17.56 The necessity for the prosecution to establish that there was a recruiting into prostitution somewhat limits the scope of this offence. However, the ambit of 'causing or inciting' may be quite wide, extending perhaps to a 'co-worker' prostitute who shows a new recruit the ropes (so long as there is an element of financial gain).[2]

---

2 See facts of *R v Paduraru* [2010] EWCA Crim 1105.

Inter-relationship with other offences

17.57 The acts amounting to an offence under this section may also fall within s 53 (controlling prostitution for gain). Where there is a question as to whether the person was already working as a prostitute, the s 53 offence may be more appropriate.

Involvement in the premises from which prostitution takes place may mean that a brothel-keeping offence has been committed (SOA 1956, s 33A).

While this section is clearly aimed at the sexual exploitation of adults, a charge under this section may be appropriate (in substitution to a charge under s 48) in circumstances where young people aged 13 to 17 have been recruited into prostitution, if the prosecution are unable to show that the defendant did not believe them to be over 18.

CLASSIFICATION

17.58 Offence is triable either way.

SENTENCING AND OTHER ORDERS

Maximum sentence

17.59 On indictment: 7 years

Summarily: 6 months imprisonment or a fine not exceeding the statutory maximum (currently £5000)

Sentencing guidelines

Determining the category

17.60

Cat	Harm	Cat	Culpability
1	• Abduction/detention	A	• Causing, inciting or controlling prostitution on significant commercial basis
	• Violence or threats of violence		• Expectation of significant financial or other gain
	• Sustained and systematic psychological abuse		• Abuse of trust

17.60 *Exploitation and trafficking*

Cat	Harm	Cat	Culpability
	• Individual(s) forced or coerced to participate in unsafe/degrading sexual • Individual(s) forced or coerced into seeing many 'customers' • Individuals(s) forced/coerced/deceived into prostitution		• Exploitation of those known to be trafficked • Significant involvement in limiting the freedom of prostitute(s) • Grooming of individual(s) to enter prostitution including through cultivation of a dependency on drugs or alcohol
		B	Close involvement with prostitute(s), for example control of finances, choice of clients, working conditions, etc (where offender's involvement is not as a result of coercion)
2	Factor(s) in category 1 not present	C	• Performs limited function under direction • Close involvement but engaged by coercion/intimidation/exploitation

Starting point and category range

17.61

Cat	A	B	C
1	Starting point: 4 yrs custody Range : 3–6 yrs custody	Starting point: 2 yrs 6 mths custody Range: 2–4 yrs custody	Starting point: 1 yr custody Range: 26 wks–2 yrs custody
2	Starting point: 2 yrs 6 mths custody Range: 2–5 yrs custody	Starting point: 1 yr custody Range: High level community order–2 yrs custody	Starting point: Medium level community order Range: Low level community order–High level community order

Additional factual elements

17.62

Aggravating factors
Statutory aggravating factors
• Previous convictions, having regard to: (a) the nature of the offence to which the conviction relates and its relevance to the current offence; and (b) the time that has elapsed since the conviction
• Offence committed whilst on bail
Other aggravating factors
• Failure to comply with current court orders
• Offence committed whilst on licence
• Deliberate isolation of prostitute(s)
• Threats made to expose prostitute(s) to the authorities (for example, immigration or police), family/friends or others
• Harm threatened against the family/friends of prostitute(s)
• Passport/identity documents removed
• Prostitute(s) prevented from seeking medical treatment
• Food withheld
• Earnings withheld/kept by offender or evidence of excessive wage reduction or debt bondage, inflated travel or living expenses or unreasonable interest rates
• Any steps taken to prevent the reporting of an incident, obtaining assistance and/or from assisting or supporting the prosecution
• Attempts to dispose of or conceal evidence
• Prostitute(s) forced or coerced into pornography
• Timescale over which the operation has been run
Mitigating factors
• No previous convictions or no relevant/recent convictions
• Remorse
• Previous good character and/or exemplary conduct*
• Age and/or lack of maturity where it affects the responsibility of the offender
• Mental disorder or learning disability, particularly where linked to the commission of the offence
• Demonstration of steps taken to address offending behaviour

* Previous good character/exemplary conduct is different from having no previous convictions. The more serious the offence, the less the weight which should normally be attributed to this factor. Where previous good character/exemplary conduct has been used to facilitate the offence, this mitigation should not normally be allowed and such conduct may constitute an aggravating factor.

Other orders

17.63

Extended and life sentence availability (CJA 2003)	Sch 15 (specified offence): yes Sch 15B (life sentence for second listed offence): no
Trigger offence for:	SOPO: yes FTO: no
Inclusion in barred lists	Children: subject to representations Vulnerable adult: subject to representations
Notification	No
Confiscation	This is a lifestyle offence within Proceeds of Crime Act 2002, Sch 2

Controlling prostitution for gain
Sexual Offences Act 2003, s 53

DEFINITION

17.64 Section 53(1):

A person commits an offence if—

(a) he intentionally controls any of the activities of another person relating to that person's prostitution in any part of the world, and

(b) he does so for or in the expectation of gain for himself or a third person.

SUMMARY

17.65 This offence is intended to criminalise those who profit by controlling prostitutes

ELEMENTS

17.66

- *Controls any of the activities*: the offence is committed even where a person other than the defendant controls some or most of the prostitute's time or activities. Control may be through a third party, but must be exercised in some form – merely, for instance, profiting from the proceeds would be insufficient. 'Control' includes, but is not limited to, one who forces another to carry out the relevant activity. It is not necessary to show that B acts under compulsion or coercion from A.[3]
- *Prostitute*: see definition at **Chapter 6** and s 51(2).
- *In any part of the world*: the offence is committed if the control takes place in the UK, albeit that the prostitution takes place outside the jurisdiction.
- *Gain* is defined at s 54(1) as including not only monetary payment but also 'the discharge of an obligation to pay or the provision of goods or services (including sexual services) gratuitously or at a discount'. The inclusion of 'sexual services' covers the situation where a pimp might receive only sexual favours for his involvement in the prostitute's activities. Further and somewhat amorphously, it includes 'the goodwill of any person which is or appears likely, in time, to bring financial advantage.'
- *Mental element*: the defendant must intentionally control another person's activities relating to prostitution. He must know that the activities he controls are prostitution-related.

PARTIES

17.67 The offence may be committed by males and females. The person controlled may be either male or female.

DISCUSSION

17.68 A wide variety of activities is likely to be caught within the ambit of this offence, including price-setting, requiring a woman to work from a particular flat or street corner or to work for a particular period of time. Within the modern context, the operation concerned may well be a sauna/

3 *R v Massey* [2007] EWCA Crim 2664.

massage parlour or escort agency, run on entirely business-like lines, with an employer/employee relationship between owner and working woman. No compulsion is necessary, other than that similar to the obligations imposed on any employee.

Designing and setting up websites, letting out accommodation, chauffeuring or providing other services are unlikely, without more, to amount to 'control'.

Inter-relationship with other offences

17.69 The acts amounting to an offence under this section may also fall within s 52 (causing or inciting prostitution for gain) where the activities involve introducing the person to prostitution.

Involvement in the premises from which prostitution takes place may mean that a brothel-keeping offence has been committed (s 33A).

While this section is clearly aimed at the sexual exploitation of adults, a charge under this section may be appropriate (in substitution to a charge under s 49) in circumstances where young people aged 13 to 17 have been recruited into prostitution, if the prosecution are unable to show that the defendant did not believe them to be over 18.

CLASSIFICATION

17.70 Offence is triable either way.

SENTENCING AND OTHER ORDERS

Maximum sentence

17.71 On indictment: 7 years

Summarily: 6 months imprisonment or a fine not exceeding the statutory maximum (currently £5000)

Sentencing guidelines

17.72 Identical to guidelines for s 52; see **17.59–17.61**.

Other orders

17.73

Extended and life sentence availability (CJA 2003)	Sch 15 (specified offence): yes Sch 15B (life sentence for second listed offence): no
Trigger offence for:	SOPO: yes FTO: no
Inclusion in barred lists	Children: subject to representations Vulnerable adult: subject to representations
Notification	No
Confiscation	This is a lifestyle offence within Proceeds of Crime Act 2002, Sch 2

Paying for sexual services of a prostitute subjected to force
Sexual Offences Act 2003, s 53

(inserted by Policing and Crime Act 2009, s 14)

DEFINITION

17.74 Section 53A:

A person (A) commits an offence if—

(a) A makes or promises payment for the sexual services of a prostitute (B),

(b) a third person (C) has engaged in exploitative conduct of a kind likely to induce or encourage B to provide the sexual services for which A has made or promised payment, and

(c) C engaged in that conduct for or in the expectation of gain for C or another person (apart from A or B).

SUMMARY

17.75 This offence is designed to penalise the customers of women forced into prostitution, whether or not the customer knew of the exploitation, with the aim of reducing demand for such services.

The offence is committed if someone pays or promises payment for the sexual services of a prostitute who has been subject to exploitation by a third party.

ELEMENTS

17.76

- *Payment* is defined at s 51(3) as including not only monetary payment but also 'the discharge of an obligation to pay or the provision of goods or services (including sexual services) gratuitously or at a discount'. Within the context of this offence, it is hard to envisage the circumstances in which sexual services would be exchanged for exploited sexual services.
- *Prostitute*: see definition at **Chapter 6** and s 51(2).
- *Exploitative conduct* includes force, threats (whether or not relating to violence), coercion or deception by C (s 53A(3)).
- The person responsible for the exploitative conduct must have been acting for or in the expectation of gain for himself or herself or another person, other than the payer or the prostitute. 'Gain' is defined at s 54(1) as the same as 'payment' (see below) but including additionally the somewhat amorphous 'goodwill of any person which is or appears likely, in time, to bring financial advantage'.
- The payment or promise of payment must be made in the jurisdiction but it does not matter where in the world the sexual services are to be provided or whether the services are actually provided (s 53A(2)(a)).
- *Mental element* – an offence is committed regardless of whether the person paying or promising payment for sexual services knows or ought to know or be aware that the prostitute has been subject to exploitative conduct. In other words the offence is one of strict liability and no mental element is required in respect of the offender's knowledge that the prostitute was forced, threatened, coerced or deceived (s 53A(2)(b)).

PARTIES

17.77 The offence may be committed by males and females. The person providing sexual services may be either male or female.

DISCUSSION

17.78 Examples of exploitative conduct are very wide ranging and could include various forms of emotional or financial pressure and threat; blackmail that B's involvement in prostitution be made public or other form of unlawful activity be reported to the authorities; exploiting an unequal relationship between B and C; or deception as to how much is to be paid for the sexual services or how they are to be provided. It is likely that such exploitative behaviour would often involve a woman's immigration status and fear of the authorities.

A customer would be caught by the offence even where the circumstances were such that they could not be expected to know or even suspect that exploitation was occurring in the background. This strict liability aspect was imposed for policy and deterrent reasons.

CLASSIFICATION

17.79 Offence is summary only.

SENTENCING AND OTHER ORDERS

Maximum sentence

17.80 A fine not exceeding level 3 on the standard scale (currently £1000).

Sentencing guidelines

17.81 There are no sentencing guidelines for this offence

Other orders

17.82

Extended and life sentence availability (CJA 2003)	Sch 15 (specified offence): no Sch 15 (life sentence for second listed offence)B: no
Trigger offence for:	SOPO: no FTO: no
Inclusion in barred lists	Children: no Vulnerable adult: no
Notification	No

Trafficking people for sexual exploitation Sexual Offences Act 2003, s 59A

(amended by Protection of Freedoms Act 2012, s 109)

DEFINITION

17.83 Section 59:

(1) A person ('A') commits an offence if A intentionally arranges or facilitates—

(a) the arrival in, or entry into, the United Kingdom or another country of another person ('B'),

(b) the travel of B within the United Kingdom or another country, or

(c) the departure of B from the United Kingdom or another country,

with a view to the sexual exploitation of B.

(2) For the purposes of subsection (1)(a) and (c) A's arranging or facilitating is with a view to the sexual exploitation of B if, and only if—

(a) A intends to do anything to or in respect of B, after B's arrival, entry or (as the case may be) departure but in any part of the world, which if done will involve the commission of a relevant offence, or

(b) A believes that another person is likely to do something to or in respect of B, after B's arrival, entry or (as the case may be) departure but in any part of the world, which if done will involve the commission of a relevant offence.

(3) For the purposes of subsection (1)(b) A's arranging or facilitating is with a view to the sexual exploitation of B if, and only if—

(a) A intends to do anything to or in respect of B, during or after the journey and in any part of the world, which if done will involve the commission of a relevant offence, or

(b) A believes that another person is likely to do something to or in respect of B, during or after the journey and in any part of the world, which if done will involve the commission of a relevant offence.

SUMMARY

17.84 This section replaces, expands and combines into one single integrated offence, the three separate trafficking offences in ss 57 to 59 of the 2003 Act,[4] which made it an offence to traffic into, within or out of the UK for the purposes of sexual exploitation. Section 59A ensures the offence encompasses trafficking anywhere in the world

ELEMENTS

17.85

- Arranges or facilitates:

  neither verb is defined in the Act, so should be given its natural meaning:

  - arrange – organise/set up
  - facilitate – make easier/assist

  The arranging or facilitating relate to B's travel, entry or departure, so arranging transport, booking tickets or helping with immigration problems would fall within the ambit of this section.

  By s 59A(2) the arranging or facilitating is done *with a view* to the sexual exploitation of B if A intends to do anything to or in respect of B, or believes that any other person is likely to do something to or in respect of B, after B's arrival, entry or departure from the UK which, if done, will involve the commission of a relevant offence. Section 59A(3) makes equivalent provision for the meaning of sexual exploitation where B is trafficked within the UK but here the exploitation may take place during or after the journey.

- *Sexual exploitation* will only occur in circumstances where a *relevant offence* is likely to occur. For activities within England and Wales, a relevant offence is an offence under Part 1 of the 2003 Act (ie ss 1 to 79) or the Protection of Children Act 1978, s 1(1) (taking or making indecent photographs of children); activities taking place outside England and Wales which would be offences under Part 1 of SOA 2003 or s 1(1) of PCA 1978 if they occurred within the jurisdiction, are also relevant offences.

- A UK national commits an offence under s 59A regardless of where in the world the arranging or facilitating takes place or regardless of which country is the country of arrival, entry, travel or departure; a non-UK

---

4 This section came into effect on 6 April 2013, repealing SOA 2003, ss 57, 58 and 59 from that day.

national commits the offence if any part of the arranging or facilitating takes place in the UK or if the UK is the country of arrival, entry, travel or departure (s 59A(4) and (5)). 'Country' and 'UK national' are defined at s 60(1).

- There is no requirement that the defendant was motivated by financial or other reward.
- *Mental element* – the defendant must intentionally arrange or facilitate the arrival, travel or departure of B, with a view to B's sexual exploitation. 'With a view' encompasses either an intention by the defendant to do something involving the commission of a relevant offence; or the belief that someone else is likely to do something involving the commission of a relevant offence.

PARTIES

17.86 The offence may be committed by males and females. Victims of trafficking may become traffickers themselves and if this appears to be the case, the prosecution will need to consider very carefully whether a defence of duress is made out and even if not, whether a prosecution is in the public interest.[5]

DISCUSSION

17.87 The arrival, travel or departure can be in or within any country in the world. Similarly, the sexual exploitation may take place in any part of the world. The only geographical limitation appears to be on a non-UK national where all the arranging takes place outside the UK and the UK is not a country of entry, travel or departure.

While the purpose of this section is to protect those who have been trafficked for sexual exploitation – largely women forced or duped into prostitution – it is of note that there is no requirement that either the travel or the 'relevant offence' be against the woman's will. A relevant offence is controlling prostitution contrary to s 53 and this requires no element of compulsion or coercion on the part of the controller. Thus, an escort agency manager booking travel tickets for women she knows from her home country to come and work for her would be committing a s 59A offence, regardless of the fact that the women were entirely willing participants. Similarly, a driver taking an 'employed' prostitute to meet a customer may be committing a trafficking offence.

---

5 *R v O* [2008] EWCA Crim 2835; *R v MB; R v LM; R v YT; R v BT; R v DG* [2010] EWCA Crim 2327.

CLASSIFICATION

17.88 Offence is triable either way.

SENTENCING AND OTHER ORDERS

Maximum sentence

17.89 On indictment: 14 years

Summarily: 6 months imprisonment or a fine not exceeding the statutory maximum (currently £5000)

Sentencing guidelines

Determining the category

17.90

Cat	Harm	Cat	Culpability
1	• Abduction/detention • Violence or threats of violence • Sustained and systematic psychological abuse • Victim(s) under 18 • Victim(s) forced or coerced to participate in unsafe/ degrading sexual activity • Victim(s) forced/coerced into prostitution • Victim(s) tricked/deceived as to purpose of visit	A	• Directing or organising trafficking on significant commercial basis • Expectation of significant financial or other gain • Significant influence over others in trafficking organisation/hierarchy • Abuse of trust
		B	• Operational or management function within hierarchy • Involves others in operation whether by coercion/ intimidation/exploitation or reward (and offender's involvement is not as a result of coercion)

17.90 *Exploitation and trafficking*

Cat	Harm	Cat	Culpability
2	Factor(s) in category 1 not present	C	• Performs limited function under direction • Close involvement but engaged by coercion/ intimidation/exploitation

Starting point and category range

17.91

Cat	A	B	C
1	Starting point: 8 yrs custody Range : 6–12 yrs custody	Starting point: 6 yrs custody Range: 4–8 yrs custody	Starting point: 18 mths custody Range: 26 wks–2 yrs custody
2	Starting point: 6 yrs custody Range: 4–8 yrs custody	Starting point: 4 yrs custody Range: 2–6 yrs custody	Starting point: 26 wks custody Range: High level community order–18 mths custody

Additional factual elements

17.92

Aggravating factors
Statutory aggravating factors
• Previous convictions, having regard to: (a) the nature of the offence to which the conviction relates and its relevance to the current offence; and (b) the time that has elapsed since the conviction • Offence committed whilst on bail
Other aggravating factors
• Failure to comply with current court orders • Offence committed whilst on licence • Deliberate isolation of victim(s)

- Children of victim(s) left in home country due to trafficking
- Threats made to expose victim(s) to the authorities (for example, immigration or police), family/friends or others
- Harm threatened against the family/friends of victim
- Exploitation of victim(s) from particularly vulnerable backgrounds
- Victim(s) previously trafficked/sold/passed around
- Passport/identity documents removed
- Victim(s) prevented from seeking medical treatment
- Food withheld
- Use of drugs/alcohol or other substance to secure victim's compliance
- Earnings of victim(s) withheld/kept by offender or evidence of excessive wage reduction, debt bondage, inflated travel or living expenses or unreasonable interest rates
- Any steps taken to prevent the reporting of an incident, obtaining assistance and/or from assisting or supporting the prosecution
- Attempts to dispose of or conceal evidence
- Timescale over which the operation has been run

Mitigating factors

- No previous convictions or no relevant/recent convictions
- Remorse
- Previous good character and/or exemplary conduct*
- Age and/or lack of maturity where it affects the responsibility of the offender
- Mental disorder or learning disability, particularly where linked to the commission of the offence

* Previous good character/exemplary conduct is different from having no previous convictions. The more serious the offence, the less the weight which should normally be attributed to this factor. Where previous good character/exemplary conduct has been used to facilitate the offence, this mitigation should not normally be allowed and such conduct may constitute an aggravating factor.

In the context of this offence, previous good character/exemplary conduct should not normally be given any significant weight and will not normally justify a reduction in what would otherwise be the appropriate sentence.

Other orders

17.93

Extended and life sentence availability (CJA 2003)	Sch 15 (specified offence): yes Sch 15B (life sentence for second listed offence): no
Trigger offence for:	SOPO: yes FTO: no
Inclusion in barred lists	Children: subject to representations Vulnerable adult: subject to representations
Notification	No
Forfeiture	The police and immigration authorities have power to detain and the courts have powers to order forfeiture of any vehicle, ship or aircraft used or intended to be used in connection with a trafficking offence (ss 60A and 60B)

Chapter 18

Preparatory sexual offences

Administering a substance with intent to stupefy or overpower Sexual Offences Act 2003, s 61

DEFINITION

18.1 Section 61(1):

A person commits an offence if he intentionally administers a substance to, or causes a substance to be taken by, another person (B)—

(a) knowing that B does not consent; and

(b) with the intention of stupefying or overpowering B, so as to enable any person to engage in a sexual activity that involves B.

SUMMARY

18.2 This section makes it an offence to administer a substance to a person without their consent, intending that they be stupefied or overpowered, so they can be exploited for sexual activity.

ELEMENTS

18.3

- The offence is committed by a defendant who *administers a substance*. Administering includes 'conduct which brought a noxious thing into contact with the victim's body, even though there was no application of direct physical force'.[1] There is no further definition or limitation

---

1 *R v Gillard* (1988) 87 Cr App Rep, [1988] Crim LR 531 (applying the term in Offences Against the Person Act 1861, s 24).

on the term 'substance', which would extend to include alcohol in the appropriate further circumstances.

- *Consent* – see **Chapter 1**. The lack of consent specifically applies to the taking of the substance, rather than the sexual activity. Consent may be vitiated by force (ie covering B's face with a drug soaked cloth) or by stealth, such as in spiking a drink. So, the offence is committed where, unbeknown to B, her drink has been laced with alcohol in order to get her to consent to sex; it is not committed by a man plying a woman with alcohol, provided she knows what she is drinking.
- *Stupefying or overpowering*: the substance must be such as to leave B incapable of giving genuine or voluntary agreement to sexual activity. Clearly, if she is rendered unconscious, she is 'stupefied'.
- *Sexual activity*: see **Chapter 2**.
- *Mental element* – the defendant must:
  - intend to administer a substance to another person
  - know that the other person does not consent;
  - intend that the substance stupefy or overpower that person, with the effect of making them succumb to sexual activity.

  The defendant must believe that the substance is likely to have properties which will 'stupefy or overpower' another person. The fact that he is wrong in practice is no defence.

PARTIES

18.4 The offence may be committed by males and females. 'B' may be either male or female. The defendant himself does not need to have or intend to have sex with B, and may administer the substance or even cause it to be taken in order that a third party can have sex with B.

DISCUSSION

18.5 This offence is aimed particularly at drug-facilitated sexual assault and those who use date rape drugs such as GHB, ketamine and Rohypnol. These can have effects such as reduction in inhibitions, loss of awareness, unconsciousness and memory loss. The amnesiac effect on the victim may create evidential difficulties in establishing the assault itself, whereas there may be better evidence of the drugging (for instance, where the defendant has a store of such materials in his medicine cabinet). The word 'substance' is undefined, ensuring that any newly developed 'legal high' will be caught by this section, if the defendant believes it to have the appropriate properties.

However, the ambit of the offence is not limited to the use of date rape drugs and would also extend to spiking a non-alcoholic drink with alcohol or, for instance, lacing beer with spirits (as the victim is still not consenting to what she is taking).

The offence is made out when the substance is administered or taken, with the necessary intention on the part of the defendant. No sexual activity needs to have taken place, thus ensuring that an offence has been committed where the 'drugging' was unsuccessful and B did not succumb. If sexual activity did occur, other specific offences, such as rape or sexual assault, will have been committed. In these circumstances, a presumption applies that B did not consent by virtue of her being drugged (s 75(2)(f)).

CLASSIFICATION

18.6 Offence is triable either way

SENTENCING AND OTHER ORDERS

Maximum sentence

18.7 On indictment: 10 years

Summarily: 6 months imprisonment or a fine not exceeding the statutory maximum (currently £5000)

Sentencing guidelines

Determining the category

18.8

Category 1	Raised harm **and** raised culpability
Category 2	Raised harm **or** raised culpability
Category 3	Administering a substance with intent **without** raised harm or culpability factors present

The court should determine culpability and harm caused or intended, by reference only to the factors below, which comprise the principal factual elements of the offence. Where an offence does not fall squarely into a category, individual factors may require a degree of weighting before making an overall assessment and determining the appropriate offence category. Where no substantive sexual offence has been committed the main consideration for the court will be the offender's conduct as a whole including, but not exclusively, the offender's intention.

Factors indicating raised harm	Factors indicating raised culpability
• Severe psychological or physical harm • Prolonged detention /sustained incident • Additional degradation/humiliation	• Significant degree of planning • Specific targeting of a particularly vulnerable victim • Intended sexual offence carries a statutory maximum of life • Abuse of trust • Recording of offence • Offender acts together with others to commit the offence • Commercial exploitation and/or motivation • Offence racially or religiously aggravated • Offence motivated by, or demonstrating, hostility to the victim based on his or her sexual orientation (or presumed sexual orientation) or transgender identity (or presumed transgender identity) • Offence motivated by, or demonstrating, hostility to the victim based on his or her disability (or presumed disability)

Starting point and category range

18.9

Category 1	Starting point: 6 yrs custody Range: 4–9 yrs custody
Category 2	Starting point: 4 yrs custody Range: 3–7 yrs custody
Category 3	Starting point: 2 yrs custody Range: 1–5 yrs custody

Additional factual elements

18.10

Aggravating factors
Statutory aggravating factors
• Previous convictions, having regard to: (a) the nature of the offence to which the conviction relates and its relevance to the current offence; and (b) the time that has elapsed since the conviction
• Offence committed whilst on bail
Other aggravating factors
• Location of offence
• Timing of offence
• Any steps taken to prevent the reporting of an incident, obtaining assistance and/or from assisting or supporting the prosecution
• Attempts to dispose of or conceal evidence
• Failure to comply with current court orders
• Offence committed whilst on licence
Mitigating factors
• No previous convictions or no relevant/recent convictions
• Remorse
• Previous good character and/or exemplary conduct*
• Age and/or lack of maturity where it affects the responsibility of the offender
• Mental disorder or learning disability, particularly where linked to the commission of the offence
• Demonstration of steps taken to address offending behaviour

* Previous good character/exemplary conduct is different from having no previous convictions. The more serious the offence, the less the weight which should normally be attributed to this factor. Where previous good character/exemplary conduct has been used to facilitate the offence, this mitigation should not normally be allowed and such conduct may constitute an aggravating factor.

Other orders

18.11

Extended and life sentence availability (CJA 2003)	Sch 15 (specified offence): yes Sch 15B (life sentence for second listed offence): no
Trigger offence for:	SOPO: yes FTO: yes, but only where V *was under 18*
Inclusion in barred lists	Children: subject to representations Vulnerable adult: subject to representations
Notification	Yes

Committing an offence with intent to commit a sexual offence
Sexual Offences Act 2003, s 62(1)

DEFINITION

18.12 Section 62(1):

> A person commits an offence under this section if he commits any offence with the intention of committing a relevant sexual offence.

SUMMARY

18.13 This offence is intended to capture the situation where a person commits a criminal offence (the 'base offence') but does so with the intention of committing a subsequent sexual offence. It is committed regardless of whether or not the substantive sexual offence is committed.

ELEMENTS

18.14

- A *relevant sexual offence* means any offence under Part 1 of the 2003 Act (ie ss 1 to 79) and includes offences of aiding, abetting, counselling or procuring such offences.
- *Mental element*: the prosecution must establish:
  - the mens rea for the base offence
  - that the base offence was committed with intent to commit a sexual offence.

DISCUSSION

18.15 This offence might be committed by a defendant kidnapping or imprisoning a victim in order to sexually assault them; physically assaulting them as a prelude to a sexual assault; or stealing a car to use in a sexual attack. The lack of any limiting definition on the term 'offence' suggests that even driving offences could constitute the base offence, if the purpose of the driving was to get at a victim for sexual purposes. It is not necessary for the prosecution to prove precisely what sexual offence was intended.

The full offence is made out by the commission of the base offence with a sexual intent – it is not necessary that the substantive sexual offence occur, although if it does, the defendant can be charged with that offence and, if appropriate, the base offence also (ie kidnapping and rape). A charge under s 62 under those circumstances is otiose.

There are significant questions about the necessity for an offence as vague and wide-ranging as s 62. Its effect, in a case of a relatively modest base offence committed with a sexual intent, is to increase the court's sentencing and ancillary powers (Sexual Offence Prevention Orders are available, and notification on the Sex Offenders' Register is likely). More serious allegations (such as kidnapping) may not result in longer sentences where a defendant is also convicted under s 62, but he may properly be categorised as a sex offender, with consequences for his treatment in custody and beyond.

There are also often likely to be evidential problems in establishing a defendant's sexual motive.

CLASSIFICATION

18.16 Offences under s 62 are triable as follows:

1. Where the offence committed was kidnapping or false imprisonment, the offence is indictable only
2. Where any other offence was committed, the offence is triable either way.

SENTENCING AND OTHER ORDERS

Maximum sentence

18.17 In category 1. above: Life imprisonment

In category 2) above:

- On indictment: 10 years

18.17 *Preparatory sexual offences*

- Summarily: 6 months imprisonment or a fine not exceeding the statutory maximum (currently £5000)

Sentencing guidelines

18.18 The starting point and range should be commensurate with that for the preliminary offence actually committed, but with an enhancement to reflect the intention to commit a sexual offence.

The enhancement will vary depending on the nature and seriousness of the intended sexual offence, but the Definitive Guideline suggests 2 years as a suitable enhancement where the intent was to commit rape or assault by penetration

Other orders

18.19

Extended and life sentence availability (CJA 2003)	Sch 15 (specified offence): yes Sch 15B (life sentence for second listed offence): yes, if offence is in category 1. above
Trigger offence for:	SOPO: yes FTO: yes, but only where intended victim *was under 18*, and D under 18 and sentenced to at least 12 months imprisonment; D over 18 and sentenced to prison or detention in hospital or community sentence of at least 12 months
Inclusion in barred lists	Children: subject to representations[2] Vulnerable adult: subject to representations
Notification	Yes, if: D under 18 and sentenced to at least 12 months imprisonment; D over 18 and • intended offence was against a person under 18, *or* • D sentenced to prison or detention in hospital or community sentence of at least 12 months

2 'Yes, if the relevant sexual offence (the 'base offence') was one specified in this Schedule and was intended to be committed in relevant circumstances, if any, specified in this Schedule in relation to that offence'.

PRACTITIONER POINTER

PROS – the Crown should properly lay two separate charges – the first being the base offence and the second the offence under s 62.

Trespass with intent to commit a sexual offence Sexual Offences Act 2003, s 63

DEFINITION

18.20 Section 63(1):

A person commits an offence if—

(a) he is a trespasser on any premises,

(b) he intends to commit a relevant sexual offence on the premises, and

(c) he knows that, or is reckless as to whether, he is a trespasser.

SUMMARY

18.21 This offence is intended to capture the situation where a person trespasses on another's premises with the intention of committing a sexual offence on the premises. It is committed regardless of whether or not the substantive sexual offence is committed.

ELEMENTS

18.22

- A person is a *trespasser* if he is on any premises without the owner's or occupier's consent, or other lawful excuse. Consent to enter may be express or implied (for instance, customers entering a shop) and may be limited to certain areas, times or purposes.
- *Premises* include a structure or part of a structure; and '*structure*' includes a tent, vehicle or vessel or other temporary or movable structure (s 63(2)). Note that this is a non-exhaustive list and the term 'premises' has a wider meaning than 'building' and is likely to include gardens, yards and land, particularly when near to buildings.[3]

3 See, for instance, Police and Criminal Evidence Act 1984, s 23: '"premises" includes any place'.

18.22 *Preparatory sexual offences*

- A *relevant sexual offence* means any offence under Part 1 of the 2003 Act (ie ss 1 to 79) and includes offences of aiding, abetting, counselling or procuring such offences.
- *Mental element* – the prosecution must establish:
  - that the defendant knows that, or is reckless as to whether, he is a trespasser, and
  - that he intended to commit a sexual offence.

  Note that while the trespass and the intention to commit a sexual offence must co-exist, it is not necessary for the purpose of the trespassing to be in order to commit a sexual offence. The defendant may have entered on the premises for an entirely different purpose or for none and subsequently, when the opportunity arose, decided to commit a sexual offence. Similarly, he will commit the offence if he has the intent to commit a relevant sexual offence at any time while he is a trespasser.

DISCUSSION

18.23 Trespass is not, in itself, a criminal offence and therefore the behaviour that constitutes this offence does not fall within s 62 (although a person who caused criminal damage in order to trespass could be committing an offence under s 62 or s 63).

The offence is intended to capture, for example, the situation where a person enters a building owned by another, or goes into someone else's garden or garage without their consent, and he intends to commit a sexual offence against the occupier. However, it may also occur when permission given to enter property is later revoked, causing the person who has entered to become a trespasser.

This offence replaces the offence of burglary with intent to rape (Theft Act 1968, s 9(2)).

CLASSIFICATION

18.24 Offence is triable either way.

SENTENCING AND OTHER ORDERS

Maximum sentence

18.25 On indictment: 10 years

Summarily: 6 months imprisonment or a fine not exceeding the statutory maximum (currently £5000)

Sentencing guidelines

Determining the category

18.26

Category 1	Raised harm **and** raised culpability
Category 2	Raised harm **or** raised culpability
Category 3	Trespassing with intent to commit a sexual offence **without** raised harm or culpability factors present

The court should determine culpability and harm caused or intended, by reference only to the factors below, which comprise the principal factual elements of the offence. Where an offence does not fall squarely into a category, individual factors may require a degree of weighting before making an overall assessment and determining the appropriate offence category. Where no substantive sexual offence has been committed the main consideration for the court will be the offender's conduct as a whole including, but not exclusively, the offender's intention.

Factors indicating raised harm	Factors indicating raised culpability
• Additional degradation/humiliation • Prolonged detention /sustained incident • Offence committed in victim's home	• Significant degree of planning • Specific targeting of a particularly vulnerable victim • Intended sexual offence carries a statutory maximum of life imprisonment • Possession of weapon or other item to frighten or injure • Abuse of trust • Offender acts together with others to commit the offence • Commercial exploitation and/or motivation • Offence racially or religiously aggravated

Factors indicating raised harm	Factors indicating raised culpability
	• Offence motivated by, or demonstrating, hostility to the victim based on his or her sexual orientation (or presumed sexual orientation) or transgender identity (or presumed transgender identity) • Offence motivated by, or demonstrating, hostility to the victim based on his or her disability (or presumed disability)

Starting point and category range

18.27

Category 1	Starting point: 6 yrs custody Range: 4–9 yrs custody
Category 2	Starting point: 4 yrs custody Range: 3–7 yrs custody
Category 3	Starting point: 2 yrs custody Range: 1–5 yrs custody

Additional factual elements

18.28

Aggravating factors
Statutory aggravating factors
• Previous convictions, having regard to: (a) the nature of the offence to which the conviction relates and its relevance to the current offence; and (b) the time that has elapsed since the conviction • Offence committed whilst on bail
Other aggravating factors
• Location of offence • Timing of offence • Any steps taken to prevent the reporting of an incident, obtaining assistance and/or from assisting or supporting the prosecution

• Attempts to dispose of or conceal evidence • Failure to comply with current court orders • Offence committed whilst on licence
Mitigating factors
• No previous convictions or no relevant/recent convictions • Remorse • Previous good character and/or exemplary conduct* • Age and/or lack of maturity where it affects the responsibility of the offender • Mental disorder or learning disability, particularly where linked to the commission of the offence • Demonstration of steps taken to address offending behaviour

* Previous good character/exemplary conduct is different from having no previous convictions. The more serious the offence, the less the weight which should normally be attributed to this factor. Where previous good character/exemplary conduct has been used to facilitate the offence, this mitigation should not normally be allowed and such conduct may constitute an aggravating factor.

Other orders

18.29

Extended and life sentence availability (CJA 2003)	Sch 15 (specified offence): yes Sch 15B (life sentence for second listed offence): no
Trigger offence for:	SOPO: yes FTO: yes, but only where intended victim *was under 18*, and D under 18 and sentenced to at least 12 months imprisonment; D over 18 and sentenced to prison or detention in hospital or community sentence of at least 12 months
Inclusion in barred lists	Children: subject to representations[4] Vulnerable adult: subject to representations

4 'Yes, if the relevant sexual offence was one specified in this Schedule and was intended to be committed in relevant circumstances, if any, specified in this Schedule in relation to that offence'.

18.29 *Preparatory sexual offences*

Notification	Yes, if: D under 18 and sentenced to at least 12 months imprisonment; D over 18 and • intended offence was against a person under 18, *or* • D sentenced to prison or detention in hospital or community sentence of at least 12 months

Chapter 19

Sex with an adult relative

Sex with an adult relative: penetration Sexual Offences Act 2003, s 64

DEFINITION

19.1 Section 64:

(1) A person aged 16 or over (A) (subject to subsection (3A)) commits an offence if—

(a) he intentionally penetrates another person's vagina or anus with a part of his body or anything else, or penetrates another person's mouth with his penis,

(b) the penetration is sexual,

(c) the other person (B) is aged 18 or over,

(d) A is related to B in a way mentioned in subsection (2), and

(e) A knows or could reasonably be expected to know that he is related to B in that way.

(2) The ways that A may be related to B are as parent, grandparent, child, grandchild, brother, sister, half-brother, half-sister, uncle, aunt, nephew or niece.

SUMMARY

19.2 This section makes it an offence for a person (A) aged 16 or over intentionally to penetrate sexually a relative (B) who is aged 18 or over if he knows or could reasonably have been expected to know that B is his relative

ELEMENTS

19.3

- *Penetration* – see **Chapter 3**.
- *Sexual* – see **Chapter 2**.
- *Related to* – the exhaustive list of relatives is contained at s 64(2). *Uncle* and *aunt* are defined at subs (3)(a) as brother and sister respectively of a person's parent (thus excluding uncles and aunts by marriage); and *nephew* and *niece*, as the child of a person's brother or sister. Adoptive parents and adopted children are included (subs (3)(za) and (zb)). An adopted child does not commit an offence in having sex with their parent, unless he or she is 18 or over (subs 3A).
- Consent is not an issue and the offence is committed by consensual sexual penetration.
- *Mental element*: The defendant must intentionally penetrate the other party in a sexual manner (see **Chapter 2**).

  The defendant must know that he is related to B, or there must be a reasonable expectation of such knowledge. However, once it is proved that he is so related there is a presumption that he knew this, which is rebutted if he can adduce evidence to raise an issue as to whether he did know or could reasonably have been expected to know (s 64(4)).

PARTIES

19.4 The offence may be committed by males and females. Both heterosexual and homosexual relationships are caught by the provision. The defendant must be 16 or over to commit the offence (18 in the case of an adopted child having penetrative sex with their adoptive parent) and party B must be 18 or over.

DISCUSSION

19.5 Specific offences under ss 25 and 26 of the 2003 Act protect children from abuse within the family. Offences contrary to ss 64 and 65 prohibit sexual behaviour between adult relatives, but the rationale for the offences lies less with societal taboo or the dangers of incestuous relationships (note the inclusion of adoptive relationships which would lead to no eugenic problems), than with protecting the vulnerable within a family relationship. CPS guidelines suggest that these offences should primarily be reserved for situations where a history of abuse against a child family member continues into adulthood or where a suspect sexually exploits an adult relative who is vulnerable.

CLASSIFICATION

19.6 Offence is triable either way.

SENTENCING AND OTHER ORDERS

Maximum sentence

19.7 On indictment: 2 years

Summarily: 6 months imprisonment or a fine not exceeding the statutory maximum (currently £5000)

Sentencing guidelines

Determining the category

19.8

Category 1	Raised harm **and** raised culpability
Category 2	Raised harm **or** raised culpability
Category 3	Sex with an adult relative **without** raised harm or culpability factors present

Factors indicating raised harm	**Factors indicating raised culpability**
• Victim is particularly vulnerable due to personal circumstances • Child conceived	• Grooming behaviour used against victim • Use of threats (including blackmail)

Starting point and category range

19.9

Category 1	Starting point: 1 yr custody Range: 26 wks–2 yrs custody
Category 2	Starting point: High level community order Range: Medium level community order–1 yr custody

19.9 *Sex with an adult relative*

Category 3	Starting point: Medium level community order Range: Band A fine–High level community order

Additional factual elements

19.10

Aggravating factors
Statutory aggravating factors
• Previous convictions, having regard to: (a) the nature of the offence to which the conviction relates and its relevance to the current offence; and (b) the time that has elapsed since the conviction • Offence committed whilst on bail
Other aggravating factors
• Failure to comply with current court orders • Offence committed whilst on licence • Failure of offender to respond to previous warnings • Any steps taken to prevent the reporting of an incident, obtaining assistance and/or from assisting or supporting the prosecution • Attempts to dispose of or conceal evidence
Mitigating factors
• No previous convictions or no relevant/recent convictions • Remorse • Previous good character and/or exemplary conduct* • Age and/or lack of maturity where it affects the responsibility of the offender • Mental disorder or learning disability, particularly where linked to the commission of the offence • Demonstration of steps taken to address offending behaviour

Other orders

19.11

Extended and life sentence availability (CJA 2003)	Sch 15 (specified offence): yes Sch 15B (life sentence for second listed offence): no

Trigger offence for:	SOPO: yes FTO: no (V must be over 18 for this offence to be committed)
Inclusion in barred lists	Children: no Vulnerable adult: no
Notification	Yes, if: D under 18 and sentenced to at least 12 months imprisonment; D over 18 and • intended offence was against a person under 18, *or* • D sentenced to prison or detention in hospital

PRACTITIONER POINTERS

1. Defence practitioners may wish to consider whether there is real evidence that the relationship in s 64(2) actually exists. For instance, paternity may be in issue, even if the parties have always believed themselves to be father and child or uncle and nephew/niece.
2. There may well be circumstances where, absent a confession, it is difficult for the prosecution to prove penetration occurred. This is particularly the case where both parties, A and B, are under investigation or where it is a truly consensual relationship. In such circumstances, defence practitioners may wish to consider carefully their advice on whether to speak in police interview.
3. In mitigation consider whether this may have been an instance of genetic sexual attraction. This is a documented psychological state in which family members who meet each other for the first time as adults subvert natural familial affection into a strong sexual attraction. Sometimes it is reciprocated.

Sex with an adult relative: consenting to penetration
Sexual Offences Act 2003, s 65

DEFINITION

19.12 Section 65:

(1) A person aged 16 or over (A) (subject to subsection (3A)) commits an offence if—

(a) another person (B) penetrates A's vagina or anus with a part of B's body or anything else, or penetrates A's mouth with B's penis,

(b) A consents to the penetration,

(c) the penetration is sexual,

(d) B is aged 18 or over,

(e) A is related to B in a way mentioned in subsection (2), and

(f) A knows or could reasonably be expected to know that he is related to B in that way.

(2) The ways that A may be related to B are as parent, grandparent, child, grandchild, brother, sister, half-brother, half-sister, uncle, aunt, nephew or niece.

SUMMARY

19.13 This section makes it an offence for a person (A) aged 16 or over to consent to being penetrated sexually by a relative (B) who is aged 18 or over if he knows or could reasonably be expected to know that B is his relative.

ELEMENTS

19.14

- *Penetration*: see **Chapter 3**.

  The offence is committed by A *consenting* to the penetration (see **Chapter 1** – in this unique situation the Crown must prove the existence of consent and the defence may seek to show that the defendant did not consent).

- *Sexual*: see **Chapter 2**.

- *Related to*: the exhaustive list of relatives is contained at s 65(2). *Uncle* and *aunt* are defined at subs (3)(a) as brother and sister respectively of a person's parent (thus excluding uncles and aunts by marriage); and *nephew* and *niece* as the child of a person's brother or sister. Adoptive parents and adopted children are included (subs (3)(za) and (zb)). An adopted child does not commit an offence in having sex with the parent, unless he or she is 18 or over (subs 3A).

- *Mental element*: The defendant must consent to a penetration which is sexual (see **Chapters 1 and 2**).

  The defendant must know that he is related to B, or there must be a reasonable expectation of such knowledge. However, once it is proved that he is so related there is a presumption that he knew this, which is rebutted if he can adduce evidence to raise an issue as to whether he did know or could reasonably be expected to know (s 65(4)).

PARTIES

19.15 The offence may be committed by males and females. Both heterosexual and homosexual relationships are caught by the provision. The defendant must be 16 or over to commit the offence (18 in the case of an adopted child consenting to penetrative sex with their adoptive parent) and B must be 18 or over.

DISCUSSION

19.16 Specific offences under ss 25 and 26 of the 2003 Act protect children from abuse within the family. Offences contrary to ss 64 and 65 prohibit sexual behaviour between adult relatives, but the rationale for the offences lies less with societal taboo or the dangers of incestuous relationships (note the inclusion of adoptive relationships which would lead to no eugenic problems), than with protecting the vulnerable within a family relationship. CPS guidelines suggest that these offences should primarily be reserved for situations where a history of abuse against a child family member continues into adulthood or where a suspect sexually exploits an adult relative who is vulnerable.

CLASSIFICATION

19.17 Offence is triable either way.

SENTENCING AND OTHER ORDERS

Maximum sentence

19.18 On indictment: 2years

Summarily: 6 months imprisonment or a fine not exceeding the statutory maximum (currently £5000)

Sentencing guidelines

19.19 Identical to guidelines for s 64; see **19.8–19.10**.

Other orders

19.20

Extended and life sentence availability (CJA 2003)	Sch 15 (specified offence): yes Sch 15B (life sentence for second listed offence): no
Trigger offence for:	SOPO: yes FTO: no (V must be over 18 for this offence to be committed)
Inclusion in barred lists	Children: no Vulnerable adult: no
Notification	Yes, if: D under 18 and sentenced to at least 12 months imprisonment; D over 18 and ● intended offence was against a person under 18, *or* ● D sentenced to prison or detention in hospital

PRACTITIONER POINTERS

1 Defence practitioners may wish to consider whether there is real evidence that the relationship in s 65(2) actually exists. For instance, paternity may be in issue, even if the parties have always believed themselves to be father and child or uncle and nephew/niece.

2 There may well be circumstances where, absent a confession, it is difficult for the prosecution to prove penetration occurred. This is particularly the case where both parties, A and B, are under investigation or where it is a truly consensual relationship. In such circumstances, defence practitioners may wish to consider carefully their advice on whether to speak in police interview.

3 In mitigation consider whether this may have been an instance of genetic sexual attraction. This is a documented psychological state in which family members who meet each other for the first time as adults subvert natural familial affection into a strong sexual attraction. Sometimes it is reciprocated.

Chapter 20

Miscellaneous sexual offences

Exposure
Sexual Offences Act 2003, s 66

DEFINITION

20.1 Section 66(1):

A person commits an offence if—

(a) he intentionally exposes his genitals; and

(b) he intends that someone will see them and be caused alarm or distress.

SUMMARY

20.2 This section makes it an offence for a person intentionally to expose his genitals where he intends that someone will see them and be caused alarm or distress.

ELEMENTS

20.3

- *Genitals* comprise the male penis or testicles and the female vulva. Buttocks or breasts are not included within the definition.
- *Alarm or distress* are greater than annoyance. Distress requires some degree of emotional disturbance.[1]
- The offence can be committed on private property as well in public places.
- *Mental element* – the prosecution must show that the defendant:

---

1 *R v DPP* [2006] EWHC 1375.

- intentionally exposed his or her genitals;
- intending that someone would see them;
- intending that the person seeing them would be caused alarm or distress.

PARTIES

20.4 The offence may be committed by males and females. The person who sees the exposure may be male or female.

DISCUSSION

20.5 It is not necessary for A's genitals to have been seen by anyone or for anyone to have been alarmed or distressed. The offence is committed by the exposure with the relevant intention, regardless of whether the intention is satisfied.

This section is aimed at 'flashers' and the requirement for an intention to alarm of distress should remove from the ambit of the offence a number of other people who may find themselves unclothed in public: naturalists, 'streakers' or people urinating publically, for instance. Each of these groups has a motive for their nudity which would not amount to alarming or distressing others. Further, the requirement of an intention to cause alarm or distress, rather than mere recklessness as to it being caused, removes from the scope of the offence those who go naked without caring what effect they have.

'Mooning' or a woman exposing her breasts could amount to an offence contrary to s 5 of the Public Order Act 1986 or the common law offence of outraging public decency (see **Chapter 25**).

There is no necessity that the defendant obtains sexual gratification from the exposure, and indeed this would be insufficient if his intention was not also to cause alarm or distress.[2]

DEFENCE

20.6 No intention to cause alarm or distress.

Many might be surprised to learn that exposure by A for his or her sexual gratification is not caught by this section in the absence of the intention to cause alarm or distress.

2 but an offence of outraging public decency might be made out.

CLASSIFICATION

20.7 Offence is triable either way.

SENTENCING AND OTHER ORDERS

Maximum sentence

20.8 On indictment: 2 years

Summarily: 6 months imprisonment or a fine not exceeding the statutory maximum (currently £5000)

Sentencing guidelines

Determining the category

20.9

Category 1	Raised harm **and** raised culpability
Category 2	Raised harm **or** raised culpability
Category 3	Exposure **without** raised harm or culpability factors present

Factors indicating raised harm	**Factors indicating raised culpability**
• Victim followed/pursued • Offender masturbated	• Specific or previous targeting of a particularly vulnerable victim • Abuse of trust • Use of threats (including blackmail) • Offence racially or religiously aggravated • Offence motivated by, or demonstrating, hostility to the victim based on his or her sexual orientation (or presumed sexual orientation) or transgender identity (or presumed transgender identity) • Offence motivated by, or demonstrating, hostility to the victim based on his or her disability (or presumed disability)

20.10 *Miscellaneous sexual offences*

Starting point and category range

20.10

Category 1	Starting point: 26 wks custody Range: 12 wks–1 yr custody
Category 2	Starting point: High level community order Range: Medium level community order–26 wks custody
Category 3	Starting point: Medium level community order Range: Band A fine–High level community order

Additional factual elements

20.11

Aggravating factors
Statutory aggravating factors
• Previous convictions, having regard to: (a) the nature of the offence to which the conviction relates and its relevance to the current offence; and (b) the time that has elapsed since the conviction • Offence committed whilst on bail
Other aggravating factors
• Location of offence • Timing of offence • Any steps taken to prevent the reporting of an incident, obtaining assistance and/or from assisting or supporting the prosecution • Failure to comply with current court orders • Offence committed whilst on licence • Commission of offence whilst under the influence of alcohol or drugs • Presence of others, especially children
Mitigating factors
• No previous convictions or no relevant/recent convictions • Remorse • Previous good character and/or exemplary conduct*

- Age and/or lack of maturity where it affects the responsibility of the offender
- Mental disorder or learning disability, particularly where linked to the commission of the offence
- Demonstration of steps taken to address offending behaviour

* Previous good character/exemplary conduct is different from having no previous convictions. The more serious the offence, the less the weight which should normally be attributed to this factor. Where previous good character/exemplary conduct has been used to facilitate the offence, this mitigation should not normally be allowed and such conduct may constitute an aggravating factor.

Other orders

20.12

Extended and life sentence availability (CJA 2003)	Sch 15 (specified offence): yes Sch 15B (life sentence for second listed offence): no
Trigger offence for:	SOPO: yes FTO: yes, but only where V *was under 18*, and D under 18 and sentenced to at least 12 months imprisonment; D over 18 and sentenced to prison or detention in hospital or community sentence of at least 12 months
Inclusion in barred lists	Children: subject to representations if committed against a child under16 Vulnerable adult: subject to representations
Notification	Yes, if: D under 18 and sentenced to at least 12 months imprisonment; D over 18 and • V under 18, *or* • D sentenced to prison or detention in hospital or community sentence of at least 12 months

Voyeurism
Sexual Offences Act 2003, s 67

DEFINITION

20.13 Section 67:

20.13 *Miscellaneous sexual offences*

(1) A person commits an offence if—

(a) for the purpose of obtaining sexual gratification, he observes another person doing a private act; and

(b) he knows that the other person does not consent to being observed for his sexual gratification.

(2) A person commits an offence if—

(a) he operates equipment with the intention of enabling another person to observe, for the purpose of obtaining sexual gratification, a third person (B) doing a private act; and

(b) he knows that B does not consent to his operating equipment with that intention.

(3) A person commits an offence if—

(a) he records another person (B) doing a private act;

(b) he does so with the intention that he or a third person will, for the purpose of obtaining sexual gratification, look at an image of B doing the act; and

(c) he knows that B does not consent to his recording the act with that intention.

(4) A person commits an offence if he installs equipment, or constructs or adapts a structure or part of a structure, with the intention of enabling himself or another person to commit an offence under subsection (1).

SUMMARY

20.14 Within s 67, subsections 1–4 set out the four ways of committing a voyeurism offence. Each involves a 'private act' being done, or contemplated to be done, by another person.

Each also necessarily involves a sexual motive by the defendant or a secondary party.

ELEMENTS

20.15

- *Observes* is interpreted widely and includes indirect observation by looking at a moving or still *image* made by any means (s 79(7) and s 79(4)). Observation can therefore encompass a range of surveillance, including viewing through a peephole, binoculars, or over a link from a remote camera.

- A *private act* is defined by s 68(1) as occurring when the person observed (or intended to be observed):

  'is in a place which, in the circumstances, would reasonably be expected to provide privacy, and–

  (a) the person's genitals, buttocks or breasts are exposed or covered only with underwear;

  (b) the person is using a lavatory; or

  (c) the person is doing a sexual act that is not of a kind ordinarily done in public'."

- *Place* in which the 'private act' is being done may be indoors or outside, subject to the reasonable expectation of privacy. Sheltered gardens, secluded beaches or woodlands might suffice, if private enough.

- *Reasonably be expected to provide privacy* – The use of the word 'reasonably' suggests that this will be a question for the jury and this was confirmed by the Court of Appeal in *R v Bassett*.[3] In that case, which involved observation of a parent and child in a shower cubicle without a door, it was held that a person may have a reasonable expectation of privacy without being wholly enclosed or sheltered from the possibility of being seen. Their Lordships cited *R v Sawyer*[4] which involved marathon runners urinating behind a hedge – to which situation the Court imparted a reasonable expectation of privacy.

- *Absence of consent* is an essential ingredient of each offence.

  To be caught by the legislation, the observation, recording etc must done with the defendant's knowledge that the person in question does not consent (see **Chapter 1**).

- *Sexual gratification* is a pre-requisite to the offence being made out. Thus, a person covertly recording sexual activity in order to cause embarrassment or distress will not amount to a voyeurism offence.

- *Structure* includes a tent, vehicle or other temporary or movable structure (s 68(2)).

PARTIES

20.16 The offence may be committed by males and females.

---

3 [2009] 1 Cr App R 7.
4 [2007] EWCA Crim 204.

The offender may be a participant as well as an observer – for example, *R v Wilkins*:[5] D installed a covert camera in a smoke alarm and recorded sex between himself and various women who consented to intercourse but not to D's recording of it for later sexual gratification.

Note that a person other than D who observes the private act under s 67(2) or who looks at the recorded image under s 67(3) does not himself commit a voyeurism offence.

DISCUSSION

Consent

20.17 Consent carries the definition applicable throughout Part 1 of the 2003 Act (see **Chapter 1**). Note that in relation to voyeurism there is no issue of absence of reasonable belief in consent – for this offence the Crown must prove *knowledge* that the person does not consent. In reality, once the pre-requisite private act is established, it is likely to be easy for the prosecution to establish that the subject did not consent to being observed or recorded for the sexual gratification of another – what could possibly have given D any notion that the other person agreed – by freedom and choice – to being observed or recorded?

Generally

20.18 A voyeurism offence can be committed irrespective of whether the person watched or filmed is aware of the observation. The wording of s 67(3) ('he does so *with* the intention') imports a requirement of contemporaneity in relation to sexual gratification, such that later sexual motivation will not suffice. The eventual distribution to others, albeit for their sexual gratification, of previously made recordings of private acts would not be caught by s 67(3).

It is curious that s 67(4) dealing with installation/construction/adaptation is referable only to s 67(1) so that, for example, installing a camera for others to make a recording which falls foul of s 67(3) does not make the installer liable under the Act, although he might be guilty of an inchoate offence.

Breasts

20.19 'Breasts', in s 68(1)(a) has been held not to include the male chest.[6]

---

5 Inner London Crown Court, March 2010.
6 *R v Bassett* [2009] 1 Cr App R 7.

Underwear

20.20 Under s 68(1)(a), 'underwear' would not include swimwear such as bikini bottoms which are typically worn externally rather than as underclothing:[7]

> 'In its ordinary connotation underwear means clothing worn next to the skin under outer clothes. Swimwear is not in its normal function underwear … some items of swimwear could be worn as underwear. A woman may choose to wear, for instance, bikini bottoms as underpants. While wearing them for this purpose … if a woman were to be filmed in circumstances where she was entitled to expect privacy, this would constitute an offence under s 67.'

Relationship with other offences

20.21 Where voyeurism involves the recording of a child doing a private act, it is likely to amount to taking/making an indecent photograph of a child in contravention of the Protection of Children Act 1978 – see **22.1**.

Examples

(*the following examples are drawn from the Explanatory Notes to the Act*)

20.22 *Section 67(1)*: A, for the purpose of his own sexual gratification, looks through a window or peephole at a person (B) having sex, knowing that the person observed does not consent to being looked at for this purpose.

Section 67(2): Landlord (A) operates a webcam to allow people on the internet to view, for their sexual gratification, live images of his tenant (B) undressing, A knowing that B does not consent to this.

Section 67(3): A secretly photographs or video-records someone (B) masturbating in B's bedroom to show to others for their sexual gratification. Proof that the intention was the sexual gratification of others could be derived from, for example, the image being posted on a pornographic website, or published in a pornographic magazine. A will be caught by the offence whether or not those looking at the image/recording know that B did not consent to being filmed with that intention.

Section 67(4): A drills a spy-hole or installs a two-way mirror in a house with the intention of spying on someone for sexual gratification or allowing others to do so. The offence would be committed by A even if the spy-hole or mirror were discovered before it was used.

---

7 *Police Service for Northern Ireland v MacRitchie* [2010] NICA 26.

CLASSIFICATION

20.23 Offence is triable either way.

SENTENCING AND OTHER ORDERS

Maximum sentence

20.24 On indictment: 2 years

Summarily: 6 months imprisonment or a fine not exceeding the statutory maximum (currently £5000)

Sentencing guidelines

Determining the category

20.25

Category 1	Raised harm **and** raised culpability
Category 2	Raised harm **or** raised culpability
Category 3	Voyeurism **without** raised harm or culpability factors present

Factors indicating raised harm	Factors indicating raised culpability
• Image(s) available to be viewed by others	• Significant degree of planning
• Victim observed or recorded in their own home or residence	• Image(s) recorded
	• Abuse of trust
	• Specific or previous targeting of a particularly vulnerable victim
	• Commercial exploitation and/or motivation
	• Offence racially or religiously aggravated

Factors indicating raised harm	**Factors indicating raised culpability**
	• Offence motivated by, or demonstrating, hostility to the victim based on his or her sexual orientation (or presumed sexual orientation) or transgender identity (or presumed transgender identity) • Offence motivated by, or demonstrating, hostility to the victim based on his or her disability (or presumed disability)

Starting point and category range

20.26

Category 1	Starting point: 26 wks custody Range: 12 wks–18mths custody
Category 2	Starting point : High level community order Range: Medium level community order–26 wks custody
Category 3	Starting point: Medium level community order Range: Band A fine–High level community order

Additional factual elements

20.27

Aggravating factors
Statutory aggravating factors
• Previous convictions, having regard to a) the nature of the offence to which the conviction relates and its relevance to the current offence; and b) the time that has elapsed since the conviction • Offence committed whilst on bail
Other aggravating factors
• Location of offence • Timing of offence • Failure to comply with current court orders

- Offence committed whilst on licence
- Distribution of images, whether or not for gain
- Placing images where there is the potential for a high volume of viewers
- Period over which victim observed
- Period over which images were made or distributed
- Any steps taken to prevent the victim reporting an incident, obtaining assistance and/or from assisting or supporting the prosecution
- Attempts to dispose of or conceal evidence

Mitigating factors

- No previous convictions or no relevant/recent convictions
- Remorse
- Previous good character and/or exemplary conduct*
- Age and/or lack of maturity where it affects the responsibility of the offender
- Mental disorder or learning disability, particularly where linked to the commission of the offence
- Demonstration of steps taken to address offending behaviour

* Previous good character/exemplary conduct is different from having no previous convictions. The more serious the offence, the less the weight which should normally be attributed to this factor. Where previous good character/exemplary conduct has been used to facilitate the offence, this mitigation should not normally be allowed and such conduct may constitute an aggravating factor.

Other orders

20.28

Extended sentence availability (CJA 2003)	Sch 15: yes Sch 15B: no
Trigger offence for:	SOPO: yes FTO: yes, but only where V *was under 18*, and D under 18 and sentenced to at least 12 months imprisonment; D over 18 and sentenced to prison or detention in hospital or community sentence of at least 12 months

Inclusion in barred lists	Children: subject to representations if committed against a child under16 Vulnerable adult: subject to representations
Notification	Yes, if: D under 18 and sentenced to at least 12 months imprisonment; D over 18 and • V under 18, *or* • D sentenced to prison or detention in hospital or community sentence of at least 12 months

Intercourse with an animal
Sexual Offences Act 2003, s 69

DEFINITION

20.29 Section 69(1):

A person commits an offence if—

(a) he intentionally performs an act of penetration with his penis,

(b) what is penetrated is the vagina or anus of a living animal, and

(c) he knows that, or is reckless as to whether, that is what is penetrated.

(2) A person (A) commits an offence if—

(a) A intentionally causes, or allows, A's vagina or anus to be penetrated,

(b) the penetration is by the penis of a living animal, and

(c) A knows that, or is reckless as to whether, that is what A is being penetrated by.

SUMMARY

20.30 This section creates two offences. The first, subs (1), makes it an offence for a man to penetrate the vagina or anus of a living animal; subs (2) makes it an offence for a person to cause or allow her vagina or his or her anus to be penetrated by the penis of a living animal.

This offence is related solely to penile penetration in relation to animals. Other forms of penetration or sexual activity with animals do not fall within this section.

ELEMENTS

20.31

- *Penetration, vagina and anus*: see **Chapter 3** and s 79. References to the vagina or anus include references to any similar part of an animal.[8]
- *Mental element*

  In relation to sub-s (1), it must be proved that the defendant:

  - intentionally penetrated an animal
  - knowing that he was penetrating an animal or being reckless as to whether he was penetrating an animal.
- In relation to sub-s (2), it must be proved that the defendant:
  - intentionally caused their vagina or anus to be penetrated
  - knowing that they were being penetrated by an animal or being reckless as to whether it was an animal that they are being penetrated by.

DISCUSSION

20.32 In the absence of penile penetration no offence under s 69 will have been committed. Oral sexual acts are excluded from the definition. However, other sexual activity with an animal may amount to an offence of causing unnecessary suffering to an animal contrary to Animal Welfare Act 2006.

This offence may come to light, and be evidenced, by the increasing tendency of people to record and film their sexual activities. In such circumstances, offences may have been committed contrary to s 64 of the Criminal Justice and Immigration Act 2008 (possession of pornographic images of a person performing sexual intercourse or oral sex with a live or dead animal – see **26.1**).

CLASSIFICATION

20.33 Offence is triable either way.

8 Commentators have speculated, without firm conclusion, on the meaning of this provision and the possible location of the mysterious orifice.

SENTENCING AND OTHER ORDERS

Maximum sentence

20.34 On indictment: 2 years

Summarily: 6 months imprisonment or a fine not exceeding the statutory maximum (currently £5000)

Sentencing guidelines

20.35 This is not an offence listed in the Sexual Offences Definitive Guideline 2014.

Comments in the earlier 2007 guidelines to the Sexual Offences Act, **which is no longer in force,** may be instructive. These stated that for a basic offence with no aggravating or mitigating factors, the starting point was a community order and the range 'an appropriate non-custodial sentence'. An aggravating factor could be the recording of the activity or circulation of pictures or videos; a mitigating factor could be that the offence was a symptom of isolation rather than depravity.

Other orders

20.36

Extended and life sentence availability (CJA 2003)	Sch 15 (specified offence): yes Sch 15B (life sentence for second listed offence): no
Trigger offence for:	SOPO: yes FTO: no
Inclusion in barred lists	Children: no Vulnerable adult: no
Notification	Yes, if: D under 18 and sentenced to at least 12 months imprisonment; D over 18 and sentenced to prison or detention in hospital

Sexual penetration of a corpse
Sexual Offences Act 2003, s 70

DEFINITION

20.37 Section 70(1):

A person commits an offence if—

(a) he intentionally performs an act of penetration with a part of his body or anything else,

(b) what is penetrated is a part of the body of a dead person,

(c) he knows that, or is reckless as to whether, that is what is penetrated, and

(d) the penetration is sexual.

SUMMARY

20.38 This section makes it an offence for a person sexually to penetrate any part of the body of a dead person with his penis, any other body part (for example his finger), or any other object.

ELEMENTS

20.39

- *Penetration*: see **Chapter 3**.

  Note that the penetration is of any part of the body of the deceased.

- The penetration must be '*sexual*' – see **Chapter 2**. Thus, those legitimately working with corpses, for instance in the course of post-mortems or laying-out, will not commit an offence.

- *Mental element* – the requirement that the defendant know that the person is dead, or be reckless about this, excludes situations where he penetrates a person believing them to be alive, or where a person dies unexpectedly during intercourse.

DISCUSSION

20.40 The circumstances in which this highly unpleasant offence could occur include both intentional necrophilia and a violent rape or drugging in which the victim dies before or during intercourse. In the latter situation the question of recklessness of the defendant as to whether his victim was alive or dead may arise.

CLASSIFICATION

20.41 Offence is triable either way.

SENTENCING AND OTHER ORDERS

Maximum sentence

20.42 On indictment: 2 years

Summarily: 6 months imprisonment or a fine not exceeding the statutory maximum (currently £5000)

Sentencing guidelines

20.43 This is not an offence listed in the Sexual Offences Definitive Guideline 2014.

Comments in the earlier 2007 guidelines to the Sexual Offences Act, **which is no longer in force,** may be instructive. These stated that for a basic offence with no aggravating or mitigating factors, the starting point was a community order and the range 'an appropriate non-custodial sentence'. For a repeat offender and/or an offence with aggravating factors, the starting point was 26 weeks with a range between 4 weeks and 18 months custody. Aggravating factors could include distress caused to relatives or friends of the deceased, physical damage caused to body of the deceased, that the corpse was that of a child or that the offence was committed in a funeral home or mortuary. The Sentencing Guidelines Council could identify no mitigating factors.

Other orders

20.44

Extended and life sentence availability (CJA 2003)	Sch 15 (specified offence): yes Sch 15B (life sentence for second listed offence): no
Trigger offence for:	SOPO: yes FTO: no

Inclusion in barred lists	Children: no Vulnerable adult: no
Notification	Yes, if: D under 18 and sentenced to at least 12 months imprisonment; D over 18 and sentenced to prison or detention in hospital

Sexual activity in a public lavatory Sexual Offences Act 2003, s 71

DEFINITION

20.45 Section 71(1):

A person commits an offence if—

(a) he is in a lavatory to which the public or a section of the public has or is permitted to have access, whether on payment or otherwise,

(b) he intentionally engages in an activity, and

(c) the activity is sexual.

SUMMARY

20.46 This section makes it an offence to engage in sexual activities in a public lavatory.

ELEMENTS

20.47

- The offence is committed in a lavatory to which the *public or a section of the public has or is permitted to have access*. This would therefore include places where the public are only admitted on certain occasions, such as lavatories in bars, hotels or shopping centres as well as genuinely 'public' local authority conveniences.
- The activity is *sexual* if 'a reasonable person would, in all the circumstances but regardless of any person's purpose, consider it to be sexual' (s 71(2)). This is a narrower definition than that provided at s 78, which defines all other sexual activity under the Act. The effect is that

only behaviour which is clearly and obviously sexual will fall within the offence.

- There is no necessity for the activity to be committed with or against any other person – solo masturbation will be caught by this section.

PARTIES

20.48 The offence may be committed by males or females. Both heterosexual and homosexual behaviour is covered by the section (unlike its predecessor offence contrary to SOA 1956, s 32, which only criminalised men persistently soliciting in public places for immoral purposes).

CLASSIFICATION

20.49 Offence is summary only.

SENTENCING AND OTHER ORDERS

Maximum sentence

20.50 6 months imprisonment or a fine not exceeding the statutory maximum (currently £5000).

Sentencing guidelines

20.51 This is not an offence listed in the Sexual Offences Definitive Guideline 2014 but is listed in the Magistrates' Courts Sentencing Guidelines.

Starting point and category range

20.52

Examples of nature of activity	**Starting point**	**Range**
Basic offence as defined in the Act, assuming no aggravating or mitigating factors	Band C fine	Band C fine
Offence with aggravating factors	Low level community order	Band C fine to Medium level community order

Aggravating and mitigating factors

20.53

Factor indicating higher culpability
• Intimidating behaviour/threats of violence to members of the public
• Blatant behaviour

The guidelines also state that this is primarily a public order offence rather than a sexual offence analogous to conduct charged as the common law offence of outraging public decency. The purpose of the legislation is to give adults and children the freedom to use public lavatories for the purpose for which they were designed, without the fear of being an unwilling witness to overtly sexual behaviour.

Other orders

20.54

Extended and life sentence availability (CJA 2003)	Sch 15 (specified offence): no Sch 15B (life sentence for second listed offence): no
Trigger offence for:	SOPO: no FTO: no
Inclusion in barred lists	Children: no Vulnerable adult: no
Notification	No

Chapter 21

Breaches of requirements and orders

Breach of notification requirements Sexual Offences Act 2003, s 91

DEFINITION

21.1 Section 91(1):

A person commits an offence if he—

(a) fails, without reasonable excuse, to comply with ss 83(1), 84(1), 84(4)(b), 85(1), 87(4), or 89(2)(b) or any requirement imposed by regulations made under s 86(1); or

(b) notifies to the police, in purported compliance with ss 83(1), 84(1) or 85(1) or any requirement imposed by regulations made under s 86(1), any information which he knows to be false.

SUMMARY

21.2 An offence is committed by a person subject to notification obligations who fails to notify police at all, or within specified time limits, or who knowingly gives false information (see **Chapter 43**).

ELEMENTS

21.3

- The obligations are:
  - Section 83(1): requirement to notify police of certain information within 3 days of 'the relevant date' (usually conviction or sentence).
  - Section 84(1): requirement to notify changes to certain information within 3 days of the change.
  - Section 84(4)(b): requirement to notify police if changes, which had been reported, do not occur.

- Section 85(1): requirement to give annual re-notification.
- Section 87(4): allowing the police to take fingerprints or photographs.
- Section 89(2)(b): obligations on parents of young offenders.
- Section 86(1): requirement to notify foreign travel plans.

- A failure to notify in one of the subs (1) circumstances is a continuing offence, committed on the first day of failure. Only one offence is committed for the same failure (s 91(3)).

CLASSIFICATION

21.4 Offence is triable either way.

SENTENCING AND OTHER ORDERS

Maximum sentence

21.5 On indictment: 5 years

Summarily: 6 months imprisonment or a fine not exceeding the statutory maximum (currently £5000)

Sentencing guidelines and factors

21.6 This is not an offence listed in the Sexual Offences Definitive Guideline 2014 but is listed in the Magistrates' Courts Sentencing Guidelines.

Starting point and category range

21.7

Examples of nature of activity	**Starting point**	**Range**
Negligent or inadvertent failure to comply with requirements	Medium level community order	Band C fine to high level community order
Deliberate failure to comply with requirements or supply of information known to be false	6 weeks custody	High level community order to 26 weeks custody

Examples of nature of activity	Starting point	Range
Conduct as described in box above and long period of non-compliance or attempts to avoid detection	18 weeks custody	6 weeks custody to Crown Court

Aggravating and mitigating factors

21.8

Factor indicating higher culpability	Factor indicating lower culpability
• Long period of non-compliance (where not in the examples above)	• Genuine misunderstanding
Factors indicating greater degree of harm	
• Alarm or distress caused to victim • Particularly serious original offence	

It is suggested that reference may be made to the Definitive Guidelines for Breach of a Protective Order and, in particular, aggravating factors where the offence is a further non-compliance, following earlier breach proceedings or where the non-compliance was committed immediately or shortly after the order was made; and the mitigating factor of a breach of the order following a long period of compliance.

See also

- *R v Clarke*:[1] failure to comply on repeated occasions. Two years reduced to 15 months on a guilty plea for a seventh non-compliance.
- *R v Grovesnor*:[2] choosing to live rough is unlikely be a mitigating factor; a sentence range of 4 to 6 months is appropriate on conviction for failing to notify a change of address for up to 3 months, absent aggravating factors. Deliberate flouting by a sexual predator or repeated breaches will merit a longer sentence.

1 [2006] EWCA Crim 491.
2 [2010] EWCA Crim 560.

Other orders

21.9

Extended and life sentence availability (CJA 2003)	Sch 15 (specified offence): no Sch 15B (life sentence for second listed offence): no
Trigger offence for:	SOPO: no FTO: no
Inclusion in barred lists	Children: no Vulnerable adult: no
Notification	No, but will already be subject to notification

Breach of sexual offences prevention order Sexual Offences Act 2003, s 113

DEFINITION

21.10 Section 113(1):

A person commits an offence if, without reasonable excuse, he does anything which he is prohibited from doing by—

(a) a sexual offences prevention order; or

(b) an interim sexual offences prevention order.

SUMMARY

21.11 An offence is committed by a person who is prohibited by virtue of a SOPO or interim SOPO from doing certain actions, who nevertheless takes those actions without reasonable excuse. (See **Chapter 44**).

CLASSIFICATION

21.12 Offence is triable either way.

SENTENCING AND OTHER ORDERS

Maximum sentence

21.13 On indictment: 5 years

Summarily: 6 months imprisonment or a fine not exceeding the statutory maximum (currently £5000)

Sentencing guidelines and factors

21.14 This is not an offence listed in the Sexual Offences Definitive Guideline 2014.

It is suggested that reference may be made to the guidelines for 'Non-compliance with notification requirements' within the Magistrates' Courts Sentencing Guidelines (s 91; see **21.6–21.8**); and the Definitive Guidelines for Breach of a Protective Order and, in particular, aggravating factors where the offence is a further non-compliance, following earlier breach proceedings or where the breach was committed immediately or shortly after the order was made; and the mitigating factor of a breach of the order following a long period of compliance. The guidelines also suggest that, where the breach comprises a further offence, and that offence is charged, consecutive sentences should be considered.

See also:

- *R v Fenton*:[3] where breach involves no real risk to those it is intended to protect, a community order may be appropriate to assist the offender to comply with the order; where there is real risk, sentences may be considered which are far higher than would have been appropriate for the specific offence or misconduct which comprised the breach. In this case two and a half years upheld for repeated breaches, where defendant was considered a risk to the public and was not amenable to probation assistance.
- *R v Morris (Richard John)*:[4] guilty plea to six breaches by having contact with a small boy. The court found real risk but also acknowledged lengthy previous compliance and the short period over which the breaches took place: 15 months reduced to 10. The court also reviewed a number of other sentencing authorities for breach of SOPOs.

3 [2007] 1 Cr App R (S) 97, CA.
4 [2013] EWCA Crim 350.

Other orders

21.15

Extended and life sentence availability (CJA 2003)	Sch 15 (specified offence): no Sch 15B (life sentence for second listed offence): no
Trigger offence for:	SOPO: no FTO: no
Inclusion in barred lists	Children: no Vulnerable adult: no
Notification	No. But note that a person made subject to a SOPO will automatically be subject also to notification for the duration of the order (s 107(3) and (4))
	Conditional discharge **is not** an available disposal (s 113(3)).

Breach of foreign travel order Sexual Offences Act 2003, s 122

DEFINITION

21.16 Section 122:

(1) A person commits an offence if, without reasonable excuse, he does anything which he is prohibited from doing by a foreign travel order.

(1A) A person commits an offence if, without reasonable excuse, the person fails to comply with a requirement under section 117A(2)

SUMMARY

21.17 An offence is committed by a person subject to a foreign travel order who travels to a country named in the order or travels out of the UK if the order prohibits him from doing so. Where it was a requirement of the order (made by virtue of s 117A(2)) that the person surrender their passports, an offence is committed if this is not done within the specified time (see **Chapter 45**).

CLASSIFICATION

21.18 Offence is triable either way.

SENTENCING AND OTHER ORDERS

Maximum sentence

21.19 On indictment: 5 years

Summarily: 6 months imprisonment or a fine not exceeding the statutory maximum (currently £5000)

Sentencing guidelines

21.20 This is not an offence listed in the Sexual Offences Definitive Guideline 2014.

It is suggested that reference may be made to the Definitive Guidelines for Breach of a Protective Order and, in particular, aggravating factors where the offence is a further non-compliance, following earlier breach proceedings or where the non-compliance was committed immediately or shortly after the order was made; and the mitigating factor of a breach of the order following a long period of compliance.

Other orders

21.21

Extended and life sentence availability (CJA 2003)	Sch 15 (specified offence): no Sch 15B (life sentence for second listed offence): no
Trigger offence for:	SOPO: no FTO: no
Inclusion in barred lists	Children: no Vulnerable adult: no
Notification	No (although as the defendant will already have been convicted of an offence against a child in order to qualify for a FTO, he may already to be subject to notification requirements)
	Conditional discharge **is not** an available disposal (s 122(3))

Breach of risk of sexual harm order
Sexual Offences Act 2003, s 128

DEFINITION

21.22 Section 128(1):

A person commits an offence if, without reasonable excuse, he does anything which he is prohibited from doing by—

(a) a risk of sexual harm order; or

(b) an interim risk of sexual harm order.

SUMMARY

21.23 An offence is committed by a person who is prohibited by virtue of a risk of sexual harm order (RSHO) or interim RSHO from doing certain actions, who nevertheless takes those actions without reasonable excuse (see **Chapter 46**).

CLASSIFICATION

21.24 Offence is triable either way.

SENTENCING AND OTHER ORDERS

Maximum sentence

21.25 On indictment: 5 years

Summarily: 6 months imprisonment or a fine not exceeding the statutory maximum (currently £5000)

Sentencing guidelines

21.26 This is not an offence listed in the Sexual Offences Definitive Guideline 2014.

It is suggested that reference may be made to the Definitive Guidelines for Breach of a Protective Order and, in particular, aggravating factors where the offence is a further non-compliance, following earlier breach proceedings or where the non-compliance was committed immediately or shortly after the order was made; and the mitigating factor of a breach of the order following a long period of compliance.

Other orders

21.27

Extended and life sentence availability (CJA 2003)	Sch 15 (specified offence): no Sch 15B (life sentence for second listed offence): no
Trigger offence for:	SOPO: no FTO: no
Inclusion in barred lists	Children: no Vulnerable adult: no
Notification	Yes. A person convicted of a breach of this order becomes subject to the notification requirements for the remaining duration of the RSHO. If he was already subject to notification which would otherwise have concluded before the expiry of the RSHO, notification will now run until the latter date (s 129).
	Conditional discharge **is not** an available disposal (s 128(3))

Part C
Other statutory and common law offences

Chapter 22

Indecent photographs of children

Taking or making indecent photographs of children Protection of Children Act 1978, s 1

DEFINITION

22.1 Section 1(1):

It is an offence for a person—

(a) to take, or permit to be taken or to make, any indecent photograph or pseudo-photograph of a child; or

(b) to distribute or show such indecent photographs or pseudo-photographs; or

(c) to have in his possession such indecent photographs or pseudo-photographs, with a view to their being distributed or shown by himself or others; or

(d) to publish or cause to be published any advertisement likely to be understood as conveying that the advertiser distributes or shows such indecent photographs or pseudo-photographs, or intends to do so.

SUMMARY

22.2 The offence is committed by a person taking, making or permitting to be taken, distributing or showing indecent photographs or pseudo-photographs of persons under 18 years of age. It is also an offence to possess such materials with a view to distributing or showing them and to advertise such materials.

ELEMENTS

22.3

- The act of taking a photograph or making a film is clearly encompassed in taking or making. However, in relation to internet usage, the term 'making' has a wider application than its everyday usage might suggest. Thus any user activity that results in an image being copied to the computer from the internet is 'making'. This includes activity where the image is simply viewed on the screen. In order for an image to be viewed on a screen, the data making up the image has to be copied to the computer, and therefore constitutes making.[1] It is sometimes suggested that images arise as a result of a 'pop-ups'. Where the defendant raises this, and discharges the evidential burden that this may have occurred, it will be necessary for the prosecution to show that the defendant knew that accessing the site was likely to result in unlawful 'pop-ups' appearing.[2]

- *Distribution* is defined at s 1(2):

  > 'a person is to be regarded as distributing an indecent photograph or pseudo-photograph if he parts with possession of it to, or exposes or offers it for acquisition by, another person.'

  Clearly, sending or exchanging images by email or file sharing will fall within s 1(1)(b). Providing a password to allow another access to material stored on a computer falls within the definition of showing that material (*R v Fellows and Arnold*[3]). No financial benefit need be derived from the distribution (or showing).

- *Photograph* includes a film, a copy of a photograph or film, a photograph comprised in a film, a negative of a photograph and data stored on a computer disc or other electronic means capable of being converted into a photograph (s 7). It also includes a 'tracing', ie a photograph which has been converted either manually or by electronic means into a graphic image (s 7(4A)).

- *Pseudo-photograph* is an image which appears to be a photograph. For these purposes it will often be an amalgam of a photograph of an adult and a photograph of a child (ie a child's face 'grafted' onto an adult's body, or vice versa) (s 7(7)).

- *Indecent photograph*. It is for the jury to consider whether the photograph itself is indecent, irrespective of the motives or intentions of the photographer/maker[4]. The test is an objective one, applying the recognised standards of propriety (*R v Stamford*[5]).

- *Child* means a person under the age of 18.[6] In the case of a pseudo-photograph, if the predominant impression is that of a child, it is to be treated as being an image of a child (s 7(8)). The court must look at the

1 See *R v Smith; R v Jayson* [2003] 1 Cr App R 13.
2 See *R v Harrison [*2008] 1 Cr App R 29.
3 [1997] 1 Cr.App.R. 244.
4 See *R v Graham-Kerr* [1988] 1 WLR 1098.
5 [1972] 2 QB 391.
6 Raised from 16 years by SOA 2003, s 45(2) with effect from 1 May 2004.

'evidence as a whole' to ascertain whether the image is of a person under the age of 18 (s 2(3)) and this is a question of fact for the tribunal, expert evidence (for instance, from a paediatrician) being inadmissible.[7]

- *Mental element*:
  - For offences under s 1(1)(a) the taking or making must be deliberate or intentional in the knowledge or belief that the image will be indecent and of a child.
  - For offences under s 1(1)(b) – no mental element required for showing or distributing, but the statutory defence under s 1(4) (below) is available if the defendant proves he did not see the images or suspect them to be indecent images of children (see *R v Price*[8] – offence is effectively one of strict liability and accidental supply of indecent images was sufficient to found the offence).
  - For offences under s 1(1)(c) the defendant must knowingly have custody or control of the item; and must do so, 'with a view to' distributing or showing them to others (see *R v Dooley*[9] – the mental element is less strong than intention and merely requires some likelihood that the images would be shown to others). The statutory defence in s 1(4) applies.
  - For offences under s 1(1)(d) the advertisement must have been published intentionally.

DISCUSSION

Indecency

22.4 Whether an image is indecent or not is a question for the jury to determine and usually, in the case of sexually explicit material relating to children, there will be little argument about this. The issue does arise in respect of less extreme images, especially simple naked photographs of young children. Since the motive of the person taking or possessing the image is irrelevant, such photographs would be equally obscene or innocuous in the hands of a predatory paedophile or the child's loving parent. The old Sentencing Guidelines (not in themselves a definition of the offence, of course) referred to 'erotic posing' as being an example of a low level indecent image. While this is not the only measure of indecency at this level, it would seem that there must be some form of context, for instance an emphasis on the child's genitalia or something

7 *R v Land* [1998] 1 Cr App R 272.
8 [2006] EWCA Crim 3363.
9 [2005] EWCA Crim 3093.

within the background or circumstance of the picture, which distinguishes an innocent naked photograph of a child from an indecent image.

In *R v Graham-Kerr*[10] the Court of Appeal approved a two-part test for the jury to apply:

1. Is it proved that the defendant took the photograph deliberately and intentionally?
2. If so, is it indecent? The defendant's motivation may be relevant to determining the first point, but is irrelevant to the second.

In *R v Dodds*[11] the jury were provided with the COPINE scale, which referred to scale 1 images as 'naked or semi-naked in legitimate settings'. The Court of Appeal deprecated this as the scale was not relevant to a test of indecency, and also criticised the admission of a police officer's opinion that the images were level 1 indecent.

The age of the child is a material consideration in determining whether a photograph was in fact indecent.[12] Thus, a topless photograph of a 14-year-old girl suggests indecency in a way that a photograph of a toddler in a bath may not.

16- and 17-year olds

22.5 The 2003 SOA included within the ambit of this offence young people aged 16 and 17. This creates the slightly anomalous situation that, while it may be lawful to have sex with a 17-year-old, it is not permitted to take an indecent photograph of them. The anomaly is partially addressed by s 1A which creates a defence for those who were married or 'living together as partners', but does not apply to those in more casual sexual relationships. In *R v M*[13] the Court of Appeal considered whether this limitation of the statutory defence was 'arbitrary, unjustified and not proportionate', but concluded that it was both compatible with Articles 8 and 10 of the ECHR and that there were no rights to make persons of 16 or 17 'the subjects of pornography'.

Inter-relationship with other offences

22.6 Section 1 (and CJA 1988, s 160) criminalises the making and possession of photographs of children. Indecent drawings and cartoons of children fall within Coroners and Justice Act 2009, ss 62–68, while written

---

10 [1988] 1 WLR 1098.
11 [2013] EWCA Crim 22.
12 See *R v Owen (Charles)* [1988] 1 WLR 134.
13 [2011] EWCA Crim 2752.

stories and descriptions may contravene the Obscene Publications Acts if they have a tendency to deprave and corrupt. Of the grey area between pseudo-images and cartoons, CPS guidelines state that 'if an image, if printed, would look like a photograph or a pseudo-photograph then it should be prosecuted as such'.

22.7

Statutory Defences and Exceptions

1. 'Marital' exemption (s 1A)

This applies only to images of children of 16 and 17 years of age.

In relation to an allegation under s 1(1)(a) – taking or permitting:

(i) the defendant must prove that the photograph in question was of the child aged 16 or over and that at the time of the taking or making of the photograph he and the child were married or living together as partners in an enduring family relationship.

(ii) the defendant must show that there is enough evidence to raise an issue as to whether the child consented to the photograph being taken or made, or as to whether the defendant reasonably believed that the child consented.

(iii) the photograph must not be one that shows a person other than the child and the defendant.

If any of these conditions is not satisfied, the prosecution need only prove the offence as set out in s 1(1)(a). But if the three conditions are satisfied, the defendant is not guilty of the offence unless the prosecution also prove that the child did not consent and that the defendant did not reasonably believe that the child consented.

In relation to an allegation under s 1(1)(b) – distributing or showing:

(i) the defendant must prove that the photograph in question was of the child aged 16 or over, and that either at the time of distributing or showing it, or at the time of obtaining it, he and the child were married or living together as partners in an enduring family relationship.

(ii) the photograph must not be one that shows a person other than the child and the defendant.

If either of these conditions is not satisfied, the prosecution need only prove the offence as set out in s 1(1)(b). But if both the conditions are satisfied, the defendant is not guilty of the offence unless the prosecution prove that the showing or distribution was to a person other than the child.

In relation to an allegation under s 1(1)(c) – possession with a view to distribution:

(i) the defendant must prove that the photograph in question was of the child aged 16 or over and that either at the time of his possession of it with a view to distributing or showing it, or at the time when he obtained it, he and the child were married or living together as partners in an enduring family relationship (s 1A(1) and (2)).

(ii) the defendant must show that there is enough evidence to raise an issue as to whether the child consented (or the defendant reasonably believed that the child consented) to the photograph's being in the defendant's possession, and also as to whether the defendant had the photograph in his possession with a view to distributing or showing it to a person other than the child (s 1A(6)).

(iii) the photograph must not be one that shows a person other than the child and the defendant.

If any of these conditions is not satisfied, the prosecution need only prove the offence as set out in s 1(1)(c). But if the three conditions are satisfied, the defendant is not guilty of the offence unless the prosecution also prove either that the child did not so consent and that the defendant did not reasonably believe that the child so consented, or that the defendant had the photograph in his possession with a view to its being distributed to a person other than the child.

2. Exemption for criminal investigations and proceedings (s 1B)

This section provides a defence to an allegation under s 1(1)(a) if the defendant can prove on the balance of probabilities that it was necessary to make the photograph for the prevention, detection or investigation of crime in any part of the world. It also applies to members of the Security Service, the Secret Intelligence Service or GCHQ, exercising the functions of their office. The *CPS and ACPO Memorandum of Understanding 2004*[14] provides information on the application of this section, particularly as it applies to individuals or organisations (including electronic communication providers) who discover unlawful activity.

(NB: the statutory exemption does not extend to defence lawyers, but see observations in *R v R(L) (Practice Note)*[15].)

3. Legitimate reason for distributing or showing (s 1(4))

This section provides a defence to allegations under s 1(1)(b) and (c) (showing and distributing/possessing with intent to show or distribute) where a defendant can prove on the balance of probabilities that he had legitimate reason for doing so. No definition is given for 'legitimate reason', but it is likely to include genuine

14 http://www.cps.gov.uk/publications/agencies/mouaccp.html
15 [2010] 2 Cr App R 9.

academic study or training for those working in the field of child abuse (but see *Atkins v DPP; Goodland v DPP*[16] – courts encouraged to view such claims with scepticism).

4. Lack of knowledge of indecent content (s **1(4)**)

This section provides a defence to allegations under s 1(1)(b) and (c) (showing and distributing/possessing with intent to show or distribute) where a defendant can prove on the balance of probabilities that he had not himself seen the images and did not know or have reason to suspect them to be indecent. The defence extends to persons who know they have pornographic material, but do not know or suspect that it contains images of children (*R v Collier*[17]).

DPP CONSENT

22.8 Proceedings under this section may not be instituted without consent of the Director of Public Prosecutions (s 1(3)).

CLASSIFICATION

22.9 Offence is triable either way.

SENTENCING AND OTHER ORDERS

Maximum sentence

22.10 On indictment: 10 years

Summarily: 6 months imprisonment or a fine not exceeding the statutory maximum (currently £5000) or both.

16 [2000] 2 Cr App R 248.
17 [2005] 1 WLR 843.

Sentencing guidelines

Determining the category

22.11

	Possession	**Distribution***	**Production****
Category A	• Possession of images involving penetrative sexual activity • Possession of images involving sexual activity with an animal or sadism	• Sharing images involving penetrative sexual activity • Sharing images involving sexual activity with an animal or sadism	• Creating images involving penetrative sexual activity • Creating images involving sexual activity with an animal or sadism
Category B	• Possession of images involving non-penetrative sexual activity	• Sharing images involving non-penetrative sexual activity	• Creating images involving non-penetrative sexual activity
Category C	• Possession of other indecent images not falling within categories A or B	• Sharing other indecent images not falling within categories A or B	• Creating other indecent images not falling within categories A or B

* Distribution includes possession with a view to distributing or sharing images.

** Production includes the taking or making of any image at source, for instance the original image. Making an image by simple downloading should be treated as possession for the purposes of sentencing.

In most cases the intrinsic character of the most serious of the offending images will initially determine the appropriate category. If, however, the most serious images are unrepresentative of the offender's conduct a lower category may be appropriate. A lower category will not, however, be appropriate if the offender has produced or taken (for example photographed) images of a higher category.

Starting point and category range

22.12

	Possession	Distribution	Production
Category A	SP: 1 yr custody Range: 26 wks–3 yrs custody	SP: 3 yrs custody Range: 2–5 yrs custody	SP: 6 yrs custody Range: 4–9 yrs custody
Category B	SP: 26 wks custody Range: High level comm. order–18 mths custody	SP: 1 yr custody Range: 26 wks–2 yrs custody	SP: 2 yrs custody Range: 1–4 yrs custody
Category C	SP: High level comm. order Range: Medium level comm. order–26 wks custody	SP: 13 wks custody Range: High level community order–26 wks custody	SP: 18 mths custody Range: 1–3 yrs custody

Additional factual elements

22.13

Aggravating factors
Statutory aggravating factors
• Previous convictions, having regard to a) the nature of the offence to which the conviction relates and its relevance to the current offence; and b) the time that has elapsed since the conviction • Offence committed whilst on bail
Other aggravating factors • Failure to comply with current court orders • Offence committed whilst on licence • Age and/or vulnerability of the child depicted* • Discernable pain or distress suffered by child depicted • Period over which images were possessed, distributed or produced • High volume of images possessed, distributed or produced

- Placing images where there is the potential for a high volume of viewers
- Collection includes moving images
- Attempts to dispose of or conceal evidence
- Abuse of trust
- Child depicted known to the offender
- Active involvement in a network or process that facilitates or commissions the creation or sharing of indecent images of children
- Commercial exploitation and/or motivation
- Deliberate or systematic searching for images portraying young children, category A images or the portrayal of familial sexual abuse
- Large number of different victims
- Child depicted intoxicated or drugged

Mitigating factors

- No previous convictions or no relevant/recent convictions
- Remorse
- Previous good character and/or exemplary conduct**
- Age and/or lack of maturity where it affects the responsibility of the offender
- Mental disorder or learning disability, particularly where linked to the commission of the offence
- Demonstration of steps taken to address offending behaviour

* Age and/or vulnerability of the child should be given significant weight. In cases where the actual age of the victim is difficult to determine, sentencers should consider the development of the child (infant, pre-pubescent, post-pubescent).

** Previous good character/exemplary conduct is different from having no previous convictions. The more serious the offence, the less the weight which should normally be attributed to this factor. Where previous good character/exemplary conduct has been used to facilitate the offence, this mitigation should not normally be allowed and such conduct may constitute an aggravating factor.

Other orders

22.14

Extended sentence availability (CJA 2003)	Sch 15: yes Sch 15B: yes
Trigger offence for:	SOPO: yes FTO: yes, if the photographs/pseudo-photographs showed persons under 16 and D was over 18, *or* is sentenced to at least 12 months
Inclusion in barred lists	Children: subject to representations Vulnerable adult: subject to representations
Notification	Yes, if the photographs/pseudo-photographs showed persons under 16 *and* D was over 18, *or* is sentenced to at least 12 months
Forfeiture of indecent materials	May be made in the usual way following conviction under PCC(S)A 2000, s 143 (which allows seizure of property used in the commission of the offence, ie computers) or under the Schedule to the PCA 1978 (which allows for forfeiture of the photographs themselves). The latter allows for forfeiture in cases where the prosecution is discontinued, the defendant cautioned or acquitted, so long as the magistrates find that the materials were indecent.

PRACTITIONER POINTERS

DEF – when advising suspects at the police station, note the tendency of police to regard all 'suspicious' images as indecent. Naked photographs and images from medical texts are unlikely to be indecent, and the suspect's motives for being in possession of them do not make them so.

From a practical point of view, the fact of indecency or level is rarely an issue at trial. It is often sensible to try to agree these elements. If they cannot be agreed, then the jury have to make the assessment, and that involves showing the images to the jury. This approach is rarely helpful to a defendant.

Notwithstanding this, where the images involve unidentified models in their teens, it is often necessary to challenge the question of whether the prosecution can in fact show that the subject is under 18. It may be possible to obtain classification material from the film makers (see discussion at **Chapter 38**).

Possession of indecent photographs of children Criminal Justice Act 1988, s 160

DEFINITION

22.15 Section 160(1):

It is an offence for a person to have any indecent photograph or pseudo-photograph of a child in his possession.

SUMMARY

22.16 Subject to the statutory defences listed below the offence is committed by a person having indecent photographs or pseudo-photographs of persons under 18 years of age in their possession.

ELEMENTS

22.17

- *Possession* involves the knowing assumption of custody or control. Whether files which have been deleted from a computer remain in the owner's custody or control depends on whether they can be retrieved. This is a question of fact for the jury to determine looking at all the circumstances, including whether the defendant has the skills and the software to retrieve the files.[18]
- *Photograph* includes a film, a copy of a photograph or film, a photograph comprised in a film, a negative of a photograph and data stored on a computer disc or other electronic means capable of being converted into a photograph. It also includes a 'tracing', ie a photograph which has been converted either manually or by electronic means into a cartoon or graphic image (s 160(4) incorporating PCA 1978, s 7).
- *Pseudo-photograph* is an image which appears to be a photograph. For these purposes it will often be an amalgam of a photograph of an adult and a photograph of a child (ie a child's face 'grafted' onto an adult's body, or vice versa) (s 160(4)).
- *Indecent photograph*. It is for the jury to consider whether the photograph itself is indecent, irrespective of the motives or intentions of the possessor

18 *R v Porter* [2006] EWCA Crim 560. In practice, it is unlikely that an 'ordinary' computer user will have such skills or software.

or maker of the photograph.[19] The test is an objective one, applying the recognised standards of propriety.[20]

- *Child* means a person under the age of 18.[21] In the case of a pseudo-photograph, if the predominant impression is that of a child, it is to be treated as being an image of a child (s 160(4)). The court must look at the 'evidence as a whole' to ascertain whether the image is of a person under the age of 18 (s 160(4)) and this is a question of fact for the tribunal, expert evidence (for instance, from a paediatrician) being inadmissible.[22]
- Mental element: the defendant must have knowledge that he is in possession of the subject material. If he knows he has indecent material, but not that it contains images of children, he may be able to avail himself of the defence in s 160(2)(b). However, it will be no defence that he believed the subjects of the photographs to be over 18, if they are held not to be. Material automatically 'cached' to a defendant's hard drive without his knowledge (even if he had previously viewed the image) does not remain in his possession.[23]

DISCUSSION

22.18 See **22.4** for discussion of indecency.

Inter-relationship with other offences

22.19 Since downloading and opening internet images equates to 'making' for the purposes of PCA 1978, s 1(1), CJA 1988, s 160 has become somewhat otiose for the prosecution of offenders viewing material on their own computers for their own purposes. The s 1(1) charge is often preferred by prosecutors since it does not allow the defendant the defence that he had deleted it and thus put it out of his possession (the *Porter* defence). It allows a defendant to be charged where the images have been deleted, and are found in unallocated clusters. Strictly, though simple presence on the hard drive should not be enough to found a case against a defendant as one of the issues with deleted files is that they do not have file attributes by which the date of creation or download can be ascertained.

See **22.6** for discussion of this offence and its relationship with 'prohibited images', Coroners and Justice Act, s 62.

19 See *R v Graham-Kerr* [1988] 1 WLR 1098.

20 *R v Stamford* [1972] 2 QB 391.

21 Raised from 16 years by SOA 2003, s 45(2) with effect from 1 May 2004.

22 *R v Land* [1998] 1 Cr App R 272.

23 *Atkins v DPP* [2000] 2 Cr App R 248.

22.20

Statutory Defences and Exceptions

1. Marital exemption (s 160A)

This applies only to images of children of 16 and 17 years of age.

(i) the defendant must prove that the photograph in question was of the child aged 16 or over and that at the time when he possessed the photograph, or at the time when he obtained it, he and the child were married or living together as partners in an enduring family relationship.

(ii) the defendant must show that there is enough evidence to raise an issue as to whether the child consented to the photograph being in his possession or as to whether the defendant reasonably believed that the child so consented.

(iii) the photograph must not be one that shows a person other than the child and the defendant.

If any of these conditions is not satisfied, the prosecution need only prove the offence as set out in s 160. But if the three conditions are satisfied, the defendant is not guilty of the offence unless the prosecution prove that the child did not consent and that the defendant did not reasonably believe that the child consented.

2. Legitimate reason for possession (s 160(2)(a))

This section provides a defence to an allegation of possession where a defendant can prove on the balance of probabilities that he had legitimate reason for having the image in his possession. No definition is given for 'legitimate reason', but it is likely to include genuine academic study or training for those working in the field of child abuse (but see *Atkins v DPP*; *Goodland v DPP*[24] – courts encouraged to view such claims with scepticism).

3. Lack of knowledge of indecent content (s 160(2)(b))

This section provides a defence to an allegation of possession where a defendant can prove on the balance of probabilities that he had not himself seen the images and did not know or have reason to suspect them to be indecent. The defence extends to persons who know they have pornographic material, but do not know or suspect that it contains images of children (*R v Collier*[25]).

24 [2000] 2 Cr App R 248.
25 [2005] 1 WLR 843.

4. Unsolicited photographs (s 160(2)(c))

This section provides a defence to an allegation of possession where a defendant can prove on the balance of probabilities that the images were sent to him unsolicited and he did not keep them for an unreasonable time. No definition is given of what amounts to a 'reasonable time'.

DPP CONSENT

22.21 Proceedings under this section may not be instituted without consent of the Director of Public Prosecutions (s 160(4)).

CLASSIFICATION

22.22 Offence is triable either way.

SENTENCING AND OTHER ORDERS

Maximum sentence

22.23 On indictment: 5 years

Summarily: 6 months imprisonment or a fine not exceeding the statutory maximum (currently £5000) or both.

Sentencing guidelines

22.24 Identical to guidelines for 'Taking or making indecent photographs of children'; see **22.11–22.13**. But note that categories for distribution or production will not be relevant to this offence.

Other orders

22.25

Extended and life sentence availability (CJA 2003)	Sch 15 (specified offence): yes Sch 15B (life sentence for second listed offence): no
Trigger offence for:	SOPO: yes FTO: yes, if the photographs/pseudo-photographs showed persons under 16 *and* D was over 18, *or* is sentenced to at least 12 months
Inclusion in barred lists	Children: subject to representations Vulnerable adult: subject to representations
Notification	Yes, if the photographs/pseudo-photographs showed persons under 16 *and* D was over 18, *or* is sentenced to at least 12 months
Forfeiture of indecent materials	May be made in the usual way following conviction under PCC(S)A 2000, s 143 (which allows seizure of property used in the commission of the offence, ie computers).

Chapter 23

Child abduction

Child Abduction Act 1984, s 2

DEFINITION

23.1 Section 2:

(1) a person, other than one mentioned in subsection (2) below, commits an offence if, without lawful authority or reasonable excuse, he takes or detains a child under the age of sixteen—

(a) so as to remove him from the lawful control of any person having lawful control of the child; or

(b) so as to keep him out of the lawful control of any person entitled to lawful control of the child.

(2) The persons are—

(a) where the father and mother of the child in question were married to each other at the time of his birth, the child's father and mother;

(b) where the father and mother of the child in question were not married to each other at the time of his birth, the child's mother; and

(c) any other person mentioned in section 1(2)(c) to (e).[1]

ELEMENTS

23.2

- *Taking* includes causing or inducing the child to accompany the defendant or any other person or causing the child to be taken (s 3(a)). It is not

---

1 This includes the child's guardian, or a person with custody of the child or in whose favour a residence order has been made.

necessary that the child be physically moved any significant distance – 'deflecting' him or her from what he would otherwise be doing without parental consent would be sufficient for the offence to be made out.[2]

- *Detaining* includes causing the child to be detained or inducing the child to remain with the defendant or any other person (s 3(c)).
- The fact that the child themselves may consent to the taking or detaining is irrelevant to the commission of the offence.
- Examples of *lawful authority* might be detention pursuant to a sentence or bail decision passed by a court or in pursuance of a power of arrest or the removal of a child to local authority care, a place of safety or immigration detention.
- *Reasonable excuse*: the defendant's conduct may reasonably excused if it appears that he has made an honest mistake, for instance in relation to the child's circumstances; or that she genuinely believed that the child taken or detained was her son or daughter.[3] In addition, the defendant's conduct is reasonably excused if he or she had a 'good motive' for the conduct, such as to protect the child from harm.
- *Mental element*: 'an intentional or reckless taking or detention of a child under the age of 16, the effect or objective consequence of which is to remove or to keep that child within the meaning of s 2(1)(a) or (b)'.[4] The defendant need not intend to remove or keep the child from lawful control, nor need he even have known that another person had or was entitled to such control.

DISCUSSION

23.3 Depending on the specific facts alleged there may be considerable overlap between this offence and a variety of other sexual and non-sexual offences, for instance false imprisonment and kidnapping (where a degree of force or a lack of consent or presumed consent is likely to be present) or meeting a child following sexual grooming (SOA 2003, s 15) where the 'meeting' may encompass a 'taking' sufficient to constitute an offence under CAA 1984. Abduction may be the preparatory offence necessary to constitute an offence under SOA 2003, s 62 (committing an offence with intent to commit a sexual offence).

In practice, despite the variety of offending envisaged by the 2003 Act, the offence of abduction may still be useful where the defendant's acts, while

2 *R v Leather* (1994) 98 Cr App R 179.
3 *R v Berry* [1996] 2 Cr App R 226.
4 *R v Leather* (1994) 98 Cr App R 179.

highly suspicious, are nevertheless not provably sexual in nature or intent – for instance, deceiving a child into accompanying the defendant.

On trial by indictment the defendant may be convicted in the alternative of common assault if the facts allow this.

23.4

Statutory Defences

Paternity (s 2(3)(a))

This section provides a defence to a man charged under section 2 where he can prove that he is the child's father or that, at the time of the alleged offence, he believed, on reasonable grounds, that he was the child's father. It applies where the father and mother of the child in question were not married to each other at the time of the child's birth.

Belief aged 16 or over (s 2(3)(b))

This section provides a defence to a person charged under section 2 if he (or she) can prove that, at the time of the alleged offence, he believed that the child had attained the age of 16.

DPP CONSENT

23.5 Proceedings under this section may not be instituted without consent of the Director of Public Prosecutions.

CLASSIFICATION

23.6 Offence is triable either way.

SENTENCING AND OTHER ORDERS

Maximum sentence

23.7 On indictment: 7 years

Summarily: 6 months imprisonment or a fine not exceeding the statutory maximum (currently £5000) or both.

Sentencing guidelines and factors

23.8 There are no sentencing guidelines for this offence

23.8 *Child abduction*

For sentencing authorities in cases where there appears to have been a sexual motive to the abduction, see:

- *R v Dean*:[5] Five years upheld after trial for defendant who attempted to abduct a four-year-old boy. Previous conviction for indecency relating to young boys
- *R v Bailey (William)*:[6] appellant with previous convictions for offences against children, including abduction, judged to be high risk and likely to reoffend. Five years not excessive for asking an eight year old to go with him
- *R v Delaney*:[7] Four years not manifestly excessive for attempted abduction of 13-year-old girl with some force, by a man of good character

Other orders

23.9

Extended and life sentence availability (CJA 2003)	Sch 15 (specified offence): no Sch 15B (life sentence for second listed offence): no
Trigger offence for:	SOPO: yes (Sch 5 offence) FTO: no
Inclusion in barred lists	Children: subject to representations Vulnerable adult: subject to representations
Notification	No

5 [2000] 2 Cr App R (S) 253.
6 [2004] EWCA Crim 3058.
7 [2007] 1 Cr App R (S) 93.

Chapter 24

Prostitution

Keeping a brothel
Sexual Offences Act 1956, s 33

DEFINITION

24.1 Section 33:

It is an offence for a person to keep a brothel, or to manage, or act or assist in the management of, a brothel.

ELEMENTS

24.2

- See **Chapter 6** for the definition of a *brothel* and the inter-relationship between this offence and s 33A.
- *Managing* a brothel requires some evidence indicating the taking of an active part in the running of the business, something suggesting control. There must be something more than the purely menial or routine duties such as cleaning the stairs or answering the door.[1]
- Whether a person is '*managing*' or '*assisting in the management* will be a question of fact and degree. A distinction arises between assisting the management and assisting *in* the management of a brothel. For the offender to assist in the management of premises they must perform acts such as negotiating and receiving payment, which are considerably beyond the menial tasks, such as cleaning and removing rubbish from the premises, which could be done without taking part in the management, so would be merely acts of assisting the managers of the premises.[2]

---

1 *Abbott v Smith* (1965) 2 QB 662.
2 *Dublides v DPP*, *The Times*, January 19, 1989, DC.

A prostitute working in a brothel may be convicted of managing or assisting if her activities go beyond the mere provision of sexual services, which in itself would not fall within s 33.

- *Mental element*: Knowledge or belief that the premises are being used by more than one prostitute for the purposes of prostitution (or some other act of 'fornication').

DEFENCES

24.3 Premises were not being used as a brothel (eg no evidence that two or more persons are involved in sexual activity, either at the same time or consecutively).

Defendant's role was insufficient to be classed as 'assisting in the management (eg working as a cleaner or 'maid' with no or limited role in making bookings, fixing prices, taking money or arranging services).

Defendant did not know that sexual activity was taking place on the premises (eg, defendant thought that the premises were a legitimate massage parlour and further sexual services were offered without his/her knowledge).

CLASSIFICATION

24.4 Offence is summary only.

SENTENCING AND OTHER ORDERS

Maximum sentence

24.5 For a first conviction: 3 months and/or a fine not exceeding level 3 (currently £1000)

For a second or subsequent conviction: 6 months and/or a fine not exceeding level 4 (currently £2500)[3].

Sentencing guidelines

24.6 There are no sentencing guidelines for this offence.

---

3 A conviction under SOA 1956, s 34, 35 or 36 is a conviction for these purposes.

Other orders

24.7

Extended and life sentence availability (CJA 2003)	Sch 15 (specified offence): yes *(probable drafting error)* Sch 15B (life sentence for second listed offence): no
Trigger offence for:	SOPO: no FTO: no
Inclusion in barred lists	Children: no Vulnerable adult: no
Notification	No
Confiscation	This is a lifestyle offence within Proceeds of Crime Act 2002, Sch 2

PRACTITIONER POINTERS

The evidence of 'test purchase' police officers is frequently deployed to prove that premises are being used as a brothel. The Crown is likely to apply for anonymity for these witnesses. Their conversations with women working in the premises (who may be neither defendants nor prosecution witnesses) go to show that offers of sexual services were made and are not hearsay for this purpose.

Massage parlours or escort agencies often operate openly for many years, and are tolerated by the authorities in the absence of concomitant criminal activity or public nuisance. A sudden change of policy and a prosecution may give rise to an argument that the prosecution be stayed as an abuse, particularly if the police (in the form of liaison officers) have given any indication of tacit approval. Even if unsuccessful, such arguments may lay the ground for significant mitigation.

Quantities of cash may be found in premises raided by police and seized under the provisions of the Proceeds of Crime Act 2002, s 294. Forfeiture is dependent on the court being satisfied that the money derived from unlawful conduct or was intended for an unlawful purpose. Where the money derived from prostitution (not a criminal activity), the test is unlikely to be met; where from brothel management, forfeiture is likely.

Unusually, this is an area of sexual offences where confiscation is a very live issue and practitioners should have this in mind from the start. Note that this will only apply in the Crown Court and thus to s 33A allegations only (see **24.8**).

Keeping a brothel used for prostitution Sexual Offences Act 1956, s 33A

(inserted by Sexual Offences Act 2003, s 55)

DEFINITION

24.8 Section 33A:

It is an offence for a person to keep, or to manage, or act or assist in the management of, a brothel to which people resort for practices involving prostitution (whether or not also for other practices).

ELEMENTS

24.9

- See **Chapter 6** for the definition of a *brothel* and the inter-relationship between this offence and s 33.
- See **Chapter 6** for the definition of *prostitution.*
- *Managing* a brothel requires some evidence indicating the taking of an active part in the running of the business, something suggesting control. There must be something more than the purely menial or routine duties such as cleaning the stairs or answering the door.[4]
- Whether a person is '*managing*' or '*assisting in the management*' will be a question of fact and degree. A distinction arises between assisting the management and assisting *in* the management of a brothel. For the offender to assist in the management of premises they must perform acts such as negotiating and receiving payment, which are considerably beyond the menial tasks, such as cleaning and removing rubbish from the premises, which could be done without taking part in the management, so would be merely acts of assisting the managers of the premises.[5]

  A prostitute working in a brothel may be convicted of managing or assisting if her activities go beyond the mere provision of sexual services, which in itself would not fall within s 33A.
- *Mental element*: Knowledge or belief that the premises are being used by more than one prostitute for the purposes of prostitution.

---

4 *Abbott v Smith* (1965) 2 QB 662.
5 *Dublides v DPP*, *The Times*, 19 January 1989, DC.

DEFENCES

24.10 Premises were not being used as a brothel (eg no evidence that two or more persons were working as prostitutes, either at the same time or consecutively).

Defendant's role was insufficient to be classed as 'assisting in the management (eg working as a cleaner or 'maid' with no or limited role in making bookings, fixing prices, taking money or arranging services).

Defendant did not know that prostitution was taking place on the premises (eg defendant thought that the premises were a legitimate massage parlour and further sexual services were being offered without his/her knowledge).

CLASSIFICATION

24.11 Offence is triable either way.

SENTENCING AND OTHER ORDERS

Maximum sentence

24.12 On indictment: 7 years

Summarily: 6 months or a fine not exceeding the statutory maximum (currently £5,000)

Sentencing guidelines

Determining the category

24.13

Cat	Harm	Cat	Culpability
1	• Under 18 year olds working in brothel	A	• Keeping brothel on significant commercial basis
	• Abduction/detention		• Involvement in keeping a number of brothels
	• Violence or threats of violence		• Expectation of significant financial or other gain
	• Sustained and systematic psychological abuse		• Abuse of trust

24.13 *Prostitution*

Cat	Harm	Cat	Culpability
	• Those working in brothel forced or coerced to participate in unsafe/degrading sexual activity • Those working in brothel forced or coerced into seeing many 'customers' • Established evidence of community impact		• Exploitation of those known to be trafficked • Significant involvement in limiting the freedom of those working in brothel • Grooming of a person to work in the brothel including through cultivation of a dependency on drugs or alcohol
		B	• Keeping/managing premises • Close involvement with those working in brothel, for example control of finances, choice of clients, working conditions, etc (where offender's involvement is not as a result of coercion)
2	Factor(s) in category 1 not present	C	• Performs limited function under direction • Close involvement but engaged by coercion/intimidation/exploitation

Starting point and category range

24.14

Cat	A	B	C
1	Starting point: 5 yrs custody Range: 3–6 yrs custody	Starting point: 3 yrs custody Range: 2–5 yrs custody	Starting point: 1 yr custody Range: High level community order–18 mths custody

Cat	A	B	C
2	Starting point: 3 yrs custody Range: 2–5 yrs custody	Starting point: 12 mths custody Range: 26 wks–2 yrs custody	Starting point: Medium level community order Range: Low level community order–High level community order

Additional factual elements

24.15

Aggravating factors
Statutory aggravating factors
• Previous convictions, having regard to a) the nature of the offence to which the conviction relates and its relevance to the current offence; and b) the time that has elapsed since the conviction • Offence committed whilst on bail
Other aggravating factors
• Failure to comply with current court orders • Offence committed whilst on licence • Deliberate isolation of those working in brothel • Threats made to expose those working in brothel to the authorities (for example, immigration or police), family/friends or others • Harm threatened against the family/friends of those working in brothel • Passport/identity documents removed • Those working in brothel prevented from seeking medical treatment • Food withheld • Those working in brothel passed around by offender and moved to other brothels • Earnings of those working in brothel withheld/kept by offender or evidence of excessive wage reduction or debt bondage, inflated travel or living expenses or unreasonable interest rates • Any steps taken to prevent those working in brothel reporting an incident, obtaining assistance and/or from assisting or supporting the prosecution • Attempts to dispose of or conceal evidence

• Those working in brothel forced or coerced into pornography
• Timescale over which the operation has been run
Mitigating factors
• No previous convictions or no relevant/recent convictions
• Remorse
• Previous good character and/or exemplary conduct*
• Age and/or lack of maturity where it affects the responsibility of the offender
• Mental disorder or learning disability, particularly where linked to the commission of the offence
• Demonstration of steps taken to address offending behaviour

* Previous good character/exemplary conduct is different from having no previous convictions. The more serious the offence, the less the weight which should normally be attributed to this factor. Where previous good character/exemplary conduct has been used to facilitate the offence, this mitigation should not normally be allowed and such conduct may constitute an aggravating factor.

Other orders

24.16

Extended and life sentence availability (CJA 2003)	Sch 15 (specified offence): no (Sch 15 refers to s 33, not s 33A) Sch 15B (life sentence for second listed offence): no
Trigger offence for:	SOPO: no FTO: no
Inclusion in barred lists	Children: no Vulnerable adult: no
Notification	No
Confiscation	This is a lifestyle offence within Proceeds of Crime Act 2002, Sch 2

PRACTITIONER POINTERS

The evidence of 'test purchase' police officers is frequently deployed to prove that premises are being used as a brothel. The Crown is likely to apply for anonymity for these witnesses. Their conversations with women working in the premises (who may be neither defendants nor prosecution witnesses) go to show that offers of sexual services were made and are not hearsay for this purpose.

Massage parlours or escort agencies often operate openly for many years, and are tolerated by the authorities in the absence of concomitant criminal activity or public nuisance. A sudden change of policy and a prosecution may give rise to an argument that the prosecution be stayed as an abuse, particularly if the police (in the form of liaison officers) have given any indication of tacit approval. Even if unsuccessful, such arguments may lay the ground for significant mitigation.

Quantities of cash may be found in premises raided by police and seized under the provisions of the Proceeds of Crime Act 2002, s 294. Forfeiture is dependent on the court being satisfied that the money derived from unlawful conduct or was intended for an unlawful purpose. Where the money derived from prostitution (not a criminal activity), the test is unlikely to be met; where from brothel management, forfeiture is likely.

Unusually, this is an area of sexual offences where confiscation is a very live issue and practitioners should have this in mind from the start. Note that this will only apply in the Crown Court.

Landlord letting premises for use as brothel Sexual Offences Act 1956, s 34

DEFINITION

24.17 Section 34:

> It is an offence for the lessor or landlord of any premises or his agent to let the whole or part of the premises with the knowledge that it is to be used, in whole or in part, as a brothel, or, where the whole or part of the premises is used as a brothel, to be wilfully a party to that use continuing.

SUMMARY

24.18 The offence is committed by a person who lets premises knowing that they are to be used as a brothel or, having let the premises, is a wilful party to their continuing use as a brothel.

ELEMENTS

24.19

- See Chapter 6 for the definition of a *brothel.*
- A landlord's *agent* may include an estate or lettings agent employed to let a flat or a porter with control over the premises.
- *Willfully* being *a party* to continued use implies that some positive action is required by the landlord and that mere acquiescence in the situation is insufficient.[6]
- *Mental element*: Both limbs of the offence would seem to require actual knowledge – either that the intention is to use the premises as a brothel, or that the premises are being used as a brothel. It is questionable whether suspicion of the motives of the tenant or the activities at the premises would be sufficient.

DISCUSSION

24.20 Sections 34 to 36 provide interlocking offences of similar gravity designed to be used against those who, while not necessarily involved in prostitution themselves, assist or profit by providing premises where the activities can take place.

Where a person is a tenant who sub-lets there would appear to be the possibility of charging under either s 34 or 35, although the former is the appropriate charge where the defendant is not resident at the premises.

CLASSIFICATION

24.21 Offence is summary only.

SENTENCING AND OTHER ORDERS

Maximum sentence

24.22 For a first conviction: 3 months and/or a fine not exceeding level 3 (currently £1000)

6 View expressed in Stones' Justices' Manual.

For a second or subsequent conviction: 6 months and/or a fine not exceeding level 4 (currently £2500)[7].

Sentencing guidelines

24.23 There are no sentencing guidelines for this offence.

Other orders

24.24

Extended and life sentence availability (CJA 2003)	Sch 15 (specified offence): no Sch 15B (life sentence for second listed offence): no
Trigger offence for:	SOPO: no FTO: no
Inclusion in barred lists	Children: no Vulnerable adult: no
Notification	No
Confiscation	This is a lifestyle offence within Proceeds of Crime Act 2002, Sch 2

Tenant permitting premises to be used as brothel Sexual Offences Act 1956, s 35

DEFINITION

24.25 Section 35:

> It is an offence for the tenant or occupier, or person in charge, of any premises knowingly to permit the whole or part of the premises to be used as a brothel.

ELEMENTS

24.26

- See **Chapter 6** for the definition of a *brothel*.

---

7 A conviction under SOA 1956, s 34, 35 or 36 is a conviction for these purposes.

- *Tenant* does not include a lessee who sublets the whole of the property without themselves remaining in occupation[8] (however, they would then be likely to be a lessor themselves and fall within s 34).
- The term *occupier* includes those who have no formal tenancy, but would include a licencee or squatter.
- *Mental element*: The offence requires actual knowledge that the premises are being or are to be used as a brothel.

DISCUSSION

24.27 Sections 34 to 36 provide interlocking offences of similar gravity designed to be used against those who, while not necessarily involved in prostitution themselves, assist or profit by providing premises where the activities can take place.

In current practice, there seems little necessity for separate offences to combat brothels and prostitution and s 35 would appear to be almost entirely subsumed within s 36 (the difference being that it is not necessary for commercial sex to take place in order to establish a brothel).

Where a person is a tenant who sub-lets there would appear to be the possibility of charging under either ss 34 or 35, although the former is the appropriate charge where the defendant is not resident at the premises.

CLASSIFICATION

24.28 Offence is summary only.

SENTENCING AND OTHER ORDERS

Maximum sentence

24.29 For a first conviction: 3 months and/or a fine not exceeding level 3 (currently £1000)

For a second or subsequent conviction: 6 months and/or a fine not exceeding level 4 (currently £2500)[9].

---

8 *Siviour v Napolitano* [1931] 1 KB 636.

9 A conviction under SOA 1956, s 34, 35 or 36 is a conviction for these purposes.

Sentencing guidelines

24.30 There are no sentencing guidelines for this offence

Other orders

24.31

Extended and life sentence availability (CJA 2003)	Sch 15 (specified offence): no Sch 15B (life sentence for second listed offence): no
Trigger offence for:	SOPO: no FTO: no
Inclusion in barred lists	Children: no Vulnerable adult: no
Notification	No

PRACTITIONER POINTER

By virtue of s 35(2), a conviction of a tenant or occupier for this offence triggers certain rights exercisable by the landlord to require the tenant to assign the lease to another person and, if he fails to do so, the landlord may determine the lease.

If the landlord fails to exercise this right, he may become party to a subsequent section 35 offence committed at the premises (s 35(3)).

Tenant permitting premises to be used for prostitution Sexual Offences Act 1956, s 36

DEFINITION

24.32 Section 36:

It is an offence for the tenant or occupier of any premises knowingly to permit the whole or part of the premises to be used for the purposes of habitual prostitution whether any prostitute involved is male or female.

ELEMENTS

24.33

- *Tenant* does not include a lessee who sublets the whole of the property without themselves remaining in occupation[10] (however, they would then be likely to be a lessor themselves and fall within s 34).
- The term *occupier* includes those who have no formal tenancy, but would include a licencee or squatter.
- *Permit* implies a permission given by the tenant or occupier to another person. A person who was working alone from premises would not be permitting herself to use the premises for prostitution.[11]
- *Habitual prostitution*: prostitution was not defined in the 1956 Act. Section 51 of the 2003 SOA provides a definition (see **Chapter 6** of this work) which is specifically reserved as the correct definition for prostitution under s 33A of the 1956 Act. While no specific reference is made to s 36, it is suggested that this is the appropriate definition. 'Habitual' implies repeated and frequent activity or behaviour established by long use.
- By virtue of amendments made in s 56 of and Sch 1 to SOA 2003, the prostitutes at the premises may be male or female.
- *Mental element*: The offence requires actual knowledge that the premises are being used for prostitution.

DISCUSSION

24.34 Sections 34 to 36 provide interlocking offences of similar gravity designed to be used against those who, while not necessarily involved in prostitution themselves, assist or profit by providing premises where the activities can take place.

In current practice, there seems little necessity for separate offences to combat brothels and prostitution and s 35 would appear to be almost entirely subsumed within s 36 (the difference being that it is not necessary for commercial sex to take place in order to establish a brothel).

Where a person is a tenant who sub-lets there would appear to be the possibility of charging under either ss 34 or 35, although the former is the appropriate charge where the defendant is not resident at the premises.

---

10 *Siviour v Napolitano* [1931] 1 KB 636.
11 *Mattison v Johnson* (1916) 80 JP 243.

CLASSIFICATION

24.35 Offence is summary only.

SENTENCING AND OTHER ORDERS

Maximum sentence

24.36 For a first conviction: 3 months and/or a fine not exceeding level 3 (currently £1000).

For a second or subsequent conviction: 6 months and/or a fine not exceeding level 4 (currently £2500)[12].

Sentencing guidelines

24.37 There are no sentencing guidelines for this offence

Other orders

24.38

Extended and life sentence availability (CJA 2003)	Sch 15 (specified offence): no Sch 15B (life sentence for second listed offence): no
Trigger offence for:	SOPO: no FTO: no
Inclusion in barred lists	Children: no Vulnerable adult: no
Notification	No

Keeping a disorderly house
Common law

DEFINITION

24.39 There is no statutory definition.

12 A conviction under SOA 1956, ss 34, 35 or 36 is a conviction for these purposes.

ELEMENTS

24.40

- A *disorderly house* is a place not regulated by the restraints of morality and which is so conducted as to violate law and good order.[13] It is not necessary that criminal behaviour or illegal activity take place on the premises. To violate good order there must be some element of 'open house' – purely private activities would appear to be exempt.
- *Keeping* requires some element of persistence or regularity in the disorderly activity – disorder occurring on one occasion only will be insufficient to meet the definition.[14] A 'keeper' suggests an element of control – being a landlord is arguably not enough if no control exercised.
- *Mental element*: the person keeping the house must have knowledge of the behaviour occurring in the premises.[15]

DISCUSSION

24.41 Conduct meeting the criterion for a disorderly house may or may not be sexual in nature. Within the context of this work, brothels, dungeons, peep shows and performances and shows of a sexual nature (either commercial or artistic) may fall within the ambit this archaic and imprecisely defined offence. In *R v Tan*[16] the appellants had been operating dungeons for the provision of sado-masochistic sexual services (without intercourse). The fact that they advertised their services met the requirement that the premises be open to the public, although the activities themselves were purely 'one-on-one'. The jury would need to find that the activities outraged public decency or injured the public interest to such an extent that condemnation and punishment were called for. In 1983, the Court of Appeal clearly felt that such 'perverted and revolting practices' fitted the bill.

While possible that a single prostitute operating alone from premises might be said to be keeping a disorderly house, it is unlikely that the necessary level of injury to the public interest or decency would be met by the provision of straightforward sexual services.[17]

---

13 *R v Berg* (1927) 20 Cr App R 38.
14 *Moores v DPP* [1992] 94 Cr App R 173.
15 *Moores v DPP* [1992] 94 Cr App R 173.
16 *R v Tan & Others* [1983] QB 1053.
17 Cf *R v Court; R v Gu* [2012] EWCA Crim 133 where 'normal sexual intercourse' was provided to individual customers, this did not fall within the scope of the common law offence.

Inter-relationship with other offences

24.42 Where two or more prostitutes are operating from the same premises, this will constitute a brothel (see Chapter 6) and those who keep it will fall within the provisions of s 33 or 33A Sexual Offences Act 1956 (see **24.1** and **24.8**).

The activity taking place within the premises may amount to acts outraging public decency (see **25.1**).

CLASSIFICATION

24.43 Offence is triable on indictment.

SENTENCING AND OTHER ORDERS

Maximum sentence

24.44 A fine or imprisonment, or both. There is no maximum punishment, but the sentence imposed must not be inordinate.

Sentencing guidelines

24.45 There are no sentencing guidelines for this offence. However, if the offence relates to commercial sexual activity, guidelines relating to brothels and controlling prostitution may be of relevance.

Other orders

24.46

Extended and life sentence availability (CJA 2003)	Sch 15 (specified offence): no Sch 15B (life sentence for second listed offence): no
Trigger offence for:	SOPO: no FTO: no
Inclusion in barred lists	Children: no Vulnerable adult: no
Notification	No

Allowing persons under 16 to be in brothels Children & Young Persons Act 1933, s 3(1)

DEFINITION

24.47 Section 3(1):

> If any person having the responsibility for a child or young person who has attained the age of four years and is under the age of sixteen years, allows that child or young person to reside in or to frequent a brothel … he shall commit an offence.

SUMMARY

24.48 The offence is committed by a person with responsibility for a child and who allows him or her to reside in or frequent a brothel.

ELEMENTS

24.49

- *Responsibility for*: defined by the Children and Young Persons Act 1933, s 17 as a person who has parental responsibility for, is legally liable for, or has care of, a child.
- See **Chapter 6** for the definition of a *brothel.*
- See **Chapter 7** for discussion of age.

CLASSIFICATION

24.50 Offence is summary only.

SENTENCING AND OTHER ORDERS

Maximum sentence

24.51 6 months imprisonment or a fine not exceeding level 2 on the standard scale (currently £500)

Sentencing guidelines

24.52 There are no sentencing guidelines for this offence

Other orders

24.53

Extended and life sentence availability (CJA 2003)	Sch 15 (specified offence): no Sch 15B (life sentence for second listed offence): no
Trigger offence for:	SOPO: no FTO: no
Inclusion in barred lists	Children: no Vulnerable adult: no
Notification	No

Loitering or soliciting for purposes of prostitution Street Offences Act 1959, s 1

(amended by Sexual Offences Act 2003, s 56 and Policing and Crime Act 2009, s 16)

DEFINITION

24.54 Section 1(1):

> It shall be an offence for a person (whether male or female) persistently to loiter or solicit in a street or public place for the purpose of prostitution.

SUMMARY

24.55 The offence is committed by a person persistently loitering or soliciting in a public place effectively offering their services (or the services of another) as a prostitute.

ELEMENTS

24.56

- *Persistently* is defined at s 1(4) of the 1959 Act:

  > 'conduct is persistent if it takes place on two or more occasions in any period of three months'.

  Prior to 2009, the offence was committed by a 'common prostitute', a derogatory term which was excised from the definition of the offence by the PCA 2009. The inclusion of the word 'persistent' (also by amendment of the 2009 Act) retained the element of repetitious behaviour. Persistence may be evidenced by previous cautions (see **24.57**).

- *Loitering* is the act of repetitive 'lingering'. No action is required and the activity seems to involve mere presence. For instance, waiting on a street corner in the hope that a client will make an advance is sufficient for the offence to be made out.

- *Soliciting* involves importuning, tempting or alluring prospective customers. No spoken word is required and soliciting may be by a smile, a gesture or a signal. The offender can smile or wink, wriggle the body or make some other gesture or signal. In order to solicit the offender must have a physical presence it is not enough to place an advertisement in a public place[18] (or presumably now to advertise on the internet).

- *Street* includes any 'bridge, road, lane, footway, subway, square, court, alley, passage … which is open to the public and the doorways and entrances of premises abutting on the street and any ground adjoining and open to a street' (s 1(4) of the 1959 Act). This is not necessarily an exhaustive list. It has also been stretched to include soliciting from a balcony or window where the person solicited was on the street.[19]

- *Public place* carries no statutory definition. It is likely to include both places where the public are admitted only on certain occasions (ie a business car park) and places the public actually frequent even when they have no right of entry.

- *For the purpose of prostitution* is defined at s 1(4) of the 1959 Act:[20]

  > 'any reference to a person loitering and soliciting for the purposes of prostitution is a reference to a person loitering or soliciting for the purposes of offering services as a prostitute'.

  This has the effect of limiting the scope of the offence to those offering services as prostitutes, and excluding those receiving such services. See **Chapter 6** for definition of 'prostitution'.

---

18 *Weisz v Monahan* [1962] 1 All ER 664.

19 *Smith v Hughes* [1960] 2 All ER 859.

20 Inserted by s 16(3) of the Policing and Crime Act 2009.

PARTIES

24.57 The offence may be committed by males and females (following amendment by SOA 2003, Sch 1). Note Home Office guidance on prosecution of those under 18 for prostitution offences.

CAUTIONS

24.58 A non-statutory cautioning system is operated by police in relation to street prostitution. A 'prostitute's caution' can be administered when two officers have witnessed a person loitering or soliciting. It requires no consent or admission from the person, nor any offence to have been committed (as there may be no persistence). This will then be evidence of persistence in a s 1 prosecution.

CLASSIFICATION

24.59 Offence is summary only.

SENTENCING AND OTHER ORDERS

Maximum sentence

24.60 For a first conviction: a fine not exceeding level 2 (currently £500)

For a second or subsequent conviction: a fine not exceeding level 3 (currently £1000).

Sentencing guidelines

24.61 There are no sentencing guidelines for this offence

Other orders

24.62

Extended and life sentence availability (CJA 2003)	Sch 15 (specified offence): no Sch 15B (life sentence for second listed offence): no
Trigger offence for:	SOPO: no FTO: no

Inclusion in barred lists	Children: no Vulnerable adult: no
Notification	No
Other orders	The Policing and Crime Act 2009 inserted a new s 1(2A) into the 1959 Act. This allows courts to make 'Engagement and Support Orders' to persons convicted of the offence instead of imposing any form of punishment. Such an order requires the offender to attend at three meetings with a supervisor. The purpose of the order is to address the causes of the conduct constituting the offence, and to find ways to cease engaging in such conduct in the future. The court may consider the imposition of an Anti-Social Behaviour Order on conviction where the behaviour of the woman is particularly persistent and anti-social.

PRACTITIONER POINTERS

1. 'Persistence'. The necessity for the prosecution to prove persistence means that at least two occasions of loitering/soliciting will be included in the particulars of an offence. These cannot then be included in any later prosecution and the Crown will need to evidence at least two following instances.
2. Formal statutory cautions and conditional cautions are available for this behaviour, notwithstanding that an informal 'prostitute's caution' has already been administered. Such a caution will also 'wipe the slate clean' in relation to establishing persistence.
3. Loitering and soliciting are separate behaviours (loitering likely to precede soliciting) and where both are alleged they should be charged separately.
4. Advocates may wish to encourage courts in the use of Engagement and Support Orders. The imposition of fines for this offence may simply have the effect of driving women back onto the streets and an ESO may be productive in assisting a person to access other support services, for instance in housing, drugs or domestic violence. As part of its rehabilitative purpose, an ESO becomes spent after 6 months.[21]

21 Policing and Crime Act 2009, s 18.

Placing an advertisement relating to prostitution Criminal Justice and Police Act 2001, s 46(1)

DEFINITION

24.63 Section 46:

(1) A person commits an offence if—

(a) he places on, or in the immediate vicinity of, a public telephone an advertisement relating to prostitution, and

(b) he does so with the intention that the advertisement should come to the attention of any other person or persons.

(2) For the purposes of this section, an advertisement is an advertisement relating to prostitution if it—

(a) is for the services of a prostitute, whether male or female; or

(b) indicates that premises are premises at which such services are offered.

SUMMARY

24.64 This offence seeks to address the nuisance of 'carding' – placing business cards for prostitutes in public telephone booths. The problem, once rife in larger cites, has reduced somewhat with the advent of internet advertising and the decline of public telephones.

ELEMENTS

24.65

- *Prostitution*: see **Chapter 6**.
- An item will be deemed to be an advertisement for prostitution if a reasonable person would consider it to be so. However this may be rebutted by the defendant showing that the advertisement was not in fact for prostitution (s 46(3)).
- A public telephone is any telephone in a public place that is made available for the use by the public and includes any structure such as a box, shelter or hood which it is located in or attached to. A 'public place' is one to which the public have access or are permitted to have access, whether on payment or otherwise (for instance, in a privately owned shopping centre). However the definition of public place excludes places

to which children under 16 are not permitted to have access or places which are wholly or mainly residential. This means, for example, that a telephone situated in a nightclub to which only adults have access or a hall of residence would not be covered (s 46(5)).

CLASSIFICATION

24.66 Offence is summary only.

SENTENCING AND OTHER ORDERS

Maximum sentence

24.67 Summarily: 6 months imprisonment or a fine not exceeding the statutory maximum (currently £5000)

Sentencing guidelines

24.68 There are no sentencing guidelines for this offence

Other orders

24.69

Extended and life sentence availability (CJA 2003)	Sch 15 (specified offence): no Sch 15B (life sentence for second listed offence): no
Trigger offence for:	SOPO: no FTO: no
Inclusion in barred lists	Children: no Vulnerable adult: no
Notification	No

Chapter 25

Public indecency

Outraging public decency
Common law

DEFINITION

25.1 It is an offence at common law to do an act of a lewd, obscene or disgusting nature in public which outrages public decency.

ELEMENTS

25.2

- The *act must be 'lewd, obscene or disgusting'*. An obscene act is more than an indecent act and is one which offends recognised (and presumably current) standards of propriety. A disgusting act is one which fills the onlooker with loathing or extreme distaste or causes annoyance.[1]
- The act must 'be of such a character that it *outrages minimum standards of public decency* as judged by the jury in contemporary society. It is not necessary to establish that any particular member of the public is outraged, and it must follow that this requirement does not mean that anyone has to see the act whilst it is being carried out'.[2] Outraging is a strong term and requires more than offending sensibilities or shocking members of the public.[3]
- It is a rule at common law that the act must be public in that the act was capable of being seen by at least two members of the public, even if it was not so seen.[4]

---

1 *R v Choi* [1999] EWCA Crim 1279.
2 *R v Hamilton* [2007] EWCA Crim 2062.
3 *Knuller (Publishing, Printing and Promoting Ltd) v DPP* [1973] AC 435.
4 *R v Hamilton* [2007] EWCA Crim 2062.

- *Mental element*: the prosecution must prove an intention to do the act and do not need to prove that the defendant had an intention to be lewd, obscene or disgusting or to outrage public decency or that he was reckless as to these outcomes.

  The defendant's intention is irrelevant to the question of whether acts are lewd, obscene or disgusting – this is an objective test and the defendant's intention to shock or offend cannot of itself render acts lewd, obscene or disgusting.

DISCUSSION

25.3 A number of offences contained within SOA 2003 now cover behaviour which might amount to outraging public decency (voyeurism, exposure, sexual activity in a public lavatory). The activities committed in the cases of *R v Hamilton* and *R v Choi* (indecent illicit filming of women) would now be offences under SOA 2003, s 67. In some circumstances, the common law offence may be wider in scope and encompass more unusual behaviour. Having sex in public and the modern phenomenon of 'dogging' would be likely to fall within the ambit of this offence.

More contentiously, the offence may be committed by those putting on artistic performances or shows of an extreme and challenging nature, including those in which self-harm or inflicting harm on others is displayed.

A person operating premises where acts take place on a regular basis may be committing the common law offence of keeping a disorderly house (see **24.39**).

CLASSIFICATION

25.4 Offence is triable either way.

SENTENCING AND OTHER ORDERS

Maximum sentence

25.5 On indictment: A fine or imprisonment, or both. There is no maximum punishment, but the sentence imposed must not be inordinate.

Summarily: 6 months' imprisonment or a fine not exceeding the prescribed sum (currently £ 5000), or both.

Sentencing guidelines and factors

25.6 There are no sentencing guidelines for this offence. However, reference may be made to guidelines for offences under the Sexual Offences Act (particularly exposure and sexual activity in a public lavatory), where the behaviour alleged is similar.

See also:

- *R v Hamilton*:[5] filming up women's skirts: Court of Appeal reduced consecutive nine-month sentences to concurrent sentences (however, the court was also mindful of totality with sentences for other offences)
- *R v Vaiculevicius*:[6] six months imprisonment reduced to three on plea of guilty for having sexual intercourse openly in a public park during the daytime. Intoxication, disregard for the presence of others and previous (unrelated) convictions were aggravating factors

Other orders

25.7

Extended and life sentence availability (CJA 2003)	Sch 15 (specified offence): no Sch 15B (life sentence for second listed offence): no
Trigger offence for:	SOPO: no FTO: no
Inclusion in barred lists	Children: no Vulnerable adult: no
Notification	No

5 [2007] EWCA Crim 2026.
6 [2013] EWCA Crim 185.

Chapter 26

Pornography

Possession of extreme pornographic images Criminal Justice and Immigration Act 2008, s 63

DEFINITION

26.1 Section 63:

(1) It is an offence for a person to be in possession of an extreme pornographic image.

(2) An 'extreme pornographic image' is an image which is both—

(a) pornographic, and

(b) an extreme image.

(3) An image is 'pornographic' if it is of such a nature that it must reasonably be assumed to have been produced solely or principally for the purpose of sexual arousal.

SUMMARY

26.2 The offence is committed by a person who knowingly possesses pornographic images which depict, for sexual purposes, acts of extreme violence, bestiality or necrophilia.

ELEMENTS

26.3

- An *extreme image* is one which is both grossly offensive, disgusting or of an otherwise obscene character and portrays, in an explicit and realistic way:
  - acts threatening a person's life
  - acts resulting in, or likely to result in, serious injury to a person's anus, breasts or genitals

- acts involving sexual interference with a human corpse
- a person performing sexual intercourse or oral sex with a living or dead animal

and a reasonable person, looking at the image, would think that the person or animal portrayed was real (s 63(6) and (7)). Acts threatening a person's life could include depictions of strangulation, hanging or suffocation. Serious injury is undefined and not necessarily equivalent to the case law definitions of an offence of grievous bodily harm. It is not necessary that the threat to a person's life or serious injury actually occur, merely that they are depicted in a realistic manner.

- The terms 'grossly offensive or disgusting' are examples of obscenity. All three terms should be given their ordinary dictionary definition (and not the statutory definition under the Obscene Publications Act 1959).[1]
- An image is *pornographic* if it can reasonably be assumed to have been produced solely or principally for the purpose of sexual arousal. In determining this, the tribunal of fact can take account of surrounding circumstances, including the context of the image. The actual purpose of the maker of the image is not necessarily determinative, and whether or not the possessor found the image arousing is irrelevant. Where it is part of a series of images – for instance, one scene from a longer film – the court must consider this and may conclude that the image in context is not pornographic, although it might have been so in isolation (s 63(4) and (5)). Thus, a series of extracts from clearly non-pornographic films or documentaries, put together out of their original context, could form a pornographic whole.
- An *image* includes a moving or still image (a film or photograph) and also data which is capable of conversion into a moving or still image. This will include data stored on disc, on computer, mobile phone or other device (s 63(8)). By virtue of the requirement that the image appear real, drawings, cartoons, paintings, physical images and 'tracings' are excluded.
- *Possession* involves the knowing assumption of custody or control. See *R v Cheung (Ping Chen)*:[2]

> 'The prosecution do not have to prove that the defendant knew that the "thing" which was to his knowledge in his custody or control had the requisite quality giving rise to the offence, in this case that the DVD contained an extreme pornographic image. Otherwise the defence under section 65(2)(b) would be otiose. It is only if there is a real doubt as to whether the defendant believed that that which he knew he had, was of a wholly different nature from that which in fact it was, that possession would not be made out.'

1 See Ministry of Justice Circular 2009/01.
2 [2009] EWCA Crim 2965.

Whether files which have been deleted from a computer remain in the owner's custody or control depends on whether they can be retrieved. This is a question of fact for the jury to determine looking at all the circumstances, including whether the defendant has the skills and the software to retrieve the files (*R v Porter*[3]).

- *Mental element*: the defendant must have knowledge that he is in possession of the subject material. If he knows he has indecent material, but not that it contains extreme images, he may be able to avail himself of the defence in s 65(2)(b). Material automatically 'cached' to a defendant's hard drive without his knowledge (even if he had previously viewed the image) does not remain in his possession (*Atkins v DPP*[4]).

DISCUSSION

26.4 The declared purpose of the extreme images legislation was to protect participants involved in the creation of very 'hard-core' pornographic material, as well as to 'protect society … from exposure to such material … which may encourage interest in violent of aberrant sexual activity'.

CPS guidance suggests circumspection in prosecuting this offence and especially that the threshold for prosecuting the 'serious injury' images should be a high one. Aggravating factors which might justify such a decision include wide circulation, evidence of exploitation of the participants and large numbers of images. Notwithstanding this, prosecutions for small numbers of images of consenting participants are not unknown.[5]

Inter-relationship with other offences

26.5 Where there is evidence that a person has published or distributed extreme pornographic images, an offence may have been committed under the Obscene Publications Act 1959 (which contains a different and potentially more restricted definition of obscenity) see **26.24**.

Where the extreme image is of a child, offences may have been committed contrary to s 1 of the Protection of Children Act 1978 (making indecent photographs) or s 160 of the Criminal Justice Act 1988 (possessing indecent photographs). Currently the Crown Prosecution Service guidelines suggest that the 1978 or 1988 Acts (which carry higher penalties) should be preferred to charges under the extreme images legislation.

3 [2006] EWCA Crim 560.

4 [2000] 2 Cr App R 248.

5 See *R v Simon Walsh* (2012) Kingston CC (unreported).

26.6

Statutory Defences and Exclusions

1. Legitimate reason for possession (s 65(2)(a))

This section provides a defence to an allegation of possession where a defendant can prove on the balance of probabilities that he had legitimate reason for having the image in his possession. No definition is given for 'legitimate reason', but it is likely to include genuine academic study (but see *Atkins v DPP; Goodland v DPP*[6] – courts encouraged to view such claims with scepticism.) Law enforcement, participation in legal processes, those involved in the classification of films and those dealing professionally with internet content should be covered by this defence.

2. Lack of knowledge of extreme pornographic content (s 65(2)(b))

This section provides a defence to an allegation of possession where a defendant can prove on the balance of probabilities that he had not himself seen the images and did not know or have reason to suspect them to be extreme pornographic images. The defence may extend to persons who know they have pornographic material, but do not know or suspect that it contains extreme images (see *R v Collier*[7] for a similar situation relating to indecent images of children).

3. Unsolicited images (s 65(2)(c))

This section provides a defence to an allegation of possession where a defendant can prove on the balance of probabilities that the images were sent to him unsolicited and he did not keep them for an unreasonable time. No definition is given of what amounts to a 'reasonable time'.

4. Participation in consensual acts (s 66)

This section provides a defence to a person charged with possession of extreme images, apart from bestiality images. The defendant must prove on the balance of probabilities that he directly participated in the acts portrayed and that the acts did not involve non-consensual harm to any person. The defendant must show that the participant did consent and that the level of the harm was such that, in law, the participant was capable of consenting to (ie, by current law, injuries below the level of actual bodily harm). Where the image is one of necrophilia, the defendant must prove that the human corpse portrayed was not in fact a corpse. The defence would not extend to an onlooker or camera operator who did not 'feature' in the film.

6 [2000] 2 Cr App R 248.
7 [2005] 1 WLR 843.

5.	**Exclusion of classified films (s 64)**
	By virtue of s 64, images which form part of a film classified by the British Board of Film Classification fall outside the scope of the offence and are therefore exempt from prosecution. However, where images from a classified film have been extracted from the main work for a purpose which must reasonably be assumed to be solely or principally for sexual arousal, the exemption is lost and the images may again fall within the ambit of s 63.

DPP CONSENT

26.7 Proceedings under this section may not be instituted without consent of the Director of Public Prosecutions (s 63(1)).

CLASSIFICATION

26.8 Offence is triable either way.

SENTENCING AND OTHER ORDERS

Maximum sentence

26.9 On indictment:

- For an offence involving images of necrophilia or bestiality (s 63(7)(c) or (d)): 2 years.
- For an offence involving images of threats to life or serious injury (s 63(7)(a) or (b)): 3 years.

Summarily: 6 months imprisonment or a fine not exceeding the statutory maximum (currently £5000).

Sentencing guidelines and factors

26.10 There are no sentencing guidelines for this offence.

For sentencing authorities, see:

- *R v Oliver (Philip)*:[8] six months reduced to two on a plea of guilty to possession of three still and eight moving images of bestiality. An aggravating factor was the installation of software allowing others access to the images. Offences of possession of extreme pornographic images under the 2008 Act, whilst serious, were not to be equated with the seriousness of similar images depicting children.
- *R v Livesey*:[9] possession of 329 still and five moving images of bestiality by a man of good character. No aggravating factors and very early admissions. The appropriate sentence was four months and 'suspension of sentence was a very serious possibility in this case'.
- *R v John Lewis*:[10] A 12 month sentence, following a guilty plea was not manifestly excessive for possession of 44 static images and 19 moving images. In addition, and importantly, the appellant in that case had two previous convictions for offences involving children.

Other orders

26.11

Extended and life sentence availability (CJA 2003)	Sch 15 (specified offence): no Sch 15B (life sentence for second listed offence): no
Trigger offence for:	SOPO: no FTO: no[11]
Inclusion in barred lists	Children: no Vulnerable adult: no
Notification	Yes, where D was over 18 and is sentenced to at least 2 years
Forfeiture	Powers of forfeiture under PCC(S)A 2000, s 143 apply to extreme images

8 [2011] EWCA Crim 3114.
9 [2013] EWCA Crim 1600.
10 [2013] 2 Cr App R(S) 121.
11 Technically, since this is an offence within SOA 2003, Sch 3, there is a trigger for a foreign travel order. However, the second requirement that the 'victim' be under 18 makes this unlikely.

Possession of prohibited images of children Coroners and Justice Act 2009, s 62

DEFINITION

26.12 Section 62:

(1) It is an offence for a person to be in possession of a prohibited image of a child.

(2) A prohibited image is an image which—

(a) is pornographic,

(b) falls within subsection (6), and

(c) is grossly offensive, disgusting or otherwise of an obscene character.

(3) An image is 'pornographic' if it is of such a nature that it must reasonably be assumed to have been produced solely or principally for the purpose of sexual arousal.

...

(6) An image falls within this subsection if it—

(a) is an image which focuses solely or principally on a child's genitals or anal region, or

(b) portrays any of the acts mentioned in subsection (7).

(7) Those acts are—

(a) the performance by a person of an act of intercourse or oral sex with or in the presence of a child;

(b) an act of masturbation by, of, involving or in the presence of a child;

(c) an act which involves penetration of the vagina or anus of a child with a part of a person's body or with anything else;

(d) an act of penetration, in the presence of a child, of the vagina or anus of a person with a part of a person's body or with anything else;

(e) the performance by a child of an act of intercourse or oral sex with an animal (whether dead or alive or imaginary);

(f) the performance by a person of an act of intercourse or oral sex with an animal (whether dead or alive or imaginary) in the presence of a child.

SUMMARY

26.13 The offence is committed by persons who knowingly possess pornographic images which depict children performing sexual acts. The definition *excludes* photographs or pseudo-photographs, but will include drawings, cartoons, computer generated images, *manga* and *anime* style images.

ELEMENTS

26.14

- To be prohibited, the image must:
  - be pornographic, and
  - offensive, disgusting or otherwise obscene, and
  - focus on a child's genitals or anal region, and
  - portray one or more of the sexual acts set out in s 62(7).
- The terms 'grossly offensive or disgusting' are examples of obscenity. All three terms should be given their ordinary dictionary definition (and not the statutory definition under the Obscene Publications Act 1959).
- An image is *pornographic* if it can reasonably be assumed to have been produced solely or principally for the purpose of sexual arousal. In determining this, the tribunal of fact can take account of surrounding circumstances, including the context of the image. The actual purpose of the maker of the image is not necessarily determinative, and whether or not the possessor found the image arousing is irrelevant. Where it is part of a series of images – for instance, one scene from a longer film – the court must consider this and may conclude that the image in context is not pornographic, although it might have been so in isolation (ss 62(4) and (5)). Thus, a series of extracts from clearly non-pornographic films or documentaries, put together out of their original context, could form a pornographic whole.
- An *image* includes a moving or still image and also data which is capable of conversion into a moving or still image. This will include data stored on disc, on computer, mobile phone or other device (s 65(2) and (3)). Indecent photographs and pseudo-photographs of children (as defined in PCA 1978 – see **22.4** and **22.5**) are specifically excluded from this offence, as will now be 'tracings'.
- *Possession* involves the knowing assumption of custody or control. Whether files that have been deleted from a computer remain in the owner's custody or control depends on whether they can be retrieved.

This is a question of fact for the jury to determine looking at all the circumstances, including whether the defendant has the skills and the software to retrieve the files (*R v Porter*[12]).

- *Child* means a person under the age of 18. An image is to be treated as that of a child if the impression or predominant impression conveyed by the image is that the person shown is a child. This is so even when some of the physical characteristics shown are not those of a child (s 65(5) and (6)). References to an image of a person include references to an imaginary person, and references to an image of a child include references to an imaginary child (s 65(7) and (8)).
- *Mental element*: the defendant must have knowledge that he is in possession of the subject material. If he knows he has indecent material, but not that it contains images of children, he may be able to avail himself of the defence in s 64(1)(b). Material automatically 'cached' to a defendant's hard drive without his knowledge (even if he had previously viewed the image) does not remain in his possession *(Atkins v DPP*[13]*)*

DISCUSSION

26.15 It was acknowledged in the Home Office 'Consultation on Possession of Non-Photographic Visual Depictions of Child Sexual Abuse' which preceded the 2009 Act, that cartoons, drawings and material created by manipulation of computer software do not harm real children. Nevertheless, there were concerns that such fantasy images reinforced potential abusers' feelings towards children and that the images themselves might be used to groom children. The offence has a higher indecency threshold than that pertaining to photographs of real children and the requirements that the images are produced solely or principally for the purposes of sexual arousal should exclude some items that have artistic merit.

Inter-relationship with other offences

26.16 Where there is evidence that a person has published or distributed prohibited images, an offence may have been committed under the Obscene Publications Act 1959 (which contains a different and potentially more restricted definition of obscenity).

---

12 [2006] EWCA Crim 560.
13 [2000] 2 Cr App R 248.

26.17

Statutory Defences and Exclusions

1. **Legitimate reason for possession (s 64(1)(a))**

   This section provides a defence to an allegation of possession where a defendant can prove on the balance of probabilities that he had legitimate reason for having the image in his possession. No definition is given for 'legitimate reason', but it is likely to include genuine academic study (but see *Atkins v DPP; Goodland v DPP*[14] – courts encouraged to view such claims with scepticism.) Law enforcement, participation in legal processes, those involved in the classification of films and those dealing professionally with internet content should be covered by this defence.

2. **Lack of knowledge of prohibited content (s 64(1)(b))**

   This section provides a defence to an allegation of possession where a defendant can prove on the balance of probabilities that he had not himself seen the images and did not know or have reason to suspect them to be prohibited images of children. The defence may extend to persons who know they have pornographic material, but do not know or suspect that it contains prohibited images (see *R v Collier*[15]).

3. **Unsolicited images (s 64(1)(c))**

   This section provides a defence to an allegation of possession where a defendant can prove on the balance of probabilities that the images were sent to him unsolicited and he did not keep them for an unreasonable time. No definition is given of what amounts to a 'reasonable time'.

4. **Exclusion of classified films (s 63)**

   By virtue of s 63, images which form part of a film classified by the British Board of Film Classification fall outside the scope of the offence and are therefore exempt from prosecution. However, where images from a classified film have been extracted from the main work for a purpose which must reasonably be assumed to be solely or principally for sexual arousal, the exemption is lost and the images may again fall within the ambit of s 62.

DPP CONSENT

26.18 Proceedings under this section may not be instituted without consent of the Director of Public Prosecutions (s 62(9)).

14 [2000] 2 Cr App R 248.
15 [2005] 1 WLR 843.

CLASSIFICATION

26.19 Offence is triable either way.

SENTENCING AND OTHER ORDERS

Sentencing guidelines

26.20 There are no sentencing guidelines for this offence.

For sentencing authorities, see:

- *R v Richard Palmer*:[16] Community order substituted for two year prison sentence upon guilty plea to three counts of possession of prohibited images by young man with Asperger's syndrome. The court drew a distinction between these and images showing abuse of real children as being of a different order of criminality.
- *R v Gregory*:[17] serving prisoner who drew pictures of child abuse (levels 4 and 5 of the *Oliver* scale applied). Some passed to another prisoner and a threat to good order in the prison. Despite a history of offending against children, two years on a plea of guilty was excessive. Reduced to 18 months.

Other orders

26.21

Extended and life sentence availability (CJA 2003)	Sch 15 (specified offence): no Sch 15B (life sentence for second listed offence): no
Trigger offence for:	SOPO: yes FTO: no[18]
Inclusion in barred lists	Children: no Vulnerable adult: no
Notification	Yes, where D was over 18 and is sentenced to at least 2 years

16 [2011] EWCA Crim 1286.
17 [2012] EWCA Crim 2099.
18 Technically, since this is an offence within SOA 2003, Sch 3, there is a trigger for a foreign travel order. However, the second requirement that the 'victim' be under 18 makes this impossible.

Forfeiture of prohibited images	May be made in the usual way following conviction under PCC(S)A 2000, s 143 (which allows seizure of property used in the commission of the offence, ie computers) or under the Schedule to the Protection of Children Act 1978, by virtue of Coroners and Justice Act 2009, s 67 (which allows for forfeiture of the images themselves). The latter allows for forfeiture in cases where the prosecution is discontinued, the defendant cautioned or acquitted, so long as the magistrates find that the materials were prohibited.

Obscene publications
Obscene Publications Act 1959, s 2

(amended by the Obscene Publications Act 1964)

DEFINITION

26.22 Section 2(1):

> Subject as hereinafter provided, any person who, whether for gain or not, publishes an obscene article or who has an obscene article for publication for gain (whether gain to himself or gain to another) shall be liable …
>
> [penalty follows – see **26.31**]

SUMMARY

26.23 The Act creates two offences:

- Where someone publishes an obscene article (gain not necessarily required)
- Where someone has an obscene article for publication (gain required)

The test of obscenity is that it will tend to deprave and corrupt its consumers

ELEMENTS

26.24

- Section 1(1) defines *obscenity*:

  'An article shall be deemed to be obscene if its effect or (where the article comprises two or more distinct items) the effect of any one of its items is, if taken as a whole, such as to tend to deprave and corrupt persons who are likely, having regard to all relevant circumstances, to read, see or hear the matter contained or embodied in it.'

- *Deprave and corrupt*: no statutory definition and various case law interpretations. Note in *R v Calder and Boyers*[19] (the 'Last Exit to Brooklyn' case) the Court of Appeal advised against attempts to re-define ordinary English phrases, but in general terms approved the trial judge's direction that:

  '"tend" obviously means "have a tendency to" or "be inclined to". "Deprave" is defined in some dictionaries … as "to make morally bad; to pervert or corrupt morally" … The essence of the matter, you may think, is moral corruption.'

  Obscenity is not confined to sexual matters, and depravity and corruption can occur by exposure to other material.

- The article must tend to deprave and corrupt *persons* who come into contact with it. The item must have this effect on 'a significant proportion of those persons likely to read it[20]'.

- *Likely, in all the circumstances, to read, etc, it*: the type of persons likely to come into contact with the material, and the effect it will have on *those* persons, is a relevant factor. However, even those accustomed to the type of material in question may be susceptible to further corruption or having their addiction deepened.[21]

- *Article* is widely defined in s 1(2) and will encompass all matter to be read, looked at or heard. Items, such as negatives, which embody the material to be published, are included by s 2 of the Obscene Publications Act 1964.

- Section 1(3) and (4) defines *publication*:

  'a person publishes an article who—

  (a) distributes, circulates, sells, lets on hire, gives, or lends it, or who offers it for sale or for letting on hire; or

  (b) in the case of an article containing or embodying matter to be looked at or a record, shows, plays or projects it or, where the matter is data stored electronically, transmits that data.

  … a person also publishes an article to the extent that any matter recorded on it is included by him in a programme included in a programme service'

---

19 [1968] 3 All ER 644.
20 *R v Calder and Boyers*.
21 *DPP v Whyte* [1972] AC 849, HL.

In *R v Barker*[22] the Court of Appeal held that there were three distinct types of publication within s 1(3)(a):

– 'sells, lets on hire, gives or lends' where publication is to an individual

– 'distributes, circulates' where publication is on a wider scale, involving more than one person

– 'offers for sale or for letting on hire' in which case the offer itself constitutes publication.

In a case falling within the first of these categories, the jury should consider whether the article would deprave and corrupt the individual to whom it was published, then whether anyone else could reasonably have been expected to see the article ('re-publication'), and, if so, whether those persons would tend to be depraved and corrupted by the exposure.

- *Mental element*: The intention of the publisher is irrelevant to the decision as to whether an item is obscene or not (but may have a bearing on the jury's decision concerning the statutory defence of 'public good').

DISCUSSION

26.25 Much of the case law surrounding this Act is concerned with the physical publication of books and magazines which would now be considered relatively mainstream and even harmless. However, its application extends to the virtual world and contemporary concerns about the protection of children. The case of *R v S (G)*[23] may be instructive here. G was the user of an internet chat room in which he discussed with another (anonymous) participant fantasies about the abuse of children. Evidence of this arose when police seized his computer and found 'chat logs', not themselves publications, but records of the conversations which had taken place. The main issue which the Court of Appeal had to deal with (on prosecution appeal against a terminatory ruling of the trial judge) was the correspondence with a single individual which, following *R v Barker*, was sufficient to amount to publication. The Court continued to apply other considerations to the questions of publication and obscenity: anonymity of the recipient, risk of re-publication and publication to an already 'depraved' reader. The Court rejected the suggestion that because 'there was only one recipient and only one likely reader of an article, the article is incapable of meeting the test of obscenity'. The fact that there was no physical product (the chat logs being only a record of electronically transmitted communications) clearly did not prevent the material falling within s 1(3)(b). Thus, communications (including text messages and emails) which may have more of a feel of private conversations between individuals fall well within the ambit of the OPA.

22 (1962) 46 Cr App R 227.
23 [2012] EWCA Crim 398.

Inter-relationship with other offences

26.26 Publication or possession of some pornographic images, especially depicting extreme sado-masochism or bestiality, will be an offence under s 64 of the Criminal Justice and Immigration Act 2008 (see **26.1**). Such images must be grossly offensive, disgusting or obscene. Indecent images of children will fall within s 1 of the Protection of Children Act 1978 (making indecent photographs – see **22.1**) or s 160 of the Criminal Justice Act 1988 (possessing indecent photographs – see **22.15**).

Limitation

26.27 Prosecution shall not be commenced more than two years after the commission of the offence (s 2(3)).

26.28

Statutory Defences

1. **Lack of knowledge of obscenity (s 2(5))**

   This section provides a defence to an allegation of publishing or having an article for publication where the defendant can prove 'that he had not examined the article in respect of which he is charged and had no reasonable cause to suspect that it was such that his publication of it would make him liable to be convicted of an offence against this section'. The burden is thus on the defendant and is discharged by satisfying the jury of the probability of this.[24]

2. **Defence of public good (s 4)**

   This section provides a defence to an allegation of publishing or having an article for publication where it is proved that the article is 'justified as being in the public good on the ground that it is in the interests of science, literature, art or learning, or other objects of general concern'. Where the article is a film or soundtrack, the test is the interests of 'drama, opera, ballet or any other art, or of literature or learning'.

   The jury should first decide whether the item is obscene and then whether its publication is in the public good. The test weighs the strength of the tendency to deprave and corrupt against the merits of the work and is determined on the balance of probability.[25]

24 *R v Carr-Briant* [1943] KB 607.
25 *DPP v Jordan* [1977] AC 699, HL.

DPP CONSENT

26.29 Proceedings relating to the publication of some moving films may not be instituted without consent of the Director of Public Prosecutions.

CLASSIFICATION

26.30 Offence is triable either way.

SENTENCING AND OTHER ORDERS

Maximum sentence

26.31 On indictment: 5 years[26]

Summarily: 6 months imprisonment or a fine not exceeding the statutory maximum (currently £5000)

Sentencing guidelines and factors

26.32 There are no sentencing guidelines for this offence.

For sentencing authorities, see:

- *R v Snowden*:[27] Defendant in possession of 55 obscene videos showing extreme sexual acts including bestiality. Admitted prior dealing in such videos on an amateur scale. Good character and guilty plea but 20% discount only as 'caught red-handed'. 30 months high but not manifestly excessive.
- *R v Tunnicliffe; R v Greenwood*:[28] sentences reduced to four and six weeks for salesmen in sex shops pleading guilty to having an obscene article for publication for gain.

26 Increased from 3 years by Criminal Justice and Immigration Act 2008, s 71.
27 [2009] EWCA Crim 1200.
28 [1999] 2 Cr App R (S) 88.

Other orders

26.33

Extended and life sentence availability (CJA 2003)	Sch 15 (specified offence): no Sch 15B (life sentence for second listed offence): no
Trigger offence for:	SOPO: no FTO: no
Inclusion in barred lists	Children: no Vulnerable adult: no
Notification	No
Forfeiture of obscene materials	Section 3 of the Act allows magistrates to issue a warrant for police to enter premises, search them and remove any suspect publications; if such publications are found the articles must then be brought before a magistrate and either forfeited by the owners or returned. The owner, author or publisher of the articles, or the person from whom they were seized, may appear before the magistrate to argue why they should not be forfeited. Note that this is not dependent upon any criminal prosecution.

Importation of indecent or obscene material Customs & Excise Management Act 1979, s 170(2)(b) Customs Consolidation Act 1876, s 42

DEFINITION

26.34 Section 170(2):

Without prejudice to any other provision of the Customs and Excise Acts 1979, if any person is, in relation to any goods, in any way knowingly concerned in any fraudulent evasion or attempt at evasion—

(b) of any prohibition or restriction for the time being in force with respect to the goods under or by virtue of any enactment,

he shall be guilty of an offence under this section and may be detained.

Section 42:

> The goods enumerated and described in the following table of prohibitions and restrictions are hereby prohibited to be imported or brought into the United Kingdom:
>
> Indecent or obscene prints, paintings, photographs, books, cards, lithographic or other engravings or any other indecent or obscene articles.

SUMMARY

26.35 An offence is committed by any person who is knowingly concerned in the fraudulent evasion (or attempt at evasion) of a prohibition on the importation of indecent or obscene goods.

ELEMENTS

26.36

- *Prohibited or restricted goods* are defined in CEMA 1979, s 1 , to mean 'goods of a class or description to which the importation, exportation or carriage coastwise is for the time being prohibited or restricted under or by virtue of any enactment'; in this respect by CCA 1876, s 42.
- The Crown must prove that an importation has taken place.
- *Concerned in the evasion*: the offence is wider than the importation itself and those who assist in the process, while not themselves bringing the goods into the country, will commit the substantive offence.[29]
- *Indecent or obscene material*: see **22.14** for a discussion of indecency; see **26.24** for definitions of obscene material.
- *Mental element*: the defendant must know that the goods imported are prohibited (as opposed to merely dutiable), but does not need to know the precise nature of the goods so long as they are still subject to prohibition (ie D believes he is importing obscene pornography, but it in fact contains indecent images of children).[30]

The defendant must behave in a fraudulent manner, in other words, by conduct deliberately intended to evade the prohibition. There is no requirement that D deceives any person directly by his words or actions.

29 *R v Neal* (1983) 77 Cr App R 283, at 288.
30 *R v Forbes (Giles)* [2002] 2 AC 512, HL.

DISCUSSION

26.37 A defendant entering the UK with images of child abuse would also be committing the offence of possession of indecent images contrary to CJA 1988, s 160 (see **22.15**). A defendant in possession of other pornographic material would be unlikely to commit an offence under the Obscene Publications Act (which requires 'publication'), but, if the images involve bestiality or sado-masochism, may commit an offence of possession of extreme pornography, contrary to Criminal Justice and Immigration Act 2008, s 67 (see **26.1**).

DEFENCES

26.38 Lack of knowledge that goods imported were of a prohibited nature. If the defendant can satisfy a jury that he believed that he was evading a duty, rather than a prohibition, a defence will lie.

Images were not indecent or obscene (see, especially, **26.24**).

CLASSIFICATION:

26.39 Offence is triable either way.

SENTENCING AND OTHER ORDERS

Maximum sentence

26.40 On indictment: 7 years

Summarily: 6 months imprisonment or a fine not exceeding the statutory maximum (currently £5000)

Sentencing guidelines and factors

26.41 There are no sentencing guidelines for this offence

For sentencing authorities, see:

- *R v Hirst*:[31] 12 months upheld on guilty plea for man of good character involved at a modest level in commercial importation of extremely hard-core pornographic videos.

31 (2001) 1 Cr App R(S) 152.

Other orders

26.42

Extended and life sentence availability (CJA 2003)	Sch 15 (specified offence): yes Sch 15B (life sentence for second listed offence): no
Trigger offence for:	SOPO: yes FTO: yes, if the prohibited goods included indecent photographs of persons under 16 *and* D was over 18, *or* is sentenced to at least 12 months
Inclusion in barred lists	Children: no Vulnerable adult: no
Notification	Yes, if the prohibited goods included indecent photographs of persons under 16 *and* D was over 18, *or* is sentenced to at least 12 months[32]

Indecent displays
Indecent Displays (Control) Act 1981, s 1

DEFINITION

26.43 Section 1(1):[32]

> If any indecent matter is publicly displayed the person making the display and any person causing or permitting the display to be made shall be guilty of an offence

SUMMARY

26.44 This Act is designed to protect members of the public from inadvertently being exposed to indecent materials, while not preventing adult establishments such as sex shops from operating.

32 *Forbes v Secretary of State for the Home Dept* [2006] EWCA Civ 962: notification was compatible with Art 8 where D knew imported goods were prohibited but not that they contained images of children.

ELEMENTS

26.45

- Display in a public place or so as to be visible from any public place is deemed to be *publicly displayed* (s 1(2)).
- *Public place* means any place to which the public have or are permitted to have access (whether on payment or otherwise) while that matter is displayed except:
  - places where only a paying adult audience has access
  - a shop or part of a shop where under 18s are not permitted and the material is only displayed behind a warning sign[33]
- There is no statutory definition of *indecent matter*, save that it does not include 'an actual human body or any part thereof' (s 1(5)).
- Other exemptions include cinemas, theatres and television broadcasting, art galleries and museums and displays by or with the authority of the Crown or a local authority.

PARTIES

26.46 The offence may be committed by corporations (s 3).

CLASSIFICATION

26.47 Offence is triable either way.

SENTENCING AND OTHER ORDERS

Maximum sentence

26.48 On indictment: 2 years

Summarily: 6 months imprisonment or a fine not exceeding the statutory maximum (currently £5000)

---

33 The terms and location of the warning sign are specified at s 1(6).

Sentencing guidelines

26.49 There are no sentencing guidelines for this offence.

Other orders

26.50

Extended and life sentence availability (CJA 2003)	Sch 15 (specified offence): no Sch 15B (life sentence for second listed offence): no
Trigger offence for:	SOPO: no FTO: no
Inclusion in barred lists	Children: no Vulnerable adult: no
Notification	No

Chapter 27

Protection of children and vulnerable persons

Barred person not to engage in regulated activity Safeguarding Vulnerable Groups Act 2006, s 7

DEFINITION

27.1 Section 7(1):

An individual commits an offence if he–

(a) seeks to engage in regulated activity from which he is barred;

(b) offers to engage in regulated activity from which he is barred;

(c) engages in regulated activity from which he is barred.

ELEMENTS

27.2 An offence is committed by a person who has been barred from working with children or vulnerable adults (the 'regulated activity') and who then engages in, or offers or seeks to engage in such work. An individual may be barred either because of their conviction or caution for a specified offence or because the Independent Barring Service considers them a risk (SVGA 2006, Sch 4, Parts 1 and 2 – see **Chapter 47**).

27.3

Statutory Defences
1. It is a defence for a person to prove that he did not know, and could not reasonably be expected to know, that he was barred from that activity (s 7(3)).
2. It is a defence for a person to prove—
(a) that he reasonably thought that it was necessary for him to engage in the activity for the purpose of preventing harm to a child or vulnerable adult (as the case may be),
(b) that he reasonably thought that there was no other person who could engage in the activity for that purpose, and
(c) that he engaged in the activity for no longer than was necessary for that purpose (s 7(4)).

CLASSIFICATION

27.4 Offence is triable either way.

SENTENCING AND OTHER ORDERS

Maximum sentence

27.5 On indictment: 5 years

Summarily: 6 months imprisonment or a fine not exceeding the statutory maximum (currently £5000)

Sentencing guidelines

27.6 There are no sentencing guidelines for this offence. It is suggested that reference may be made to the Magistrates' Courts Sentencing Guidelines for failure to comply with notification requirements (see **21.6–21.8**).

Reference may also be made to the relevant factors in the Definitive Guidelines for Breach of a Protective Order.

Other orders

27.7

Extended and life sentence availability (CJA 2003)	Sch 15 (specified offence): no Sch 15B (life sentence for second listed offence): no
Trigger offence for:	SOPO: no, although SOPO may have been made at the same time as individual was placed on barred list. FTO: no
Inclusion in barred lists	D will already be barred
Notification	No, although D may already be subject to notification as a result of the conviction/caution which caused him to be placed on the barred list.

Part D
Repealed offences commonly encountered in historic sex cases

Chapter 28

Sexual Offences Act 1956

Rape
Sexual Offences Act 1956, s 1 etc

INTRODUCTION

28.1 'Historic' rape cases in which an alleged offence predates the 2003 Act will continue to come before the courts for the foreseeable future. It is even possible that we have not seen the last case involving allegations going back to a time before the 1956 legislation.

There follows a brief history of the development, in our lifetime, of the law concerning rape. Thereafter we set out, in familiar form, the required elements of the offence of rape according to the era in which it falls.

Which version of the law applies to any given rape allegation is determined by its timing within the following periods:

A. any date before 3 November 1994 (see **28.3**)

B. 3 November 1994 to 30 April 2004 (see **28.4**)

C. 1 May 2004 onwards (see **Chapter 8**)

HISTORY

28.2 Before 1976 there was no statutory definition of rape. In its original form the Sexual Offences Act 1956 simply stated 'it is felony for a man to rape a woman' and 'a man who induces a married woman to have sexual intercourse with him by impersonating her husband commits rape' without further defining the offence. The House of Lords considered the topic in *DPP v Morgan*[1] and that judgment should be taken as stating the ingredients of the offence under both the 1956 Act and previously at common law. The *actus reus* was vaginal intercourse without the woman's consent; the *mens rea* involved

1 [1976] AC 182.

either knowledge that the woman did not consent or recklessness as to consent ('having intercourse willy-nilly not caring whether the victim consents or no[2]'). Notably, the offence was not made out if a defendant held (or might have held) a genuine belief in consent, however unreasonable that belief was. The reasonableness or otherwise of a professed belief in consent would merely be evidence as to whether or not such a belief had genuinely been held.

A year after *Morgan*, Parliament passed the Sexual Offences (Amendment) Act 1976 which encapsulated these points and gave the first statutory definition of rape:

> s 1(1) For the purposes of section 1 of the Sexual Offences Act 1956 (which relates to rape) a man commits rape if—
>
> (a) he has unlawful sexual intercourse with a woman who at the time of the intercourse does not consent to it; and
>
> (b) at that time he knows that she does not consent to the intercourse or he is reckless as to whether she consents to it;
>
> and references to rape in other enactments (including the following provisions of this Act) shall be construed accordingly.
>
> (2) It is hereby declared that if at a trial for a rape offence the jury has to consider whether a man believed that a woman was consenting to sexual intercourse, the presence or absence of reasonable grounds for such a belief is a matter to which the jury is to have regard, in conjunction with any other relevant matters, in considering whether he so believed.

This section clarified the meaning of rape and consent rather than changing the substantive law, so this legislation applies not just to subsequent cases but to all rapes alleged to have occurred before 3 November 1994. That was the commencement date for s 142 of the Criminal Justice and Public Order Act 1994 which substituted the following replacement s 1 into the 1956 Act (emphasis added):

> s 1(1) It is an offence for a man to rape a woman or *another man*.
>
> (2) A man commits rape if–
>
> (a) he has sexual intercourse with a person (whether vaginal or *anal*) who at the time of the intercourse does not consent to it; and
>
> (b) at the time he knows that the person does not consent to the intercourse or is reckless as to whether that person consents to it.

---

2 Per Lord Hailsham.

(3) A man also commits rape if he induces a married woman to have sexual intercourse with him by impersonating her husband.

We can safely ignore subsection (3). Even before improvements in domestic lighting, husband impersonation rape must have been extremely rare and it is inconceivable that such a case will now arise on an historic basis. In any event, the subsection was arguably superfluous because the wife would have been consenting to sex with her husband, not the imposter.

Until this amendment of SOA 1956 only women could be raped and only by penile penetration of the vagina. Anal rape (of either gender) was now acknowledged as rape. Oral rape was not to be recognised for another decade.

An important topic, although not (as explained below) date-specific, is the removal of the marital exception. Historically a wife could not be raped by her husband. The House of Lords in *R v R*[3] re-interpreted the common law such that this exception was removed. The omission in 1994 of the surplus word 'unlawful' (before the phrase 'sexual intercourse') in the amended s 1 of the SOA 1956 is seen as confirming that change.

Significantly, because *R v R* had clarified the common law, rather than created a new offence, the ruling has retrospective effect. This was challenged in *SW v UK; CR v UK*[4] as a potential violation of Article 7(1) of the European Convention of Human Rights ('No one shall be guilty of any criminal offence … which did not constitute a criminal offence … at the time when it was committed'). The European Court rejected the submissions, saying that Article 7(1) does not prevent gradual judicial clarification of the law and observing that this adjustment had been foreseeable.

The *SW* and *CR* marital rapes had been carried out within a year or two of the decision in *R v R*. However, the retrospective effect of the ruling appears to be unlimited. The Court of Appeal has since endorsed cases stretching back to the 1960s.[5]

ELEMENTS

Period A – any date before 3 November 1994

28.3 Common law and s 1 of the Sexual Offences Act 1956. The elements of offence are identical, the only difference being whether the allegation is indicted as 'contrary to Common Law' (up to 31 December 1956) or 'contrary to s 1(1) of the Sexual Offences Act 1956' (from 1 January 1957).

3 [1991] UKHL 12, [1992] 1 AC 599.
4 [1996] 21 EHRR 363.
5 *R v Barry C* [2004] EWCA Crim 292.

- A is male

  (the offence can only be committed as a principal by a male, although a woman may aid and abet the offence)

- Age of A

  'man' does not exclude 'boy' (SOA 1956, s 46)

  – before 19 September 1993 – A aged at least 14

    (irrebuttable presumption at common law that a boy under 14 is incapable of sexual intercourse – although his actions could amount to indecent assault for which he is deemed capable)

  – from 20 September 1993 – A aged at least 10

    (age of criminal responsibility – presumption abolished by SOA 1993, s 1)

- B is female (any age)

- 'Sexual intercourse' – penetration of B's vagina [not anus or mouth] with the penis

  – Vagina – any penetration 'within the labia of the pudendum' suffices. Even the slightest penetration suffices[6]

    > '... it shall not be necessary to prove the completion of the intercourse by the emission of seed, but the intercourse shall be deemed complete upon proof of penetration only' (SOA 1956, s 44)

  Sexual intercourse is a continuing act[7] and if consent is withdrawn (or absence of consent belatedly realised) continued penetration suffices.

- B does not consent – see **Chapter 1**

  There is no marital exception[8]

- Mental element – A either:

  – knows that B does not consent; or

  – is reckless as to consent ('couldn't care less, but pressed on regardless'[9]);

  – A's genuine, albeit mistaken, belief that B consents would defeat this element;

---

6 *R v R'Rue* (1838) 8 C & P 641; *R v Allen* (1839) 9 C & P 31.
7 *Kaitamaki* [1985] AC 147, PC.
8 See discussion of *R v R* at **28.2**.
9 *R v Taylor (Robert)* (1985) 80 Cr App R 327, CA, per Lord Lane CJ, at 332.

– Such a belief in consent need not be reasonable, so long as it was genuinely held;

– A mistaken belief in consent where the mistake arises through voluntary intoxication is no defence.

Period B – 3 November 1994 to 30 April 2004

28.4 Section 1 of the Sexual Offences Act 1956, as amended by s 142 of the Criminal Justice and Public Order Act 1994.

- A is male

  (the offence can only be committed as a principal by a male, although a woman may aid and abet the offence)

- A is aged at least 10 – the age of criminal responsibility

  ("man" does not exclude "boy" (s 46 SOA 1956))

- B is female or male (any age)

- 'Sexual intercourse' – penetration of B's vagina or anus (not mouth) with the penis

  Even the slightest penetration suffices[10]

  Where vaginal – any penetration "within the labia of the pudendum"

  > '... it shall not be necessary to prove the completion of the intercourse by the emission of seed, but the intercourse shall be deemed complete upon proof of penetration only' (SOA 1956, s 44)

  Sexual intercourse is a continuing act[11] and if consent is withdrawn (or absence of consent belatedly realised) continued penetration suffices.

- B does not consent – see **Chapter 1**

  There is no marital exception[12]

- Mental element – A either:

  – knows that B does not consent, or

  – is reckless as to consent ('couldn't care less, but pressed on regardless'[13])

  A's genuine, albeit mistaken, belief that B consents would defeat this element.

10 *R v R'Rue* (1838) 8 C & P 641; *R v Allen* (1839) 9 C & P 31.
11 *Kaitamaki* [1985] AC 147, PC.
12 See discussion of *R v R* at **28.2**.
13 *R v Taylor (Robert)* (1985) 80 Cr App R 327, CA, per Lord Lane CJ, at 332.

Such a belief in consent need not be reasonable, so long as it was genuinely held.

A mistaken belief in consent where the mistake arises through voluntary intoxication is no defence.

Period C – 1 May 2004 onwards

28.5 Section 1 of the Sexual Offences Act 2003.

See **Chapter 8**.

CLASSIFICATION

28.6 For all rape cases, whatever the date, the offence is triable on indictment only.

SENTENCING AND OTHER ORDERS

Maximum sentence

28.7 Maximum sentence (completed offence, any date): life imprisonment.

For attempted rape the maximum sentence is also life imprisonment, except from 24 March 1948[14] until 15 September 1985[15] (inclusive) when the maximum was 7 years.

Other orders

28.8

Extended and life sentence availability (CJA 2003)	Sch 15 (specified offence): yes Sch 15B (life sentence for second listed offence): yes
Trigger offence for:	SOPO: yes FTO: yes, but only where V was under 18

14 Attempted Rape Act 1948, s 1 ('7 years penal servitude'), Criminal Justice Act 1948, s 1 (imprisonment replaced penal servitude) and Sexual Offences Act 1956, s 51 and Sch 4 (maintained maximum of 7 years).

15 Sexual Offences Act 1985, s 3(2) (restored life imprisonment as the maximum sentence for attempted rape).

Inclusion in barred lists	Children: automatic if V is a child Subject to representations if V adult Vulnerable adult: subject to reps if V child
Notification	Yes

Sexual intercourse with a girl under 13 Sexual Offences Act 1956, s 5 etc

INTRODUCTION

28.9 Here we deal with 'historic' allegations involving vaginal intercourse girls under the age of 13.

Which version of the law applies to any given allegation of intercourse with a girl under 13 is determined by its timing within the following periods:

A any date up to and including 31 December 1956:

Carnal knowledge of a girl under 13, contrary to s 4 of the Criminal Law Amendment Act 1885

B 1 January 1957 to 30 April 2004 inclusive:

Sexual intercourse with a girl under 13, contrary to s 5 of the Sexual Offences Act 1956

C 1 May 2004 onwards (see **Chapter 10**)

Whatever the date, it was an offence for a male to have vaginal intercourse with a girl under 13, irrespective of consent.

For periods A and B the elements of the offence are identical, only the statement of offence differs.

LEGISLATION

28.10 Criminal Law Amendment Act 1885, s 4:

> Any person who unlawfully and carnally knows any girl under the age of 13 years shall be guilty.....

Sexual Offences Act 1956, s 5

> It is an offence for a man to have unlawful sexual intercourse with a girl under the age of thirteen.

ELEMENTS

28.11

- A is male (the offence could only be committed as a principal by a male, although a woman could aid and abet).

  'Man' does not exclude 'boy' (SOA 1956, s 46)

- Age of A:

  - before 19 September 1993 – A aged at least 14

    (irrebuttable presumption at common law that a boy under 14 is incapable of sexual intercourse – although his actions could amount to an indecent assault of which he is deemed capable)

  - from 20 September 1993 – A aged at least 10

    (age of criminal responsibility – presumption abolished by SOA 1993, s 1)

- Sexual *intercourse* – penetration of the B's vagina by A's penis.

  Any penetration suffices, however slight.

  Ejaculation is not required.

- Age[16] of B: *under 13.*

  There is strict liability as to the girl's age, even a reasonable belief in her being older is no defence.

- *Consent is irrelevant*

DISCUSSION

28.12 No statutory time-limits attach to bringing a prosecution for these offences.

CLASSIFICATION

28.13 Both offences are triable only on indictment.

---

16 See **Chapter 7**.

SENTENCING AND OTHER ORDERS

Maximum sentence

28.14 Period A (s 4 Criminal Law Amendment Act 1885):

- Completed offence, maximum: Life imprisonment
- For an attempt, maximum: 2 years

Period B (s 5 Sexual Offences Act 1956):

- Completed offence, maximum: Life imprisonment
- For an attempt 1 January 1957 to 1 July 1960, maximum: 2 years[17]
- For an attempt 2 July 1960 to 30 April 2004, maximum: 7 years[18]

Other orders

28.15

Extended and life sentence availability (CJA 2003)	Sch 15 (specified offence): yes Sch 15B (life sentence for second listed offence): yes
Trigger offence for:	SOPO: yes FTO: yes
Inclusion in barred lists	Children: automatic Vulnerable adult: subject to reps
Notification	Yes

Buggery
Sexual Offences Act 1956, s 12 etc

INTRODUCTION

28.16 Over the history of sexual offences law, the expression 'buggery' has covered a wide range of conduct, including consensual anal intercourse (illegal even between consenting spouses until 3 November 1994[19]), anal rape

17 Sexual Offences Act 1956, Sch 2, Part1, para 2(b) as enacted.
18 Indecency With Children Act 1960, s 2(3).
19 Criminal Justice and Public Order Act 1994.

and bestiality. It is highly unlikely that practitioners will need to deal with any animal sex cases from before SOA 2003, so we exclude them. Section 7 of the Sexual Offences Act 1967 introduced a 12-month time-limit for commencing proceedings for an offence of buggery of a man aged 16 or over unless the alleged behaviour amounted to an assault, so we will disregard all s 12 buggery between consenting adults and focus only on anal intercourse with children (under 16) and non-consenting adults.

Until 1994 only a woman could be raped and then only vaginally. Cases of what would now be categorised as anal rape could only be prosecuted as buggery or indecent assault. The same will continue to apply to historic cases.

Selection of charges in historic cases may be guided by the penalties available. The maximum penalty for buggery of a child under 16 was life imprisonment. Maximum sentences for other forms of buggery varied according to type and date.

DEFINITIONS

28.17 Offences Against the Person Act 1861, s 61:

> Whosoever shall be convicted of the abominable crime of buggery, committed either with Mankind or with any animal, shall be liable … to be kept in Penal Servitude[20] for life …

Sexual Offences Act 1956, s 12(1):

> It is (an offence) for a person to commit buggery with another person or with an animal.

ELEMENTS

28.18 All dates – limited so as to exclude bestiality.

- Penetration of B's anus by A's penis[21]

  Any degree of penetration will suffice

  No emission or ejaculation is necessary[22]

- Note that absence of consent is *not* an element of this offence, but affects sentencing provisions at some dates

---

20 Criminal Justice Act 1948 s 1(1) provides that penal servitude is replaceable by imprisonment of the same maximum term.

21 *R v Jacobs* (1817) R & R 331.

22 *R v Reekspear* (1832) 1 Mood CC 342; *R v Cozins* (1834) 6 C & P 351; Offences Against the Person Act 1861, s 63.

PARTIES

28.19 The offence could only be committed as a principal by a male, although a woman could aid and abet.

At common law a boy under the age of 14 was deemed incapable of sexual intercourse. This remained a conclusive presumption until its abolition on 20 September 1993 by s 1 of the Sexual Offences Act 1993.

Complainants may be male or female.

DISCUSSION

28.20 Buggery without consent, whether of a male or female, on or after 3 November 1994 (commencement date for Criminal Justice & Public Order Act 1994) should be charged as rape.

Varying penalty provisions have the effect of creating a number of different offences, so the indictment particulars should make clear which is alleged. Alternative counts may be laid if necessary.[23]

DPP's consent is required before instituting proceedings for an offence of buggery with a male if either party was under 16 at the time.[24]

CLASSIFICATION

28.21 Offence is triable only on indictment

SENTENCING AND OTHER ORDERS

28.22 Sentencing for non-consensual buggery in historic cases should be in line with modern sentencing for rape.[25]

Maximum sentences

28.23 Buggery:

- With a female (of any age and at any date): Life

  (from 3 November 1994 charge as rape – same maximum)

---

23 *R v Reakes* [1974] Crim LR 615; *R v Courtie* [1984] AC 463.

24 Sexual Offences Act 1967, s 8 amended by Sexual Offences (Amendment Act 2000), s 1(2)(b).

25 *A-G Ref (No 39 of 2006) R v Rodney Clive* [2007] Cr App R(S) 34.

- With a male under 16 (at any date): Life

  (from 3 November 1994 charge as rape – same maximum)
- With a male 16 or over

  Until 31 December 1956: Life

  From 1 January 1957 to 2 November 1994: 10 years

  From 3 November 1994 onwards (charge as rape): Life

Attempted Buggery (of male or female, of any age):

Until 2 November 1994: 10 years

From 3 November 1994 onwards (charge as attempted rape): Life

Other orders

28.24

Extended and life sentence availability (CJA 2003)	Sch 15 (specified offence): no Sch 15B (life sentence for second listed offence): yes
Trigger offence for:	SOPO: yes FTO: yes, where D over 20 and V under 18
Inclusion in barred lists	Children: subject to representations if V under 16 or non-consent Vulnerable adult: subject to representations if V under 16 or non-consent
Notification	If D over 20 and V under 18

Indecent assault on a woman Sexual Offences Act 1956, s 14 etc

INTRODUCTION

28.25 Here we deal with 'historic' allegations involving sexual assaults on females. The offences apply to all females irrespective of age.

Which version of the law applies to any given allegation of indecent assault on a female is determined by its timing within the following periods:

A. any date up to and including 31 December 1956:

Indecent assault, contrary to s 52 of the Offences Against the Person Act 1861

B. 1 January 1957 to 30 April 2004 inclusive:

Indecent assault on a woman, contrary to s 14 of the Sexual Offences Act 1956

C. 1 May 2004 onwards (see **Chapter 9**)

LEGISLATION

28.26 *Period A*: Offences Against the Person Act 1861, s 52:

> Whosoever shall be convicted of any indecent assault upon any female … shall be liable…to be imprisoned for any term not exceeding two years.

Period B: Sexual Offences Act 1956, s 14:

> (1) It is an offence … for a person to make an indecent assault on a woman.
>
> (2) A girl under the age of sixteen cannot in law give any consent which would prevent an act being an assault for the purposes of this section.

ELEMENTS

Period A

28.27

- An assault (a non-consensual touching – actual or apprehended)
- Accompanied by circumstances of indecency on the part of A towards B[26]

---

26 *Beal v Kelley* (1951) 35 Cr App R 128, at 130, per Lord Goddard CJ, dealing with s 15.

- Consent is a defence, but not if the assault involved blows intended or likely to cause bodily harm[27]
- Consent is no defence if B was under 16,[28] unless A genuinely believed A to have attained that age[29]
- Invitation/incitement alone is insufficient[30] – contrast Indecency with Children Act 1960, s 1

Period B[31]

28.28

- B is female, of any age – 'woman' does not exclude 'girl' (SOA 1956, s 46)
- An intentional assault (a non-consensual touching – actual or apprehended)
- The assault (or the assault and the circumstances accompanying it) is capable of being considered by right-minded persons as indecent
- A intended not merely an assault, but one that was indecent
- Consent is a defence, but not if the assault involved blows intended or likely to cause bodily harm[32]
- Consent is no defence if B was under 16,[33] unless A genuinely believed A to have attained that age[34]

DISCUSSION

28.29 These offences may be committed by males or females[35].

No time-limits attach to prosecuting these offences, but the House of Lords in *R v J*[36] ruled that it is impermissible to bring a charge under this section

27 *R v Donovan* [1934] 2 KB 498, 25 Cr App R 1.
28 Not in OAPA 1861, but Criminal Law Amendment Act 1880 (age 13) and then Criminal Law Amendment Act 1922 (age 16) introduced this provision.
29 *R v Maughan (Reginald)* (1934) 24 Cr App R 130 was to contrary effect, but we suggest that this is overtaken by the House of Lords' reasoning in *R v K* [2002] 1 AC 462.
30 *Fairclough v Whipp* (1951) 35 Cr App R 138, compare *Beal & Kelley* (1951) 35 Cr App R 128.
31 Stated in *R v Court* [1988] 2 All ER 221, per Lord Ackner.
32 *R v Donovan* [1934] 2 KB 498, 25 Cr App R 1.
33 SOA 1956, s 14(2).
34 *R v K* [2002] 1 AC 462.
35 *R v Hare* [1934] 1 KB 354; 24 Cr App R 108; and SOA 1956, s 14 reads '… a person …'.
36 [2004] UKHL 42, [2005] 1 AC 562.

in order to circumvent the 12-month time-limit on initiating prosecution for unlawful sexual intercourse ('USI') with a girl under 16 contrary to s 6 SOA 1956. Where a defendant in an historic case is charged with rape, the trial judge is permitted to leave USI as an alternative verdict, but it may not be put on the indictment. This state of affairs was described in *R v Cottrell & Fletcher*[37] as "a shambles".

It is quite remarkable that a man could still be prosecuted for, say, having kissed or fondled a girl of almost sixteen, but would escape any liability for full sexual intercourse with a child on her thirteenth birthday. There remains an available option where a position of trust existed, namely an offence under s 3 Sexual Offences (Amendment) Act 2000. This was in force from 8 January 2001 until 30 April 2004[38] (inclusive) and provided a maximum penalty of 5 years imprisonment. There is no time limit in relation to that offence.

Historically, there has been divergent opinion as to whether the complainant's age should be stated in the indictment. In *R v Hodgson*[39] the Court of Appeal deprecated such averment, although surely it was essential for female complainants under 13 when increased penalties applied (from 2 July 1960 to 15 September 1985, see **28.31**).

CLASSIFICATION

28.30 Both offences are triable either-way.

A consolidated Practice Direction in 2002[40] indicated that indecent assault should be tried summarily unless the court considered its sentencing powers insufficient and one or more of the following factors applied:

- Substantial age disparity and a 'more serious' assault;
- Breach of trust;
- Several 'more serious' offences;
- Particularly vulnerable complainant;
- Serious nature of the alleged assault.

Nonetheless, careful consideration should be given before jurisdiction is retained in the Magistrates' Court for any 'historic' cases, given the legal complexities that invariably arise. Furthermore, seldom will summary trial provide adequate sentencing powers in those historic cases for which, despite their age, prosecution remains in the public interest.

---

37 [2007] EWCA Crim 2016, per Sir Igor Judge (President QBD), at [38].
38 Repealed by Sexual Offences Act 2003.
39 [1973] 57 Cr App R 502.
40 [2002] 3 All ER 904, at [51].

SENTENCING AND OTHER ORDERS

Maximum sentence

28.31

- *Period A* (Offences Against the Person Act 1861, s 52):

  Maximum: 2 years imprisonment[41]

- *Period B* (Sexual Offences Act 1956, s 14):

  Maximum sentence depends on the offence date and age of victim:

1 January 1957 to 1 July 1960 (inclusive)	
Victim any age:	2 years imprisonment[42]
2 July 1960 to 15 September 1985 (inclusive)	
Victim aged 13 or over:	2 years imprisonment[43]
2 July 1960 to 15 September 1985 (inclusive)	
Victim aged under 13 (and so stated on indictment):	5 years imprisonment[44]
16 September 1985 to 30 April 2004 (inclusive):	
Victim any age:	10 years imprisonment[45]

Where an allegation date straddles the periods before and after an increased penalty, the lower maximum applies.

Other orders

28.32

Extended and life sentence availability (CJA 2003)	Sch 15 (specified offence): yes Sch 15B (life sentence for second listed offence): yes
Trigger offence for:	SOPO: yes FTO: yes, where V under 18

41 Offences Against The Person Act 1861, s 52.
42 SOA 1956, s 37 and Sch 2(17).
43 SOA 1956, s 37 and Sch 2(17).
44 Indecency With Children Act 1960, s 2(1)(b) and (3)(c).
45 Sexual Offences Act 1985, s 3(3).

Inclusion in barred lists	Children: subject to representations Vulnerable adult: subject to representations
Notification	If V under 18 or D given 30 months imprisonment or restriction order

Indecent assault on a man
Sexual Offences Act 1956, s 15 etc

INTRODUCTION

28.33 Here we deal with 'historic' allegations involving sexual assaults on males.

The offences apply to all males irrespective of age.

Which version of the law applies to any given allegation of indecent assault on a male is determined by its timing within the following periods:

A. any date up to and including 31 December 1956:

Indecent assault, contrary to s 62 of the Offences Against the Person Act 1861

B. 1 January 1957 to 30 April 2004 inclusive:

Indecent Assault on a Man, contrary to s 15 of the Sexual Offences Act 1956

C. 1 May 2004 onwards [see **Chapter 9**]

LEGISLATION

28.34 *Period A*: Offences Against the Person Act 1861, s 62:

> Whosoever shall attempt to commit the said abominable crime,[46] or shall be guilty of any assault with intent to commit the same, or of any indecent assault upon any male person…shall be liable…to be kept in Penal Servitude for any term not exceeding ten years…or to be imprisoned for any term not exceeding two years.[47]

46 The 'abominable crime' is buggery, referring to the preceding section, OAPA 1861, s 61.

47 For current effect of the sentencing provisions, see **28.39** and fn 59.

Period B: Sexual Offences Act 1956, s 15:

(1) It is an offence for a person to make an indecent assault on a man.

(2) A boy under the age of sixteen cannot in law give any consent which would prevent an act being an assault for the purposes of this section.

ELEMENTS

Period A

28.35

- An assault (a non-consensual touching – actual or apprehended)
- Accompanied by circumstances of indecency on the part of A towards B[48]
- Consent is a defence, but not if the assault involved blows intended or likely to cause bodily harm[49]
- Consent is no defence if B was under 16,[50] unless A genuinely believed A to have attained that age[51]
- Invitation/incitement alone is insufficient[52] – contrast Indecency with Children Act 1960, s 1

Period B[53]

28.36

- B is male, of any age – 'man' does not exclude 'boy' (SOA 1956, s 46)
- An intentional assault (a non-consensual touching – actual or apprehended)
- The assault (or the assault and the circumstances accompanying it) is capable of being considered by right-minded persons as indecent
- A intended not merely an assault, but one that was indecent

---

48 *Beal v Kelley* (1951) 35 Cr App R 128, at 130, per Lord Goddard CJ.

49 *R v Donovan* [1934] 2 KB 498, 25 Cr App R 1.

50 Not in OAPA 1861, but Criminal Law Amendment Act 1880 (age 13) and then Criminal Law Amendment Act 1922 (age 16) introduced this provision.

51 *R v Maughan* (1934) 24 Cr App R was to contrary effect, but we suggest that this is overtaken by the House of Lords' reasoning in *R v K* [2002] 1 AC 462.

52 *Fairclough v Whipp* (1951) 35 Cr App R 138, compare *Beal & Kelley* (1951) 35 Cr App R 128.

53 Stated in *R v Court* [1988] 2 All ER 221, per Lord Ackner, dealing with s 14.

- Consent is a defence, but not if the assault involved blows intended or likely to cause bodily harm[54]
- Consent is no defence if B was under 16,[55] unless A genuinely believed A to have attained that age[56]

DISCUSSION

28.37 These offences may be committed by males or females.[57]

No time-limits attach to prosecuting these offences.

CLASSIFICATION

28.38 Both offences are triable either-way.

A consolidated Practice Direction in 2002[58] indicated that indecent assault should be tried summarily unless the court considered its sentencing powers insufficient and one or more of the following factors applied:

- substantial age disparity and a 'more serious' assault;
- breach of trust;
- several 'more serious' offences;
- particularly vulnerable complainant;
- serious nature of the alleged assault.

Nonetheless, careful consideration should be given before jurisdiction is retained in the Magistrates' Court for any 'historic' cases, given the legal complexities that invariably arise. Furthermore, seldom will summary trial provide adequate sentencing powers in those historic cases for which, despite their age, prosecution remains in the public interest.

54 *R v Donovan* [1934] 2 KB 498; 25 Cr App R 1.
55 SOA 1956, s 15(2).
56 *R v K* [2002] 1 AC 462.
57 *R v Hare* [1934] 1 KB 354, 24 Cr App R 108 – and SOA 1956, ss 14 and 15 read '... a person ...'.
58 [2002] 3 All ER 904, at [51].

SENTENCING AND OTHER ORDERS

Maximum sentence

28.39

- *Period A* (Offences Against the Person Act 1861, s 62):

  Maximum: 10 years imprisonment[59]

- *Period B* (Sexual Offences Act 1956, s 15):

  Maximum: 10 years imprisonment[60]

In contrast to the penalty provisions for indecent assault of a female, the maximum under s 15 has remained constant and does not vary according to the victim's age.

Other orders

28.40

Extended and life sentence availability (CJA 2003)	Sch 15 (specified offence): yes Sch 15B (life sentence for second listed offence): yes
Trigger offence for:	SOPO: yes FTO: yes, where V under 18
Inclusion in barred lists	Children: subject to representations Vulnerable adult: subject to representations
Notification	If V under 18 or D given 30 months imprisonment or restriction order

59 Offences Against The Person Act 1861, s 62 – two years imprisonment or penal servitude 3–10 years, but Criminal Justice Act 1948, s 1(1) provides that penal servitude is replaceable by imprisonment of the same maximum term.

60 SOA 1956, s 37(3) and Sch 2(18).

Chapter 29

Gross indecency with a child

Indecency with Children Act 1960, s 1 in force 2 July 1960 until 30 April 2004

DEFINITION

29.1 Section 1(1):

> Any person who commits an act of gross indecency with or towards a child under the age of sixteen,[1] or who incites a child under that age to such an act with him or another, shall be liable on conviction on indictment to imprisonment for a term not exceeding ten years,[2] or on summary conviction to imprisonment for a term not exceeding six months, to a fine not exceeding £400,[3] or to both.

ELEMENTS

29.2

- commits or incites
- an *act*

  The authorities show a very broad interpretation of 'commits an act', including the case of *R v Speck*[4] in which *inactivity* sufficed. The appellant had allowed, with no express encouragement, an 8-year-old girl's hand to remain on his clothed penis for some minutes, causing an erection. The Court of Appeal identified his inertia as an implied

---

1 Under 14 from 2 July 1960 until 11 January 2001, when amended by Criminal Justice and Court Services Act 2000, s 39.
2 2 years from 2 July 1960 until 1 October 1997, when increased by Crime (Sentences) Act 1997, s 52.
3 Originally £100, increased by Criminal Justice Act 1967 (s 92 and Sch 3).
4 [1977] 2 All ER 859.

invitation to the child to continue her behaviour and judged that this could constitute the requisite 'act' by D.

- of gross indecency

  Gross indecency is not defined in this statute, nor in others where the phrase is used. Interpretation will be a matter for the tribunal.

  By way of non-exhaustive example only, we note that the Wolfenden Committee[5] said of the same phrase in SOA 1956, s 13 (gross indecency between men) 'it usually takes the form of mutual masturbation, inter-crural contact or oral-genital contact'.

- With or towards

  The words 'with or towards' are to be read collectively.[6]

  Assistance with this element is found in *R v Francis*[7] which held that masturbating in the presence of a child sufficed, so long as D knew that the child was aware of his act, even if he had not deliberately sought such attention, sufficed. Conversely, if D believed the child to be unaware, he would not commit the offence. It is clear that the offence does not require any physical contact between D and a child.

- a child under the *age* of:

  - 14: 2 July 1960 until 11 January 2001
  - 16: 11 January 2001 until 30 April 2004

  The age of the child is a material averment (see Specimen Indictment, **Appendix 1**).

  A genuine belief (even if unreasonable) that the child had attained the relevant age would be a complete defence.

DISCUSSION

29.3 It was confirmed by the House of Lords in *B (A Minor) v DPP*[8] that this offence is one requiring *mens rea*, rather than being an offence of strict liability. Hence, as stated above, a genuine mistake concerning the essential age element negatives liability.

5 Wolfenden Report 4 September 1957 at paras 104–105.
6 *B (A Minor) v DPP* [1999] 3 WLR 116 (Divisional Court).
7 (1988) 88 Cr App R 127.
8 [2000] 2 AC 428.

DEFENCES

29.4 Honest belief that the child had attained the relevant age.

Activity not being 'with or towards' the child: for example, child observes D masturbating without D intending or being aware of the observation.

CLASSIFICATION

29.5 Offence is triable either way, but careful consideration should be given before retaining jurisdiction in the magistrates' court for any 'historic' cases, given the complexities that invariably arise. It is unlikely, if the circumstances make such a late prosecution in the public interest, that summary trial would provide adequate sentencing powers.

SENTENCING AND OTHER ORDERS

Maximum sentence

29.6 Maximum sentence depends on the offence date:

- 2 July 1960 to 30 September 1997 (inclusive): 2 years imprisonment[9]
- 1 October 1997 to 30 April 2004 (inclusive): 10 years imprisonment[10]

Where an allegation date straddles the periods before and after the increased penalty, the lower maximum applies.

Other orders

29.7

Extended sentence availability (CJA 2003)	Sch 15: yes Sch 15B: yes
Trigger offence for:	SOPO: yes FTO: yes
Inclusion in barred lists	Children: subject to representations Vulnerable adult: subject to representations
Notification	Yes

9 Indecency with Children Act 1960, s 1(1).
10 Increased from 2 years by Crime (Sentences) Act 1997, s 52, in force 10 October 1997.

Part E
Topics

Chapter 30

Police station attendance

30.1 Advice proffered at the police station can have far reaching consequences and it is a commonplace to say that guilt or innocence is often decided at this stage.

We cannot here deal with the full range of issues that arise in advising suspects at the police station. Probably the most important matters that legal advisors must consider in these situations relate to the provision of samples and advice on whether to speak in interview. We set out the law on these two areas and offer guidance concerning the key decisions.

Bearing in mind the seriousness of sexual allegations and the fact that those accused are often strangers to the criminal justice system, we provide the following checklist.

INITIAL ATTENDANCE AT THE POLICE STATION – A CHECKLIST

30.2

- Prior to attendance, obtain brief details of the offences being alleged.
- Consider the statutory and other potential defences to the alleged offences.

Attending the police station

30.3

- Important to keep accurate notes including details of times
- View custody record. Check and record the following:
  - Client's personal details
  - Place and time of arrest
  - Details of the alleged offence as stated on custody record
  - Whether any significant comments have been made by client during booking in procedure

- Check property sheet – record items, in particular items seized as evidence (including clothing and shoes)
- Check if any samples (intimate and non-intimate) have already been taken
- Check if client has been drug tested – result
- Check if client has been seen by FME ('Forensic Medical Examiner') – note any medical conditions (note: may have to get client's authority before allowed to view)
- Check if client fit to be interviewed/detained or if they require an appropriate adult
- Check custody log to see if there have been any incidents while the client has been in custody
- Check the custody log to see if the officer in the case has spoken to the client
- Check to see if client has asked for anyone to be notified of the arrest and if they have been allowed to speak to anyone
- Check if home address has been searched

Obtaining disclosure from the officer in the case

30.4

- Obtain the full name and contact details of the officer in the case
- Often written disclosure will be provided – this does not prevent the lawyer asking additional questions. Keep full record of questions asked and responses given, even if the officer refuses to comment
- Keep a note of the time disclosure was given and who gave the disclosure
- Obtain as much information about the alleged offence as is possible including:
  - Date, time and location of alleged offence
  - When the matter was reported to the police and by whom?
  - What forensic evidence has been obtained?
  - Complainant's name
  - Whether complainant has provided a statement or a videoed interview
  - What injuries, if any, the complainant has
  - Any other witnesses, if so have these witnesses have provided statements?

- Any other evidence – eg CCTV footage, mobile phone evidence
- Whether the complainant and the suspect are known to each other – if so the nature of their relationship – whether there have been any past incidents
- If the complainant and client do not know each other, ask how the client was identified
- Client's previous convictions
- Any significant comments made to the police – check if the suspect has signed officer's notebook
- Any significant silences
- Reply made by client after being informed of the reasons for arrest
- Reply made by client after caution
- Whether anyone else was present when client was arrested
- Whether client's home address, work or place of arrest were searched – if so the results of this search
- Ask if the officer intends to provide staged disclosure

Attending the client

30.5

- Introduce self and outline role
- Go through the disclosure provided – warning the client that the disclosure given is unlikely to be the entire case against him or her as police may have withheld information, investigations may be at an early stage, further investigations may need to be undertaken, etc
- Go through any information as obtained from the custody record

Advising the client generally

30.6

- Advise on the law – the elements of the offence(s) and available defences
- Advise client that should the matter progress further, final charges may be different from that arrested for
- Advice on caution
- Advice on interview procedure

Taking instructions

30.7

- Only need to take initial instructions, but ensure a full note is kept
- Confirm client's instructions
- Make a careful and full note of client's demeanour, eg is client anxious, tired, suffering from any mental health or physical health problem?

Advising client whether or not to answer questions

30.8 See **30.14**.

FAILURE TO MENTION FACTS AND ADVERSE INFERENCES

30.9

> 'Where, in any proceedings against a person for an offence, evidence is given that the accused … on being questioned under caution by a constable trying to discover whether or by whom the offence had been committed, failed to mention any fact relied on in his defence in those proceedings … being a fact which in the circumstances existing at the time the accused could reasonably have been expected to mention when so questioned … the court or jury … may draw such inferences from the failure as appear proper' (Criminal Justice & Public Order Act 1994, s 34).

Consider what a suspect could *reasonably* be expected to mention when questioned or charged.

- It is doubtful whether an adverse inference can be drawn if questioning relates to extremely old matters as it can be argued that due to the passage of time it may be unreasonable for the suspect to mention a fact
- The same may apply to complex cases or circumstances
- No adverse inference should be drawn if very limited disclosure given prior to interview as it is not reasonable to expect a client to mention a fact when he is unaware of the full details of the allegation against him.
- However, be aware that police often disclose additional information during the actual interview which could trigger an adverse inference if questions are not answered. Consequently during the interview the advisor should constantly review advice given and if need be should stop the interview to further advise the client.

Prepared statements

30.10 Note, a prepared statement or answering questions does not automatically stop an adverse inference being raised, as the issue is whether the defendant 'failed to mention any fact relied on in his defence'.

- An adverse inference can be drawn if D departs from his prepared statement, gives a different explanation at trial or fails to mention a fact in his/her answers/prepared statement which is then raised at trial.

Pre-conditions for an adverse inference

30.11 *R v Argent*[1] details the conditions that must be satisfied before an adverse inference can be drawn:

1. there must be proceedings against a person for an offence;
2. the alleged failure to mention a fact at trial must have occurred before charge, or on charge;
3. the alleged failure must have occurred during questioning under caution;
4. the questioning must have been directed to trying to discover whether or by whom the alleged offence was committed;
5. the alleged failure of the accused must have been to mention any fact relied on in his defence in those proceedings
6. the alleged failure must have been to mention a fact which in the circumstances existing at the time the accused could reasonably have been expected to mention when so questioned.

R v Howell[2] held that 'in the circumstance existing at the time' can be construed so as to include, when relevant, time of day, defendant's age, experience, mental capacity, state of health, sobriety, tiredness, knowledge, personality and legal advice.

The effect of legal advice

30.12 D when giving evidence can state that he remained silent on legal advice.

- *R v Beckles*[3] details the two-stage test for the jury to consider before drawing an adverse inference namely:

---

1 [1997] 2 Cr App R 27.
2 [2003] EWCA Crim 1.
3 [2004] EWCA Crim 2766.

1. did the defendant genuinely rely on the legal advice, ie did the defendant accept the advice and believe that he was entitled to follow it; and
2. was it reasonable for the defendant to rely on the advice?

- Reasonableness does not depend on whether the advice was legally correct
- The defendant will have to waive legal privilege if doubts are raised by the Crown of the reasonableness or otherwise of his reliance on legal advice
- Also legal privilege will be waived if the defendant explains the reasons why he was advised to remain silent
- However *Condron*[4] – privilege not waived if the advisor is called to rebut inference of subsequent fabrication
- Always keep a careful note of the advice given and why, bearing in mind that, in certain circumstances, the advisor's note may be disclosed to the Crown

Adverse inferences are only relevant if the matter will proceed to trial. If the suspect admits the offence and then fails to answer questions, no adverse inference can be drawn and no reduction in credit can be made.

Finally, what inference can be drawn is dependent on the facts of the case and on the jury but a defendant cannot be found guilty of an offence based solely on an adverse inference.

POLICE INTERVIEW – ADVISING THE CLIENT

30.13 No two police station attendances are the same, and no two sets of allegations are the same. Each case turns on its particular facts and there are no strict rules as to when a client should or should not answer questions. As with non-sexual allegations, when in doubt always advise client to answer no comment.

There are three options for the police interview

- Silence
- Prepared statement
- Full comment

4 [1997] 1 WLR 827.

What option is taken will depend on the circumstance of each case. Also the advice given should be under constant review as further information is disclosed during the course of the police interview.

If the decision is taken to advice the client *not to answer questions*, then a careful note of why this advice was given should be made. In addition:

- the client should be advised that he or she should give no answers to all questions asked, no matter how innocuous some may appear. Answers to some questions and not others simply highlights the questions not answered.
- The client should be advised that the police sometimes give a 'special warning' to clients who are not answering questions. The client should be advised about this and advised that the special warning does not change the advice given.
- The client should be advised that the police still have to ask the questions even though the client has made the decision not to answer.
- Further that it is better to answer 'no comment' rather than to remain silent as this simply prolongs the interview process.
- Some police officers will question the validity of the advice given and will seek to undermine the legal advisor. The client should be warned that this may happen.

If the decision is made to *draft a prepared statement* then care must be taken that the statement correctly records the client's instructions since a prepared statement will not prevent an adverse inference being drawn if it is inconsistent with evidence given by the client at trial and/or does not mention facts which are later mentioned at trial.

- The prepared statement must be signed by the client.
- The prepared statement should be read by the advisor at the beginning of the interview after the client has been cautioned and informed of his rights and entitlements by the officers.
- The client should be advised firmly that no questions should be answered after the prepared statement has been read.
- As stated above, the detail contained in the prepared statement may need to be added to if further disclosure is provided during the police interview.

Perhaps the most difficult decision is that of *advising the client to answer questions* because, as stated in the caution, anything the client says in interview may be used against them. It is therefore crucial that the client is advised that his or her account will be subject to scrutiny by the police and any inconsistencies commented upon both during the course of the interview and at trial.

30.13 *Police station attendance*

Should a suspect accused of a sexual offence answer questions? Subject to all the caveats above, there are three reasons which, we suggest, make speaking in interview a more attractive option than in relation to many non-sexual offences. First, in sexual offence allegations, the area of contention is frequently not what the suspect *did*, but what he *believed*. So, the truth or reasonableness of the defendant's belief in the complainant's consent or belief that she was over a certain age limit are often the issues which a jury are asked to decide upon. These are matters which are fully within the suspect's knowledge, are relatively uncomplicated and are difficult for the police or prosecution to gainsay with any authority. In short, if the advisor's view is that the suspect will be able to conduct himself well in interview, the advice is likely to be to answer the questions.

Secondly, being entirely within the suspect's personal knowledge, these are matters which he might usually be expected to mention. Arguing that there was a good reason for the suspect not mentioning his properly and reasonably held belief (absent some unusual circumstances) is likely to be difficult, creating the very strong likelihood that the jury would be invited to draw an adverse inference if he fails to do so.

Thirdly, the strength of the inference which is drawn from silence, or the effect on the jury of hearing that the defendant made no comment in interview, is likely to be very damaging. In serious sexual offences more than any others, we would suggest that jurors are likely to be very unimpressed that the defendant could not put his account down promptly, particularly on issues of knowledge and belief. The jury are likely to think that the issue is a relatively simple one – 'did she or didn't she consent?'; 'did he genuinely believe she consented?' – and perhaps expect an innocent accused to answer the allegation at the first opportunity.

SAMPLES

30.14 Provisions relating to the taking of samples can be divided into the following sections:

1. Fingerprints
2. Photographs
3. Search for identifying marks
4. Intimate samples
5. Non-intimate samples

Fingerprints

PACE s 65 and Code D section 4

30.15 The police have extensive powers to take fingerprints with or without consent.

As a basic guide, a suspect in custody after being arrested for a recordable offence, should be advised to consent to having their fingerprints taken.

The lawyer should advise their client that refusal to consent will allow the police to use reasonable force to take their fingerprints and this could result in additional charges of obstructing or assaulting a police officer acting in the execution of their duty.

Note, that if a suspect has attended the police station as a volunteer and is questioned about a recordable offence, there is no power at that point to take his/her fingerprints. However, the police can subsequently take fingerprints without consent if the person is later arrested, charged or informed that they will be reported for a recordable offence.

The provisions relating to the retention and destruction of fingerprints (and DNA samples) are contained within the Protection of Freedoms Act 2012. The length of time fingerprints are retained is dependent on the nature of the offence, whether person was arrested, charged, convicted and previous convictions.

Finally, the suspect should be advised that fingerprints will be subject to speculative comparison with those held on the police database.

Photographs

PACE s 64A and Code D section 5

30.16 As with fingerprints, the police have extensive powers to take photographs with or without consent.

Again, as a basic guide, a client in custody after being arrested for a recordable offence should be advised to consent to having their photograph taken. As above, the police have the power to use reasonable force and any refusal to co-operate could result in charges of obstructing or assaulting a police officer acting in the execution of their duty.

Note, unlike the provisions for the taking fingerprints from volunteers, the police do have the power to take a photograph of a suspect who attends the police station as a volunteer; however, force may not be used.

Clients should also be advised that the police can ask them to remove any head covering or item which obscures their face. In addition, if this request is not complied with, then a police officer or designated civilian may remove the item.

Photographs taken of people detained in custody generally do not have to be destroyed unless they have attended the police station as a volunteer and no further action is to be taken against them.

In addition to taking photographs of a person's face, the police also have powers to photograph other parts of the body (see below), however a person should not be required to remove other forms of clothing to facilitate the taking of photographs.

Search for identifying marks

PACE s 54A and Code D section 5

30.17 Identifying marks are any marks or features which assist in either establishing the detained person's identity or identification as a person involved in the commission of an offence.

An identifying mark may be photographed.

A search for an identifying mark may be conducted with the consent of the detained person or if this consent is refused then a search can be conducted with the authorisation of an officer of at least inspector rank.

If consent is refused and authorisation for a search has been given by an inspector then the police may use reasonable force.

A person attending as a volunteer may also be subject to a search or examination; however, force cannot be used.

Whether or not a suspect should consent to the police searching for an identifying mark will depend on individual circumstances. If there is any doubt whether they should consent, it would be sensible to refuse consent thereby requiring the officers to obtain authorisation from their inspector. The grounds for the authorisation should be considered; however, if the authorisation is given then the client should be advised to co-operate.

The provisions governing the destruction of any photographs taken of identifying marks are identical to those relating to photographs of a person's face.

Intimate samples

PACE s 62 and Code D section 6

30.18 Intimate samples are defined as samples of:

1. Blood, semen, urine or other tissue fluid (not saliva)

2. Pubic hair
3. Dental impression
4. Swabs from any part of a person's genitals (including pubic hair) or from a person's body orifice other than their mouth

The basic requirements before an intimate sample can be taken are that authorisation must be given by an officer of at least the rank of inspector *and* appropriate consent has been given.

Authorisation may only be given in the following circumstances:

(a) for a person detained at a police station for a recordable offence:
 - (i) the officer has reasonable grounds for suspecting the person's involvement in a recordable offence; and
 - (ii) the officer believes an intimate sample will tend to confirm or disprove that person's involvement;

(b) for a person not detained at a police station:
 - (i) from whom, in the course of an investigation for an offence, two or more non-intimate samples suitable for the same means of analysis have been taken which proved to be insufficient; and
 - (ii) the officer has reasonable grounds for believing that the sample will tend to confirm or disprove involvement;

(c) in the case of any person whether detained or not:
 - (i) two or more non-intimate samples suitable for the same means of analysis have been taken after conviction for offences outside of England and Wales, which have proved insufficient.

Before a sample is taken, the suspect must be informed of the following:

1. the reason for the sample being taken;
2. the fact that authorisation has been given;
3. the provisions under which this authorisation was given; and
4. if the sample is being taken at a police station, the client must be informed that it will be subject to a speculative search.

In addition to the above the suspect should be cautioned before an intimate sample is taken.

Note: An intimate sample can never be taken without the consent of the suspect; however they must be warned that refusal to consent could result in an adverse inference being drawn at trial. Further, if at the time the request for an intimate sample is made the suspect is detained in custody and is unrepresented, they must be reminded of their entitlement to free legal advice.

The police also have powers to require a person to attend a police station for an intimate sample to be taken or face arrest in default. However it should be noted that a sample cannot be taken unless the necessary conditions have been satisfied and appropriate consent has been given.

It is sometimes the case that officers will insist a defendant on court bail returns to the police station to provide an intimate sample. Any such requests should be scrutinised to ensure the police have the power to make this request, in particular whether two or more non-intimate samples have been taken which proved to be insufficient.

Advising on consenting to giving intimate samples

30.19 Advising a client on whether or not they should consent to the giving of an intimate sample depends on the circumstances of the case. Often this issue will arise before the lawyer's attendance at the police station and before full details of the case have been provided by the officer.

Whenever the issue of intimate samples arises it is important to obtain as much information about the request as is possible and to check if the conditions for this request have been met. This would include:

1. confirming the client has been arrested for a recordable offence;
2. checking the grounds upon which authorisation has been given;
3. asking whether the police are in possession of forensic evidence and the nature of this evidence (see below);
4. asking what intimate sample is to be taken and considering whether the taking of a sample have any probative effect; for instance in a rape allegation where the client accepts sexual intercourse and the issue is that of consent it is arguable that an intimate sample of, say, a genital swab would be of no probative benefit;
5. considering whether a sample would tend to confirm or disprove the client's involvement; for example a urine sample in a rape allegation could be analysed for the presence of drugs or alcohol but would not, by itself, confirm or disprove a client's involvement;
6. Consider whether it is necessary for an intimate sample to be taken, for example if an intimate sample is required for DNA profile to be obtained then this could be obtained by the taking of a non-intimate sample (see **30.21**).

An adverse inference can be drawn if the statutory conditions are satisfied and the client subsequently refuses without good cause to provide appropriate consent. What adverse inference will be made at trial and how this will impact on the case is difficult to predict therefore the client must always be warned about the dangers of refusing consent.

The adverse inference provisions are different from those relating to failure to answer questions or account for an object/mark or presence at a location in a police interview under caution as an adverse inference in those circumstances is based on the reasonableness of the decision. Adverse inferences with reference to intimate samples can only be drawn if consent was refused without good cause. It is therefore arguable that a decision made on legal advice could prevent an adverse inference being drawn. However care should be taken in giving this advice as the jury may take such a refusal as an indication the client had something to hide and could affect the client's credibility at trial.

In cases where the evidence against a client is weak then the decision whether or not to advise the client to consent should be carefully considered as an intimate sample may actually assist the police and provide the evidential missing link to the offence; for example in cases of 'stranger rape'.

It should also be borne in mind that often, samples are requested at a very early stage of the police investigation and therefore before the police are in possession of all or indeed any of the forensic evidence.

Clients may also feel embarrassed or fearful if providing an intimate sample, for example a genital swab. Various safeguards surrounding who and in what circumstances an intimate sample can be taken are contained within Code D. It is therefore unlikely that the courts will take a refusal based on grounds of embarrassment, religious objection or fearfulness as a good cause. If the client does raise such an issue then a careful note of the client's reasons for refusing consent should be made and in certain circumstances the reasons for refusing consent could be noted on the custody record (subject to the client's authorisation).

The provisions governing the destruction of intimate samples are contained in the Protection of Freedoms Act 2012. The length of time an intimate sample is kept depends on the same factors as those outlined for the retention of fingerprint evidence.

Non-intimate samples

PACE s 63 and Code D section 6.

30.20 Non-intimate samples are:

1. Hair, other than pubic hair;
2. Sample taken from nails or from under nails;
3. A swab from any part of the body, including the mouth but not any other body orifice;
4. Saliva;

5. Footprint or other similar impression of any part of a person's body other than that of a hand.

The main difference between non-intimate and intimate samples is that an adverse inference cannot be drawn for refusing to provide a non-intimate sample. However, as with fingerprints, the police may use reasonable force to take a non-intimate sample and as above, clients must be advised that refusal to co-operate could potentially result in additional charge of assaulting or obstructing a police officer in the execution of their duty.

Non-intimate samples can always be taken if the client consents. The police also have extensive powers to take non-intimate samples without consent and without requiring authorisation.

In general terms authorisation is not needed if a person has been arrested on suspicion of a recordable offence and is in police detention. Further, a person who attends the police station as a volunteer and is later charged or informed that they will be reported or cautioned (if they have admitted the offence) can have a non-intimate sample taken without consent and without the authorisation of an inspector.

In addition to the above, the police have wide powers to require a person released on bail or a person who has been convicted to return to the police station for a non-intimate sample to be taken (PACE s 63A(4)).

When advising on non-intimate samples it is important to check that any relevant conditions have been satisfied and, if required, authorisation has been given. If the conditions have been met then a client should be advised to provide the sample requested. The client should also be advised that the sample would be subject to a speculative search against crimes recorded on the police database.

Chapter 31

Jurisdiction

Sexual Offences Act 2003, s 72 and Sch 2

31.1 A number of sections of the Sexual Offences Act deal, directly or indirectly, with the abuse of children and others outside the UK, including the trafficking legislation and the imposition of foreign travel orders. Section 72 of the Act deals most directly with the problem and extends the jurisdictional scope of child sexual offences to activities which occur anywhere in the world. The provision applies to a UK national or resident who does an act outside the UK which would constitute a relevant sexual offence in England and Wales.

SEXUAL OFFENCES TO WHICH S 72 APPLIES[1]

31.2 Schedule 2:

- Rape and other offences against children under 13 (ss 5 to 8)
- Child sex offences (ss 9 to 15)
- Abuse of positions of trust (ss 16 to 19)
- Familial child sex offences (ss 25 and 26)
- Abuse of children through prostitution and pornography (ss 47 to 50)
- Rape, assault by penetration, sexual assault, sexual activity without consent (ss 1 to 4) where the victim was under 18
- Sexual offences against people with a mental disorder (ss 30 to 41) where the victim was under 18
- Preparatory offences (ss 61 to 63) where the victim or intended victim was under 18
- Taking or making indecent photographs of children (Protection of Children Act 1978, s 1)

---

1 Including attempts, conspiracies or incitements to commit these offences and aiding and abetting, counselling or procuring the commission of the offences.

- Possession of indecent photograph of children (Criminal Justice Act 1988, s 160)

APPLICATION

31.3 The section applies to a UK national or resident who does an act outside the UK which would constitute a Sch 2 offence if done in the UK. It also applies to those who become UK nationals or residents after doing the act. In relation to residents and those who later become UK nationals or residents, there is a further requirement that the act must constitute an offence in the country in which it took place. This is not a requirement for UK nationals who are deemed to know, and required to abide by, English laws when travelling overseas, irrespective of local law.

Definitions of a UK national and resident are contained at s 72(9).

EXAMPLES

31.4 The section will cover both predatory paedophiles who travel abroad in order to abuse children and those who commit offences against child family members while they are on holiday in a foreign country. In the latter instance, offences within and outside the jurisdiction may be contained on the same indictment (the terms of which should contain both s 72 and the substantive offence – see Specimen Indictment, **Appendix 1**).

PRACTICALITIES

31.5 There may be few evidential problems where, for instance, a foreign allegation forms just one of a number of complaints of continuing sexual abuse made by a child against a family member. Such an instance may be important to the Crown as something that happens on holiday has a degree of specificity in relation to time and place that is often lacking in child sex allegations. Where the allegation relates to foreign children, for instance in 'sex tourism' cases, there will be the added complexity of evidence gathering and co-operation between UK and extra-national police forces. It will usually be possible for foreign witnesses, especially children, to give evidence via video link from their own country.

Where it is a requirement that the act constitute an offence in the foreign country, there is a presumption that this is so, unless the defendant takes issue with this interpretation of the foreign law and serves a notice to that effect on the prosecution. It is then a question of law for the judge to decide whether the overseas offence is the equivalent to an offence in Sch 2 (s 72(6)–(8)).

HISTORIC CONSIDERATIONS

31.6 Section 72 replaced the provisions of s 7 of the Sex Offenders Act 1997, extending it to cover the offences in the 2003 Act. The original s 72 was in itself substituted by s 72(1) of the Criminal Justice and Immigration Act 2008, which removed the necessity that, for UK nationals, the act be an offence in the country in which it was committed and increased the Sch 2 'age limit' to 18 years. These are not retrospective provisions and any historic extra-jurisdictional prosecutions must be brought under the legislation in force at the time:

- 1 September 1997–30 April 2004: Sex Offenders Act 1997, s 7
- 1 May 2004–13 July 2008: SOA 2003, s 72
- 14 July 2008–present: SOA 2003, s 72 as amended by CJIA 2008

OTHER PROVISIONS

31.7 Note the provisions of s 59A in relation to trafficking people for sexual exploitation:

- A UK national commits an offence under s 59A regardless of where in the world the arranging or facilitating takes place and irrespective of which country is the country of arrival, entry, travel or departure. A non-UK national commits the offence if any part of the arranging or facilitating takes place in the UK or if the UK is the country of arrival, entry, travel or departure.

Note also the availability of foreign travel orders (SOA 2003, ss 114–122) as a method of controlling those who, it is feared, may abuse children in other jurisdictions (see **Chapter 45**). A 'trigger offence' for a FTO may be a conviction in a foreign jurisdiction for a sexual offence against a person under 18.

Chapter 32

Bail

32.1 The general presumption that bail will be granted in accordance with s 4(1) of the Bail Act 1976 applies to sexual offences as to all other criminal cases. Bail may only be withheld if one of the exceptions to bail, listed in Sch 1, is found.

In one circumstance only serious sexual offences are dealt with in a different fashion affecting the presumption of bail. Section 25 of the Criminal Justice and Public Order Act 1994 provides that a defendant charged with or convicted of one of a number of serious offences, who has a previous conviction for one of those offences, shall not be granted bail unless the court is satisfied that there are exceptional circumstances which justify it. The offences are:

- murder
- manslaughter
- rape (SOA 1956, s 1 and SOA 2003, s 1)
- assault by penetration (SOA 2003, s 2)
- causing a person to engage in sexual activity without consent, where the activity involved penetration (SOA 2003, s 4(4)(a)–(d))
- rape of child under 13 (SOA 2003, s 5)
- assault of a child under 13 by penetration (SOA 2003, s 6)
- causing or inciting a child under 13 to engage in sexual activity, where the activity involved penetration (SOA 2003, s 8(3)(a)–(d))
- sexual activity with a person with a mental disorder impeding choice, where the touching involved penetration (SOA 2003, s 30(3)(a)–(d))
- causing or inciting a person, with a mental disorder impeding choice, to engage in sexual activity, where the activity involved penetration (SOA 2003, s 31 (3)(a)–(d))
- attempting to commit any above offence

The list includes Scottish and Northern Irish offences. Convictions for relevant corresponding offences under EU jurisdictions will also trigger the presumption against bail (s 25(3B)).

The burden placed on the defendant in such circumstances is a limited one. A court in considering an application in these circumstances should first apply the provisions of the Bail Act and consider the conditions under which bail should be refused. Only if the court was unsure under the Bail Act test (in which case bail should normally be granted) would the defendant need to rebut the provision of s 25.[1]

These provisions apply also to the grant or refusal of bail by police upon charge.

1 *R (on the application of O) v Crown Court at Harrow* [2006] UKHL 42.

Chapter 33

Public interest immunity: information held by third parties

by Alison Lambert

INTRODUCTION

33.1 Issues of Public Interest Immunity arise in respect of information which exists and could be liable for disclosure but which it may not be in the public interest to disclose. This is because there is a risk of serious prejudice to an important public interest. For the purposes of this chapter, Public Interest Immunity will be discussed in respect of Social Services files. It should be remembered, however, that linked files held by the Youth Offending Service and Education Departments may also be relevant. It is obviously vitally important that information contained within such files, relating to children, should be protected and the confidentiality of the child is of paramount importance. Further, Social Workers and other professionals should be free to record information about children without fear that this may be disclosed without proper scrutiny by the Court.

Public Interest Immunity often arises in cases involving sexual offences. This is especially true in historic rape and sexual abuse cases where there is often the need to examine material gathered at the time the relevant offences are alleged to have occurred. The passage of time will affect the memories of those involved and the Social Care records will contain a contemporaneous record and, potentially, material which is accurate and pertinent to the offences charged.

DUTY OF THE PROSECUTOR

33.2 The prosecutor is under an obligation to consider whether there is material held by a third party which might be relevant to the duty of disclosure under the Criminal Procedure and Investigations Act 1996.

Prosecutors should always be alive to the possibility that relevant material may be contained within the files of third parties such as Social Services, Education

Departments and the Youth Offending Service. It is especially important for a prosecutor to consider whether there may be relevant material in sexual offences cases. The complainants in such cases are often vulnerable, from troubled backgrounds and have had extensive contact with Social Services Departments during their childhood. However, this will not be the situation in every case and fishing expeditions should be avoided.

LOCAL AUTHORITY PROTOCOLS

33.3 The procedure which needs to be followed will depend on the protocol of the local authority holding the relevant files. Some local authorities surprisingly do not assert Public Interest Immunity on their files and will be happy to hand information directly to the prosecutor. If the local authority does not have a protocol they may have already supplied material to the prosecutor and it is then for the prosecutor to assert Public Interest Immunity. The content of these files is treated as sensitive material and appears as a specific example at (xii) of the Code of Practice under Part II of the Criminal Procedure and Investigation Act 1996 – 'material supplied to an investigator during a criminal investigation which relates to a child or young person and which has been generated by a local authority social services department'.

It is far more common for local authorities to assert Public Interest Immunity on the files that they hold. The prosecutor should ensure that they are familiar with the protocol for the relevant local authority and be aware that there may be more than one local authority involved as the child may have moved between different local authority areas during their childhood.

The vast majority of local authorities do have protocols, which often allow police officers to attend at their offices to examine Social Services files. The police can then indicate to the prosecutor whether there is any potentially qualifying material thus enabling the prosecutor to make the necessary applications to the court. It is here that the first warning note is sounded. The police do not always identify or apply the disclosure test correctly when examining files. They sometimes miss critical material and an example of this is of a 14-year-old girl who accused a man who was a family friend of sexually assaulting her on numerous occasions. On examination of the files it was revealed that he had rejected her and she had then fabricated the allegations. Without the Public Interest Immunity exercise being carried out this information would have been missed entirely and an innocent man could have ended up in prison. Another commonly missed scenario is where there is information within the files which clearly points to another individual within the child's circle who could have been the perpetrator. This is of particular relevance if the defendant is raising transference.

The prosecutor should then make an application for a witness summons for Social Care files requiring the local authority to attend at court at the time and date specified in the summons and to produce their files. This is the most common method of Social Care files being produced.

STEPS WHICH CAN BE TAKEN BY THE DEFENCE

33.4 Sometimes the prosecutor will advise the defence that there is no third-party material or that there is third party material but none which assists the defence. A defence practitioner may have a feeling or even information that this is not the case. The client (if it is a historic sex abuse case or a stepfather sex abuse case) is in the ideal position to know if there was Social Services involvement with the family. The client will know if there is someone else within the family or outside of the family who might be responsible and the client will know the complainant and any likely reasons why the complainant might make up the allegations. Defence practitioners who think the prosecutor does have files or material should then make an application under s 8 of the Criminal Procedure and Investigations Act 1996 for disclosure.

The defence may be told by the prosecution that they have not made any enquiries regarding third-party material and in these circumstances the prosecution should be asked why they have not sought to obtain any third-party disclosure. If the practitioner is not satisfied with the response and feels that there is or might be relevant material held by a third party it may be necessary to make an application for a third party summons requiring the third party (the local authority, Education Authority or Youth Offending Service) to attend court with the information that is sought. This is done under s 2 of the Criminal Procedure (Attendance of Witnesses) Act 1965. The local authority is entitled to apply to have the witness summons set aside on the grounds of Public Interest Immunity but in reality will usually attend with the files and assert Public Interest Immunity on any material which may be liable for disclosure. However, this should not be used as a fishing expedition and a defence practitioner should be ready to give the judge sound reasons why the witness summons should be issued.

THE DISCLOSURE EXERCISE

33.5 Once a summons is received the local authority may go through the files themselves, but will usually instruct counsel to go through the files and identify material which is liable or potentially liable for disclosure meeting the usual test. The test to be applied is 'material which undermines the case for the prosecution or assists the defendant'. It is vital that both the prosecution and defence assist disclosure counsel by providing as much information as possible and the defence statement should always be provided. This will be used to assist in the disclosure task and is vitally important. If there is an unusual defence or a specific piece of information that is sought the practitioner needs to make counsel for the local authority aware.

At hearings for the return of a third party summons it is also very important that the defence practitioner instructs the trial counsel or trial advocate to attend if at all possible or alternatively to have fully briefed the person attending. The judge will normally ask what information is sought over and above the usual information. The usual information being evidence of previous false allegations, lie telling, attention-seeking behaviour, triggers for disclosure, evidence that another might be to blame or evidence of transference. It is a long list but one which disclosure counsel will bear in mind while undertaking the disclosure exercise. It is therefore important that any specific information sought which falls outside of this list is communicated to disclosure counsel. It is here that the next warning note is sounded. If the counsel or advocate who attends the Public Interest Immunity hearing does not have sufficient information on the relevant issues they are likely to sit mute when the judge asks them what specific material is sought and important information pertinent to the defendant may be missed.

The judge will consider the material identified by counsel for the local authority and decide, applying the seven questions in *R v H*[1] whether all or some of the material should be disclosed. Any disclosure ordered will be redacted or supplied in the form of a disclosure note. The over-riding factor is the ability of the defendant to have a fair trial.

It is important to remember that the judge has the final say as to what use the material can be put during the trial including making directions to limit the cross examination.

If there is any material within the Social Care files which relates to proceedings within the Family Court then the permission of the presiding Family Judge on the relevant circuit will additionally be required before any disclosure is made.

It is here that the final warning note is sounded. The local authority will not generally hold medical information pertaining to the complaint. The exception to this relates to counselling which may have been provided as part of the Social Care function. It is more usual that this counselling will have been outsourced so if the defence practitioner has knowledge that counselling has taken place then a request will need to be made in order to identify the relevant organisation. It will then be necessary to request that the prosecutor makes an application for a witness summons in respect of that third party or for a Criminal Procedure and Investigations Act 1996 s 8 application to be made. Counsel examining the files will always endeavour to make a judge aware if there is information suggesting counselling has been undertaken in order to assist the parties in pinpointing additional potential third parties. Specific or

---

1 [2004] UKHL 3, [2004] 2 AC 134.

general medical information will be held by the Primary Care Trust and not Social Services.

Practitioners should note that the new CPS 2013 Protocol & Good Practice Model[2] has been issued and came into force on 1 January 2014. It is intended to streamline the procedure for disclosure into Family and Criminal proceedings. The Protocol addresses 'child abuse' and therefore includes cases both where the abuse is sexual and non-sexual and applies where the child was aged 17 or under at the time of the alleged offences.

2 http://www.cps.gov.uk/publications/docs/third_party_protocol_2013.pdf

Chapter 34

Case preparation checklist – prosecution

INTRODUCTION

34.1 In this and the following chapter, we attempt to give an overview of the various steps that practitioners preparing a sex case, on both prosecution and defence sides, may be required to take. So far as the prosecution checklist is concerned, we can do no better than that provided on the CPS website and have effectively reproduced it here, although we have unravelled many of the acronyms. The lists envisages a non-consensual offence such as rape.

CHECKLIST

34.2

EVIDENCE (quality, strengths and weaknesses)

- Visually Recorded Interview (confirm viewed/comment on quality, admissibility, transcribing and editing)
- Consent/Capacity
- Evidential/Conclusive presumptions
- Medical evidence (forensic physician should attend conference and give live evidence unless there are particular/considered reasons)
- DNA and other scientific evidence (consult with forensic scientist)
- Fingerprints
- CCTV
- Phone analysis/records/texts/images/cell site/computer records
- Birth certificates
- YJCEA 1999, s 41 applications (required to be in writing)

- Bad character of the accused (previous convictions and complaints including foreign)
- Hearsay
- Consideration of any defence put forward
- Possible collusion between witnesses
- Potential abuse of process

BAIL/CUSTODY ISSUES

THRESHOLD TEST/FULL CODE TEST (evidential and public interest)

CHARGES/INDICTMENT

- Old/new legislation
- Which behaviour is covered by which charge
- Adequate sentencing powers
- Acceptability of pleas (taking account of views expressed by the victim)
- DPP consent

UNUSED MATERIAL

- MG6C, D, and E
- Previous complaints by the alleged victim
- Witnesses previous convictions
- Tendered witnesses
- Criminal Injuries Compensation Authority claims

THIRD PARTY MATERIAL (consents or court order required for disclosure)

- Social Services, Educational, Medical, Therapy, Counselling, Adult and Child Disability Services
- Care proceedings/family/disciplinary proceedings
- Sexual Assault Referral Centre records
- Independent Sexual Violence Advisor records

'NO WITNESS, NO JUSTICE' (WITNESS CARE)

- Special measures for vulnerable/intimidated witnesses (including intermediaries)
- Early special measures meeting

- Meeting with witness
- Other measures (breaks, medication, secure entrance to court)
- Witness summons/reluctant witness hearing

APPLICATIONS

- Hearsay
- Bad Character
- Special Measures

DECISION TO NFA OR TO PROCEED ON LESSER CHARGE (Second rape specialist to be consulted and their opinion recorded)

DIRECT COMMUNICATION WITH COMPLAINANT (is a letter/ meeting required?)

SENTENCING

- Plea and Sentencing document (in accordance with AG's guidelines)
- Dangerousness provisions, extended sentences, life sentences
- Victim personal statement

ANCILLARY ORDERS (SOPO, Restraining Order)

TRIAL ADVOCATE (rape panel counsel, rape specialist HCA)

INSTRUCTIONS TO COUNSEL

- Analysis of the evidence
- Confirm visually recorded interview viewed, comment on quality, admissibility, transcribing and editing
- Which behaviour is covered by which charge
- Acceptability of pleas (taking account of views expressed by the complainant)
- Reminder to counsel to make introductions and provide explanations/ updates to witnesses
- Reminder that offensive and irrelevant cross-examination should be challenged
- Reminder to tackle inappropriate cross-examination about previous sexual history
- Reminder to consider sentencing and ancillary orders including SOPOs and compensation

- Information on third party material with instructions that disclosure should only be made in accordance with the statutory tests
- Reminder to consider seeking an adverse inference where CPIA, s 11 allows
- Request a written report on any case that results in an acquittal

CONFERENCE WITH COUNSEL (to include OIC and forensic physician)

PROACTIVE CASE MANAGEMENT

(Action dates, pre-trial checks and trial readiness)

OUTSTANDING MATTERS

Chapter 35

Case preparation checklist – defence

INTRODUCTION

35.1 In this and the preceding section, we attempt to provide trial preparation checklists. This defence checklist comprises the authors' own thoughts and experiences. It is based on preparing for trial on a non-consensual offence such as rape.

We are acutely aware that many of our readers will be highly experienced practitioners who will have their own tried, tested and well considered processes. To such readers we apologise for our apparent presumption but hope that this may provide food for thought, perhaps an *aide memoire*, or a useful teaching aid when guiding junior colleagues in this area of work.

We are also aware that the lists are counsels of perfection: practitioners would never need to undertake every step for any one client and the real skill lies in determining which elements need to be addressed to make a significant difference in a particular case. Finally, we hope that the funding difficulties faced by us all do not make attention to the details listed here a thing of the past.

CHECKLIST

35.2

ATTENDANCE AT POLICE STATION

- (see **Chapter 30**)

BAIL/CUSTODY

- Take instructions on potential conditions to address objections to bail (alternative residence, geographic restrictions, securities/sureties).

PRELIMINARY INSTRUCTIONS

- Ensure preliminary instructions are taken based on Advance Information served at allocation hearing.

- Client advised on the law.
- Client advised on credit for guilty plea.
- Client advised on venue, where this is in issue.
- Early identification of potential defence witnesses and other lines of enquiry (eg CCTV).
- Assess client: do you need any reports on the defendant – medical, psychiatric, psychological?

ANALYSIS OF PROSECUTION CASE

- Check indictment carefully. Is it properly drafted? What exact offences are being alleged and what are the elements of the offences?
- Are these current offences or is there a historic element? If so, are the counts properly selected with that in mind?
- Are there any issues of joinder, where there are multiple offences or different sorts of offending?
- Any jurisdictional issues? (but see s SOA 2003, s 72 at **Chapter 31**)
- Consider the evidence (likely to be contained in a Visually Recorded Interview).
- Any obvious strengths and weaknesses (for instance, multiple complainants unknown to each other making similar allegations)?
- Set this against what the defendant says, to make an initial assessment of the overall strengths and weaknesses of the case.
- Obtain and review Visually Recorded Interview (note that undertaking will be required and sensitive recording must be stored safely and copies not made).
- Consider manner in which interview was conducted and whether it was guideline compliant. Any obvious editing submissions to be made?
- Consider multiple complainants or other prosecution witnesses of fact – any suggestion or hint of collusion? Any reason for bias?

BUILDING THE DEFENCE CASE

- Prepare proof of evidence and comments on relevant prosecution statements.
- Why complainant would lie?
- Full background – what information does the defendant know about the complainant?

- Explanation for silence in interview or inconsistencies with instructions.
- Unused material – review schedule
- Defence Statement – think ahead, what information might there be and what do you want to trigger?
- How much do you need to disclose to obtain this information?
- Is there any relevant material that might be contained on Facebook, Twitter or in phone records? Can you obtain this yourself or via Defence Statement disclosure request?
- In particular, what does the complainant disclose on Facebook?
- Do you need to obtain defence expert evidence – DNA/injuries (see **Chapters 36** and **37**)?
- Is there scientific or medical evidence either relied on or unused – if so is it helpful to you?
- Consider whether the absence of incriminating evidence (for instance, lack of vaginal injuries, absence of semen) can be a positive feature in your client's defence.
- Do you need an expert to speak to this or challenge prosecution assertions?
- Defence witnesses of fact. In historic/family cases, those who knew the parties well and had no suspicions.
- Can you call spouses or partners (impermissible to comment on absence, but the jury may speculate if they do not attend).
- Character witnesses. Defendants in sex cases are often of good character and can marshal excellent character witnesses.
- Is it possible to call witnesses who were in a similar position to the complainant and were not abused?
- Any alibi or partial alibi evidence? How firm is the complainant's account of the date of any incident? CCTV, ANPR, cell site.
- Do banking records assist with the defendant's whereabouts?
- In historic cases, any possibility of an abuse argument? Substantial loss of evidence, witnesses who now cannot be traced/have died, such that defendant cannot have a fair trial?

TACTICAL CONSIDERATIONS

- Defendant bad character – more than in any other type of case, you may advise your client to put previous convictions before the jury if they are non-sexual.

- Juries consistently demonstrate that they are prepared to overlook even quite serious offences where they are unrelated to the present allegations.
- Any scope for negotiating on plea? If complainant does not have to give evidence it will have a real effect on credit.
- In borderline custody/non-custody cases, there is a very significant difference in how a defendant is dealt with if they are not 'in denial'.

PROCEDURAL

- Diarise key dates from PCMH questionnaire.
- Consider any special measures, bad character or hearsay applications and object if appropriate.

Chapter 36

DNA evidence

36.1 DNA (deoxyribonucleic acid) is a complex chemical present in the cells of the body. It carries the genetic information necessary for the development and functioning of all living organisms.

The vast majority of the genetic information (more than 99%) is identical for every member of a given species, including human beings. Crucially, however, individual characteristics are also encoded, within discrete parts of the DNA. These zones of variability are the areas of forensic interest. Although varying widely between individuals, they are identical throughout any one person's biological cells, forming a genetic blueprint for the individual.

36.2 Physically, DNA comprises long ribbon-like structures, the chromosomes, in a tightly coiled double helix. There are 46 of these chromosomes: 23 derived from each parent. Laboratory examination of a sample is undertaken at selected areas ('loci') along the genetic chain. The chosen areas are those where wide variations between individuals are expected. In order to facilitate examination, a chemical technique known of DNA amplification or 'PCR' (polymerase chain reaction) is used to copy these informative regions of the DNA many times so as to enhance their concentration relative to the remaining DNA.

At each locus there are two 'alleles', one derived from each parent, composed of what can conveniently be thought of as 'building blocks'. These building blocks are called STRs (Short Tandem Repeats). The number of such blocks in any particular allele is an identifying factor. Under current standard tests,[1] ten loci are examined, designated D3, VWA, D16, D2, D8, D21, D18, D19, THO1, and FGA. The allelic blocks are counted at each. If, for example, at locus 'D3' the parental alleles have 14 and 16 blocks respectively, the notation is: 'D3 14, 16'. A full table can then be compiled, as in this example:[2]

1 SGM+ ('Second Generation Multiplex Test'), introduced in 1999.
2 Given in the appeal case of *R v Reed & Another; R v Garmson* [2009] EWCA Crim 2698, at [42].

STR site examined	Gender test	D3	VWA	D16	D2	D8	D21	D18	D19	THO1	FGA
	XY (male)	14 16	15 17	12 12	24 25	11 12	30 32	13 14	13 16	7 9	20 23

From this numerical matrix something effectively resembling a barcode can be established. This is the DNA profile.

The standard test also identifies the gender of the person from whom the DNA has originated. That is achieved by analysis of a marker called Amelogenin found on the sex chromosomes: expressed as XY for males and XX for females.

36.3 DNA profiles obtained from 'crime stains' are compared with those drawn from reference samples, either from a suspect or a database, in order to assist in the task of identification. In the absence of any technical faults, where the comparison reveals anything other than a 'perfect' match at all points, it is possible to eliminate the individual as the source of the crime sample. The converse is not true. Where two profiles match perfectly it is possible to say that the two samples *may* have come from the same person. The question of what, if anything, can properly be said about the probability that they actually *did*, has generated considerable debate and misunderstanding.

Evaluation of the evidential significance of matching profiles involves assessing the probability of them matching by chance, known as the 'match probability'. Theoretically, it would be possible, if every single person's profile was known, to say 'there are only *x* number of people in the world with this profile', or perhaps even 'there is no-one else alive with this profile'. But we do not have everyone's profile. In the UK we have the data for about a tenth of the population. Statistical methods have to be applied in order to extrapolate an *estimated* match probability.

Because of the multiplicity of variables in the DNA code, the possible permutations are very numerous indeed. Early methods of analysis typically involved examination of six loci and gave rise to a million or so combinations. Present systems routinely use eleven, one of which is the identifier of gender. By using this number of reference points, the permutations are increased a thousand fold.

The quality of crime-scene DNA samples varies, sometimes generating only a 'partial' profile. A good sample produces results at all eleven chosen loci, providing a 'full' profile. A match at that level will commonly give rise to a match probability (even cautiously calculated) of one in a billion (one thousand million). But what does that mean? What it does *not* mean is that 'there is only a one in a billion chance of the crime sample not coming from the suspect'. That is an example of the error which has become known as the 'prosecutor's fallacy'. A correct way to express the situation of a one in a billion type match is to say that 'the probability of this profile arising by random chance (conveniently termed the 'random occurrence ratio') is one in a billion'.

The error of the 'prosecutor's fallacy' is easier to appreciate if we consider the situation where (perhaps because only a partial profile is obtained) the random occurrence ratio is one in a million. Let us assume that the crime sample comes from semen found at the scene or swabbed from a victim. If we know nothing else about the perpetrator, we know that semen means he is male. The UK population is about 63 million, of whom just under half are males. A match with a random occurrence ratio of one in a million would give rise to an estimate that there might be around 31 men in the UK whose profiles would match that of the crime sample. That can only be an estimate. Not having a 100% database we cannot say that there *are* 31 men with matching profiles. There could be more, there could be fewer: it is a logical estimation, nothing more. In conjunction with other evidence, though, this could become compelling. For example, if the suspect lives only two streets away from the crime scene the composite evidence of identity becomes very strong.

Conceptually the advance from one/million to one/billion type matches is highly significant. Again, consider our population. The standard match figure has moved from being approximately 1⁄63rd of the number of people in the UK to a number equating to 16 times our population total. With a one in a billion random occurrence ratio, it becomes highly unlikely (though not impossible) that there is *any* person in the country with a matching profile other than the suspect.

36.4 Monozygotic ('identical') twins have matching profiles. Other people who are related to each other are more likely than non-related persons to have profiles which match each other. Sometimes DNA evidence seems very strong against a suspect, but becomes less so when it is realised that there is a sibling who cannot be ruled out. Obviously the best way to 'rule in' or 'rule out' a relative is by obtaining that individual's own profile. Where no sample is available from them, one relies again on best estimates. For full profiles using current technology, the estimated match probabilities are as follows:[3]

Non-relative	1: 1,000,000,000	1 in a billion
Brother	1: 10,000	1 in ten thousand
Parent/child	1: 1,000,000	1 in a million
Half-sibling	1: 10,000,000	1 in ten million
Uncle/Nephew	1: 10,000,000	1 in ten million
First cousin	1: 100,000,000	1 in a hundred million

36.5 Having been very careful, as one must, to avoid saying that a DNA 'match' means the suspect has been identified, it is unrealistic to suppose that in

3 The male versions are shown, but broadly similar estimates apply between female relatives.

the collective mind of a jury a one in a billion random occurrence ration is not going to mean precisely that. Attention must then turn to potential explanations for such very strong DNA evidence other than those denoting guilt:

- **Transference** – if the DNA at the crime scene did indeed originate from the suspect, could it have arrived there by some means other than his or her presence/involvement?

  DNA can be transferred in the following ways:

  (i) Primary transfer – by a person directly to the object from which the sample was taken;

  (ii) Secondary transfer – by one person to another and by that other person to the object from which the sample was taken; and

  (iii) Tertiary transfer – by a person to an object and from that object to another person and by that person to the object from which the sample was taken.

- **Contamination** – could the apparent match be the result of accidental or malicious crossover of material somewhere along the line? Enquiry can be made into the process of retrieving, transporting, storing and examining samples. Laboratories doubtless have rigorous protocols aimed at ensuring that crime scene samples are stored and examined well away from reference samples, but are the correct procedures always followed without exception (are they in any profession?). Could contamination have occurred in transit? Were police officers unqualified in scientific techniques involved in collecting samples? Might someone (a corrupt police officer or the 'real' offender) have 'planted' the defendant's DNA in an incriminating place?

- **Misinterpretation** – are the laboratory results open to a different explanation? The chemical analysis is represented in a graphical form known as an electrophoretogram, expert reading of which is an interpretive exercise that might be described as 'an art as well as a science'. The various loci can react differently on amplification and the process can generate results, known as 'artefacts', which are consequent upon the process itself rather than the DNA being tested. Two of the most common artefacts are 'pull up' (comparable to over-exposure in photography) and 'stutter' (small additional peaks caused by the amplification process – it is sometimes difficult to distinguish between stutter and the presence of a secondary contributor).

- **Technical limitations** – some DNA analysis is particularly challenging because:

  (a) the crime stain contains material from more than one person (a 'mixed profile'); or

  (b) the available sample is phenomenally small.

A mixed profile is indicated by the presence of more than two alleles at one (or more) of the tested loci. Within a mixed profile, the person contributing the greater amount of the DNA is referred to as the major contributor, with the corresponding profile being termed the major profile.

Where there two contributors and four alleles at a locus, this will be because each of the persons has two different alleles at that locus. However, if the individuals have alleles in common at a given locus, they will overlap each other and not be shown separately. This is referred to as masking.

Interpretation of mixed profiles calls for particular care and skill.

36.6 Using what has been the standard test since 1999 (SGM+), it is possible to obtain a DNA profile from a sample containing less than 1 nanogram (a billionth of a gram) of DNA, such as might be obtained from a tiny blood spot, barely visible to the naked eye, comprising perhaps just 100 cells.

Newer techniques have been developed enabling meaningful analysis of even smaller samples, comprising just a few cells and containing as few as 200 picograms (one-fifth of a nanogram, ie a five-billionth of a gram). Generically, these techniques are referred to as 'Low Template DNA' and the best known is 'LCN' ('Low Copy Number') pioneered by the Forensic Science Service.[4] The reliability of LCN was challenged following criticism in the Omagh bombing case of *R v Hoey*.[5] However, the Court of Appeal gave the following guidance in the conjoined appeals of *R v Reed & Reed; R v Garmson*:[6]

> 'Low Template DNA can be used to obtain profiles capable of reliable interpretation if the quantity of DNA that can be analysed is above the stochastic threshold – that is to say where the profile is unlikely to suffer from stochastic effects which prevent proper interpretation of the alleles.
>
> There is no agreement among scientists as to the precise line where the stochastic threshold should be drawn, but it is between 100 and 200 picograms.
>
> A challenge to the validity of the method of analysing Low Template DNA by the LCN process should no longer be permitted at trials where the quantity of DNA analysed is above the stochastic threshold of 100–200 picograms in the absence of new scientific evidence. A challenge should only be permitted where new scientific evidence is

4 The government-owned agency, closed on 31 March 2012.
5 [2007] NICC 49, the defendant Sean Hoey was acquitted.
6 [2009] EWCA Crim 2698, at [74].

> properly put before the trial court at a Plea and Case Management Hearing (PCMH) or other pre-trial hearing for detailed consideration by the judge.
>
> There may be cases where reliance is placed on a profile obtained where the quantity of DNA analysed is within the range of 100-200 picograms where there is disagreement on the stochastic threshold on the present state of the science. We would anticipate that such cases would be rare and that, in any event, the scientific disagreement will be resolved as the science of DNA profiling develops. If such a case arises, expert evidence must be given as to whether in the particular case, a reliable interpretation can be made. We would anticipate that such evidence would be given by persons who are expert in the science of DNA and supported by the latest research on the subject. We would not anticipate there being any attack on the good faith of those who sought to adduce such evidence.'

Expert assistance will inevitably be required where any of the topics detailed above are live issues in a case. As all instructed experts should be aware, r 33 of the Criminal Procedure Rules 2013 sets out the requirements for expert evidence, including providing[7] that where there is a range of opinion on the matters dealt with in the report the expert must summarise the range of opinion.

36.7 An additional area of interest is the analysis of sexually transmitted infection where it can be possible for scientists to isolate particular strains of an infection (a virus or bacterium). Matching results are capable of supporting the identification of the defendant where this is in dispute. As with standard DNA profiling, an exact match will not conclusively prove identity, but it will form part of the overall evidence upon which a jury could be sure that the defendant has been correctly identified, whereas a disparity will exclude the suspect.

This kind of analysis, as well as assisting with identity, is of special interest in cases of alleged deliberate or criminally reckless infection. In 1998 in the US a doctor[8] was convicted of attempted murder after he intentionally injected a former partner (under the guise of giving a vitamin B shot) with blood he had taken from an HIV-infected patient. Despite the added complication of HIV's potential to mutate rapidly, analysis of the relative viral DNA samples showed a marked similarity not found with control samples, sufficient to support the prosecution case. In conjunction with the evidence of the doctor having on the relevant date taken blood from the patient that never arrived at the test laboratory, the 'strain' analysis proved conclusive.

---

7 Rule 33.3(1)(f)(i).

8 Richard J Schmidt.

Chapter 37

Medical evidence and toxicology

INTRODUCTION

37.1 We do not seek to provide all the material that might be of interest to a practitioner dealing with medical evidence, or its absence, in sex cases.

'SEXUAL' INJURIES

37.2 This is a topic where it might help to 'start at the end'. There are two widely accepted key principles:

- absence of injury following alleged penetrative sexual activity does not demonstrate that penetration did not occur or that there was consent;
- presence of genito-anal injury following sexual penetration does not demonstrate the absence of consent.

The combination of these two principles rather begs the question as to why evidence of such presence/absence of injury is nonetheless routinely adduced.

Perhaps the answer is that parties in criminal trials do not trust juries to accept completely these principles, or even that practitioners themselves remain sceptical.

In practice, where there is no injury the defence will want to adduce its absence. Where there is injury, or features that could be interpreted as injury, the prosecution will generally wish to adduce that.

In each case, the opposing party will no doubt rely on expression (either through a witness or an agreed admission) of the standard principles above, in order to establish that the findings are neutral.

If the evidence, properly understood, is neutral – how does it help? It could be argued that neutral evidence is not relevant and, on basic rules, therefore not admissible. However, such 'neutral' evidence is routinely called.

Perhaps this is an area where a standard judicial direction could be crafted, akin to the 'avoiding false assumptions/avoidance of stereotypes' directions now routinely given on other topics. For now, though, practitioners will need to address the problem directly. It is vital to ensure that no prejudicial one-sided view of the findings goes unchallenged.

GLOSSARY OF TERMS – ANOGENITAL ANATOMY

37.3

Anus	Opening through which faeces pass from the body.
Anal canal	The part of the intestine between the anus and rectum.
Anal sphincter	Muscle surrounding the anal canal – it comprises an internal and external part.
Clitoris	Mound of erectile tissue situated below the mons pubis near the upper junction of the labia minora, above the opening of the urethra.
Corona	The circumference at the base of the glans penis, projecting beyond the line of the penile shaft.
Coronal sulcus	See 'sulcus'
Fossa navicularis	In females, the shallow depression between the hymen and the posterior fourchette. In males, the final part of the urethra before its emergence through the meatus.
Glans (or 'glans penis')	Penile head – the sensitive bulbous structure at the distal end of the penis.
Hart's line	Edge of the vulval vestibule.
Hymen	Membrane surrounding the opening to the vagina, with a central opening of varying size.
Introitus	Opening of the vagina.
Labia majora	('Outer lips') The two larger folds of skin forming the outer external genitalia in females.
Labia minora	('Inner lips') The two inner folds of skin of the external female genitalia.
Meatus	Opening slit at the end of the urethra through which is expelled urine in both sexes and semen in males.
Mons pubis	Triangular area of skin above the pubic bone, bearing pubic hair from puberty.

Penis	The male external sex organ, doubling as the urinary tract. In simple terms, it comprises the shaft and head (or glans).
Perineum	Area between the anus and vagina in females and between the anus and scrotum in males.
Posterior fourchette	Area where the Labia Minora join at the bottom of the vulva. Sometimes referred to as 'frenulum of labia minora' or 'posterior commissure'.
Rectum	Portion of intestine above the anus, a temporary store for faeces.
Scrotum	In males, the dual-chambered protuberance of skin and muscle, containing the testicles divided by a septum. It is an extension of the perineum.
Sulcus	The 'neck' of the penis, at the top of the shaft immediately below the 'head' (glans). Referred to as the coronal sulcus.
Urethra	Tube from the urinary bladder to the outside of the genitalia. In females it carries urine out from the bladder to just below the clitoris. In males it carries urine from the bladder to the end of the penis and also semen through the penis.
Vagina	It is important to note that the medical and legal definitions of 'vagina' differ significantly. Doctors use the word to refer to the tube-shaped canal between the uterus and the introitus (opening). Legally the term also encompasses the external vulva, so that penetration merely of the labia qualifies as penetration of the vagina. See **Chapter 3**
Vestibule	Innermost part of the vulva, opening into the urethra and vagina.
Vulva	Collective term describing the external female genitalia.

GLOSSARY OF TERMS – INJURIES AND OTHER PRESENTATIONS

37.4

Abrasion	Superficial injury to upper layers of skin caused by tangential action (rubbing/scraping).
Anal fissure	Split in the perianal surface or the mucosa around the anal opening. Capable of being caused by intrusion/extrusion of items or material (innocently or otherwise) – may result from constipation and other natural causes.
Anal/perianal laceration	Acute tear in the anus or the immediately surrounding tissues.
Artefactual dermatitis	Self-inflicted skin lesions caused, for example, by repeated scratching – often driven by underlying psychiatric conditions. The symptoms might be mistaken for direct signs of abuse, although of course the indirect (psychiatric) cause might indeed be sexual or physical abuse.
Bruise (or 'contusion')	Localised collection of blood under the skin, resulting from physical trauma to blood vessels. Colour sequence is red/purple – yellow -brown – fading. The only accepted indicator is that yellow indicates bruising at least 18 hours old.
Dermatitis	General term describing inflammation of the skin.
Ecchymosis	Collection of blood in tissues under the skin but, unlike a bruise/contusion, not caused by trauma. Designation depends on size: petechiae < 3 mm; purpura 3-10 mm; ecchymoses > 1 cm.
Eczema	General term used to describe a variety of conditions that cause an itchy, inflamed skin rash.
Erythema	Redness (non-specific) – it can be caused by trauma, but regularly arises through other causes.
Female genital mutilation	Previously known as 'female circumcision' – practice of removing part or all of the external female genitalia, particularly the clitoris, for non-medical reasons. It is prohibited by the Female Genital Mutilation Act 2003.

Hymenal observations	Forensic analysis of clefts, notches and lacerations to the hymen and the implications of the absence of injury to this area is beyond the scope of this work. Reference may be made to the Royal College of Paediatrics and Child Health's publication, *Physical Signs of Child Sexual Abuse*,[1] but expert opinion is generally required.
Incised wound	Wound (breakage of the skin) caused by cutting edge, such as blade or glass.
Laceration	Term is frequently misunderstood to mean a cut. In general medical usage, a laceration is a breach of skin caused by blow(s) by hard object against skin, causing tearing. In the genital context, the term can refer to tearing of skin or other membranes (such as the hymen).
Oedema	Swelling caused by fluid accumulation.
Petechiae	Tiny red or purple spots, between pinpoint and pinhead size, resulting from tiny haemorrhages within the dermal or submucosal layers. See also the larger features, purpura and ecchymosis.
Psoriasis	Chronic skin disease characterised by red, flaky, crusty patches covered with silvery scales.
Purpura	Collection of blood in tissues under the skin but, unlike a bruise/contusion, not caused by trauma. Designation depends on size: petechiae < 3 mm; purpura 3-10 mm; ecchymoses > 1 cm.

TOXICOLOGICAL INVESTIGATION

37.5 Where complaints of sexual offences are made promptly, blood and urine samples are routinely taken from complainants. Rather less frequently, such samples are taken from suspects as well.

In relation to both, analysis can be undertaken with a view to detecting whether the subject was likely to have been under the influence of any intoxicating substance, illicit or otherwise, at the material time.

With complainant samples a particular interest will be the possible presence of so-called 'date-rape drugs' such as GHB (gammahydroxybutyric acid), GBL (gammabutyrolactone) and Rohypnol (flunitrazepam). These substances

1 2008, revised edition in preparation – meanwhile see Interim Statement July 2011.

can have a dual impact, first removing capacity to consent, secondly causing amnesia. However, it is right to say that these drugs feature only in a tiny percentage of cases. The reason for this is not clear. It may be because their detection times are relatively short in the context of victims who, by definition, will be suffering from physical restrictions after the event and may be slower than otherwise to contact the police. Equally it might simply be that the incidence of drug-facilitated sexual assault is much lower than was originally feared.

Proof of illicit drug use by a defendant might help assessment of his likely perceptions and behaviour at the material time and the accuracy or otherwise of his later recollections.

Detection of Viagara (sildenafil citrate) might be relevant, for example where a suspect has asserted a lack of any prior intention to engage in sex.

Alcohol is, of course, the intoxicant most commonly associated with sexual offences, either alone or in combination with other substances. Assessment of samples of urine or blood taken after an alleged incident will necessarily rely on 'back-calculation' to gauge the likely reading at the material time and (more contentiously) to estimate the possible effect on the person. Timeframes are usually longer with sexual allegations than in drink-driving cases. This leads to difficulty because the further back the calculation has to go, the wider the estimation has to be. Typically the evidence will suggest such a wide range of estimated effects as to provide little illumination. The following example is taken from a case where the complainant made an immediate report to police, so samples were taken more promptly than is often the case:

The incident was stated to have occurred between 03:30 and 05:00.

The blood sample was taken approximately 3.5 hours after the incident ended whilst the urine sample was taken approximately 2.5 hours after the incident ended.

The presence of ethanol (alcohol) in X's blood and urine specimens (78 and 164 mg%[2] *respectively) demonstrates that X had consumed alcohol at some time prior to specimen collection. Based on certain assumptions, calculations show that X's blood alcohol concentration at around 05:00 could have been between 110 and 180 mg% with a most likely concentration of 145 mg%, based on an average elimination rate.*

Note, even with immediate reporting and fairly prompt sampling, the extent of the range: *'between 110 and 180 mg%'* – and these are merely estimates.

2 Milligrams percent – also expressed as mg/dL (milligrams per deciliter), the values are identical.

Likewise, when one seeks an indication of the likely effect of the calculated level, the answer is beset with 'estimation/average' and other caveats. A standard table 'for general guidance only' shows as follows:

10–50 mg%	Little outward effects, feelings of relaxation and well-being, increased sociability
50–100 mg%	Increased self-confidence and talkativeness, mild euphoria, educed co-ordination and slightly slowed reactions *Legal driving limit is 80 mg%*
100–150 mg%	Impaired balance, thickened speech, clumsiness, reduced alertness, lowered social reserve, increased garrulousness and volubility
150–200 mg%	Drunkenness, slurred speech, glazed eyes, flushed complexion, staggered gait, drowsiness, exaggerated emotional responses, impaired co-ordination, reduced inhibitions, dizziness, nausea, disorientation
200–250 mg%	Marked or heavy drunkenness, confusion, grossly impaired co-ordination, vomiting, reduced awareness, short-term memory may be impaired
250–300 mg%	Extreme drunkenness, stupor, impaired consciousness, reduced reflexes, depressed respiration, incontinence
300–400 mg%	Unconsciousness, absence of reflexes, coma
c. 400 mg% +	Possible death by respiratory depression or cardiac arrest

However, the table is subject to the qualification that the listed symptoms can overlap considerably and, in any event, the estimations may not apply to any specific individual because of differences in 'habituation' (the regularity with which the person drinks) and tolerance. It is expressly 'not possible to determine a particular level of alcohol that could cause memory loss in a specific individual, or render an individual unable to form an intent, or to give informed consent to, sexual activity'.

An expert suggests associated signs that *might* have arisen at the crucial time – these are necessarily very tenuous estimates and, invariably cover a broad range. Returning to our example, with its estimated range of 110–180 mg%, we see that this covers three different categories within the table of possible effects. The expert would have to accept the equal possibilities that the complainant might have been only very slightly affected by alcohol or, at the other end of the scale, affected to a marked degree.

Detection of other substances can be of interest. Voluntarily ingested illicit drugs might have caused a complainant to consent to activity to which they might not have agreed when sober. Again, some of these drugs could have been taken involuntarily, through 'spiking' of drinks.

How long after administration a drug can be detected varies depending on a number of factors, including dosage, frequency of use and the individual's metabolism. The following table gives approximate detectability times for a selection of drugs based on typical usage:

Drug	Time detectable in urine	Time detectable in blood
Amphetamine	1–2 days	12–24 hours
Cannabis	Occasional – 12 hours Regular – days or weeks	Occasional–a few hours Regular–hours or days
Cocaine	1–2 days	12–24 hours
Diazepam/Temazepam	4–6 days	2–3 days
Ecstasy (MDMA)	1–2 days	12–24 hours
Heroin/Morphine	1–2 days	12–24 hours
Ketamine	2–3 days	12–24 hours
Methadone	2–3 days	24–36 hours

Detection is often possible over much longer periods in hair samples, but this will not assist with the question of when a drug was taken or the duration and degree of its effects. Hair testing could be significant, however, where a person claims never to have used drugs.

A common feature is denial of illicit drug use and understatement of alcohol intake and its effects. Many a prosecution case has been scuppered by damage to the credibility of a complainant who denies, for example, taking cocaine before the incident, only for the toxicology results to suggest otherwise. Another weakness that arises is where the complainant asserts that the assailant 'must have spiked my drink' and there is nothing to support the suggestion in the analysis.

Prescription drugs can be of interest, particularly any commonly prescribed for mental health conditions. Detection of drugs such as the antidepressant Citalopram should trigger an enquiry into mental health records for possible disclosure.

Chapter 38

Computer interrogation and analysis of images

38.1 In this section we largely refer to child abuse images and investigations into offences contrary to PCA 1978, s 1 and CJA 1988, s 160. However, extreme pornographic images and prohibited images of children may also be detected and investigated in similar fashion.

Hitherto, for sentencing purposes, the severity of child abuse images has been categorised in the 5 level SAP (Sentencing Advisory Panel) scale. This was adapted from the ten level COPINE project ('Combating Paedophile Information Networks in Europe') categorisation which is sometimes erroneously referred to, but is not a sentencing or categorising tool used by the courts. New sentencing guidelines in force from 1 April 2014 have reduced the scale to 3 categories:

- Category A: images involving penetrative sexual activity/images involving sexual activity with an animal or sadism
- Category B: images involving non-penetrative sexual activity
- Category C: other indecent images not falling within categories A or B

It should be noted that neither the SAP scale nor the new guideline categories apply to extreme or prohibited images.

It should be noted that the SAP scale does not apply to extreme or prohibited images.

DETECTION OF ILLEGAL IMAGES

38.2 Illegal images can come to the attention of police and other authorities in a variety of ways. The most significant and biggest UK police investigation into computer crime, Operation Ore, commenced in 1999 and was based around a list of credit card subscribers to an online pornography portal, Landslide Productions, supplied to police by the US authorities. While Landslide provided access to child abuse websites, it also accessed numerous legitimate sites and many people were arrested who had never sought or possessed illegal images. In addition, access to the sites using stolen credit card details was rife and some people were arrested whose cards had been used fraudulently. The damage of accusations and arrests for matters of this nature can hardly be underestimated.

The detection of users of illegal pornography is often accidental – family members, flatmates, work colleagues or computer repairers find unlawful images (or what they think are unlawful images) and report them. Images may be found on lost mobile phones or on computers seized by police for other reasons, in particular perhaps following arrest for internet grooming.

Increasingly, internet service providers police their own users. For instance, Microsoft monitor online storage facilities (such as Dropbox or SkyDrive) and will search for files which match known child abuse images, reporting these to police where appropriate. In addition there is now a very proactive online police presence, for instance by the Child Exploitation and Online Protection Centre (CEOP) or the US-based National Centre for Missing and Exploited Children (NCMEC). Intelligence led operations are frequently mounted on known internet sites, chatrooms and forums where suspected paedophile activity is taking place. In these cases the IP addresses of subscribers undertaking suspicious activity can be obtained, and a search warrant obtained on the back of it. Increasingly police are deploying undercover officers in teen chat rooms.

SEIZURE AND INTERROGATION OF COMPUTERS

38.3 If, as result of monitoring online activity, police suspect that illegal images have been accessed, then they will identify the Internet Protocol (IP) address and the Internet Service Provider may, if records are still held provide them with the corresponding physical location of the subscriber allocated that IP address at the relevant time.[1] They are then likely to obtain a search warrant and seize computers and other devices capable of accessing the internet at that location. The suspect may not be arrested at this point, and this can potentially happen many months later following a positive result from the interrogation of the devices. It is not unusual for a period of years to elapse between the initial seizure of the equipment and the eventual charging of the suspect.

Interrogation of a seized computer or mobile phone falls within the remit of a force Hi Tech Crime Unit which may carry out the work itself or outsource to one or more private forensic agencies. Individual exhibits should be photographed and the hard-drive removed from the computer. The hard-drive is connected to

1 Establishing the IP address is not a complete answer to the question of which specific computer was being used to access the internet. The IP address provided by a service provider relates to the IP address assigned to the *router*, or *fibre modem* which connects to the service. On the domestic side of that device, all connected addresses will have their own local IP address internally on the network. However all devices operating through the router will share the same IP address the other side of the router. The importance is that in most domestic settings the IP identifies the subscriber address and not the precise machine.

a write-blocking device. This is a piece of hardware that is situated between the forensic analyst's computer and the exhibit device. (Ordinarily, if a hard drive is connected to the computer there is a risk that the computer can alter the data on the exhibit. A write-blocker stops this by preventing any instructions to write data being passed on to the device.) The objective of the first connection of the device is to generate a verifiable byte for byte copy of the entire hard-drive in its original. By comparing the hash-values of the hard-drive itself and that of the image, the examiner can ensure that the copy is an exact one which can then safely be used for further examination and there is no risk of damage or contamination to the original hard-drive.

Examination of the computer for illegal images is normally done by use of software, typically 'Encase' or 'Categorizer for All' (C4A). These programs are purposely designed forensic tools. The programme first identifies anything which could be a picture or movie file (by looking for appropriate hash-value 'headers' which signify the start of a picture/movie file and 'footers' which mark the end of such files) and will identify both live and deleted files. These are exported as files and stored, the end result being a series of folders containing all images on the hard-drive.

There is similar dedicated software to allow the forensic examination of mobile phone handsets, and media cards should be treated in the same way as a computer.

Secondly, C4A (not Encase) compares the hash-values of each image against the values of previously seen and graded images kept on a national Police database (the 'hash' database). Each image is categorised in one of three ways:

(i) Previously seen images which contain innocent material

(ii) Previously seen images which have been identified as indecent images of children and graded according to the SAP scale 1 to 5 (The database also records images which have been identified as extreme or prohibited)

(iii) Unknown images

Images in category (iii) must then be viewed individually, discarded as innocent, or graded as indecent. A case report and category report are then generated along with a further report to update the values on the hash database.

In an ideal world the Police Examiner, or Officer in Charge, should also manually inspect the images identified as illegal (in category (ii)) to verify that they have been accurately graded. Cost constraints mean that this is rarely done, or may be completed by persons with little or no training.

DEFENCE EXAMINATIONS

38.4 Even when defendants charged with unlawful image offences accept their guilt, it is important that the prosecution case is not agreed without some analysis. In itself, this is not easy. Funding problems, embarrassment and shame on the part of the defendant and the need for early pleas of guilty (or the 'Stop Delaying Justice' promotion in the magistrates' courts) militate against full examination of the materials or their provenance. The situation is particularly acute when proper disclosure is not made until a later stage of the proceedings.

We would suggest that courts should be asked for adjournments of plea hearings until such times that the images can be examined. If necessary, an indication can be given that guilty pleas are likely to be forthcoming, but it is the professional duty of defence lawyers in these circumstances to ensure that the prosecution allegations are made out. Experience shows that frequently they are not. Where the national database method detailed above has been used to identify and grade images, historical errors are likely to be repeated.

If it is not provided in initial disclosure, the prosecution should be asked at the earliest stage to provide a report showing the exact location on the defendant's computer or phone of each image and its categorisation.

Content and categorisation reports

38.5 At a minimum, the defence must examine the images to ensure that (a) they are indecent; (b) they are of children and (c) they are correctly categorised.

Many solicitors feel uncomfortable, or lacking in experience, viewing the illegal images and often prefer that this task is carried out by an experienced defence expert.

Questions of indecency arise most often in relation to images which the prosecution allege are in category (a), but do not fulfil the requirement of indecency, even if they depict nudity.

It is often difficult to say whether images are of under 18s rather than young adults. Certain websites specialise in adult models who look youthful (so called 'twink' or 'barely legal' pornography, for instance). It may be possible in these cases to trace the website from which the images have been taken. United States law requires the makers of pornography to maintain 'USC 2257 Title 18 records'. These are records of photo or film shoots with age verification of the models concerned (typically photographs of the models holding their passports) and the details of the USC 2257 Title 18 Compliance Notice will be displayed on the associated websites. Non-US film makers will often also keep such records to enable them to sell within the United States. Such records can sometimes be obtained from the webmaster. In some cases it may be appropriate to request that the Crown carry out this investigation, as they may be better placed to obtain the co-operation of overseas film makers than defence lawyers.

Context may be important in age verification. Taken in isolation, a single image may look young. However, if this is part of a series, it may become apparent that the image is anomalous and that the subject is in fact an adult (see below).

The difficulties in determining the content or grading of an image can be compounded where the police are relying on tiny thumbnail images. These images, in their original size, are often as small as 96 by 96 pixels, thus making it impossible to identify any details using the naked eye.

Finally, the same images occur again and again in indecency prosecutions and previous investigations may have been carried out into the subjects of the photographs or films. Here, an experienced defence forensic examiner may have knowledge of the images and may be able to identify the actual subjects as being models over the age of 18.

Categorisation

38.6 Because seriousness and sentencing are based on the quantity of images at particular categories (A, B and C) it is important that defence practitioners check and challenge the prosecution's suggested gradings. These may not be entirely accurate and assumptions should not be made about the activity that is occurring in a photograph (for instance, penetrative sexual activity) if that is not explicitly shown in the image.

Similar investigations should be carried out in respect of extreme or prohibited images:

Technical reports

38.7 Technical reports should be commissioned where there is any question surrounding the defendant's making or possession of the images. They may also assist with the question of context above. A technical report may deal with:

- When – dates and times of access to the images – what else was being viewed in the seconds before and after the image was accessed? If entirely legal material, this may be illustrative that the images have been automatically downloaded without the knowledge of the user.
- Whether the images have been viewed or not.
- Whether the images are part of a large body of files which have been copied, for instance from someone else's hard-drive or disc.
- How the images have been downloaded

- Attribution – who was responsible for the downloads? It may be possible to see activity taking place either side of suspect activity that points to a particular user, ie access to Hotmail or online banking.
- The search terms in the browser history – has the defendant been searching against terms which are likely to produce illegal material? A negative finding may be helpful here (although it is always possible that the browser history may be on a different computer).
- Multiple copies of the same image, sometimes in different sizes. While each separate copy is an individual 'making' or 'possession', it may provide mitigation that many images are merely duplicates.

Chapter 39

Evidence

Previous sexual history
Youth Justice and Criminal Evidence Act 1999, s 41

INTRODUCTION

39.1 In the 1962 edition of *Archbold*, the rape chapter explained, 'evidence may be given by the prisoner that the prosecutrix is a woman of notoriously bad character for want of chastity or common decency'. There has been some progress since those days. Developments over the past half century have sought to address concerns that juries were reaching unfair conclusions based on the 'twin myths' that sexually-experienced complainants were more likely to have consented to sexual activity and that they were inherently less worthy of belief.

No doubt many alleged victims still feel that they themselves are being inappropriately 'put on trial', but the law has striven to ensure that the invasion of privacy in these most intimate areas is limited only to what is really necessary and that juries focus on the proper issues.

The current restrictions on defence examination of a complainant's sexual history appear to have 'bedded in'. The resultant position is that while judicial leave is always required, which will only be considered after a properly reasoned application, such leave should not be withheld where this would genuinely interfere with the right to a fair trial.

THE RESTRICTIONS

39.2 After development through common law rules and earlier legislation, the current restrictions are enacted in s 41 of the Youth Justice and Criminal Evidence Act 1999 (YJ&CEA 1999), which came into force on 4 December 2000. This detailed and complex provision is set out below. Two features should be noted at the outset:

- restrictions attach only to the defence: the statute places no constraint upon the prosecution;
- in contrast to (for example) the bad character provisions, there is no scope for agreement between the parties: the question of leave has to be decided by the Court following a formal application.

LEGISLATION

39.3 YJ&CEA 1999, s 41:

(1) If at a trial a person is charged with a sexual offence, then, except with the leave of the court—

(a) no evidence may be adduced, and

(b) no question may be asked in cross-examination, by or on behalf of any accused at the trial, about any sexual behaviour of the complainant.

(2) The court may give leave in relation to any evidence or question only on an application made by or on behalf of an accused, and may not give such leave unless it is satisfied—

(a) that subsection (3) or (5) applies, and

(b) that a refusal of leave might have the result of rendering unsafe a conclusion of the jury or (as the case may be) the court on any relevant issue in the case.

(3) This subsection applies if the evidence or question relates to a relevant issue in the case and either—

(a) that issue is not an issue of consent; or

(b) it is an issue of consent and the sexual behaviour of the complainant to which the evidence or question relates is alleged to have taken place at or about the same time as the event which is the subject matter of the charge against the accused; or

(c) it is an issue of consent and the sexual behaviour of the complainant to which the evidence or question relates is alleged to have been, in any respect, so similar—

(i) to any sexual behaviour of the complainant which (according to evidence adduced or to be adduced by or on behalf of the accused) took place as part of the event which is the subject matter of the charge against the accused, or

(ii) to any other sexual behaviour of the complainant which (according to such evidence) took place at or about the same time as that event, that the similarity cannot reasonably be explained as a coincidence.

(4) For the purposes of subsection (3) no evidence or question shall be regarded as relating to a relevant issue in the case if it appears to the court to be reasonable to assume that the purpose (or main purpose) for which it would be adduced or asked is to establish or elicit material for impugning the credibility of the complainant as a witness.

(5) This subsection applies if the evidence or question—

(a) relates to any evidence adduced by the prosecution about any sexual behaviour of the complainant; and

(b) in the opinion of the court, would go no further than is necessary to enable the evidence adduced by the prosecution to be rebutted or explained by or on behalf of the accused.

(6) For the purposes of subsections (3) and (5) the evidence or question must relate to a specific instance (or specific instances) of alleged sexual behaviour on the part of the complainant (and accordingly nothing in those subsections is capable of applying in relation to the evidence or question to the extent that it does not so relate).

(7) Where this section applies in relation to a trial by virtue of the fact that one or more of a number of persons charged in the proceedings is or are charged with a sexual offence—

(a) it shall cease to apply in relation to the trial if the prosecutor decides not to proceed with the case against that person or those persons in respect of that charge; but

(b) it shall not cease to do so in the event of that person or those persons pleading guilty to, or being convicted of, that charge.

(8) Nothing in this section authorises any evidence to be adduced or any question to be asked which cannot be adduced or asked apart from this section.

WHEN DOES S 41 APPLY?

39.4 The provisions of s 41 apply in all courts to trials, appeals and 'Newton' hearings[1] when the remaining charges[2] include at least one sexual offence. They also apply, less significantly, to dismissal hearings and when a magistrates' court is inquiring into an offence as examining justices.[3]

---

1 YJ&CEA 1999, s 42(3)(d).
2 See s 41(7) above.
3 YJ&CEA 1999, s 42(3)(a).

TO WHICH OFFENCES DOES S 41 APPLY?

39.5 As enacted, the statute provided a list[4] of 'sexual offences' to which the provisions applied. When the Sexual Offences Act 2003 was passed, all of its substantive offences were brought under the s 41 umbrella.[5] Unfortunately, a drafting error purported to *substitute* rather than *add* these offences. However, this 'vacuum' has been effectively removed by the Court of Appeal ruling in *R v Cartwright*[6] and s 41 should be taken to apply to cases involving any sexual offence, whether under the 2003 Act or the 'old regime'.

WHAT IS COVERED?

39.6 The provisions restrict (a) adducing evidence (for example, testimony from the defendant) and (b) asking questions in cross-examination (whether of the complainant or anyone else) about any 'sexual behaviour' of the complainant.

This is defined by s 42(1)(c):

> 'sexual behaviour' means any sexual behaviour or other sexual experience, whether or not involving any accused or other person, but excluding (except in section 41(3)(c)(i) and (5)(a)) anything alleged to have taken place as part of the event which is the subject matter of the charge against the accused.

Whether particular behaviour is 'sexual' will usually be a straightforward question, but in borderline cases the analysis is 'really a matter of impression and common sense'[7] informed now by the statutory definition under s 78 of the Sexual Offences Act 2003 (see **Chapter 2**).

'Sexual behaviour' includes a situation in which the complainant is the victim of a sexual offence but does not herself do anything.[8]

Implied sexual behaviour is also covered, for example where there are proposed questions about a pregnancy. The Explanatory Notes to the legislation suggest that 'evidence' in this context is 'to be understood as including secondary evidence of sexual behaviour such as abortions'.

---

4 YJ&CEA 1999, s 62.
5 SOA 2003, s 139 and Sch 6 para 41.
6 [2007] EWCA Crim 2581.
7 *R v Mukadi* [2003] EWCA Crim 3765.
8 *R v V* [2006] EWCA Crim 1901 at [20].

ALLEGEDLY FALSE STATEMENTS ABOUT SEXUAL BEHAVIOUR

39.7 An important contrast is to be made between actual behaviour and false statements about sexual behaviour. Evidence or questioning about a false allegation of sexual activity is not 'about any sexual behaviour of the complainant' and therefore would not be caught by s 41. This view was confirmed by the Court of Appeal in the conjoined appeals of *R v RT; R v MH*:[9]

> 'It seems to this Court that normally questions or evidence about false statements in the past by a complainant about sexual assaults or such questions or evidence about a failure to complain about the alleged assault which is the subject matter of the charge, while complaining about other sexual assaults, are not ones "about" any sexual behaviour of the complainant. They relate not to her sexual behaviour but to her statements in the past or to her failure to complain.' (per Keane LJ)

The difficulty for the defence comes, however, in establishing the falsity of the complainant's earlier statement. Important guidance on this point was given in the same judgment:[10]

> 'The defence, wishing to put questions about alleged previous false complaints, will need to seek a ruling from the judge that s 41 does not exclude them. It would be professionally improper for those representing the defendant to put such questions in order to elicit evidence about the complainant's past sexual behaviour as such under the guise of previous false complaints. But in any case the defence must have a proper evidential basis for asserting that any such previous statement was (a) made and (b) untrue. If those requirements were not met, then the questions would not be about lies but would be "about the sexual behaviour of the complainant" within the meaning of s 41(1). The judge is entitled to seek assurances from the defence that it has a proper basis for asserting that the statement was made and was untrue.'

It has sometimes been thought that the defence would be 'stuck with the answer' if the allegedly false statement was denied. However, the Court of Appeal in *R v V*[11] clarified that s 4 of the Criminal Procedure Act 1865 (Lord Denman's Act) was applicable to these situations to enable other evidence to be called to prove the inconsistent statement.

Assertions that a complainant has made a false allegation may engage the bad character provisions (Criminal Justice Act 2003, s 100). It was pointed out in *R v V*[12] that cross-examination about an allegedly false sexual allegation

9 [2001] EWCA Crim 1877, at [33].
10 At [41].
11 [2006] EWCA Crim 1901, at [32]–[35].
12 [2006] EWCA Crim 1901, at [25].

may require a ruling in relation to s 41 as well as leave under s 100, but the Court observed that in many cases s 41 will be the more formidable obstacle to overcome.

NINE GATEWAYS AND THREE HURDLES

39.8 Once it is ascertained that s 41 is engaged, the proposed evidence or questioning has to pass through one of the gateways and clear all applicable hurdles.

The gateways

39.9 Section 41 provides four express gateways.

The landmark House of Lords case of *R v A (No. 2)* in effect creates five further openings.

In short form, the four statutory gateways may conveniently be labelled as follows:

- s 41(3)(a) — not consent
- s 41(3)(b) — consent, contemporaneity
- s 41(3)(c) — consent, similarity
- s 41(5) — rebuttal

The next four gateways derive from *R v A* and are actually sub-sets of s 41(3)(a) – Lord Hope's non-exhaustive examples of admissibility where the issue is not consent:

- belief in consent
- bias/motive to fabricate
- explaining physical evidence
- explaining unexpected knowledge (very young children)

The final and, perhaps, most significant gateway is the fair trial safety net creatively developed by Lord Steyn in *R v A*. Technically it derives from s 41(3)(c) and we label it here as:

- Human Rights Act 1998, s 3 and ECHR Article 6

These gateways will be examined in turn (the numbering is ours):

(1) Relates to a relevant issue in the case and that issue is not an issue of consent (s 41(3)(a))

A 'relevant issue in the case' is defined by s 42(1)(a) as 'any issue falling to be proved by the prosecution or defence in the trial of the accused'.

See further under (5) to (8) below – the four examples given by Lord Hope of such issues.

(2) Relates to a relevant issue in the case – it is an issue of *consent* – alleged sexual behaviour *at or about the same time* (s 41(3)(b))

A 'relevant issue in the case' is defined by s 42(1)(a) as 'any issue falling to be proved by the prosecution or defence in the trial of the accused'.

The Explanatory Notes to the Act foresaw that 'at or about the same time' will generally be interpreted no more widely than 24 hours before or after the offence. Such insistence on narrow contemporaneity was affirmed in *R v A (No. 2)*.[13]

(3) Relates to a relevant issue in the case – it is an issue of *consent* – alleged sexual behaviour, in any respect, *so similar* to any sexual behaviour of the complainant which (allegedly) took place as part of the event which is the subject of the charge, or to any other any sexual behaviour of the complainant which (allegedly) took place at or about the same time as that event, that the similarity *cannot be explained by coincidence.* (s 41(3)(c))

A 'relevant issue in the case' is defined by s 42(1)(a) as 'any issue falling to be proved by the prosecution or defence in the trial of the accused'.

Careful reading of s 41(3)(c)(i) reveals that no temporal limitation attaches to this gateway.[14] If sufficient similarity is established, the previous sexual behaviour can have occurred at any time.

The required level of similarity was described by Lord Clyde in *R v A*:

> '... does not necessitate that the similarity has to be in some rare or bizarre conduct. So long as the particular factor is of a significance which goes beyond the realm of what could reasonably be explained as a coincidence it should suffice. Something about the sexual behaviour of the complainant on each of the occasions, such as something said or done by him or her which is not so unremarkable as to be reasonably explained as a coincidence has to be found ... some kind of connection or relationship with the behaviour which on a reasonable view is not a mere matter of chance.'

This gateway is the one that has been widened by the House of Lords' judgment in *R v A* to ensure the compliance of s 41 with Article 6, as required under the Human Rights Act (see (9) below).

13 [2002] 1 AC 45, per Lord Slynn, at 55.
14 Confirmed in *R v T* [2004] EWCA Crim 1220.

(4) Relates to evidence adduced by the prosecution about sexual behaviour of the complainant – necessary to enable the evidence to be *rebutted* or *explained* (s 41(5))

This gateway can apply irrespective of whether or not the issue is consent. Also, in contrast to other subsections, it is no barrier to the opening of this gateway that the purpose of the proposed evidence or questioning is to impugn the complainant's credibility.

Examples of the rebuttal gateway arising would include where an unmarried complainant insists in her evidence in chief that she would never have consented to sexual intercourse outside of wedlock whereas medical records revealed that she had obtained contraceptive services and told medical professionals that she was having sex.

In *Rooney*,[15] in a retrial three months after s 41 came into force, the complainant said in her evidence in chief that she had done as the defendant had asked 'because I felt I had to; I had never had a sexual experience before and I thought it was something that I had to do.'

She had given almost identical evidence in the original trial (in April 2000 – before the commencement date for s 41), but had then admitted in cross-examination that she and another teenage friend had in fact given a 'blow job' to two youths on a beach in Cornwall when she was only 13. The Court of Appeal (although dismissing the appeal) found that the retrial judge should have allowed the questions to be put. It was irrelevant that the aim of seeking to cross-examine about this was to attack the complainant's credibility, because the s 41(5) rebuttal gateway is not subject to the s 41(4) hurdle.

(5) Belief in consent (sub-set of s 41(3)(a))

This is the first of Lord Hope's examples for admission where the issue is not consent.

His Lordship referred in this regard to *DPP v Morgan*, but of course where a trial is dealing with alleged non-consensual offences under the SOA 2003, the scope for a Morgan-style defence will be reduced because of the requirement that a defendant's belief in consent must now be reasonable. That change will bite particularly where it is sought to bring up alleged sexual behaviour between the complainant and third parties. It will seldom be possible for a defendant successfully to claim 'because she had sex with A and B, I believed she'd consent to sex with me'.

---

15 [2001] EWCA Crim 2844.

(6) Bias/motive to fabricate (sub-set of s 41(3)(a))

This is the second of Lord Hope's sample categories for admission where the issue is not consent.

A useful example of its operation is found in *R v Martin*[16] in which the Court of Appeal found that the appellant should have been able to advance his case that the complainant had made a false allegation against him in response to his hurtful rejection of her after she had performed oral sex on him at her own instigation.

(7) Explaining physical evidence (sub-set of s 41(3)(a))

This is the third 'Lord Hope' category.

Physical evidence consistent with sexual activity, such as where semen (though unsuitable for DNA profiling) is detected upon examination of a child, might be explained by evidence of sexual experience at the hands of another.

(8) Explaining unexpected knowledge (very young children) (sub-set of s 41(3)(a))

There is an obvious implied, rhetorical question when a very young child describes in graphic detail intimate sexual activity – 'how on earth would they know about these things other than through experiencing the alleged offending'. One answer might be, 'because the child had experienced sexual activity, but with someone other than the defendant'.

This gateway, the fourth and final of Lord Hope's 'not-consent' examples, is only likely to apply to very young children. As the Court of Appeal has recognised (for example in *R v MF*[17] in which the complainant was 14), it is almost inevitable that older children will be able to describe acts of masturbation and sexual intercourse from sources other than direct experience, such as the media or 'playground talk'.

(9) Human Rights Act 1998, s 3 & ECHR Article 6 (sub-set of s 41(3)(c))

This is so important that we describe it as a further gateway, although it is technically an extension of the s 41(3)(c) path. Lord Steyn created it with these words:

> 'In my view s 3[18] requires the court to subordinate the niceties of the language of s 41(3)(c), and in particular the touchstone of coincidence, to broader considerations of relevance judged by logical and common sense criteria of time and circumstances … the legislature would not … have wished to deny the right to an accused to put forward a full

16 [2004] EWCA Crim 916.
17 [2005] EWCA Crim 3376.
18 Human Rights Act 1998, s 3.

> and complete defence by advancing truly probative material. It is therefore possible under s 3 to read s 41, and in particular s 41(3)(c), as subject to the implied provision that evidence or questioning which is required to ensure a fair trial under Article 6 of the Convention should not be treated as inadmissible … Where the line is to be drawn must be left to the judgment of trial judges. On this basis a declaration of incompatibility can be avoided.'

His Lordship continued:

> 'It is of supreme importance that the effect of the speeches today should be clear to trial judges who have to deal with problems of the admissibility of questioning and evidence on alleged prior sexual experience between an accused and a complainant. The effect of the decision today is that under s 41(3)(c) of the 1999 Act, construed as necessary by applying the interpretive obligation under s 3 of the Human Rights Act 1998, and due regard always being paid to the importance of seeking to protect the complainant from indignity and from humiliating questions, the test of admissibility is whether the evidence (and questioning in relation to it) is nevertheless so relevant to the issue of consent that to exclude it would endanger the fairness of the trial under Article 6 of the convention. If this test is satisfied the evidence should not be excluded.'

The hurdles

Section 41(6) – specific instance

39.10 This subsection requires that the evidence or question for which leave is sought must relate to a specific instance (or specific instances). There is no scope for scattergun approaches or fishing expeditions.

The s 41(6) limitation applies to all gateways.

Section 41(4) – credibility

39.11 This subsection places a limitation on s 41(3) and is, therefore, applicable to all gateways except the 'rebuttal' gateway under s 41(5).

It deems irrelevant (and therefore inadmissible) any evidence or questioning whose main purpose appears to the court to be impugning the complainant's credibility.

It was recognised in *R v A* that 'issues of consent and issues of credibility may well run so close to each other as almost to coincide'.[19] This maintains the

19 Per Lord Clyde.

long established acknowledgement that in disputed sex cases 'the difference between questions going to credit and questions going to the issue is reduced to vanishing point'.[20]

This topic might be ripe for further development by the higher courts. The appeal in *Martin* (see Gateway (9) above) overcame this hurdle because although it was *one* purpose of the questions to impugn the credibility of the complainant, it was not *the* purpose or the *main* purpose. The Court of Appeal added that, otherwise, it would have been necessary to consider whether this subsection should be 'read down' to ensure a fair trial.

Section 41(2)(b) – refusal of leave might render unsafe

39.12 Each of the gateways is subject to this hurdle. Section 41(2)(b) requires that before any evidence of a complainant's previous sexual behaviour is allowed to be introduced, the court must be satisfied that if that evidence were not heard, its absence might lead to an unsafe decision by the tribunal on an issue that had to be proved in the case (ie an element of the offence).

PRACTITIONER POINTERS

PROS – beware of adducing evidence that triggers rebuttal

PROS – have the witness informed if leave is granted (make defence and judge aware)

DEF – follow procedure and formulate questions (focus)

20 *R v* Funderburk (1990) 90 Cr App R 467.

FLOWCHARTS

39.13 Two diagrams follow:

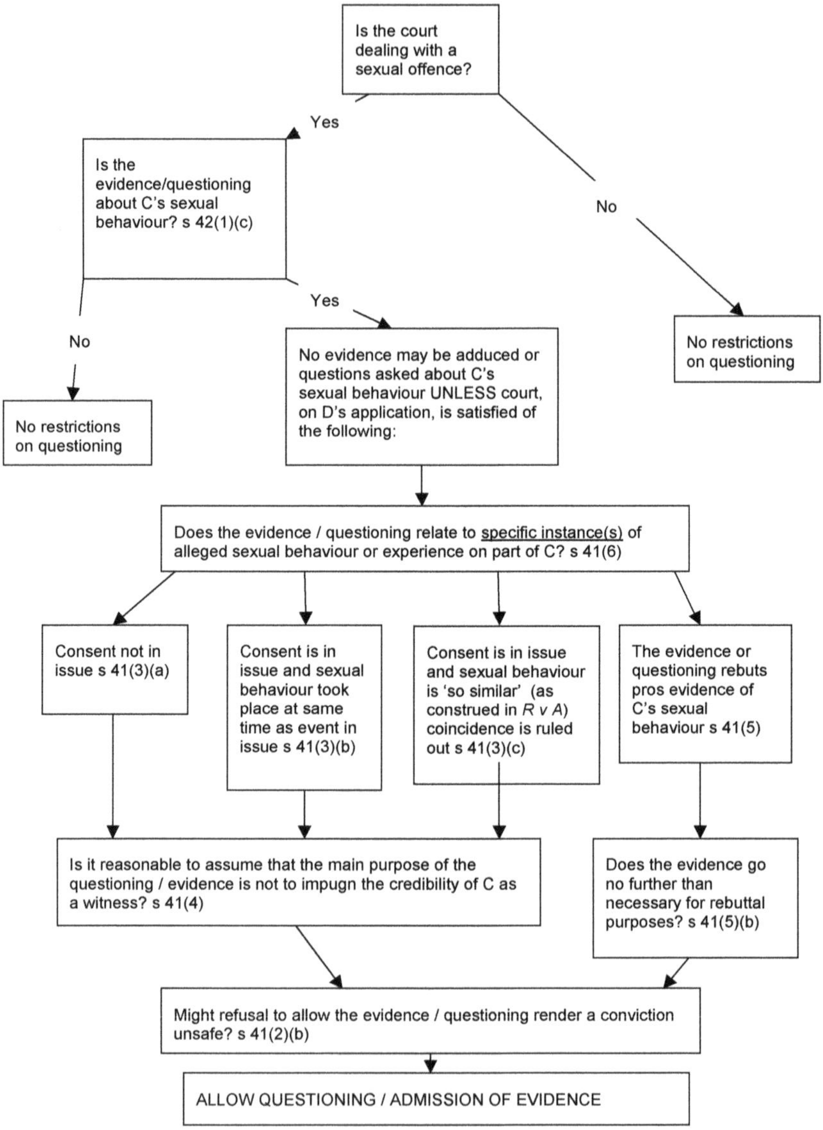

Gateway/Hurdle Flowchart

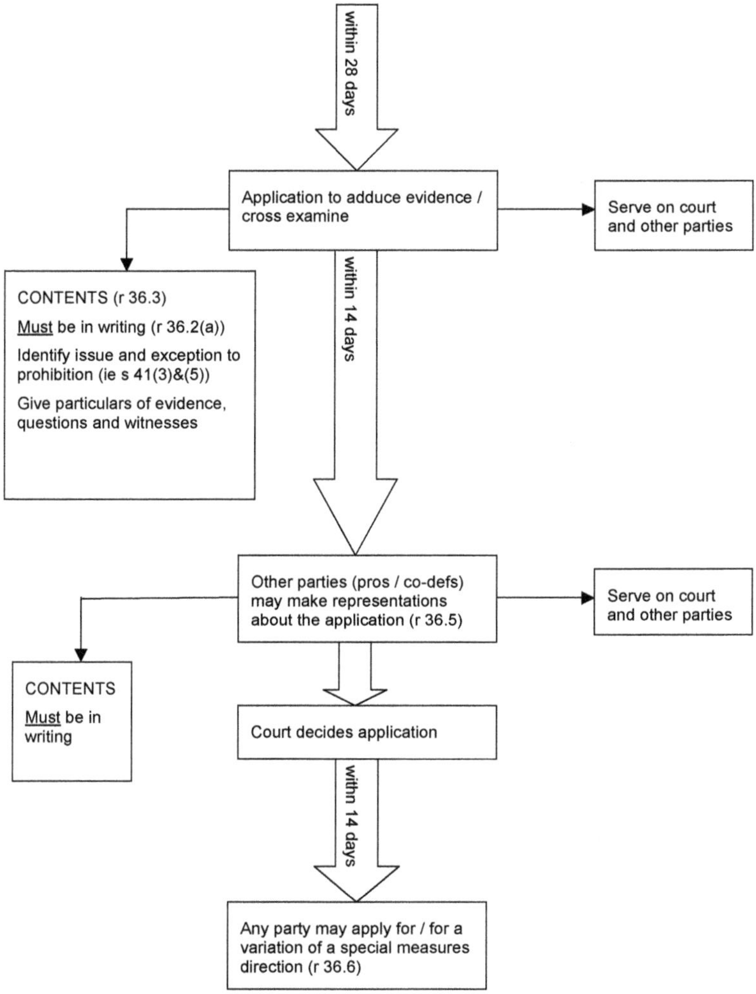

Procedure – YJ&CEA 1999, s 43

Previous inconsistent statements Criminal Justice Act 2003, s 119

INTRODUCTION

39.14 Section 120 of the Criminal Justice Act 2003 is set out in full at **39.20**, where we discuss the modern replacement of the 'recent complaint' rules. Here we consider another matter arising from Part 11 of the Act, namely the changed status of previous inconsistent statements.

LEGISLATION

39.15 Section 119 of the Criminal Justice Act 2003 *(emphasis added)*:

(1) If in criminal proceedings a person gives oral evidence and—

(a) he admits making a previous inconsistent statement, or

(b) a previous inconsistent statement made by him is proved by virtue of section 3, 4 or 5 of the Criminal Procedure Act 1865 (c. 18),

the statement is *admissible as evidence of any matter stated* of which oral evidence by him would be admissible.

EFFECT OF s 119

39.16 Before the statutory intervention, the common law rule was that a previous inconsistent statement was not evidence of its contents, instead its relevance was limited to the weight to be attached to the witness's testimony at trial. That position is now transformed. Once admitted or proved, the previous inconsistent statement is not only evidence to undermine the 'credibility' of the witness (as someone who makes inconsistent statements) but also evidence as to the truth of what was said.

It often occurs that a complainant's evidence in chief (whether through a video-recorded interview or live) fails to match previous accounts. Typically there will be revelations to a friend, a 999 call, a first account to a police officer and answers to questions from a medical professional. There may be differences between these various accounts, as noted, and the evidence at trial. Some aspects might be omitted from one version to another, or they will be described differently. The defence will usually wish to capitalise on such inconsistency.

Where things were previously said which were favourable to the defendant, there may be no difficulty. The problem comes where the earlier account included aggravating features. For example, if the complainant originally described being punched in the face before being raped but fails to repeat the punch allegation in evidence, the defence might wish to submit that the inconsistency denotes untruthfulness – perhaps the punch claim was a lie, abandoned when the witness realised that the absence of any injury would be undermining. There has always been the danger in such a situation that the complainant might confirm the accuracy of the omitted feature and give a convincing explanation for leaving it out. However, by virtue of s 119, once the making of the previous statement is adduced, the punch allegation is 'in evidence' against the defendant, even if completely disavowed by the complainant at trial (but see below).

DISCUSSION

39.17 In the Court-Martial case of *R v Coates*,[21] the complainant agreed that her first account of the alleged rape had not been accurate. At trial she put her allegation on a different basis. However, because the defence had (perfectly understandably) cross-examined about the inaccurate earlier statement, it became evidence of the truth of its content. The defendant was convicted. Only because this was a court-martial case, the basis of the tribunal's decision is known. The Board based the conviction on the first version of events, despite it having been disclaimed by the complainant.

The Court of Appeal quashed the conviction as being unsafe, suggesting that the proper course would have been an application to exclude the first account under s 78 of the Police and Criminal Evidence Act 1984. Such a technical exclusion, notwithstanding that the making of the earlier inconsistent statement needs to be adduced by the defence, is potentially an extremely useful device enabling the defence fairly and properly to 'have its cake and eat it'. If a s 78 application succeeds in such circumstances, the judge would have to make it clear to the jury that they may not convict on the basis of the withdrawn account and, no doubt, would explain its remaining relevance of potentially undermining the credibility of the complainant.

Previous consistent statements
Complaint evidence

INTRODUCTION

39.18 We focus here on what was traditionally termed 'recent complaint' evidence, this being the category of 'previous consistent statement' evidence most commonly relied upon in connection with sexual offences. In fact, as

21 [2007] EWCA Crim 1471.

discussed below, such evidence is no longer confined to sex cases, but it will continue to have particular prominence in this area.

HISTORY

39.19 Notoriously, in medieval times a rape allegation could only be sustained if the woman (only females could then be raped) immediately raised the 'hue and cry'. Over time the rule was moderated so that, rather than there being an absolute requirement for immediate complaint, its absence gave rise to 'a strong, though not conclusive, presumption that her testimony is feigned'. Evolution continued to the point where, in the late nineteenth century, evidence of recent complaint was simply admissible to support allegations of rape and other sexual offences. Prompt complaints could be adduced by the prosecution, but their relevance was expressly limited. As stated in 1896 in *R v Lillyman*;[22]

> 'It is clearly not admissible as evidence of the facts complained of … the complaint can only be used as evidence of the consistency of the conduct of the prosecutrix with the story told by her in the witness box, and as being inconsistent with her consent to that of which she complains.'

It took over a century for the penny to drop that this rule was absurd. It required juries to be directed that a recent complaint is not evidence that an alleged victim was sexually assaulted, but merely evidence that he or she is now telling the truth when repeating the complaint. Surely, if consistency of complaint is barred from helping jurors to decide whether the complaint is actually true, it has no relevance at all. The Criminal Law Revision Committee eventually recognised that the established law was 'wholly unrealistic' and, from 4 April 2005, s 120 of the Criminal Justice Act 2003 significantly changed the position.

LEGISLATION

39.20 For convenience, we set out the section (as amended) in full. The 'complaint' provision is created by subss (1), (4) and (7).

Section 120 of the Criminal Justice Act 2003:

> (1) This section applies where a person (the witness) is called to give evidence in criminal proceedings.
>
> (2) If a previous statement by the witness is admitted as evidence to rebut a suggestion that his oral evidence has been fabricated, that statement

22 [1896] 2 QBD 167, per Hawkins J.

is admissible as evidence of any matter stated of which oral evidence by the witness would be admissible.

(3) A statement made by the witness in a document—

(a) which is used by him to refresh his memory while giving evidence,

(b) on which he is cross-examined, and

(c) which as a consequence is received in evidence in the proceedings,

is admissible as evidence of any matter stated of which oral evidence by him would be admissible.

(4) A previous statement by the witness is admissible as evidence of any matter stated of which oral evidence by him would be admissible, if—

(a) any of the following three conditions is satisfied, and

(b) while giving evidence the witness indicates that to the best of his belief he made the statement, and that to the best of his belief it states the truth.

(5) The first condition is that the statement identifies or describes a person, object or place.

(6) The second condition is that the statement was made by the witness when the matters stated were fresh in his memory but he does not remember them, and cannot reasonably be expected to remember them, well enough to give oral evidence of them in the proceedings.

(7) The third condition is that—

(a) the witness claims to be a person against whom an offence has been committed,

(b) the offence is one to which the proceedings relate,

(c) the statement consists of a complaint made by the witness (whether to a person in authority or not) about conduct which would, if proved, constitute the offence or part of the offence,

(d) [*repealed – temporal requirement, see below**]

(e) the complaint was not made as a result of a threat or a promise, and

(f) before the statement is adduced the witness gives oral evidence in connection with its subject matter.

(8) For the purposes of subsection (7) the fact that the complaint was elicited (for example, by a leading question) is irrelevant unless a threat or a promise was involved.

*Subsection 120(7)(d), repealed by s 112 of the Coroners & Justice Act 2009,[23] had imposed a condition that 'the complaint was made as soon as could reasonably be expected after the alleged conduct'. This had been given a wide interpretation[24] in view of the experience of the courts as to delayed reporting of allegations. In any event, the temporal restriction has now disappeared.

DISCUSSION

39.21 The following points should be noted:

- Complaints are now evidence of the truth of their content.
- Nonetheless, complaints cannot be *independent* evidence of the truth of their content – juries must be so directed.[25]
- To be admissible, complaints do not need to have been 'recent' – there is no longer any timing requirement.
- Section 120(4)(b) makes a precondition for admissibility under this head that the complainant reaffirms the contents of the statement. This section does not provide a route to admit evidence omitted by the complainant.
- Evidence of multiple complaints by the same witness are admissible, although there is 'obviously a need in fairness to restrict evidence of "complaint upon complaint" which may merely be self-serving'.[26]

Corroboration

INTRODUCTION

39.22 As every student knows, there is no longer a requirement that juries must be warned of the danger of convicting on the basis of the uncorroborated testimony of the complainant of a sexual offence.

LEGISLATION

39.23 In force since 3 February 1995, s 32(1) of the Criminal Justice and Public Order Act 1994 provides as follows:

---

23 From 1 February 2010.

24 See *R v Openshaw* [2006] EWCA Crim 556.

25 *R v AA* [2007] EWCA Crim 1779, per Laws LJ.

26 *R v Openshaw* [2006] EWCA Crim 556, per McCombe J, at 23.

Section 32(1):

> Any requirement whereby at a trial on indictment it is obligatory for the court to give the jury a warning about convicting the accused on the uncorroborated evidence of a person merely because that person is -
>
> (a) ...
>
> (b) where the offence charged is a sexual offence, the person in respect of whom it is alleged to have been committed, is hereby abrogated.

A like provision covering summary trials is contained in s 32(3).

DISCUSSION

39.24 The statutory intervention is not the end of the subject.

Soon after the legislation came into force, the Court of Appeal considered this topic in *R v Makanjuola*.[27] Taylor CJ clarified that a discretion remained as to whether a trial judge should give any warning and, where given:

> 'its strength and terms must depend upon the content and manner of the witness's evidence, the circumstances of the case and the issues raised. The judge will often consider that no special warning is required at all. Where, however, the witness has been shown to be unreliable, he or she may consider it necessary to urge caution. In a more extreme case, if the witness is shown to have lied, to have made previous false complaints, or to bear the defendant some grudge, a stronger warning may be thought appropriate and the judge may suggest it would be wise to look for some supporting material before acting on the impugned witness's evidence. We stress that these observations are merely illustrative of some, not all, of the factors which judges may take into account in measuring where a witness stands in the scale of reliability and what response they should make at that level in their directions to the jury.'

Given the discretionary nature of any direction, the Court of Appeal indicated that it would be disinclined to interfere with a trial judge's decision unless it was *Wednesbury* unreasonable. Therefore, it is all the more important for defence advocates to argue persuasively at first instance for any direction sought. It was said in *Makanjuola* to be desirable that the question of any special warning be resolved by discussion before closing speeches.

---

27 *R v Makanjuola & Easton* [1995] 2 Cr App R 469.

Special measures directions in sexual offence cases YJ&CEA 1999 (amended by Coroners and Justice Act 2009) Part 29, Criminal Procedure Rules

39.25 The YJ&CEA 1999 introduced into criminal proceedings a statutory regime of 'special measures directions'. These measures are intended to protect vulnerable and intimidated witnesses and to help them give their 'best evidence'. Although some of the provisions have still not been implemented even after 15 years, those that are available are by now so familiar that some judges decline to refer to them as 'special' measures: they have become entirely routine.

A court may make a measures direction of its own motion or, more usually, on application by a party – almost invariably the Crown.

ELIGIBILITY

39.26 Complainants in sexual offence cases are automatically eligible by virtue of s 17(4) unless they elect to 'opt out'. Those aged under 18 are covered (additionally) by s 16(1)(a).[28]

SELECTION OF MEASURES

39.27 Having determined that a witness is eligible for special measures, the court should then consider whether any of the special measures available would be likely to improve the quality of evidence given by the witness (s 19(2)(a)) and if so which of those measures (s 19(2)(b)(i)). There are significant presumptions, discussed below.

MEASURES AVAILABLE

39.28 The statute provides for the following measures in respect of eligible witnesses:

- s 23 screening witness from accused
- s 24 evidence by live link
- s 25 evidence given in private

28 As amended by s 98: Coroners and Justice Act 2009 (Commencement No 7) Order 2011 (SI 2011/1452).

- s 26 removal of wigs and gowns
- s 27 video recorded evidence in chief
- s 29 examination of witness through intermediary
- s 30 aids to communication

Section 28, which provides for video-recorded cross-examination or re-examination has not yet been implemented but, at the time of writing, is being piloted in a number of areas.

PRESUMPTIONS

39.29 Section 21, as amended by s 100 of the Coroners and Justice Act 2009,[29] gives a presumption for all child witnesses that they will give evidence in chief through a video-recorded interview and any further evidence by live video link, unless the court were satisfied that this would not improve the quality of the child's evidence. The child may 'opt out' of this 'primary rule', subject to the court's agreement. If that occurs, there is a further presumption that the alternative will be evidence from behind a screen, although this is subject to a further 'opt out' with the court's agreement.

Section 22A (a new section inserted by s 101 of the Coroners and Justice Act 2009[30]) makes particular provision for adult complainants in sexual offence trials in the Crown Court for the automatic admissibility of a video-recorded interview as evidence in chief, unless that would not be in the interests of justice or would not maximise the quality of the complainant's evidence.

VIDEO-RECORDED EVIDENCE

39.30 The admissibility of video-recorded evidence in chief is always subject to s 27 of the YJ&CEA 1999, by which:

> (2) A special measures direction may, however, not provide for a video recording, or a part of such a recording, to be admitted under this section if the court is of the opinion, having regard to all the circumstances of the case, that in the interests of justice the recording, or that part of it, should not be so admitted.
>
> (3) In considering for the purposes of subsection (2) whether any part of a recording should not be admitted under this section, the court must consider whether any prejudice to the accused which might result from that part being so admitted is outweighed by the desirability

29 In force from 27 June 2011.
30 In force from 27 June 2011.

> of showing the whole, or substantially the whole, of the recorded interview.

Timely editing of interviews can, of course, alleviate many difficulties.

One further point to note is the sensible relaxation of the earlier rules relating to the availability of supplementary questions following video-recorded evidence in chief. The new s 27(5)(b)[31] provides that:

> The witness may not without the permission of the court give evidence in chief otherwise than by means of the recording as to any matter which, in the opinion of the court, is dealt with in the witness's recorded testimony.

PRACTITIONER POINTERS

There is seldom any point in trying to object to special measures sought by the prosecution. It is sometimes worth exploring the evidential basis for assertions made in written applications – 'the witness has been spoken to and says …' – when did that conversation take place, what else was discussed, are there notes?

What often happens is that measures are granted for a complainant – 'ABE and live link', but on the day of trial this evolves into a suggestion of 'ABE and screens' on the basis that the complainant 'has said she wants to give evidence in court' – almost invariably this indicates that someone other than the witness has decided that the evidence will have greater impact if received from the witness box, rather than over a de-personalising video link. Again, this can merit further enquiry.

Early submission of proposals for editing video interviews is good practice. Prosecutors should not wait to be invited to remove lengthy descriptions of things that are not in dispute or the interviewer's tedious recitation of her own TV viewing habits. Likewise a 'truth and lies' phase with an adult witness is normally completely superfluous. When defending, reflect carefully before demanding that leading questions or hearsay are removed – sometimes it can be useful to say in a closing speech 'you saw how even the experienced specialist police officer fell into the trap of assuming such and such' or 'the child readily adopted the interviewer's suggestion – does that reveal how easily she can be influenced?'

WARNING TO JURY

39.31 Section 32 of the YJ&CEA 1999 requires that:

> Where on a trial on indictment evidence has been given in accordance with a special measures direction, the judge must give the jury such warning (if any) as the judge considers necessary to ensure that the fact that the direction was given in relation to the witness does not prejudice the accused.

31 Substituted by Coroners and Justice Act 2009, s 103 from 27 June 2011.

MEASURES FOR DEFENDANTS

39.32 Measures for assisting defendants to maximise the quality of their evidence have been much slower to arrive in our courts. Section 33A of the YJ&CEA 1999, inserted by s 47 of the Police and Justice Act 2006 from 5 January 2007, makes it possible for vulnerable defendants to give evidence via a live-link:

> (1) This section applies to any proceedings (whether in a magistrates' court or before the Crown Court) against a person for an offence.
>
> (2) The court may, on the application of the accused, give a live link direction if it is satisfied—
>
> > (a) that the conditions in subsection (4) or, as the case may be, subsection (5) are met in relation to the accused, and
> >
> > (b) that it is in the interests of justice for the accused to give evidence through a live link.
>
> (3) A live link direction is a direction that any oral evidence to be given before the court by the accused is to be given through a live link.
>
> (4) Where the accused is aged under 18 when the application is made, the conditions are that—
>
> > (a) his ability to participate effectively in the proceedings as a witness giving oral evidence in court is compromised by his level of intellectual ability or social functioning, and
> >
> > (b) use of a live link would enable him to participate more effectively in the proceedings as a witness (whether by improving the quality of his evidence or otherwise).
>
> (5) Where the accused has attained the age of 18 at that time, the conditions are that—
>
> > (a) he suffers from a mental disorder (within the meaning of the Mental Health Act 1983) or otherwise has a significant impairment of intelligence and social function,
> >
> > (b) he is for that reason unable to participate effectively in the proceedings as a witness giving oral evidence in court, and
> >
> > (c) use of a live link would enable him to participate more effectively in the proceedings as a witness (whether by improving the quality of his evidence or otherwise).

Section 33BA of the YJ&CEA 1999, to be inserted by s 104 of the Coroners and Justice Act 2009, will enable courts to allow for an intermediary to assist a defendant (as with other witnesses under YJ&CEA 1999, s 29), but this is not yet in force. Note, however, s 19(6) of the 1999 Act:

(6) Nothing in this Chapter is to be regarded as affecting any power of a court to make an order or give leave of any description (in the exercise of its inherent jurisdiction or otherwise)—

(a) in relation to a witness who is not an eligible witness, or

(b) in relation to an eligible witness where (as, for example, in a case where a foreign language interpreter is to be provided) the order is made or the leave is given otherwise than by reason of the fact that the witness is an eligible witness.

That statutory observation is significant, because it serves as a reminder that the court is able, through its inherent fair trial regulation powers, to consider accommodating the needs of a defendant as a witness in the case, where the statutory provisions do not yet provide the necessary help. On this topic the following cases are relevant:

- *R v SH*[32] – in *obiter* remarks when dealing with an interlocutory application (which in fact the Court declined to hear for jurisdictional reason) the Court of Appeal said:

  'we can see no reason at all why such a person in the exercise of the court's inherent powers should not, if the judge finds it necessary and appropriate, be allowed to act in a role equivalent to an interpreter when the defendant is in the witness box'.

- *R (on application of D, a minor) v Camberwell Green Youth Court*:[33]

  '... if there are steps which the court can take in the exercise of its inherent powers to assist the defendant to give his best quality evidence, the 1999 Act does not exclude this.'[34]

- *C v Sevenoaks Youth Court*[35]

  'In my judgment, when trying a young child, and most particularly a child such as 'C' who is only 12 with learning and behavioural difficulties, notwithstanding the absence of any express statutory power, the Youth Court has a duty under its inherent powers and under the Criminal Procedure Rules to take such steps as are necessary to ensure that he has a fair trial, not just during the proceedings, but beforehand as he and his lawyers prepare for trial'.[36]

---

32 [2003] EWCA Crim 1208.
33 [2005] UKHL 4.
34 Per Baroness Hale, at [63].
35 [2009] EWHC 3088.
36 Per Openshaw J. at [17].

- *R (on application of AS) v Great Yarmouth Youth Court*[37] – the Administrative Court (Mitting J) quashed the justices' decision to refuse to allow a defendant with ADHD to have an intermediary.

Cross-examination of children and other vulnerable witnesses

39.33 As mentioned at **39.28**, piloting is currently under way of pre-recorded cross-examination and re-examination of vulnerable witnesses as provided for under s 28 of the YJ&CEA 1999. These measures lay on the statute book for 14 years before being trialled and it will be interesting to see how they might operate in practice. Practitioners have long harboured concerns regarding the practicability of pre-recording evidence, but there is a strong appetite in many quarters for change. The outgoing Lord Chief Justice, Lord Judge, said in November 2013 that the requirement for the physical presence of a child witness in the court building should be 'regarded as an antediluvian hangover from laughable far off days of the quill pen and the ink well.'

The use of technology represents only part of the changing landscape regarding evidence from children and other vulnerable witnesses. Over the recent past, the style of cross-examination of vulnerable witnesses, especially young complainants, has been subject to critical scrutiny. In-depth research has been undertaken into how children and people with learning difficulties process information and the extent to which they are able to understand different verbal constructions. Flowing from the research, expert guidance is now available on how to frame questions so as to maximise comprehension. Such guidance alarms many advocates. Steeped in the adversarial system, our objective has always been to obtain answers that support our case, rather than helping the tribunal to 'get to the truth', which is the natural aim of 'best evidence' measures.

The big change is that advocates are being told that favourable answers obtained from traditional cross-examination techniques, such as leading questions, may be unfairly obtained. Trial judges, supported by the Court of Appeal, are encouraged to control the way questions are asked. Out go leading and tagged questions (eg 'he never touched your willy at all, did he?') and the established imperative to 'put the case' to the witness is deemed not only unnecessary, but even regarded sometimes as inappropriate.

Three Court of Appeal cases chart the new attitude.

37 [2011] EWHC 2059.

In *R v Barker*[38] the witness was aged four when giving evidence about events when she was just two. The Lord Chief Justice said[39] as follows:

> 'Aspects of evidence which undermine or are believed to undermine the child's credibility must, of course, be revealed to the jury, but it is not necessarily appropriate for them to form the subject matter of detailed cross-examination of the child and the advocate may have to forego much of the kind of contemporary cross-examination which consists of no more than comment on matters which will be before the jury in any event from different sources ... comment on the evidence, including comment on evidence which may bear adversely on the credibility of the child, should be addressed after the child has finished giving evidence.'

In *R v Wills*,[40] the Court of Appeal rejected the submission that the trial judge's limitations imposed on cross-examination rendered the trial unfair, with the following observations:

> 'In this case there was, in our judgment, every need for there to be clear limitations imposed on the cross-examination of the vulnerable young complainants'[41]

> '...in cases where it is necessary and appropriate to have limitations on the way in which the advocate conducts cross-examination, there is a duty on the judge to ensure that those limitations are complied with. This is important to ensure that vulnerable witnesses are able to give the best evidence of which they are capable. Where appropriate the judge, in fairness to defendants, should explain the limitations to the jury and the reasons for them.'[42]

> '... for vulnerable witnesses, the traditional style of cross-examination where comment is made on inconsistencies during cross-examination must be replaced by a system where those inconsistencies can be drawn to the jury at or about the time when the evidence is being given and not, in long or complex cases, for that comment to have to await the closing speeches at the end of the trial. One solution would be for important inconsistencies to be pointed out, after the vulnerable witness has finished giving evidence, either by the advocate or by the judge, after the necessary discussion with the advocates. This was, we think, envisaged by what the Lord Chief Justice said in *R v B* at [42].'[43]

38 [2010] EWCA Crim 4.
39 At [42].
40 [2011] EWCA Crim 1938.
41 At [23].
42 At [36].
43 At [39].

In *R v E*,[44] a child cruelty case, the Court of Appeal upheld the trial judge's restrictions in relation to cross-examination of a witness aged five:

> 'The real complaint here, in our view, is that the defence was deprived of the opportunity to confront (the child witness) in what we might venture to call "the traditional way". It is common, in the trial of an adult, to hear, once the nursery slopes of cross-examination have been skied, the assertion: "You were never punched, hit, kicked as you have was suggested, were you?" It was precisely that the judge was anxious to avoid and, in our view, rightly. It would have risked confusion in the mind of the witness whose evidence was bound to take centre stage, and it is difficult to see how it could have been helpful. Putting the same thing a different way, we struggle to understand how the defendant's right to a fair trial was in any way compromised simply because (Counsel) was not allowed to ask: "Simon did not punch you in the tummy, did he?"'

These changed attitudes to cross-examination techniques will make many experienced advocates feel very uncomfortable, but they are here to stay and practitioners should anticipate important discussions in which judges will seek to establish 'ground rules' for cross-examination.

Excellent resources are available from the website hosted by the Advocacy Training Council at www.theadvocatesgateway.org which provides the extensive toolkits (updated in October 2013) such as 'Ground rules hearings: planning to question someone with communication needs' and 'Planning to question a child or young person'.

Prohibitions on cross-examination by defendant in person
YJ&CPA 1999, ss 34–39
Part 31, Criminal Procedure Rules, Part 31

39.34 Further protection is given to complainants and witnesses in sexual offences by ss 34 to 36 YJCPA 1999, which prevent the defendant from cross-examining in person. Sections 34 and 35 provide absolute bars on cross-examination once the statutory criteria are met; s 36 requires an exercise of discretion by the court.

In appropriate circumstances, the court will appoint a legal representative to represent the interests of the defendant for the purposes of cross-examination.

44 [2011] EWCA Crim 3028.

SECTION 34

39.35 This applies to the complainant in a sexual offence[45] and provides that no person charged with a sexual offence may in any criminal proceedings cross-examine in person the complainant. Where the defendant is charged with sexual and non-sexual offences, the prohibition applies to both.

SECTION 35

39.36 This applies to 'protected witnesses', effectively child complainants and witnesses to defined sexual and other offences. Age is determined either at the time of giving evidence or at the time any video recording was made which forms the child's evidence in chief.

The offences to which this section applies are:

- All the offences within Part 1 (ss 1 to 71) SOA 2003 and the offences which it replaced (SOA 1956, ss 1 to 32; Indecency With Children Act 1960; SOA 1967; Criminal Law Act 1977, s 54)
- Sections 33 to 35, Sexual Offences Act 1956 (offences relating to brothels), and the Protection of Children Act 1978 (indecent images of children)

  In relation to these offences a child is defined as being under the age of 18[46]
- Child Abduction Act 1984, ss 1 or 2 (kidnapping, false imprisonment)
- Children and Young Persons Act 1933, s 1 (child cruelty)
- Any offence involving an assault on, or injury or threat of injury to, any person

  In relation to these offences a child is defined as being under the age of 14

As with s 34, the prohibition on cross-examination applies to all offences where the defendant is charged with offences falling both within and outside s 35 (s 35(1)). Where the witness is also a co-defendant, the prohibition applies (s 35(5)).

---

45 YJ&CEA 1999, s 62: Any offence under SOA 2003 Part 1, or any relevant superseded offence.

46 YJ&CEA 1999, s 35, as amended by Coroners and Justice Act 2009, s 105.

SECTION 36

39.37 Where neither ss 34 or 35 apply, the prosecution may apply for, or the court may of its own volition give, a direction prohibiting the defendant from cross-examining a witness in person. The test for the court to apply is whether the quality of the evidence is likely to be diminished by direct cross-examination or improved if a direction were to be given (s 36(2)). The court must consider a number of statutory criteria, including the views of the witness, the likely nature of the questioning, the witness's relationship to the defendant and any relevant behaviour of the defendant (s 35(3)).

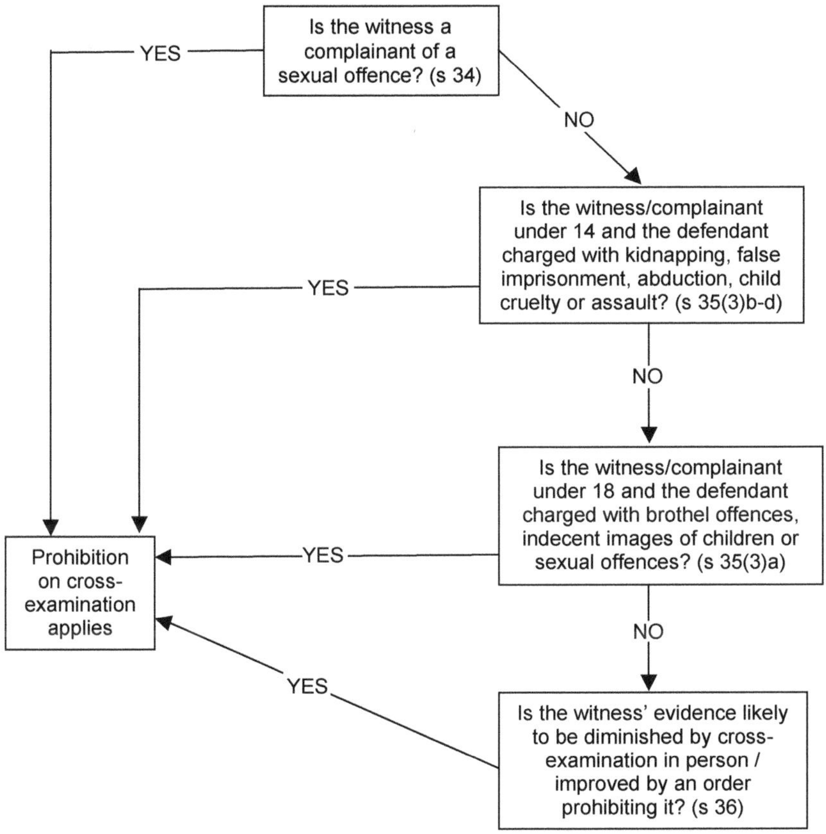

Where a defendant is prohibited from cross-examining in person under any of these provisions, he must be invited to arrange for a legal representative to cross-examine on his behalf and required to notify the court that this has be done. In the absence of such positive notification, the court must consider whether the appointment of a legal representative is necessary and, if so, make an appointment.

The representative chosen and appointed by the court, acts in the interests of the accused, but is not responsible to him (s 38).

Section 39 provides for a judicial direction to the jury on a trial in indictment in order that the defendant is not prejudiced by these measures.

The procedure to be followed where a person is prohibited by any of these sections from cross-examining in person is contained in Part 31 of the Criminal Procedure Rules. This provides for time limits, and sets out who is to be notified and what should be contained in a prosecution application under s 36. Note that, where the appointment is made by the court, it terminates at the conclusion of the relevant cross-examination, unless the court deems otherwise (r 32.2(2)).

PRACTITIONER POINTERS

In practice, the trigger for these provisions is the appearance before the court of an unrepresented defendant.

While relatively rare in the Crown Court, it is all too common in the Magistrates' Court, particularly at the first hearing.

Courts may make a 'pre-emptive' order at the first hearing where funding of the case by the defendant is in doubt.

Solicitors or counsel instructed to cross-examine under s 38 will receive an order appointing them. At the conclusion of their involvement they may claim costs at the appropriate private client rate. Claims are submitted to the National Taxing Team.

Spouse/civil partner of defendant Police and Criminal Evidence Act 1984, ss 80 and 80A

INTRODUCTION

39.38 The scope of rules governing the compellability of a spouse to give evidence for or against a defendant has been extended, so as to apply additionally to registered same-sex civil partners.[47]

47 Civil Partnership Act 2004, s 261(1) and Sch 27(9).

LEGISLATION

39.39 The witness compellability provisions, as amended, are set out below:

Police and Criminal Evidence Act 1984, s 80:

(2) In any proceedings the spouse or civil partner of a person charged in the proceedings shall, subject to subsection (4) below, be compellable to give evidence on behalf of that person.

(2A) In any proceedings the spouse or civil partner of a person charged in the proceedings shall, subject to subsection (4) below, be compellable—

(a) to give evidence on behalf of any other person charged in the proceedings but only in respect of any specified offence with which that other person is charged; or

(b) to give evidence for the prosecution but only in respect of any specified offence with which any person is charged in the proceedings.

(3) In relation to the spouse or civil partner of a person charged in any proceedings, an offence is a specified offence for the purposes of subsection (2A) above if—

(a) it involves an assault on, or injury or a threat of injury to, the spouse or civil partner or a person who was at the material time under the age of 16;

(b) it is a sexual offence alleged to have been committed in respect of a person who was at the material time under that age; or

(c) it consists of attempting or conspiring to commit, or of aiding, abetting, counselling, procuring or inciting the commission of, an offence falling within paragraph (a) or (b) above.

(4) No person who is charged in any proceedings shall be compellable by virtue of subsection (2) or (2A) above to give evidence in the proceedings.

(4A) References in this section to a person charged in any proceedings do not include a person who is not, or is no longer, liable to be convicted of any offence in the proceedings (whether as a result of pleading guilty or for any other reason).

(5) In any proceedings a person who has been but is no longer married to the accused shall be competent and compellable to give evidence as if that person and the accused had never been married.

(5A) In any proceedings a person who has been but is no longer the civil partner of the accused shall be compellable to give evidence as if that person and the accused had never been civil partners.

(6) Where in any proceedings the age of any person at any time is material for the purposes of subsection (3) above, his age at the material time shall for the purposes of that provision be deemed to be or to have been that which appears to the court to be or to have been his age at that time.

(7) In subsection (3)(b) above 'sexual offence' means an offence under the Protection of Children Act 1978 or Part 1 of the Sexual Offences Act 2003.

A defendant's current spouse or partner, unless he or she is also an accused, is always a compellable witness for that defendant.

Police and Criminal Evidence Act 1984, s 80A:

> The failure of the spouse or civil partner of a person charged in any proceedings to give evidence in the proceedings shall not be made the subject of any comment by the prosecution.

DISCUSSION

39.40 An accused's current spouse or civil partner, unless also a defendant, is compellable as a witness by any party in respect of a 'specified offence'. That category comprises sexual offences against a child under 16 plus allegations involving assault, injury or threat of injury against a child or against the spouse/civil partner.

It is notable that the definition of 'specified offences' provided in s 80(3) does not expressly include sexual offences alleged to have been committed against the spouse/civil partner, only against children. However, it is submitted that most sexual offences would be encompassed by the description 'involves an assault'.

An amendment introduced by s 139 of and Sch 6, para 28 to the Sexual Offences Act 2003 made a surprising change. It removed from the definition of 'sexual offence' in subs 80(7) all those offences under the Sexual Offences Act 1956, the Indecency with Children Act 1960, the Sexual Offences Act 1967 and s 54 of the Criminal Law Act 1977. It seems likely that the effect on trials of 'historic' allegations was overlooked. The only 'sexual offences' now listed are those under Part 1 of the Sexual Offences Act 2003 and the Protection of Children Act 1978. The solution to the apparent oversight may, again, be to rely on the alternative categorisation, offences 'involving an assault'. Depending on the circumstances, that interpretation might allow these compellability provisions to be applied to cases involving charges under the Child Abduction Act 1984, which was never included in the s 80(7) list.

Tricky tactical decisions can be faced as to whether to call evidence from a defendant's spouse/civil partner. For example, in cases of alleged parental sexual abuse the evidence of the other parent can be highly significant. Feelings of loyalty will often dictate whether such evidence will be forthcoming voluntarily. Compelling the witness to give evidence will be a step to be taken only after carefully weighing up the risks. A witness 'going hostile' may be a significantly different prospect these days, now that previous inconsistent statements are evidence of the truth of their contents.

The statutory prohibition on comment by the prosecution about the failure of a defendant's spouse or civil partner to give evidence is a rule not infrequently disregarded. In *Naudeer*[48] a conviction for theft was overturned on appeal because the trial judge had failed to intervene and direct the jury to disregard the barred comment. In that particular case the issue that the absent wife's evidence might have addressed was central. The uncorrected comment was held to render the conviction unsafe.

Contrastingly in *Whitton*,[49] far from correcting prosecution counsel's error, the trial judge had made similar observation in the summing-up. The Court of Appeal found that prosecuting counsel's clear breach was subsumed by the judicial comments which, not being covered by the statutory prohibition, were unobjectionable. That ruling highlights a curious incongruity. Giving general guidance, Purchas LJ in *Naudeer* observed: 'if a judge in the exercise of his discretion decides to comment upon the failure of the accused to call his spouse … he must, except in exceptional circumstances, do this with a great deal of circumspection.'

The extension of the statutory prohibition to cover civil partners is entirely logical, but it begs the question why the same rules should not apply to other long-term partners. In fact, in *Weller*[50] it was suggested that similar restraint should be applied to cohabitees.

We suggest that, given that comment on the topic (in a closing speech) is forbidden, a question in cross-examination of a defendant 'are we going to hear from your wife?' is equally objectionable.

---

48 [1984] 3 All ER 1036.
49 [1998] Crim LR 492.
50 [1994] Crim LR 856.

Chapter 40

Historic sex cases and abuse of process

INTRODUCTION

40.1 In the absence of any general statute of limitations covering serious offences under our jurisdiction, 'historic' sex cases come before the courts without temporal constraint. These old cases are extremely challenging. They bring legal complexity, both in relation to the substantive law and, where it arises, to sentencing. We endeavour to unravel those technical intricacies in Part D (**Chapters 28** and **29**).

Historic cases place huge strain on defendants, the majority of whom are of previous good character, often of considerable standing in the community. The stakes are high, usually with the potential for extremely long sentences being passed on people of advanced age. Unless there are obvious financial motives or family disputes, juries will wonder why late allegations would be made unless they are true. Notwithstanding the burden and standard of proof, defendants can face a mountain to climb, one that steepens exponentially when similar allegations come from multiple complainants.

INITIAL CHECKS

40.2 At the outset, the parties need to check various important matters:

Dates

40.3 How specific is the evidence in terms of dating the allegations? Are the allegations framed under offences that were current at the material times?

Charging

40.4 Are the charges correct? Subject to the applicable law, do they provide the appropriate sentencing scope?

Jurisdiction

40.5 Is there any jurisdictional deficiency concerning location? Are incidents said to have occurred during holidays – overseas? Scotland?

Defendant age

40.6 Where allegations date back to childhood, practitioners should explore whether the defendant was actually of an age to incur criminal liability at the material time. The age of criminal responsibility in English law has been set at 10 since 1 February 1964.[1] For three decades before then it had been just eight years[2]. Below the minimum age, there was (as now) a conclusive presumption that the child was *doli incapax* (incapable of crime).

Usually of greater significance is the further *rebuttable* presumption that a child from the age of 10 until 14 was incapable of crime. That presumption was only displaced if the prosecution proved to the criminal standard that the child knew his action was seriously wrong. Otherwise, the child had to be acquitted, however strong the evidence might be in other respects.

This common law rule remained in force until its abolition on 30 September 1998.[3] It will continue to apply to historic cases from before that date.

Another vitally important presumption was that at common law a boy under the age of 14 was deemed incapable of sexual intercourse. This remained a conclusive presumption until its abolition on 20 September 1993 by s 1 of the Sexual Offences Act 1993. Evidence of penetration might remain admissible in support of a lesser charge of indecent assault, or potentially as 'bad character' evidence.

Consents

40.7 Is the consent of the DPP required for any of the selected charges?[4] Have the procedures been undertaken?

Time-bars

40.8 Do any of the proposed counts fall foul of a time-bar? Examples would include an allegation of unlawful sexual intercourse with a girl under 16, contrary to s 6(1) of the Sexual Offences Act 1956 (see discussion of SOA 1956, s 14 at **28.29**).

---

1 Children and Young Persons Act 1963, s 16(1) commencement date.
2 Children and Young Persons Act 1933.
3 By Crime and Disorder Act 1998, s 34.
4 The CPS website carries helpful information: under *'Consents To Prosecute'*.

INDICTMENTS

40.9 The prosecution will have to decide, and the defence scrutinise, whether counts cover single incidents or a course of conduct. Are there to be 'specimen' counts? Significant dates must be identified. Where the age of any party is an essential ingredient, the dates should not straddle landmark birthdays. Likewise, where sentencing powers have changed over the years, the dates should enable a judge to identify which provisions apply.

Because the 1956 Sexual Offences Act was immediately repealed when replaced by its 2003 counterpart, problems arose in cases where there was uncertainty whether an alleged offence took place before or after 1 May 2004 (the commencement date for the 2003 Act). Initially there was a lacuna and such cases could not be sustained. This has been remedied by s 55 of the Violent Crime Reduction Act 2006. Both 'old' and 'new' offences should be charged and the relevant date will be presumed to have been after the coming into force of the new offence, unless the old offence carried a lower maximum penalty.

PROBLEMS

40.10 Anxious consideration must always be given, by defence and prosecution, to the question of whether the circumstances of each case permit a fair trial.

Obvious difficulties can arise:

- Missing witnesses
- Missing records
- Imperfect memory – whether resulting merely from the passage of time, or arising from medical conditions

ABUSE OF PROCESS

40.11 Application may be made, on the basis of impediments to the defendant having a fair trial on the delayed allegations, to stay the case for abuse of process.

The Consolidated Practice Direction issued in 2006 sets out the procedure:

> 'IV.36.1 In all cases where a defendant in the Crown Court proposes to make an application to stay an indictment on the grounds of abuse of process, written notice of such application must be given to the prosecuting authority and to any co-defendant not later than 14 days before the date fixed or warned for trial ("the relevant date"). Such notice must:
>
> (a) give the name of the case and the indictment number;

(b) state the fixed date or the warned date as appropriate;

(c) specify the nature of the application;

(d) set out in numbered sub-paragraphs the grounds upon which the application is to be made;

(e) be copied to the chief listing officer at the court centre where the case is due to be heard.

IV.36.2 Any co-defendant who wishes to make a like application must give a like notice not later than seven days before the relevant date, setting out any additional grounds relied upon.

IV.36.3 In relation to such applications, the following automatic directions shall apply:

(a) the advocate for the applicant(s) must lodge with the court and serve on all other parties a skeleton argument in support of the application at least five clear working days before the relevant date. If reference is to be made to any document not in the existing trial documents, a paginated and indexed bundle of such documents is to be provided with the skeleton argument;

(b) the advocate for the prosecution must lodge with the court and serve on all other parties a responsive skeleton argument at least two clear working days before the relevant date, together with a supplementary bundle if appropriate.

IV.36.4 All skeleton arguments must specify any propositions of law to be advanced (together with the authorities relied upon in support, with page references to passages relied upon) and, where appropriate, include a chronology of events and a list of dramatis personae. In all instances where reference is made to a document, the reference in the trial documents or supplementary bundle is to be given.

IV.36.5 The above time limits are minimum time limits. In appropriate cases the court will order longer lead times. To this end in all cases where defence advocates are, at the time of the plea and directions hearing, considering the possibility of an abuse of process application, this must be raised with the judge dealing with the matter, who will order a different timetable if appropriate, and may wish, in any event, to give additional directions about the conduct of the application.'

PRINCIPLES

40.12 *A-G's Ref (No 1 of 1990)*[5] laid down some general principles. That authority seemed to recognise a burden on the defendant to establish an abuse

5 (1992) 95 Cr App R 296.

of process, albeit to the civil standard. That judgment predated, of course, the Human Rights Act. In *R v EW*,[6] the Court of Appeal said:

> '… once the issue has been raised it must be for the Crown to satisfy the court that a fair trial is still possible. Nevertheless it must be for the defendant to raise the issue and to identify those respects in which he says that a fair trial is not possible. We are not persuaded that this approach is in substance different from that adopted in Attorney General's Reference No 1 of 1990.'

The test, ultimately, is whether a fair trial is possible in the particular circumstances of any given case.

In *R v Stephen Paul S*[7] Rose LJ summarised as follows:

> 'In the light of the authorities, the correct approach for a judge to whom an application for a stay for abuse of process on the ground of delay is made, is to bear in mind the following principles:
>
> (i) Even where delay is unjustifiable, a permanent stay should be the exception rather than the rule;
>
> (ii) Where there is no fault on the part of the complainant or the prosecution, it will be very rare for a stay to be granted;
>
> (iii) No stay should be granted in the absence of serious prejudice to the defence so that no fair trial can be held;
>
> (iv) When assessing possible serious prejudice, the judge should bear in mind his or her power to regulate the admissibility of evidence and that the trial process itself should ensure that all relevant factual issues arising from delay will be placed before the jury for their consideration in accordance with appropriate direction from the judge;
>
> (v) If, having considered all these factors, a judge's assessment is that a fair trial will be possible, a stay should not be granted.'

The principles were affirmed by a five-judge Court of Appeal in *R v F(S)*,[8] which held as follows:

- An application to stay for abuse of process on grounds of delay and a submission of 'no case to answer' are two distinct matters. They must receive distinct and separate consideration.
- An application to stay for abuse of process on the grounds of delay has to be determined in accordance with *A-G's Ref (No 1 of 1990)*. It cannot succeed unless, exceptionally, a fair trial is no longer possible owing to prejudice to the defendant occasioned by the delay which cannot fairly

---

6 [2004] EWCA Crim 2901, per Clarke LJ, at [23].
7 [2006] EWCA Crim 756, at [21].
8 [2011] EWCA Crim 1844; 2 Cr App R 28.

be addressed in the normal trial process. The presence or absence of explanation or justification for the delay is relevant only insofar as it bears on that question,

- An application to stop the case on the ground that there is no case to answer must be determined in accordance with *R v Galbraith*.[9] The question is whether the evidence, viewed overall, is such that the jury could properly convict.
- There is no different *Galbraith* test for offences which are alleged to have been committed some years ago, whether or not they are sexual offences.
- An application to stay for abuse of process ought ordinarily to be heard and determined at the outset of the case, and before the evidence is heard, unless there is a specific reason to defer it because the question of prejudice and fair trial can better be determined at a later stage.

The decision on abuse of process is a matter for the discretion of the individual trial judge. The Court of Appeal will be very slow to overturn the decision at first instance. Given the need to focus on the facts of each individual case, the citation of authorities is unlikely to inspire such intervention. In *R v F(S)* the Court observed *per curiam* that all necessary discussion about the applicable principles was contained within these cases:

- *Galbraith*
- *A-G Ref (No 1 of 1990)*
- *R v S(SP)*
- *R v F(S)*

and it would no longer be necessary or appropriate for reference to be made to any other appellate decisions.

TIMING

40.13 After *R v Smolinski*,[10] it was widely understood that abuse applications in respect of delay should ordinarily be decided *after* evidence had been called, so that the judge would be better able to assess the significance of missing evidence and any inconsistencies. However that interpretation was corrected in *R v F(S)* and, as stated above, an application to stay for abuse of process ought ordinarily to be determined at the outset of the case, before evidence is heard, unless there is some specific reason to adopt the alternative course.

---

9 (1981) 73 Cr App R 124.
10 [2004] EWCA Crim 1270.

COMMENT

40.14 The Court of Appeal's response to the recent case of *R v RD*[11] may be instructive. The appellant, a man of previous good character, faced charges dating back to 1949.

It was submitted on his behalf that a fair trial was not possible without missing evidence, including lost documents (such as work and school records to indicate people's whereabouts on particular dates) and significant witnesses who had died or were infirm.

Dismissing the appeal, the Court acknowledged that the 63-year delay was 'extreme even by the standards of courts in this jurisdiction which are used to trying allegations of historic sexual abuse' but, having examined carefully the potential effect of missing material, ultimately decided:

> 'Although this matter required careful scrutiny because of the very substantial delay in this case, we are entirely satisfied that the judge was correct in her assessment that the trial process could properly cope with the difficulties faced by this appellant and that there would be and indeed was no prejudice to him of a type which would mean that he could not and did not get a fair trial. On an analysis of the missing material and on an analysis of the evidence given at the trial and the issues before the jury, we are satisfied that this appellant received a fair trial, and was not disadvantaged in a way that could properly be described as amounting to serious prejudice to his ability to mount a proper defence to the allegations brought against him.'

In 2006 in *R v R*[12] the trial judge reached similar conclusions when an application to stay on account of delay was made at the start of the trial. The complainant had dated her alleged abuse by reference to the school that she recalled attending at the time. She went on to say that she could not report her brother's sexual offending against her because their parents always favoured him and she had no-one else to turn to: she would have confided in her nanny to whom she was very close, but nanny had died by then. Purely by chance old documents had been hoarded (including school reports and a funeral invoice) enabling the defence to demonstrate that 'nanny' had not died until after the child had moved on to senior school. The complainant when confronted by the documents acknowledged the incongruity, but simply said 'according to my childhood memory, I was at that school and nanny had already died'. Following this, the judge reconsidered matters and ruled that the witness's 'childhood memory' was unreliable and withdrew the case from the jury.

It is troubling that the defendant's acquittal depended on the chance hoarding of the documentary evidence. Taking into account *R v RD*, one can be fairly confident that the Court of Appeal would not have overturned convictions if

---

11 [2013] EWCA 1592.

12 Peterborough Crown Court, unreported.

the documents had no longer existed. In *RD*, even though ancient electoral rolls had been found which contradicted some of the evidence and led to RD's acquittal on two counts, the Court of Appeal took this approach to potential evidence that remained unavailable:

> 'In considering the question of prejudice to the defence, it seems to us that it is necessary to distinguish between mere speculation about what missing documents or witnesses might show, and missing evidence which represents a significant and demonstrable chance of amounting to decisive or strongly supportive evidence emerging on a specific issue in the case. The court will need to consider what evidence directly relevant to the appellant's case has been lost by reason of the passage of time. The court will then need to go on to consider the importance of the missing evidence in the context of the case as a whole and the issues before the jury. Having considered those matters, the court will have to identify what prejudice, if any, has been caused to the appellant by the delay and whether judicial directions would be sufficient to compensate for such prejudice as may have been caused or whether in truth a fair trial could not properly be afforded to a defendant ... on an analysis of the missing material and on an analysis of the evidence given at the trial and the issues before the jury, we are satisfied that this appellant received a fair trial, and was not disadvantaged in a way that could properly be described as amounting to serious prejudice.'

The problem remains that if evidence is missing, whether in the form of documents or people, it is impossible to prove what it would have revealed.

Part F
Sentencing and orders following conviction

Chapter 41

Sentencing guidelines

SEXUAL OFFENCES DEFINITIVE GUIDELINE

41.1 The majority of offences detailed in this work are covered by the Sentencing Council's *Sexual Offences Definitive Guideline*.[1] It includes most offences created by the 2003 Act[2] plus offences contrary to s 160 of the Criminal Justice Act 1988, s 1 of the Protection of Children Act 1978 (indecent photographs of children) and s 33A of the Sexual Offences Act 1956 (keeping a brothel used for prostitution).

The guideline applies to all sentencing decisions in relevant cases after 1 April 2014 irrespective of when the offence took place. It applies only to offenders aged 18 and older. General principles relating to the sentencing of youths are contained in the Sentencing Guidelines Council's definitive guideline *Overarching Principles – Sentencing Youths*.[3]

Section 125(1) of the Coroners and Justice Act 2009 provides that when sentencing for offences committed on or after 6 April 2010:[4]

> 'Every court—
>
> (a) must, in sentencing an offender, follow any sentencing guideline which is relevant to the offender's case, and
>
> (b) must, in exercising any other function relating to the sentencing of offenders, follow any sentencing guidelines which are relevant to the exercise of the function,

1 Published on 12 December 2013 and effective from 1 April 2014.

2 It does not include s 51A (soliciting); s 53A (paying for sexual services of a prostitute subject to force); s 69 (intercourse with an animal); s 70 (penetration of a corpse); s 71 (sexual activity in a public lavatory); or breaches of notification requirements or other orders.

3 http://sentencingcouncil.judiciary.gov.uk/docs/web_overarching_principles_sentencing_youths.pdf

4 For offences prior to this date s 172(1) of the Criminal Justice Act 2003 applies, requiring the court to '*have regard to* any guidelines which are relevant to the offender's case' (emphasis added).

unless the court is satisfied that it would be contrary to the interests of justice to do so.'

Operation of the Guideline

41.2 The 2014 Guideline requires that a court, sentencing an offender for one of the offences listed within the guidelines, follows a process involving nine steps. We deal only with steps 1 and 2 within the individual offence chapters of this work, and do so in table form. Steps 3 to 9 are applicable to all offences.

- Step 1: **Determining the offence category**

  Within each offence, the Council has specified different categories reflecting varying degrees of seriousness. The court must categorise the offence by reference only to the tables within this step. These usually determine seriousness by reference to degrees of harm and culpability (although a different determination is used in offences of possession or making of indecent images of children).

- Step 2: **Arriving at the starting point and category range**

  Having determined the category, the sentencer should use the corresponding starting points in the next table to reach a sentence within a category range. The starting point applies to all offenders irrespective of plea or previous convictions.

  A case of particular gravity, characterised by multiple features of culpability or harm in step one, could merit upward adjustment from the starting point before further adjustment for aggravating or mitigating features.

  Having determined the starting point, further adjustment may be made for aggravating or mitigating features, using a further table. This contains a non-exhaustive list of additional factual elements providing the context of the offence and factors relating to the offender. The court should identify whether any combination of these, or other relevant factors, should result in an upward or downward adjustment from the starting point. In particular, relevant recent convictions are likely to result in an upward adjustment. In some cases, having considered these factors, it may be appropriate to move outside the identified category range.

- Step 3: **Factors which indicate a reduction, such as assistance to the prosecution**. The court should take into account ss 73 and 74 of the Serious Organised Crime and Police Act 2005 (assistance by defendants: reduction or review of sentence) and any other rule of law by virtue of which an offender may receive a discounted sentence in consequence of assistance given (or offered) to the prosecutor or investigator.

- Step 4: **Reduction for guilty pleas**. The court should take account of any potential reduction for a guilty plea in accordance with s 144 of the Criminal Justice Act 2003 and the *Guilty Plea guideline*.[5]
- Step 5: **Dangerousness**. The court should consider whether, having regard to the criteria contained in Chapter 5 of Part 12 of the Criminal Justice Act 2003, it would be appropriate to impose a life sentence (s 224A or s 225(2)) or an extended sentence (s 226A). When sentencing offenders to a life sentence under these provisions, the notional determinate sentence should be used as the basis for the setting of a minimum term.
- Step 6: **Totality principle**. If sentencing an offender for more than one offence, or where the offender is already serving a sentence, the court should consider whether the total sentence is just and proportionate to the offending behaviour.
- Step 7: **Ancillary orders**. The court must consider whether to make any ancillary orders. The court must also consider what other requirements or provisions may automatically apply.
- Step 8: **Reasons**. Section 174 of the Criminal Justice Act 2003 imposes a duty to give reasons for, and explain the effect of, the sentence.
- Step 9: **Consideration for time spent on bail**. The court must consider whether to give credit for time spent on bail in accordance with s 240A of the Criminal Justice Act 2003.

OTHER GUIDELINES AND FACTORS

41.3 Other guidelines include the *Magistrates' Court Sentencing Guidelines 2008*,[6] which provide for offences contrary to ss 71 and 91 SOA 2003 (as well as other sexual offences in the magistrates' courts); and the *Breach of a Protective Order Definitive Guideline7* which may assist in the consideration of breach offences under the 2003 Act.[8]

The new sexual offence guidelines are almost comprehensive in the range of sexual offences that they encompass. The Sentencing Council has consulted widely and the guidelines show a thorough understanding of the elements of harm and culpability which aggravate sexual offences – in particular, the

---

5 http://sentencingcouncil.judiciary.gov.uk/docs/Reduction_in_Sentence_for_a_Guilty_Plea_-Revised_2007.pdf

6 http://sentencingcouncil.judiciary.gov.uk/docs/MCSG_Update9_October_2012.pdf and its update to take account of the new Definitive Guideline: http://sentencingcouncil.judiciary.gov.uk/docs/Final_MCSG_Update_10_-_December_2013_(web).pdf

7 http://sentencingcouncil.judiciary.gov.uk/docs/web_breach_of_protective_order.pdf

8 Note *R v Kavanagh* (2008) EWCA Crim 855 – where an offence is not within guidelines, but is similar to one which is, it is appropriate to have reference to the latter.

long-term psychological effect upon victims and the various ways in which offenders manipulate their victims to their own ends.

The guidelines have rendered obsolete the body of previous sentencing authority. Indeed, the Lord Chief Justice gave the following guidance in the case of *Erskine*:[9]

> 'Advocates must expect to be required to justify the citation of any authority. In particular where a definitive Sentencing Guidelines Council guideline is available there will rarely be any advantage in citing an authority reached before the issue of the guideline, and authorities after its issue which do not refer to it will rarely be of assistance.'

Only where there are no applicable guidelines have we cited some sentencing authorities.

9 [2009] EWCA Crim 1425, at [80].

Chapter 42

Extended and life sentences

Criminal Justice Act 2003, ss 224A–226A

42.1 The Criminal Justice Act 2003, as amended by the Legal Aid Sentencing and Punishment of Offenders Act 2012, creates the regime by which extended and life sentences may be imposed upon certain offenders, particularly those who pose a perceived danger to the public. Reference is made to Schs 15 and 15B to the 2003 Act (see Part G, **Appendix 5**).

EXTENDED SENTENCES

42.2 Section 226A allows courts to pass extended sentences of imprisonment for violent and sexual offences.

An offence is a 'specified offence' if it is a specified violent offence (Sch 15, Pt 1) or a specified sexual offence (Sch 15, Pt 2).

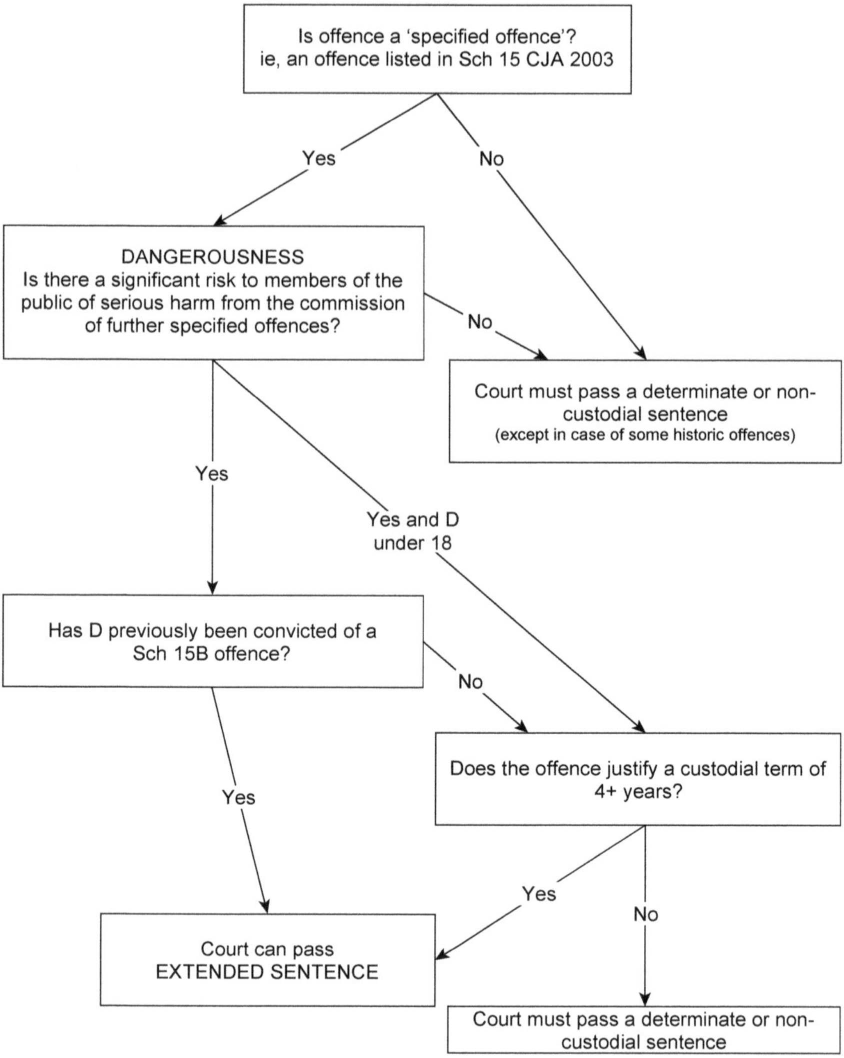

- *Assessment of dangerousness*: There must be a 'significant risk to members of the public of serious harm occasioned by the commission of further specified offences by the offender'. 'Serious harm' means 'death or serious personal injury, whether physical or psychological'.

  Note that even where the conditions for an extended sentence are fulfilled, the sentence is discretionary. A determinate sentence may be appropriate even following a finding of dangerousness.

- *Length of sentence*: An extended sentence of imprisonment is a sentence of imprisonment the term of which is equal to the aggregate of:
  - (a) the appropriate custodial term, and
  - (b) a further period (the 'extension period') for which the offender is to be subject to a licence (s 226A(5)).

The extension period must be a period of such length as the court considers necessary for the purpose of protecting members of the public from serious harm occasioned by the commission by the offender of further specified offences, and must not exceed:

(a) 5 years in the case of a specified violent offence, and

(b) 8 years in the case of a specified sexual offence (s 226A(8)).

Furthermore, the term of an extended sentence of imprisonment must not exceed the term that, at the time the offence was committed, was the maximum term permitted for the offence (s 226A(9)).

LIFE IMPRISONMENT FOR A SECOND LISTED OFFENCE

42.3 Section 224A provides that a sentence of imprisonment for life must be imposed upon a person aged 18 or over who is convicted for a second time of an offence listed in Sch 15B if certain conditions are met relating to the gravity of the new offence and the sentence imposed for the earlier offence. The court need not impose a life sentence if particular circumstances relating to either offence or to the offender make it unjust to do so.

Note that there is no requirement under this provision that the court make a finding of dangerousness or seriousness.

LIFE IMPRISONMENT FOR SERIOUS OFFENCES

42.4 Life sentences are not restricted to repeat offenders. Section 225 provides that where a person is convicted of a specified violent or sexual offence (Sch 15) which is punishable by imprisonment for life; and the court is of the opinion that there is a significant risk to members of the public of serious harm occasioned by the commission by him of further specified offences; then, if the court considers that the seriousness of the offence is such as to justify the imposition of a sentence of life imprisonment, it must impose such a sentence.

Clearly, this provision requires an assessment of dangerousness, but once that is found and the conditions relating to life sentences and seriousness are met, there is no discretion but for a life sentence to be passed.

APPLICABILITY

42.5 These provisions are in force from 3 December 2012 following enactment of provisions of the LASPOA 2012. Note that:

- Extended sentences (s 226A) are available whatever the date of the offence provided that the conviction was on or after 3 December 2012.
- Life sentences for a second offence (s 224A) may not be imposed unless the new offence was committed on or after 3 December 2012.
- Life sentences for serious offences (s 225) are available whatever the date of the offence provided that the conviction was on or after 3 December 2012.

Chapter 43

Notification and notification orders

Sexual Offences Act 2003, ss 80–92

43.1 A register of known and convicted sex offenders was introduced in Part 1 of the Sex Offenders Act 1997 and this was then replaced by the provisions of ss 80 to 92 of the 2003 Act. The purpose of the legislation is to allow the authorities to keep track on potentially dangerous sex offenders by requiring that those persons regularly report their whereabouts and personal circumstances to the police. The length of the period during which they must report is directly related to the penalty the court has imposed on them, but the court has no other role in the notification process. Schedule 3 comprises a list of the offences which trigger a requirement for notification (see **Appendix 6**).

WHO IS SUBJECT TO NOTIFICATION? (s 80)

43.2 A person becomes subject to notification requirements (termed a 'relevant offender') is he or she is:

(a) convicted of an offence listed in Sch 3;

(b) found not guilty of such an offence by reason of insanity;

(c) found to be under a disability and to have done the act charged against him in relation to an offence listed in Sch 3;

(d) cautioned for an offence listed in Sch 3. (s 80)

Schedule 3 to the SOA comprises a list of the majority of sexual offences likely to be prosecuted in the UK. All offences created by the 2003 are included, save those relating to prostitution, pornography and trafficking (ss 48–59), sexual activity in a public lavatory (s 71) and breaches of orders. Offences under earlier legislation which have been superseded by the SOA 2003 are included.

The list is wide ranging and covers a variety of offences, some relatively modest in seriousness. However, the inclusion of these offences in the Schedule is tempered in the following ways:

- The age or apparent age of the victim, or disparity in age between the victim and perpetrator, is relevant to the inclusion of certain offences on the Schedule. So, an offence under SOA 1956, s 13 (indecency between men) is included if the offender was over 20 and the victim under 18. Where this is the case paras 95 and 97 of the Schedule provide guidance as to determination of age.

- The penalty imposed on the offender is relevant to the inclusion of many offences on the Schedule. For example, an offence under SOA 2003, s 69 (intercourse with an animal) is included only if an adult offender has been sentenced to a term of imprisonment or detained in a hospital.

The purpose of these proviso is to ensure that only more predatory or serious offenders are subject to the notification requirements. The proviso are often combined, so a person convicted for the common offence of sexual assault (SOA 2003, s 3) is only subject to notification if:

- the victim was under 18, or
- the offender is or has been sentenced to a term of imprisonment, detained in a hospital or made subject to a community sentence of at least 12 months.[1]

NOTIFICATION OBLIGATIONS (ss 83–86)

43.3 A relevant offender has notification obligations which take effect in three different ways: initial notification; when changes occur to the information provided; and regular periodic notification.

Initial notification (s 83)

43.4 Within three days of 'the relevant date' (which will usually be conviction, but see below), the relevant offender must notify the police of specific information set out in ss 83(4):

(a) date of birth

(b) national insurance number

(c) name on the relevant date (ie other aliases)

(d) home address on relevant date

(e) name on the date notification is given

(f) home address on date of notification

(g) other addresses at which he regularly resides

1 *R v Davidson* [2009] 2 Cr App R (S) 13, CA: the relevant period is the duration of the order itself, rather than the duration of the requirements imposed under the order, or the time taken to complete those requirements.

If the offender is remanded in custody, sentenced to a term of imprisonment, detained in hospital or outside the UK, the three-day period commences on his release from custody or hospital or his re-entry into the UK (s 83(6)). Of course, where a prison sentence is imposed, the three-day period may commence many months or years after conviction and sentence.

Note that, for those offences within Sch 3 which are sentence-dependent (ie sexual assault which only becomes a Sch 3 offence where the sentence is one of imprisonment or a community sentence in excess of 12 months), the relevant date will be the date of sentence, rather than the date of conviction.

The requirement for initial notification is waived for a 'repeat' offender' who is already subject to notification, provided that he gave initial notification in respect of the earlier offence and he remains subject to notification for at least three days after the relevant date for the latter offence (s 83(2)).

Changes to information given (s 84)

43.5 The relevant offender is required by s 84 to notify police of:

- a change to their home address,
- release from custody,
- their use of a different name (not notified to police under s 83(1)
- the fact that they have resided or stayed for a qualifying period at an address not notified to police under s 83(1).

The notification must be given within three days of the change taking effect, but may be given in advance of an expected change (s 83(2)). If advanced notice is given and the actual change takes effect more than two days before the anticipated date, fresh notification is required (s 83(3)). Similarly, if advanced notice is given and the anticipated change does not take effect within three days of the date specified for the change, the relevant offender must notify the police of this within six days of that date (s 83(4)).

Regular periodic notification (s 85)

43.6 A relevant offender must re-notify police of the information set out in s 83(5) each year, even if no change to that information has occurred. If change has occurred and been notified under s 84, the 12-month period runs from the date of that notification.

In addition to the obligation to notify, a relevant offender must allow a police officer or other authorised person to take his fingerprints, photographs or both at the request of the officer in order to verify identity (s 87(4)).

FURTHER NOTIFICATION REQUIREMENTS

43.7 Section 86 requires relevant offenders to notify all foreign travel arrangements (including destination, carrier and accommodation) in advance of the date of travel.

The Sexual Offences Act 2003 (Notification Requirements) Regulations 2012[2] introduces new notification requirements, both in terms of initial notification and changes to circumstances. There is a requirement to notify:

- on a weekly basis if the relevant offender does not regularly reside or stay at one place;
- if the relevant offender has resided, or stayed for the period of at least 12 hours, at a household or other private place where a child resides or stays;
- information in relation to any bank accounts, credit and debit cards held by the relevant offender; and
- information contained in any passport or other form of identification held by the relevant offender.

LENGTH OF NOTIFICATION PERIOD (S 82)

43.8 The length of time during which a relevant offender remains subject to the notification requirements is dependent on the penalty or order made by the court.

TABLE	
Description of relevant offender	*Notification period*
A person who, in respect of the offence, is or has been sentenced to **imprisonment for life or for a term of 30 months or more**	**An indefinite period** beginning with the relevant date
A person who, in respect of the offence, has been made the subject of an order under section 210F(1) of the Criminal Procedure (Scotland) Act 1995 (order for lifelong restriction)	**An indefinite period** beginning with the relevant date
A person who, in respect of the offence or finding, is or has been **admitted to a hospital subject to a restriction order**	**An indefinite period** beginning with the relevant date

2 SI 2012/1876.

A person who, in respect of the offence, is or has been sentenced to **imprisonment for a term of more than 6 months but less than 30 months**	**10 years** beginning with the relevant date
A person who, in respect of the offence, is or has been sentenced to **imprisonment for a term of 6 months or less**	**7 years** beginning with the relevant date
A person who, in respect of the offence or finding, is or has been **admitted to a hospital without being subject to a restriction order**	**7 years** beginning with the relevant date
A person within section 80(1)(d) [a person who receives a caution]	**2 years** beginning with the relevant date
A person in whose case an order for **a conditional discharge** or, in Scotland, a probation order, is mad in respect of the offence	The period of the conditional discharge or, in Scotland, the probation period
A person of any other description	**5 years** beginning with the relevant date

The relevant date is the date of conviction, finding or caution (s 82(6)).

The 'indefinite period' is the length of the offender's life.

For offenders under 18 years old on the relevant date, the 10, 7, 5 and 2-year notification periods are halved.

Where an offender is sentenced to consecutive terms of imprisonment for Sch 3 offences, those terms are aggregated in determining the length of sentence. For an offender who is sentenced to partly concurrent sentences (ie where he or she is already serving a sentence when a fresh sentence is imposed) the two periods are aggregated, less the period during which the two sentences overlap.

There is no right of appeal against the imposition of notification requirements. However, ss 91A–91F (inserted by the Sexual Offences Act 2003 (Remedial) Order 2012[3]) provide a framework for those subject to indefinite notification to apply to the police for a review of the necessity for notification to continue in order to protect the public from sexual harm. Application may be made 15 years after the first notification and every eight years thereafter (eight years after first notification for a person under 18).

NOTIFICATION AND SENTENCING

43.9 Notification is an administrative function and an obligation on the convicted person and no order or direction is required of the convicting or

3 SI 2012/1883.

sentencing tribunal (apart from the issue of a certificate under s 92, essentially certifying salient facts upon which the operation of notification depends). The Criminal Procedure Rules 2012, r 42.3 require the court to tell the defendant that notification requirements apply, but this should form no part of the sentence itself or the sentencing decision. The effect of the notification requirement on a defendant is not a justification for leniency on the part of the sentencing tribunal (*AG Ref (No 50 of 1997)*[4]). Notification is not a penalty or punitive measure (*Ibbotson v UK* (1999)[5]).

Defence advocates and representatives should be alive to the notification requirements and be ready to advise their clients of the necessity for prompt notification, even if the court fails to mention this. For many offences in Sch 3, the requirement arises on conviction rather than following the sentence hearing when minds are more readily turned to the consequences for the defendant.

BREACH OF NOTIFICATION REQUIREMENTS (S 91)

43.10 An offence is committed by a relevant offender who fails without reasonable excuse to make the initial or periodic notification (ss 83(1) and 85(1)), to notify of relevant changes within the statutory timescale (ss 84(1) and 84(4)(b)) or to allow an officer to take his fingerprints or photograph (s 87(4)). Similarly it is an offence to knowingly give false information in purported compliance with any of the relevant sections.

In each case the offence is punishable:

(a) On summary conviction, to imprisonment up to 6 months or a fine not exceeding the statutory maximum or both;

(b) On conviction on indictment, to imprisonment up to 5 years.

Section 91, see **21.1**.

NOTIFICATION ORDERS (S 97–101)

43.11 Section 97 of the Act makes provision for persons convicted of sexual offences abroad to be subject to notification requirements if they enter the UK. The provision applies to both foreign and UK nationals. The offender must have been convicted (or found not guilty by reason of insanity, etc) of an offence which would have been the equivalent of a Sch 3 offence in the UK. The appropriate notification period which would have applied in the UK must not have already expired when the offender enters the UK.

4 [1998] 2 Cr App R(S) 155.
5 [1999] Crim LR 153.

Application for an order is made to the magistrates' court by a chief officer of police for the area in which the offender is either in, or it is believed he is planning to enter.

If an order is made, the requirements last for the period equivalent to that in the Table in s 82 (see **43.8**), starting from the actual date of conviction in the foreign jurisdiction

An order made under s 97 makes the defendant subject to the notification requirements detailed above and thereby any failure to notify will be an offence contrary to s 91.

Chapter 44

Sexual offences prevention order (SOPO)

Sexual Offences Act 2003, ss 104–113

INTRODUCTION

44.1 Sexual Offences Prevention Orders (SOPOs) are civil preventative orders designed to protect the public from serious sexual harm. They may be made:

- on sentence for certain scheduled offences

  ('where the court deals with the defendant in respect of an offence' – s 104(2))

- on mental health disposal for certain scheduled offences

  ('where the court deals with the defendant in respect of a finding…' – s 104(3))

- by complaint to a magistrates' court by local police (s 104(6) to (8)) in view of a person's behaviour since conviction/caution/finding (s 104(1)(a) and s 106(8))

REQUIREMENTS FOR MAKING AN ORDER – ON CONVICTION OR FINDING

44.2 The court may make an order:

(a) if it is satisfied that it is necessary for the purpose of protecting the public or any particular members of the public from serious sexual harm from the defendant (s 104(1)(b)), and

(b) it is dealing with him in respect of an offence listed under Schedules 3 or 5 (see **Appendix 6**) or where, in respect of such an offence, he is found not guilty by reason of insanity or found to be under a disability but to have done the act charged against him (s 104(2) and (3)).

Note that, by virtue of changes made by s 141 of the Criminal Justice & Immigration 2008, the various 'qualifiers' in Schedule 3 relating to the ages of the victim and the offender and the length of sentence imposed are *not* relevant to the availability of a SOPO.

'Serious sexual harm' is defined by s 106 to mean serious physical or psychological harm, caused by the defendant committing one or more offences listed in Schedule 3'[1].

REQUIREMENTS FOR MAKING AN ORDER – ON APPLICATION

44.3 A chief officer of police may apply to a magistrates' court for an order in respect of a person who resides in his police area or who the chief officer believes is in, or is intending to come to, his police area if it appears to the chief officer that:

(a) the person is a qualifying offender, and

(b) the person has, since the date when he was convicted of a relevant offence, acted in such a way as to give reasonable cause to believe that it is necessary for such an order to be made (s 104(4) and (5)).

A 'qualifying offender' is a person who has been convicted of or cautioned for an offence listed under Schedules 3 or 5 or where, in respect of such an offence, he was found not guilty by reason of insanity or found to have been under a disability but to have done the act charged against him. Convictions and findings in foreign jurisdictions for offences similar to those listed in Schedules 3 and 5, will also qualify (s 106(5)-(7)).

The court may make an order if it is satisfied that the defendant's behaviour since the date he was first convicted of a relevant offence makes it necessary to make such an order, for the purpose of protecting the public or any particular members of the public from serious sexual harm from him (s 104(1)(a)).

Section 127 of the Magistrates' Courts Act 1980 does not apply and there is no requirement that the behaviour took place within 6 months of the application for an order[2].

---

1 Note that this poses a different test from that of 'serious harm' under the dangerous offender provisions of the Criminal Justice Act 2003.

2 SOA 2003, s 132A as amended by Policing and Crime Act 2009, s 22.

KEY CASES

44.4

- *R v Smith, Clarke, Hall & Dodd*[3]
- *R v Terrell*[4]

THE TEST

44.5

- Is the making of an order *necessary* to protect from serious sexual harm through the commission of (Sch 3) sexual offences?

  The order must be necessary, not merely desirable – *R v Halloren*[5]
- If some order is necessary, are the terms proposed nevertheless oppressive?
- Overall are the terms proportionate?

RELATIONSHIP OF SOPO TO TYPES OF SENTENCE (INDETERMINATE/EXTENDED)[6]

44.6 The usual rule is that an indefinite sentence needs no SOPO.

The availability of a SOPO would not always render an indefinite sentence unnecessary.

RELATIONSHIP TO OTHER REGIMES

44.7 No SOPO restriction is required if it merely duplicates a provision of one of the other (automatic) regimes:

- *Notification Requirements*

  SOPO must not conflict with notification requirements. There should be little or no overlap between them.

  It is not normally proper to use a SOPO merely to extend the notification requirements beyond the periods prescribed by law.

---

3 [2011] EWCA Crim 1772.
4 [2008] 2 Cr App R (S) 49.
5 [2004] EWCA Crim 233.
6 See *R v Smith & others*, at [12]–[13].

- *Disqualification from Working with Children*

  Where offences involve children, the defendant will almost inevitably be barred (SVGA 2006) or disqualified (CJ&CSA 2000) from working with children. Therefore SOPO provision(s) covering the same prohibition are unnecessary. Inconsistent SOPO/disqualification prohibitions must be avoided.

DRAFTING

44.8 Although the applicable Criminal Procedure Rule, Part 50, does not demand an advance draft SOPO, Court of Appeal guidance in *R v Smith* in effect does. Observing that sentence will not ordinarily follow immediately upon conviction, the Court indicated that advance service of a properly considered written draft is essential: '... we suggest not less than two clear days before but in any event not *at* the hearing'. Refer to **Appendix 4** for specimen order.

TERMS AND TOPICS

44.9

- *Computer use/internet access*

  A blanket prohibition on computer use or internet access is impermissible – nowadays these are an essential part of everyday living/employment requirement for many.

  Terms governing access for inspection by police or prohibiting history deletion may be useful.

- *Personal contact with children* (including <16 and <18)

  Any SOPO term must be tailored to the necessity to prevent sexual offending causing serious harm. Although prohibitions on contact with persons aged 16 or 17 may be justified, contact restrictions are much more likely to be applicable only in relation to children under 16.

  Where SOPO restrictions are necessary, proper account must be taken of:

  - children in the family (immediate/extended);
  - practicalities of everyday life (proximity on public transport, youth workers/work experience students in shops and other public situations).

PRACTITIONER POINTERS

PROS – never assume that terms proposed by CPS/police will be *Smith* compliant

DEF – there is nothing to stop the defence preparing a draft order – it is a tactically astute move that can gain the upper hand. At least prepare counter-proposals to argue

BOTH – have paper and electronic versions available – amendments are likely to be required

EFFECT OF THE SOPO (S 107)

44.10 The order has effect for a fixed period of not less than 5 years.

The order is prohibitive, preventing the defendant from doing anything described, but only such prohibitions may be included which are necessary to protect the public, or particular members of the public, from serious sexual harm from the defendant.

The imposition of a SOPO makes the defendant subject to the notification requirements of ss 80 – 92 for the duration of the order (s 107(3)-(5)) – see chapter 41.

BREACH OF THE ORDER (S 113)

44.11 Breach of a SOPO ('without reasonable excuse') is an offence punishable:

(a) On summary conviction, to imprisonment up to 6 months or a fine not exceeding the statutory maximum or both;

(b) On conviction on indictment, to imprisonment up to 5 years.

Section 113, see **21.10**.

OTHER PROVISIONS

44.12 A SOPO may be varied, renewed or discharged on application by the defendant or a relevant chief officer of police. Application will generally be to the court which made the order. Renewal or variation to impose additional prohibitions may only be made if it is necessary to protect the public, or any particular members of the public, from serious sexual harm from the defendant (and varied orders must also be to that end). A SOPO may not be discharged within 5 years of commencement without police consent (s 108).

An appeal against a SOPO made by application lies to the Crown Court. An appeal against a SOPO made following conviction is equivalent to an appeal against sentence and therefore lies either to the Crown Court or Court of Appeal (s 110).

Chapter 45

Foreign travel order (FTO)

Sexual Offences Act 2003, ss 114–122

45.1 A foreign travel order (FTO) is not an order made on conviction but may be made by complaint to a magistrates' court by a chief of police in respect of a person ('the defendant') who resides in that police area or who the chief officer believes is in, or is intending to come, to his police area. The officer must have reasonable cause to believe that an order is necessary.

PURPOSE OF THE ORDER

45.2 The purpose of the order is to protect children (ie persons under 18 years) from serious sexual harm from the defendant taking place outside the UK. It seeks to address the problem of 'sex tourism' to countries where children are more easily exploited.

REQUIREMENTS FOR MAKING THE ORDER (SS 114–116)

45.3 The court may make an order if it is satisfied that:

(a) the defendant is a 'qualifying offender', and

(b) the defendant's behaviour since the appropriate date makes it necessary to make a FTO, for the purpose of protecting children generally or any child from serious sexual harm from the defendant outside the UK (s 114(3)).

A qualifying offender is a person who, in respect of any offence listed in s 116, has been found guilty, found not guilty by reason of insanity, found to be under a disability but to have done the act charged against him, or cautioned. The offences listed in s 116 comprise:

- any offence under Sch 3 to the Act (see **Appendix 6**) where the victim was under 18 at the time of the offence;
- possession, taking, making, distributing and importing of indecent photographs of children under 18 (PCA 1978, s 1; CJS 1988, s 160);

- committing an offence with intent to commit a sexual offence (SOA 2003, s 62), or trespassing with intent to commit a sexual offence (SOA 2003, s 63), against a person under 18.

The appropriate date is the date upon which the defendant was convicted, found or cautioned for the qualifying offence.

'Serious sexual harm' means serious physical or psychological harm caused by the defendant doing acts which would constitute a Sch 3 offence if done in the UK (s 115(2)).

Section 127 of the Magistrates' Courts Act 1980 does not apply and there is no requirement that the behaviour took place within six months of the application for an order.[1]

EFFECT OF THE ORDER (S 117)

45.4 The order has effect for a fixed period of not more than five years.

The order is prohibitive, preventing the defendant from:

- travelling to specific countries;
- travelling to all countries save those named in the order; or
- travelling to all countries outside the UK (s 117(2)).

Where the order imposes a blanket ban it is also a requirement that the individual surrender their passport at a police station. Only such travel prohibitions may be imposed so as to protect a child or children from serious sexual harm from the defendant outside the UK (s 117(3)).

The imposition of a FTO makes the defendant subject to the notification requirements of s 86(1) – he becomes a 'relevant offender' for the purpose only of notifying his travel arrangements to the police (s 117(4)). (see **Chapter 43**).

BREACH OF THE ORDER (S 122)

45.5 Breach of a FTO ('without reasonable excuse') is an offence punishable:

(a) on summary conviction, to imprisonment up to six months or a fine not exceeding the statutory maximum or both;

(b) on conviction on indictment, to imprisonment up to five years.

Section 122, see **21.16**.

1 SOA 2003, s 132A as amended by Policing and Crime Act 2009, s 22.

OTHER PROVISIONS

45.6 A FTO may be made in respect of a defendant who has convictions for offences in other jurisdictions which are the equivalent of s 116 offences in the UK (s 116(3)–(7)).

A FTO may be varied, renewed or discharged on application by the defendant or a relevant chief officer of police. Renewal or variation to impose additional prohibitions may only be made if it is necessary to protect children or a child from serious sexual harm from the defendant outside the UK (s 118).

Appeals against the making of a FTO lie to the Crown Court (s 119).

PRACTITIONER POINTERS

1 In essence, the test for the making of an order is three-fold:
   (i) the defendant is a qualifying offender;
   (ii) that he has behaved since the qualifying offence, in a way such as to pose a risk;
   (iii) that it is necessary to make the order – in other words that the risk continues.

2 Note that the activity abroad which it is feared the defendant will engage in does not have to be an offence in that country (ie where there is a lower age of consent in the foreign jurisdiction).

3 Applications under Part 2 of the 2003 Act are civil in nature and civil rules of evidence, including hearsay, will apply.

4 The imposition of an order under Part 2 of the 2003 Act may be a significant infringement on the private and family life of the defendant and Art 8 rights are engaged. It should be argued that only such restrictions as are proportionate for the prevention and detection of crime, the rights of others and the protection of health and morals should be imposed.

5 Parties should consider making an application for prohibitions on publication of details of the proceedings (Contempt of Court Act 1981, s 11) if there is a potential danger to the defendant or risk of public unrest in view of the controversial nature of the hearing.

6 Means-tested legal aid is available to represent the defendant on applications for FTOs, applications to vary or discharge or appeals against the imposition of an FTO. The interests of justice test will apply.

7 Assistance may be found in the Home Office Guidance on Part 2 of the Sexual Offences Act:

http://www.homeoffice.gov.uk/publications/police/operational-policing/sexual-offences-2003

Chapter 46

Risk of sexual harm order (RHSO)

Sexual Offences Act 2003, ss 123–129

46.1 A risk of sexual harm order (RSHO) is not an order made on conviction but may be made by complaint to a magistrates' court by a chief of police in respect of a person aged 18 or over ('the defendant') who resides in that police area or who the chief officer believes is in, or is intending to come, to his police area. The officer must have reasonable cause to believe that an order is necessary.

PURPOSE OF THE ORDER

46.2 The purpose of the order is to protect children (ie persons under 16 years) from harm from the defendant.

REQUIREMENTS FOR MAKING THE ORDER (S 123)

46.3 The court may make an order if it is satisfied that the defendant on at least two occasions has:

(a) engaged in sexual activity involving a child or in the presence of a child;

(b) caused or incited a child to watch a person engaging in sexual activity or to look at a moving or still image that is sexual;

(c) given a child anything that relates to sexual activity or contains a reference to such activity;

(d) communicated with a child, where any part of the communication was sexual.

Further the court must find it necessary to make such an order, for the purpose of protecting children or a specific child from harm from the defendant (s 123(3) and (4)).

The activity alleged may have taken place before or after the commencement of the 2003 Act. It is not necessary that the defendant be convicted of an offence, and an order may be applied for in circumstances where the evidence does not support criminal charges or where a criminal prosecution is inappropriate.

Section 127 of the Magistrates' Courts Act 1980 does not apply and there is no requirement that the acts took place within six months of the application for an order.[1]

EFFECT OF THE ORDER

46.4 The order has effect for at least two years and may be for a fixed period or until further order.

The order is prohibitive, preventing the defendant from 'doing anything' the court deems necessary to protect children or any child from harm from the defendant (s 123(5) and (6)). 'Harm' is described as physical or psychological (s 124(2)). Definitions of 'sexual image', 'sexual activity' and 'sexual communication' are given in s 124(4)–(7).

The terms of the order will be circumstance specific, but examples might include:

- having no contact with a particular child, either in person or over the internet
- not going to a particular location where the offender has previously had contact with a child
- other geographic restrictions, such as not entering public parks or going within a specific distance of schools.

BREACH OF THE ORDER (S 128)

46.5 Breach of an RSHO or interim RSHO ('without reasonable excuse') is an offence punishable:

(a) on summary conviction, to imprisonment up to six months or a fine not exceeding the statutory maximum or both;

(b) on conviction on indictment, to imprisonment up to five years.

A person convicted of such a breach becomes subject to the notification requirements of s 80 for the duration of the RSHO (s 129) (see **Chapter 43**).

Section 128, see **21.22**.

1 SOA 2003, s 132A as amended by Policing & Crime Act 2009, s 22.

OTHER PROVISIONS

46.6 A court may grant an interim RSHO prior to the determination of an application for a full order, 'if it considers it just to do so'. As with a full order, it may prohibit the defendant from doing anything described in the order. However, the interim order has effect only for a specific period and ceases to have effect on the determination of the main application (s 126).

A RSHO may be varied, renewed or discharged on application by the defendant or a relevant chief officer of police. Renewal or variation to impose additional prohibitions may only be made if it is necessary to protect children or a child from harm from the defendant. Discharge within two years of the making of the order requires consent of the defendant and a relevant chief officer of police (s 125).

Appeals against the making of a RSHO or interim RSHO lie to the Crown Court (s 127).

PRACTITIONER POINTERS

1 The court may consider in detail the behaviour alleged and the defendant's circumstances. In applying for or opposing an order it may be helpful to consider the defendant's previous convictions (if any), compliance with other orders or therapeutic assistance, help from family members (or isolation from assistance) and any changes to his circumstances (moving home, employment) which may make him a greater or lesser risk.

2 Applications under Part 2 of the 2003 Act are civil in nature and civil rules of evidence, including hearsay, will apply.

3 An order is preventative only – it cannot compel the defendant to comply with conditions requiring positive action.

4 If conceding that an order may be made, it may be helpful to prepare your own draft, ensuring that the prohibitions are proportionate to the risk likely to be found by the court. The imposition of a RSHO may be a significant infringement on the private and family life of the defendant and Art 8 rights are engaged. It should be argued that only such restrictions as are proportionate for the prevention and detection of crime, the rights of others and the protection of health and morals should be imposed.

5 Parties should consider making an application for prohibitions on publication of details of the proceedings (Contempt of Court Act 1981, s 11) if there is a potential danger to the defendant or risk of public unrest in view of the controversial nature of the hearing.

6 Orders should be specific as to time and place in order that a defendant subject to a RSHO knows exactly what does, and what does not, constitute a breach.

7 Means-tested legal aid is available to represent the defendant on applications for RSHOs, applications to vary or discharge or appeals against the imposition of an RSHO. The interests of justice test will apply.

8 Assistance may be found in the Home Office Guidance on Part 2 of the Sexual Offences Act:

http://www.homeoffice.gov.uk/publications/police/operational-policing/sexual-offences-2003

Chapter 47

Bars from working with children and vulnerable adults

Safeguarding Vulnerable Groups Act 2006 Safeguarding Vulnerable Groups Act 2006 (Prescribed Criteria and Miscellaneous Provisions) Regulations 2009

PURPOSE OF THE PROVISIONS

47.1 The purpose of these provisions is to prevent those who might be a danger to children and vulnerable adults from working with those groups. The Independent Barring Service (IBS), which came into existence on 1 December 2012 as an amalgam of the Criminal Records Bureau and the Independent Safeguarding Authority, is tasked with maintaining a children's barred list and an adults' barred list.

INCLUSION ON THE BARRED LISTS

47.2 Inclusion on the barred lists is primarily triggered by conviction or caution for a specified offence. The SVGA 2006 (Prescribed Criteria and Miscellaneous Provisions) Regulations 2009[1] creates, in its schedule, four lists of offences:

- Para 1: automatic inclusion in children's barred list
- Para 2: inclusion in children's barred list, subject to representations
- Para 3: automatic inclusion in the adults' barred list
- Para 4: inclusion in the adults' barred list, subject to representations

1 SI 2009/37.

The lists are long and comprehensive, particularly those under paras 2 and 4, and contain offences relating to violence and other abuse as well as sexual offences. Some offences are included subject to the proviso that they were committed against or in respect of a child.

There is also provision for the IBS to include a person on the list without caution or conviction if is seems to the service that the person has engaged in relevant conduct – essentially behaviour that endangers or would endanger a child or vulnerable adult or inappropriate sexual conduct towards a child or vulnerable adult.[2]

EFFECT OF INCLUSION

47.3 Inclusion on a barred list prevents an individual from engaging in regulated activities as defined in SVGA 2006, Sch. 4, Part 1 (children) and Part 2 (adults). In relation to children, these are likely to include teaching, training, instructing or caring for children and working in schools or children's homes. Family arrangements and personal, non-commercial arrangements are excluded.

PROCEDURE

47.4 A person convicted of or cautioned for an offence that falls within paras 1 or 3 will be referred to the IBS for automatic inclusion on the relevant list. A person falling within paras 2 or 4 will be referred to the IBS which will consider them for inclusion. Representations may be made to the IBS by the convicted person as to why he or she should not be included on the barred list, prior to inclusion.

In order for a person to be included on the barred lists there is no requirement for the court which convicted a person of a specified offence to make any order (but see below). However, the Criminal Procedure Rules 2012, r 42.3 require the court to tell the defendant that they are to be or may be included in a barred list.

Since the provision is preventative rather than punitive, it may be applied to offences committed before the 2006 Act came into force without breaching Article 7 ECHR.[3]

---

2 Cf SVGA 2006, Sch 4, Parts 1 and 2.

3 *R v G* [2005] EWCA Crim 1300.

RELATIONSHIP OF THIS REGIME WITH CRIMINAL JUSTICE AND COURT SERVICES ACT 2000, S 28 (DISQUALIFICATION FROM WORKING WITH CHILDREN)

47.5 Under s 28 of the 2000 Act, judges were obliged to disqualify from working with children any person convicted of a qualifying offence against a child where the sentence was 12 months or more, unless satisfied that it was unlikely that the defendant would commit a further offence against a child. The disqualification was indefinite. The convicted person was immediately disqualified and a notice notified him or her of the general effect of the order.

The SVGA 2006 was intended to replace the 2000 Act and has now fully done so. From 17 June 2013, courts no longer have power to disqualify offenders from working with children pursuant to the CJSA 2000.[4]

WORKING WHILE BARRED (SVGA 2006, S 7)

47.6 An individual commits an offence if he—

(a) seeks to engage in regulated activity from which he is barred;

(b) offers to engage in regulated activity from which he is barred;

(c) engages in regulated activity from which he is barred.

In each case the offence is punishable:

- on summary conviction, by imprisonment up to six months, or a fine not exceeding the statutory maximum, or to both;
- on conviction on indictment, by imprisonment up to five years.

Section 7, see **27.1**.

PRACTITIONER POINTERS

1 Prosecutors should ready to advise the court that the barring provisions may apply on conviction for a range of offences, in order that the court can remind the defendant of this in accordance with CPR r 42.3.

2 Defence lawyers need to be aware of the application of the barring provisions in advising their clients. Particular care should be taken in advising clients on accepting a caution for an offence falling within the Schedule to the 2009 Regulations.

4 Safeguarding Vulnerable Groups Act 2006 (Commencement No 8 and Saving) Order 2012, SI 2012/2231.

Chapter 48

Sentencing in historic sex cases

GENERAL PRINCIPLES

48.1 The principles were comprehensively set out by the Court of Appeal in the guideline case of *R v H & others*:[1]

- No specific provision is made for 'historic' or 'cold' cases. The purposes of sentencing expressed in s 142(1) of the Criminal Justice Act 2003 apply equally to such cases, namely:
  - (a) the punishment of offenders;
  - (b) the reduction of crime (including its reduction by deterrence);
  - (c) the reform and rehabilitation of offenders;
  - (d) the protection of the public; and
  - (e) the making of reparation by offenders to persons affected by their offences.
- Sentence is constrained by the maximum penalty applicable at the date of the offence, unless the current maximum is lower (in which case that lower limit applies).
- Within the applicable maximum, sentence should be passed in accordance with current guidelines. In relation to repealed offences not specifically covered by the Definitive Guideline, comparison should focus on the elements of an offence rather than the name given to it (for example, the rape guideline applies to non-consensual buggery).

Particular care is required when dealing with an offence for which the maximum sentence was changed. An example is gross indecency with a child, contrary to s 1 of the Indecency with Children Act 1960: from implementation on 2 July 1960 until 30 September 1997 the maximum was two years imprisonment, but this was thereafter increased to 10 years[2] until repeal by Sexual Offences Act 2003, from 1 May 2004.

---

1 [2011] EWCA Crim 2753, [2012] 2 Cr App R(S) 21.
2 By Crime (Sentences) Act 1997, s 52.

Maximum sentences for attempts have been the subject of some particularly wild fluctuations over time. For example, attempted rape from 24 March 1948 to 15 September 1985[3] carried a maximum sentence of seven years: thereafter there is parity with the completed offence (life imprisonment). One of the cases in *R v H & others* involved an unlawful sentence in excess of the seven year maximum which had gone unnoticed even on an earlier appeal hearing in the Court of Appeal.

Even more extreme variation is found with attempted sexual intercourse with a girl under 13, the maximum penalty at various dates[4] being two years, seven years and life.

Maximum sentences applicable at varying dates are set out within the substantive offence chapters in Parts B, C and D of this book.

'SPECIAL' SENTENCING PROVISIONS

48.2 A labyrinth of provisions has been enacted over the years, aimed at dealing with offenders perceived to present a particular danger through reoffending. The regimes include the following:

- 1 October 1992 to 29 September 1998 – extended sentences

  Criminal Justice Act 1991, s 44 and Powers of Criminal Courts (Sentencing) Act 2000, s 86(1)

- 30 September 1998 to 3 April 2005 – extended sentences

  Powers of Criminal Courts (Sentencing) Act 2000, s 85

- 1 October 1992 to 3 April 2005 – longer than commensurate sentences

  Criminal Justice Act 1991, s 2(2)(b) and Powers of Criminal Courts (Sentencing) Act 2000, s 80(2)(b) – as amended by Sexual Offences Act 2003

Continuing applicability of these regimes when historic offences are being sentenced today is likely to be almost exclusively of academic interest only. We say that because even the most recent offences falling within the scope of these old provisions will have been committed nearly a decade ago. If there has been no serious offending since that time it is unlikely, however grave the old offence, that the offender would be properly assessed as posing an ongoing danger in respect of future offending. Conversely, if there has been a later serious sexual offence, the current 'dangerousness' provisions can be invoked to address ongoing risk. Having said that, there could arise a scenario where the old powers will need to be revisited, perhaps where there is a

---

3 See **28.7**.
4 See **28.14**.

delayed conviction for a grave historic offence and there is recent disturbing behavior, albeit not amounting to 'triggering' offences. A particular concern, often bemoaned by the Court of Appeal but habitually ignored by Parliament, is the failure to categorise the offence of child abduction as a sexual offence. If a recent sexually motivated offence of child abduction were sentenced now alongside an historic sexual offence, it might be very useful to invoke the old dangerousness provisions. Such a course would, however, be unnecessary if proper use were made of overlapping offences, such as that under s 62 of the SOA 2003 (committing an offence with intent to commit a sexual offence) – see discussion at **18.15**.

SENTENCING COUNCIL GUIDANCE

48.3 The new Sexual Offences Definitive Guideline gives the following guidance on the correct approach to sentencing historic sexual offences:

> 'When sentencing sexual offences under the Sexual Offences Act 1956, or other legislation pre-dating the 2003 Act, the court should apply the following principles:[5]
>
> 1 The offender must be sentenced in accordance with the sentencing regime applicable at the *date of sentence*. Under the Criminal Justice Act 2003[6] the court must have regard to the statutory purposes of sentencing and must base the sentencing exercise on its assessment of the seriousness of the offence.
>
> 2 The sentence is limited to the maximum sentence available at the *date of the commission of the offence*. If the maximum sentence has been reduced, the lower maximum will be applicable.
>
> 3 The court should have regard to any applicable sentencing guidelines for equivalent offences under the Sexual Offences Act 2003.
>
> 4 The seriousness of the offence, assessed by the culpability of the offender and the harm caused or intended, is the main consideration for the court. The court should not seek to establish the likely sentence had the offender been convicted shortly after the date of the offence.
>
> 5 When assessing the culpability of the offender, the court should have regard to relevant culpability factors set out in any applicable guideline.
>
> 6 The court must assess carefully the harm done to the victim based on the facts available to it, having regard to relevant harm factors set

5 *R v H and others* [2011] EWCA Crim 2753.
6 Section 143.

out in any applicable guideline. Consideration of the circumstances which brought the offence to light will be of importance.

7 The court must consider the relevance of the passage of time carefully as it has the potential to aggravate or mitigate the seriousness of the offence. It will be an aggravating factor where the offender has continued to commit sexual offences against the victim or others or has continued to prevent the victim reporting the offence.

8 Where there is an absence of further offending over a long period of time, especially combined with evidence of good character, this may be treated by the court as a mitigating factor. However, as with offences dealt with under the Sexual Offences Act 2003, previous good character/exemplary conduct is different from having no previous convictions. The more serious the offence, the less the weight which should normally be attributed to this factor. Where previous good character/exemplary conduct has been used to facilitate the offence, this mitigation should not normally be allowed and such conduct may constitute an aggravating factor.

9 If the offender was very young and immature at the time of the offence, depending on the circumstances of the offence, this may be regarded as personal mitigation.

10 If the offender made admissions at the time of the offence that were not investigated this is likely to be regarded as personal mitigation. Even greater mitigation is available to the offender who reported himself to the police and/or made early admissions.

11 A reduction for an early guilty plea should be made in the usual manner.'

Part G
Appendices

Appendix 1

Specimen Indictments

INTRODUCTORY NOTES

A properly drafted indictment is a prerequisite for any Crown Court case, setting out a route map for judge, jury and parties. Any trial that begins with the jury being asked to pencil in amendments or the judge querying the indictment during the prosecution opening is starting on a very poor footing.

These are the essentials:

- count(s) properly reflecting what is alleged;
- law applicable at the material time;
- appropriate sentencing scope provided;
- essential matters included, surplusage omitted.

We provide in this appendix sample counts for all the indictable offences covered in the book, which we hope busy practitioners will find useful. Our specimens are, of course, guides rather than prescriptions, but we trust that each will 'pass muster'.

Inevitably stylistic considerations arise. For example, we steadfastly refuse to include in the particulars of any indictment the phrase 'the said', which we consider to be anathema in the 21st century, but we have yet to settle on an alternative to 'namely'. Likewise we retain the traditional mode of expressing a date, 'on the 1st day of January 2014', although we can see no objection to a modernised 'on 1 January 2014'. After all, one wouldn't say 'in the year' 2014.

Some of the offences created under the 2003 Act pose a real challenge to achieving plain English. It helps if repetition of parties' names is limited: where obvious, for instance where there is a male defendant and female complainant, 'he/she' and 'his/her' can be substituted.

By tradition, indictments are framed so as to refer to the defendant in the third person, although of course upon arraignment the clerk switches to 'you'. We sincerely hope that the enduring error on some CPS pro forma material has finally been eradicated so that juries will no longer face the alarming suggestion that 'the defendant penetrated with *your* penis'.

As a rule, we have not laboriously indicated alternative gender. Where a defendant can only be male or an alleged victim only female, this is set out within the substantive sections under the heading 'parties'.

When drafting indictments for aggravated versions of offences, such as the penetrative form of sections 4, 8, 9 and 10 of the Sexual Offences Act 2003, it is good practice to include in the Statement of Offence a reference to the relevant enabling subsection. See, as an example, the penetrative version of s 4 on page 531.

Likewise, where appropriate, the word 'penetrative' should be included in the Statement of Offence (see same example).

What is crucial in each case is that statutory aggravating features are reflected in the particulars.

PART B – SEXUAL OFFENCES ACT 2003

Section 1

(see Chapter 8)

STATEMENT OF OFFENCE

RAPE, contrary to section 1(1) of the Sexual Offences Act 2003.

PARTICULARS OF OFFENCE

AA, on the 1st day of January 2014, intentionally penetrated with his penis the vagina [anus/mouth] of BB who did not consent to the penetration and AA did not reasonably believe that she [he] did consent to it.

Section 2

(see Chapter 9)

STATEMENT OF OFFENCE

ASSAULT BY PENETRATION, contrary to section 2(1) of the Sexual Offences Act 2003.

PARTICULARS OF OFFENCE

AA, on the 1st day of January 2014, intentionally penetrated the vagina [anus] of BB [with a vibrator] with a part of his body, namely his fingers, the penetration was sexual and BB did not consent to the penetration and AA did not reasonably believe that she did consent to it.

Section 3

(see Chapter 9)

STATEMENT OF OFFENCE

SEXUAL ASSAULT, contrary to section 3(1) of the Sexual Offences Act 2003.

PARTICULARS OF OFFENCE

AA, on the 1st day of January 2014, intentionally touched BB, the touching was sexual, BB did not consent to the touching and AA did not reasonably believe that she did consent to it.

Section 4 – non penetrative

(see Chapter 9)

STATEMENT OF OFFENCE

CAUSING A PERSON TO ENGAGE IN SEXUAL ACTIVITY WITHOUT CONSENT, contrary to section 4(1) of the Sexual Offences Act 2003.

PARTICULARS OF OFFENCE

AA, on the 1st day of January 2014, intentionally caused BB to engage in a sexual activity, namely to perform a 'striptease', when BB did not consent to the sexual activity and AA did not reasonably believe that BB did consent to it.

Section 4 – penetrative

(see Chapter 9)

STATEMENT OF OFFENCE

CAUSING A PERSON TO ENGAGE IN PENETRATIVE SEXUAL ACTIVITY WITHOUT CONSENT, contrary to section 4(1) and (4) of the Sexual Offences Act 2003.

PARTICULARS OF OFFENCE

AA, on the 1st day of January 2014, intentionally caused BB to engage in a sexual activity, namely penetrating the anus of CC with a broom handle, when BB did not consent to the sexual activity and AA did not reasonably believe that he did consent to it.

Section 5

(see Chapter 10)

STATEMENT OF OFFENCE

RAPE OF A CHILD UNDER 13, contrary to section 5(1) of the Sexual Offences Act 2003.

PARTICULARS OF OFFENCE

AA, on the 1st day of January 2014, intentionally penetrated with his penis the vagina [anus/mouth] of BB, a child under the age of 13 years.

Section 6

(see Chapter 10)

STATEMENT OF OFFENCE

ASSAULT BY PENETRATION OF A CHILD UNDER 13, contrary to section 6(1) of the Sexual Offences Act 2003.

PARTICULARS OF OFFENCE

AA, on the 1st day of January 2014, intentionally penetrated the vagina [anus] of BB, a child under the age of 13, [with an object unknown] with a part of his body, namely his fingers and the penetration was sexual.

Section 7

(see Chapter 10)

STATEMENT OF OFFENCE

SEXUAL ASSAULT OF A CHILD UNDER 13, contrary to section 7(1) of the Sexual Offences Act 2003.

PARTICULARS OF OFFENCE

AA, on the 1st day of January 2014, intentionally touched BB, a child under the age of 13, and the touching was sexual.

Section 8 – causing, non penetrative

(see Chapter 10)

STATEMENT OF OFFENCE

CAUSING A CHILD UNDER 13 TO ENGAGE IN SEXUAL ACTIVITY, contrary to section 8(1) of the Sexual Offences Act 2003.

PARTICULARS OF OFFENCE

AA, on the 1st day of January 2014, intentionally caused BB, a child under the age of 13, to engage in a sexual activity, namely to expose her naked genitalia over a webcam for viewing by a person or persons unknown.

Section 8 – causing, penetrative

(see Chapter 10)

STATEMENT OF OFFENCE

CAUSING A CHILD UNDER 13 TO ENGAGE IN PENETRATIVE SEXUAL ACTIVITY, contrary to section 8(1) and (2) of the Sexual Offences Act 2003.

PARTICULARS OF OFFENCE

AA, on the 1st day of January 2014, intentionally caused BB, a child under the age of 13, to engage in a sexual activity, namely to penetrate with his fingers the vagina of CC.

Section 8 – inciting, non penetrative

(see Chapter 10)

STATEMENT OF OFFENCE

INCITING A CHILD UNDER 13 TO ENGAGE IN SEXUAL ACTIVITY, contrary to section 8(1) of the Sexual Offences Act 2003.

PARTICULARS OF OFFENCE

AA, on the 1st day of January 2014, intentionally incited BB, a child under the age of 13, to engage in a sexual activity, namely to take a naked photograph of herself and send it to him via a mobile phone.

Section 8 – inciting, penetrative

(see Chapter 10)

STATEMENT OF OFFENCE

INCITING A CHILD UNDER 13 TO ENGAGE IN PENETRATIVE SEXUAL ACTIVITY, contrary to section 8(1) and (2) of the Sexual Offences Act 2003.

PARTICULARS OF OFFENCE

AA, on the 1st day of January 2014, intentionally incited BB, a child under the age of 13, to engage in a sexual activity, namely to penetrate with a carrot the anus of BB.

Section 9 – non penetrative

(see Chapter 11)

STATEMENT OF OFFENCE

SEXUAL ACTIVITY WITH A CHILD, contrary to section 9(1) of the Sexual Offences Act 2003.

PARTICULARS OF OFFENCE

AA, a person aged [over] 18, on the 1st day of January 2014, intentionally touched BB, a person aged under 16 years, namely 15 years, whom AA did not reasonably believe was aged 16 or over, and the touching was sexual.

Section 9 – penetrative

(see Chapter 11)

STATEMENT OF OFFENCE

PENETRATIVE SEXUAL ACTIVITY WITH A CHILD, contrary to section 9(1) and (2) of the Sexual Offences Act 2003.

PARTICULARS OF OFFENCE

AA, a person aged [over] 18, on the 1st day of January 2014, intentionally touched BB, a person aged under 16 years, namely 14 years, whom AA did not reasonably believe was aged 16 or over, and the touching was sexual and involved the penetration of BB's vagina with a part of AA's body, namely his finger.

Section 10 – causing

(see Chapter 11)

STATEMENT OF OFFENCE

CAUSING A CHILD TO ENGAGE IN SEXUAL ACTIVITY, contrary to section 10(1) and (2) of the Sexual Offences Act 2003.

PARTICULARS OF OFFENCE

AA, a person aged [over] 18, on the 1st day of January 2014, intentionally caused BB, a person aged 14 years, to engage in sexual activity, namely to penetrate[1] with his penis the vagina of CC.

Section 10 – inciting

(see Chapter 11)

STATEMENT OF OFFENCE

INCITING A CHILD TO ENGAGE IN SEXUAL ACTIVITY, contrary to section 10(1) of the Sexual Offences Act 2003.

---

1 This specimen provides an example of the aggravated offence (therefore triable only on indictment – see **11.18** and **11.21**). For non-aggravated version omit 'penetrative' and omit 'and (2)' from Statement of Offence.

PARTICULARS OF OFFENCE

AA, a person aged [over] 18, on the 1st day of January 2014, intentionally incited BB, a person aged 14 years, to engage in sexual activity, namely to expose her naked breasts over a webcam for viewing by CC.

Section 11

(see Chapter 11)

STATEMENT OF OFFENCE

ENGAGING IN SEXUAL ACTIVITY IN THE PRESENCE OF A CHILD, contrary to section 11(1) of the Sexual Offences Act 2003.

PARTICULARS OF OFFENCE

AA, a person aged [over] 18, on the 1st day of January 2014, intentionally engaged in a sexual activity, namely masturbating herself, and for the purpose of obtaining sexual gratification she engaged in that activity when BB, a boy aged 14 and whom AA did not reasonably believe was 16 or over, was in a position to observe her over a webcam, AA intending that BB should be aware that she was engaging in the activity.

Section 12

(see Chapter 11)

STATEMENT OF OFFENCE

CAUSING A CHILD TO WATCH A SEXUAL ACT, contrary to section 12(1) of the Sexual Offences Act 2003.

PARTICULARS OF OFFENCE

AA, a person aged [over] 18, on the 1st day of January 2014, for the purpose of obtaining sexual gratification, intentionally caused BB, a girl aged 14 and whom AA did not reasonably believe was 16 or over, to look at an image of himself engaging in a sexual activity, namely having oral sex with another person.

Section 13

(see Chapter 11)

STATEMENT OF OFFENCE

SEXUAL ACTIVITY WITH A CHILD, contrary to section 13(1) of the Sexual Offences Act 2003.

PARTICULARS OF OFFENCE

AA, a person aged under 18, on the 1st day of January 2014, intentionally touched BB, a person aged 14 years whom AA did not reasonably believe was aged 16 or over, and the touching was sexual.

Section 14

(see Chapter 11)

STATEMENT OF OFFENCE

FACILITATING THE COMMISSION OF A CHILD SEX OFFENCE, contrary to section 14(1) of the Sexual Offences Act 2003.

PARTICULARS OF OFFENCE

AA, between the 1st day of January 2014 and 10th January 2014, intentionally facilitated an act which he believed BB would do and which would involve the commission of an offence of sexual activity with a child, contrary to section 9 Sexual Offences Act 2003, in that he arranged airline and hotel bookings for BB to travel to Indonesia intending to have sex with prostitutes under the age of 16.

Section 15

(see Chapter 11)

STATEMENT OF OFFENCE

MEETING A CHILD FOLLOWING SEXUAL GROOMING, contrary to section 15(1) of the Sexual Offences Act 2003.

PARTICULARS OF OFFENCE

AA, a person aged [over] 18, on the 1st day of January 2014, having on at least two occasions met or communicated with BB, a child under the age of 16, namely 12 years, whom he did not reasonably believe to be aged 16 years or over, travelled with the intention of meeting her, intending to do something to her during or after the meeting that would have constituted an offence as defined in section 15(2)(b) Sexual Offences Act 2003.

Section 16

(see Chapter 12)

STATEMENT OF OFFENCE

SEXUAL ACTIVITY WITH A CHILD BY A PERSON IN A POSITION OF TRUST, contrary to section 16(1) of the Sexual Offences Act 2003.

PARTICULARS OF OFFENCE

AA, a person aged [over] 18, on the 1st day of January 2014, intentionally and sexually touched BB, a person aged under 18 whom AA did not reasonably believe was 18 or over, when AA was in a position of trust in relation to BB by virtue of his looking after persons under 18 receiving education at an educational institution, BB was receiving education at that institution and AA knew or could reasonably have been expected to know of the circumstances by which he was in a position of trust in relation to BB.

Section 17 – causing

(see Chapter 12)

STATEMENT OF OFFENCE

CAUSING A CHILD TO ENGAGE IN SEXUAL ACTIVITY BY A PERSON IN A POSITION OF TRUST, contrary to section 17(1) of the Sexual Offences Act 2003.

PARTICULARS OF OFFENCE

AA, a person aged [over] 18, on the 1st day of January 2014, intentionally caused BB, a person aged under 18 whom AA did not reasonably believe was 18 or over, to engage in a sexual activity, namely to touch his clothed groin area, when AA was in a position of trust in relation to BB by virtue of his looking after persons under 18 receiving education at an educational institution, BB was receiving education at that institution and AA knew or could reasonably have been expected to know of the circumstances by which he was in a position of trust in relation to BB.

Section 17 – inciting

(see Chapter 12)

STATEMENT OF OFFENCE

INCITING A CHILD TO ENGAGE IN SEXUAL ACTIVITY BY A PERSON IN A POSITION OF TRUST, contrary to section 17(1) of the Sexual Offences Act 2003.

PARTICULARS OF OFFENCE

AA, a person aged [over] 18, on the 1st day of January 2014, intentionally incited BB, a person aged under 18 whom AA did not reasonably believe was 18 or over, to engage in a sexual activity, namely to send him via an internet connection images of her in underwear, when AA was in a position of trust in relation to BB by virtue of his looking after persons under 18 receiving education at an educational institution, BB was receiving education at that institution and AA knew or could reasonably have been expected to know of the circumstances by which he was in a position of trust in relation to BB.

Section 18

(see Chapter 12)

STATEMENT OF OFFENCE

SEXUAL ACTIVITY IN THE PRESENCE OF A CHILD BY A PERSON IN A POSITION OF TRUST, contrary to section 18(1) of the Sexual Offences Act 2003.

PARTICULARS OF OFFENCE

AA, a person aged [over] 18, on the 1st day of January 2014, for the purpose of obtaining sexual gratification, intentionally engaged in sexual activity, namely dancing naked outside a bedroom window, when BB, a person aged under 13, was in a place from which AA could be observed and AA intended BB to be aware that she was engaging in the activity, AA being in a position of trust in relation to BB by virtue of looking after children living in a children's home, BB residing in that home and AA knowing of the circumstances by which she was in a position of trust in relation to BB.

Section 19

(see Chapter 12)

STATEMENT OF OFFENCE

CAUSING A CHILD TO WATCH A SEXUAL ACT BY A PERSON IN A POSITION OF TRUST, contrary to section 19(1) of the Sexual Offences Act 2003.

PARTICULARS OF OFFENCE

AA, a person aged [over] 18, on the 1st day of January 2014, for the purpose of obtaining sexual gratification, intentionally caused BB, a person aged under 18 whom AA did not reasonably believe was 18 or over, to look at an image of a person engaging in a sexual activity, when AA was in a position of trust in relation to BB by virtue of looking after persons aged under 18 detained in an institution under court order, BB was detained in that institution and AA knew of the circumstances by which he was in a position of trust in relation to BB.

Section 25

(see Chapter 13)

STATEMENT OF OFFENCE

[PENETRATIVE] SEXUAL ACTIVITY WITH A CHILD FAMILY MEMBER, contrary to section 25(1) and (6) of the Sexual Offences Act 2003.[2]

---

2 For non-aggravated version omit 'penetrative ' and remove 'and (6)' from the Statement of Offence.

PARTICULARS OF OFFENCE

AA, a person aged [over] 18, on the 1st day of January 2014, intentionally touched his niece BB, a person under 18 years, by penetrating her anus with his finger: the touching was sexual, he knew or could reasonably have been expected to know that she was his niece and he did not reasonably believe that she was 18 or over.

Section 26

(see Chapter 13)

STATEMENT OF OFFENCE

INCITING A CHILD FAMILY MEMBER TO ENGAGE IN [PENETRATIVE] SEXUAL ACTIVITY, contrary to section 26(1) and (6) of the Sexual Offences Act 2003.[3]

PARTICULARS OF OFFENCE

AA, a person aged [over] 18, on the 1st day of January 2014, intentionally incited his niece BB, a person under 18 years, to touch him sexually by penetrating his anus with her finger, when he knew or could reasonably have been expected to know that she was his niece and he did not reasonably believe that she was 18 or over.

Section 30

(see Chapter 14)

STATEMENT OF OFFENCE

[PENETRATIVE][4] SEXUAL ACTIVITY WITH A PERSON WITH A MENTAL DISORDER IMPEDING CHOICE, contrary to section 30(1) and (3) of the Sexual Offences Act 2003.

PARTICULARS OF OFFENCE

AA, on the 1st day of January 2014, intentionally touched BB sexually, [by penetrating his anus with her finger], when BB was unable to refuse because of or for a reason related to a mental disorder, and AA knew or could reasonably have been expected to know that BB had a mental disorder and that because of it or for a reason related to it BB was likely to be unable to refuse.

---

3 For non-aggravated version, omit 'penetrative' and remove 'and (6)' from the Statement of Offence.

4 For non-aggravated version, omit 'penetrative' and remove 'and (3)' from the Statement of Offence..

Section 31

(see Chapter 14)

STATEMENT OF OFFENCE

[CAUSING/INCITING] A PERSON WITH A MENTAL DISORDER IMPEDING CHOICE TO ENGAGE IN [PENETRATIVE] SEXUAL ACTIVITY, contrary to section 31(1) and (3) of the Sexual Offences Act 2003.[5]

PARTICULARS OF OFFENCE

AA, on the 1st day of January 2014, intentionally [caused/incited] BB to engage in a [penetrative] sexual activity, namely [penetrating the vagina of CC with a vibrator] exposing her breasts, when BB was unable to refuse because of or for a reason related to a mental disorder, and AA knew or could reasonably have been expected to know that BB had a mental disorder and that because of it or for a reason related to it BB was likely to be unable to refuse.

Section 32

(see Chapter 14)

STATEMENT OF OFFENCE

SEXUAL ACTIVITY IN THE PRESENCE OF A PERSON WITH A MENTAL DISORDER IMPEDING CHOICE, contrary to section 32(1) of the Sexual Offences Act 2003.

PARTICULARS OF OFFENCE

AA, on the 1st day of January 2014, for the purpose of obtaining sexual gratification intentionally engaged in a sexual activity, namely masturbating herself, when BB was present, BB being unable to refuse because of or for a reason related to a mental disorder, AA knowing or believing that BB was aware that she was engaging in the activity and AA knew or could reasonably have been expected to know that BB had a mental disorder and that because of it or for a reason related to it BB was likely to be unable to refuse.

Section 33

(see Chapter 14)

STATEMENT OF OFFENCE

CAUSING A PERSON WITH A MENTAL DISORDER IMPEDING CHOICE TO WATCH A SEXUAL ACT, contrary to section 33(1) of the Sexual Offences Act 2003.

---

5 For non-aggravated version, omit 'penetrative' and remove 'and (3)' from the Statement of Offence.

PARTICULARS OF OFFENCE

AA, on the 1st day of January 2014, for the purpose of obtaining sexual gratification intentionally caused BB to look at an image of a person engaging in a sexual activity, BB being unable to refuse because of or for a reason related to a mental disorder and AA knew or could reasonably have been expected to know that BB had a mental disorder and that because of it or for a reason related to it was likely to be unable to refuse.

Section 34

(see Chapter 15)

STATEMENT OF OFFENCE

SEXUAL ACTIVITY WITH A PERSON WITH A MENTAL DISORDER WHOSE AGREEMENT WAS PROCURED BY INDUCEMENT, THREAT OR DECEPTION contrary to section 34(1) of the Sexual Offences Act 2003.[6]

PARTICULARS OF OFFENCE

AA, on the 1st day of January 2014, with the agreement of BB, a person with a mental disorder, intentionally touched BB by penetrating her mouth with his fingers, the touching was sexual and AA had obtained BB's agreement by [giving her an inducement/making a threat] practising a deception, namely telling her that he was a dentist, where AA knew or could reasonably have been expected to know that BB had a mental disorder.

Section 35

(see Chapter 15)

STATEMENT OF OFFENCE

CAUSING A PERSON WITH A MENTAL DISORDER TO ENGAGE IN [PENETRATIVE] SEXUAL ACTIVITY BY THREAT [INDUCEMENT/ DECEPTION] contrary to section 35(1) and (2) of the Sexual Offences Act 2003.[7]

PARTICULARS OF OFFENCE

AA, on the 1st day of January 2014, intentionally caused BB, a person with a mental disorder, to [agree to] engage in a sexual activity, namely to lick the feet of AA [namely the penetration of CC's vagina with BB's penis], by making a threat, where AA knew or could reasonably have been expected to know that BB had a mental disorder.

---

6 If aggravated by penetration, include details and add reference to subsection (2).

7 For non-aggravated version, omit 'penetrative' and remove 'and (2)' from the Statement of Offence.

Section 36

(see Chapter 15)

STATEMENT OF OFFENCE

ENGAGING IN SEXUAL ACTIVITY IN THE PRESENCE, PROCURED BY INDUCEMENT [THREAT/DECEPTION], OF A PERSON WITH A MENTAL DISORDER contrary to section 36(1) of the Sexual Offences Act 2003.

PARTICULARS OF OFFENCE

AA, on the 1st day of January 2014, for the purpose of obtaining sexual gratification, intentionally engaged in a sexual activity, namely masturbating himself, in the presence of BB, a person with a mental disorder, intending that BB should be aware that he was engaging in the activity, where BB agreed to be present because of an inducement given by AA for the purpose of obtaining his agreement and AA knew or could reasonably have been expected to know that BB had a mental disorder.

Section 37

(see Chapter 15)

STATEMENT OF OFFENCE

CAUSING A PERSON WITH A MENTAL DISORDER TO [WATCH] LOOK AT AN IMAGE OF A SEXUAL ACT BY [INDUCEMENT/THREAT] DECEPTION, contrary to section 37(1) of the Sexual Offences Act 2003.

PARTICULARS OF OFFENCE

AA, on the 1st day of January 2014, for the purpose of obtaining sexual gratification, intentionally caused BB, a person with a mental disorder, to look at an image of persons unknown engaging in a sexual activity, where BB agreed to look because of a deception practised by AA for the purpose of obtaining BB's agreement and AA knew or could reasonably have been expected to know that BB had a mental disorder.

Section 38

(see Chapter 16)

STATEMENT OF OFFENCE

[PENETRATIVE] SEXUAL ACTIVITY WITH A PERSON WITH A MENTAL DISORDER BY A CARE WORKER, contrary to section 38(1) and (3) of the Sexual Offences Act 2003.[8]

---

8 For non-aggravated version, omit 'penetrative' and remove 'and (3)' from the Statement of Offence.

PARTICULARS OF OFFENCE

AA, on the 1st day of January 2014, intentionally and sexually touched BB, a person with a mental disorder, [by penetrating her vagina with his penis], where AA knew or could reasonably have been expected to know that BB had a mental disorder, and where AA was involved in BB's care in a way falling within section 42 of the Sexual Offences Act 2003.

Section 39

(see Chapter 16)

STATEMENT OF OFFENCE

[CAUSING] INCITING [PENETRATIVE} SEXUAL ACTIVITY BY A PERSON WITH A MENTAL DISORDER BY A CARE WORKER, contrary to section 39(1) and (3) of the Sexual Offences Act 2003.[9]

PARTICULARS OF OFFENCE

AA, on the 1st day of January 2014, intentionally [caused] incited BB, a person with a mental disorder, to engage in a sexual activity [namely to have sexual intercourse with CC], where AA knew or could reasonably have been expected to know that BB had a mental disorder, and where AA was involved in BB's care in a way falling within section 42 of the Sexual Offences Act 2003.

Section 40

(see Chapter 16)

STATEMENT OF OFFENCE

ENGAGING IN SEXUAL ACTIVITY IN THE PRESENCE OF A PERSON WITH A MENTAL DISORDER BY A CARE WORKER, contrary to section 40(1) of the Sexual Offences Act 2003.

PARTICULARS OF OFFENCE

AA, on the 1st day of January 2014, intentionally engaged in a sexual activity, namely masturbating herself, and for the purpose of obtaining sexual gratification she engaged in that activity when BB, a person with a mental disorder, was in a position to observe her over a webcam and she intended that he should be aware that she was engaging in the activity, and she knew or could reasonably have been expected to know that he had a mental disorder, and where she was involved in his care in a way falling within section 42 of the Sexual Offences Act 2003.

---

9 For non-aggravated version, omit 'penetrative' and remove 'and (3)' from the Statement of Offence.

Section 41

(see Chapter 16)

STATEMENT OF OFFENCE

CAUSING A PERSON WITH A MENTAL DISORDER TO WATCH A SEXUAL ACT BY A CARE WORKER, contrary to section 41(1) of the Sexual Offences Act 2003.

PARTICULARS OF OFFENCE

AA, on the 1st day of January 2014, for the purpose of obtaining sexual gratification, intentionally caused BB, a person with a mental disorder, to look at an image of AA engaging in a sexual activity, namely having oral sex with another person, where AA knew or could reasonably have been expected to know that BB had a mental disorder, and where AA was involved in his care in a way falling within section 42 of the Sexual Offences Act 2003.

Section 47[10]

(see Chapter 17)

STATEMENT OF OFFENCE

PAYING FOR SEXUAL SERVICES OF A CHILD, contrary to section 47(1) of the Sexual Offences Act 2003.

PARTICULARS OF OFFENCE

AA, on the 1st day of January 2014, intentionally obtained for himself the sexual services of BB who was under 18 and AA did not reasonably believe that she was 18 or over, and before obtaining those services AA knew that CC had promised payment to another for those services.

Section 48

(see Chapter 17)

STATEMENT OF OFFENCE

[CAUSING] INCITING CHILD PROSTITUTION [PORNOGRAPHY], contrary to section 48(1) of the Sexual Offences Act 2003.

PARTICULARS OF OFFENCE

AA, on the 1st day of January 2014, intentionally incited [caused] BB, a person under 18, to become a prostitute [to be involved in pornography] and AA did not reasonably believe that BB was 18 or over.

---

10 Where it is alleged that penetration brings the offence within subsection (6), this should be reflected in indictment (statement and particulars).

Section 49

(see Chapter 17)

STATEMENT OF OFFENCE

CONTROLLING A CHILD PROSTITUTE [CHILD INVOLVED IN PORNOGRAPHY], contrary to section 49(1) of the Sexual Offences Act 2003.

PARTICULARS OF OFFENCE

AA, between the 1st day of January 2013 and the 27th day of August 2014, intentionally controlled the activities of BB, a person under 18, relating to BB's prostitution [involvement in pornography] and AA did not reasonably believe that BB was 18 or over.

Section 50

(see Chapter 17)

STATEMENT OF OFFENCE

[ARRANGING] FACILITATING CHILD PROSTITUTION [PORNOGRAPHY], contrary to section 50(1) of the Sexual Offences Act 2003.

PARTICULARS OF OFFENCE

AA, on the 1st day of January 2014, intentionally [arranged] facilitated the prostitution [involvement in pornography] of BB, a person under 13 [under 18, and AA did not reasonably believe that BB was 18 or over].

Section 51A

(see Chapter 17)

summary only

Section 52

(see Chapter 17)

STATEMENT OF OFFENCE

[CAUSING] INCITING PROSTITUTION FOR GAIN, contrary to section 52(1) of the Sexual Offences Act 2003.

PARTICULARS OF OFFENCE

AA, on the 1st day of January 2014, intentionally [caused] incited BB to become a prostitute and did so for, or in the expectation of, gain for himself [a third person, CC].

Section 53

(see Chapter 17)

STATEMENT OF OFFENCE

CONTROLLING PROSTITUTION FOR GAIN, contrary to section 53(1) of the Sexual Offences Act 2003.

PARTICULARS OF OFFENCE

AA, on the 1st day of January 2014, intentionally controlled BB's activities relating to prostitution and did so for, or in the expectation of, gain for himself [a third person, CC].

Section 53A

(see Chapter 17)

summary only

Section 59A

(see Chapter 17)

STATEMENT OF OFFENCE

TRAFFICKING FOR SEXUAL EXPLOITATION, contrary to section 59A(1) of the Sexual Offences Act 2003.

PARTICULARS OF OFFENCE

AA, on the 1st day of January 2014, intentionally [arranged] facilitated the arrival in the United Kingdom of BB with a view to the sexual exploitation of her.

Section 61

(see Chapter 18)

STATEMENT OF OFFENCE

ADMINISTERING A SUBSTANCE WITH INTENT, contrary to section 61(1) of the Sexual Offences Act 2003.

PARTICULARS OF OFFENCE

AA, on the 1st day of January 2014, intentionally administered a substance to [caused a substance to be taken by] BB, knowing that she did not consent and with the intention of stupefying or overpowering her so as to enable CC to engage in sexual activity involving BB.

Section 62[11]

(see Chapter 18)

STATEMENT OF OFFENCE

COMMITTING AN OFFENCE WITH INTENT TO COMMIT A SEXUAL OFFENCE, contrary to section 62(1) of the Sexual Offences Act 2003.

PARTICULARS OF OFFENCE

AA, on the 1st day of January 2014, committed the offence of child abduction alleged in Count One with the intention of committing a relevant sexual offence.

Section 63

(see Chapter 18)

STATEMENT OF OFFENCE

TRESPASS WITH INTENT TO COMMIT A SEXUAL OFFENCE, contrary to section 63(1) of the Sexual Offences Act 2003.

PARTICULARS OF OFFENCE

AA, on the 1st day of January 2014, while trespassing on premises, namely the King John School, knowing or being reckless that he was a trespasser, intended to commit a relevant sexual offence on the premises.

Section 64

(see Chapter 19)

STATEMENT OF OFFENCE

SEXUAL PENETRATION WITH AN ADULT RELATIVE, contrary to section 64(1) of the Sexual Offences Act 2003.

PARTICULARS OF OFFENCE

AA, a person aged (over) 16, on the 1st day of January 2014, intentionally penetrated the vagina of BB with a part of his body, namely his finger, the penetration was sexual, BB was aged (over) 18, and AA is the uncle of BB, she being the daughter of his sister, and AA knew or could reasonably be expected[12] to know that he is related to BB in that way.

---

11 Where the base offence is kidnapping or false imprisonment, engaging subsection (3), this should be reflected in the indictment (statement and particulars).

12 In a case where the existence of the relationship is perfectly clear, the 'reasonable expectation' alternative may be omitted

Section 65

(see Chapter 19)

STATEMENT OF OFFENCE

CONSENTING TO SEXUAL PENETRATION BY AN ADULT RELATIVE, contrary to section 65(1) of the Sexual Offences Act 2003.

PARTICULARS OF OFFENCE

AA, a person aged (over) 16, on the 1st day of January 2014, consented to the penetration of her mouth by BB with his penis, the penetration was sexual, BB was aged (over) 18, and AA is the aunt of BB, she being the sister of his father, and AA knew or could reasonably be expected[13] to know that he is related to BB in that way.

Section 66

(see Chapter 20)

STATEMENT OF OFFENCE

EXPOSURE, contrary to section 66(1) of the Sexual Offences Act 2003.

PARTICULARS OF OFFENCE

AA, on the 1st day of January 2014, intentionally exposed his genitals, intending that someone would see them and be caused alarm or distress.

Section 67 – observing

(see Chapter 20)

STATEMENT OF OFFENCE

VOYEURISM, contrary to section 67(1) of the Sexual Offences Act 2003.

PARTICULARS OF OFFENCE

AA, on the 1st day of January 2014, for the purpose of obtaining sexual gratification, observed BB doing a private act, namely being in a place which, in the circumstances, would reasonably be expected to provide privacy while his buttocks were covered only in underwear, and AA knew that BB did not consent to being observed for AA's sexual gratification.

---

13 Ibid.

Section 67 – operating equipment

(see Chapter 20)

STATEMENT OF OFFENCE

VOYEURISM, contrary to section 67(2) of the Sexual Offences Act 2003.

PARTICULARS OF OFFENCE

AA, on the 1st day of January 2014, operated equipment with the intention of enabling a person or persons to observe, for the purpose of obtaining sexual gratification, BB doing a private act, namely being in a place which, in the circumstances, would reasonably be expected to provide privacy while her breasts were exposed, and AA knew that BB did not consent to his operating equipment with that intention.

Section 67 – recording

(see Chapter 20)

STATEMENT OF OFFENCE

VOYEURISM, contrary to section 67(3) of the Sexual Offences Act 2003.

PARTICULARS OF OFFENCE

AA, on the 1st day of January 2014, recorded BB doing a private act, namely being in a place which, in the circumstances, would reasonably be expected to provide privacy when doing a sexual act not of a kind ordinarily done in public, namely masturbating, AA intending for the purpose of obtaining sexual gratification to look at an image of BB doing the act and AA knowing that BB did not consent to his recording the act with that intention.

Section 67 – installing/constructing/adapting

(see Chapter 20)

STATEMENT OF OFFENCE

VOYEURISM, contrary to section 67(4) of the Sexual Offences Act 2003.

PARTICULARS OF OFFENCE

AA, on the 1st day of January 2014, adapted a structure, by fitting a 'spy hole' into the wall of a shower cubicle, with the intention of enabling a person or persons unknown to commit an offence contrary to section 67(1) of the Sexual Offences Act 2003, namely observing, for the purpose of obtaining sexual gratification, a person doing a private act, knowing that the person does not consent to being observed for the other's sexual gratification.

Section 69 – active

(see Chapter 20)

STATEMENT OF OFFENCE

INTERCOURSE WITH AN ANIMAL, contrary to section 69(1) of the Sexual Offences Act 2003.

PARTICULARS OF OFFENCE

AA, on the 1st day of January 2014, intentionally performed an act of penetration with his penis of the [vagina] anus of a living animal, namely a donkey, knowing or being reckless as to whether that is what was penetrated.

Section 69 – passive

(see Chapter 20)

STATEMENT OF OFFENCE

INTERCOURSE WITH AN ANIMAL, contrary to section 69(2) of the Sexual Offences Act 2003.

PARTICULARS OF OFFENCE

AA, on the 1st day of January 2014, intentionally allowed his anus to be penetrated by the penis of a living animal, namely a dog, knowing or being reckless as to whether that was what he was penetrated by.

Section 70

(see Chapter 20)

STATEMENT OF OFFENCE

SEXUAL PENETRATION OF A CORPSE, contrary to section 70(1) of the Sexual Offences Act 2003.

PARTICULARS OF OFFENCE

AA, on the 1st day of January 2014, intentionally performed an act of sexual penetration of a part of the body, namely the vagina, of a dead person with part of his body, namely his penis, knowing or being reckless as to whether that is what was penetrated.

Section 71

(see Chapter 20)

summary only

Section 72 – UK national

(see Chapter 31)

STATEMENT OF OFFENCE

RAPE OF A CHILD UNDER 13 OUTSIDE THE UNITED KINGDOM, contrary to sections 5 and 72(1) of the Sexual Offences Act 2003.

PARTICULARS OF OFFENCE

AA, a United Kingdom national, on the 1st day of January 2014, in Barbados, intentionally penetrated with his penis the vagina of BB, a child under the age of 13 years, such as would constitute an offence listed in Schedule 2 to the Sexual Offences Act 2003 if done in England and Wales.

Section 72 – UK resident

(see Chapter 31)

STATEMENT OF OFFENCE

RAPE OF A CHILD UNDER 13 OUTSIDE THE UNITED KINGDOM, contrary to sections 5 and 72(2) of the Sexual Offences Act 2003.

PARTICULARS OF OFFENCE

AA, a United Kingdom resident, on the 1st day of January 2014, in Barbados, intentionally penetrated with his penis the vagina of BB, a child under the age of 13 years, such act constituting an offence under the law in force in Barbados and such as would constitute an offence listed in Schedule 2 to the Sexual Offences Act 2003 if done in England and Wales.

Section 91 – failure

(see Chapter 21)

STATEMENT OF OFFENCE

BREACH OF NOTIFICATION REQUIREMENTS, contrary to section 91(1)(a) of the Sexual Offences Act 2003.

PARTICULARS OF OFFENCE

AA, being a person subject to the notification requirements under section 80 of the Sexual Offences Act 2003, on the 1st day of January 2014,[14] failed without reasonable excuse to comply with the requirement under section 84(1)(b) of that Act to notify police of a change of his home address within three days of that change.

Section 91 – false information

(see Chapter 21)

STATEMENT OF OFFENCE

BREACH OF NOTIFICATION REQUIREMENTS, contrary to section 91(1)(b) of the Sexual Offences Act 2003.

PARTICULARS OF OFFENCE

AA, being a person subject to the notification requirements under section 80 of the Sexual Offences Act 2003, on the 1st day of January 2014 notified, in purported compliance with section 83(1) of that Act, information which he knew to be false, namely that his home address was 123 High Street.

Section 113

(see Chapter 21)

STATEMENT OF OFFENCE

BREACH OF A SEXUAL OFFENCES PREVENTION ORDER, contrary to section 113(1) of the Sexual Offences Act 2003.

PARTICULARS OF OFFENCE

AA, on the 1st day of January 2014, without reasonable excuse, used the internet to attempt to contact a girl he knew or suspected to be under the age of 16, which he was prohibited from doing by virtue of a Sexual Offences Prevention Order made by the Crown Court at Bolton on the 30th day of September 2013.

Section 122 – prohibited travel

(see Chapter 21)

STATEMENT OF OFFENCE

BREACH OF A FOREIGN TRAVEL ORDER, contrary to section 122(1) of the Sexual Offences Act 2003.

---

14 Failure to notify contrary to ss (1)(a) is a continuing offence committed from the first day of failure.

PARTICULARS OF OFFENCE

AA, on the 1st day of January 2014, without reasonable excuse, travelled to Morocco, which he was prohibited from doing by virtue of a Foreign Travel Order made by the Leicester Magistrates' Court on the 30th day of September 2013.

Section 122 – failure to comply with a requirement

(see Chapter 21)

STATEMENT OF OFFENCE

BREACH OF A FOREIGN TRAVEL ORDER, contrary to section 122(1A) of the Sexual Offences Act 2003.

PARTICULARS OF OFFENCE

AA, on the 29th day of October 2013,[15] without reasonable excuse, failed to comply with the requirement that he surrender his passport(s) to the police by 28th October 2013, such requirement being imposed by virtue of a Foreign Travel Order made by the Leicester Magistrates' Court on the 30th day of September 2013 and pursuant to section 117A(2) of the Sexual Offences Act 2003.

Section 128

(see Chapter 21)

STATEMENT OF OFFENCE

BREACH OF A RISK OF SEXUAL HARM ORDER, contrary to section 128(1) of the Sexual Offences Act 2003.

PARTICULARS OF OFFENCE

AA, on the 1st day of January 2014, without reasonable excuse, entered Elm Park, which he was prohibited from doing by virtue of a Risk of Sexual Harm Order made by the Swansea Magistrates' Court on the 30th day of September 2013.

PART C – OTHER STATUTORY & COMMON LAW OFFENCES

Protection of Children Act 1978, s 1

(see Chapter 22)

STATEMENT OF OFFENCE

[TAKING] MAKING AN INDECENT PHOTOGRAPH OF A CHILD, contrary to section 1(1)(a) of the Protection of Children Act 1978.

---

15 Failure to comply contrary to s 122(1A) is a continuing offence committed from the first day of failure.

PARTICULARS OF OFFENCE

AA, on the 1st day of January 2014, [took] made an indecent photograph [pseudo-photograph] of a child.[16]

Criminal Justice Act 1988, s 160

(see Chapter 22)

STATEMENT OF OFFENCE

POSSESSION OF AN INDECENT PHOTOGRAPH OF A CHILD, contrary to section 160(1) of the Criminal Justice Act 1988.

PARTICULARS OF OFFENCE

AA, on the 1st day of January 2014, had in his possession an indecent photograph [pseudo-photograph] of a child.[17]

Child Abduction Act 1984, s 2

(see Chapter 23)

STATEMENT OF OFFENCE

CHILD ABDUCTION, contrary to section 2(1)(a) of the Child Abduction Act 1984.

PARTICULARS OF OFFENCE

AA, on the 1st day of January 2014, without lawful authority or reasonable excuse, detained BB, a child under the age of 16, so as to remove him from the lawful control of his parents.

Sexual Offences Act 1956, s 33

(see Chapter 24)

summary only

Sexual Offences Act 1956, s 33A

(see Chapter 24)

STATEMENT OF OFFENCE

KEEPING A BROTHEL USED FOR PROSTITUTION, contrary to section 33A of the Sexual Offences Act 1956.

---

16 Any identifier, such as a sequential number, should be stated.
17 Ibid.

PARTICULARS OF OFFENCE

AA, on the 1st day of January 2014, [kept/managed/acted] assisted in the management of a brothel to which people resorted for practices involving prostitution.

Sexual Offences Act 1956, s 34

(see Chapter 24)

summary only

Sexual Offences Act 1956, s 35

(see Chapter 24)

summary only

Sexual Offences Act 1956, s 36

(see Chapter 24)

summary only

Keeping a disorderly house – common law

(see Chapter 24)

STATEMENT OF OFFENCE

KEEPING A DISORDERLY HOUSE, contrary to Common Law.

PARTICULARS OF OFFENCE

AA, between the 31st day of December 2013 and 31st day of January 2014, at 123 Lancing Lane, Oakham, kept a disorderly house.

Children & Young Persons Act 1933, s 3

(see Chapter 24)

summary only

Street Offences Act 1959, s 1

(see Chapter 24)

summary only

Criminal Justice and Police Act 2001, s 46

(see Chapter 24)

summary only

Outraging public decency – common law

(see Chapter 25)

STATEMENT OF OFFENCE

OUTRAGING PUBLIC DECENCY, contrary to Common Law.

PARTICULARS OF OFFENCE

AA and BB, on the 1st day of January 2014, committed an act of a lewd, obscene or disgusting nature which outraged public decency, namely having sexual intercourse in open public view in Priory Park, Ventnor.

Criminal Justice and Immigration Act 2008, s 63

(see Chapter 26)

STATEMENT OF OFFENCE

POSSESSION OF AN EXTREME PORNOGRAPHIC IMAGE, contrary to section 63(1) of the Criminal Justice and Immigration Act 2008.

PARTICULARS OF OFFENCE

AA, on the 1st day of January 2014, had in her possession an extreme pornographic image.[18]

Coroners and Justice Act 2009, s 62

(see Chapter 26)

STATEMENT OF OFFENCE

POSSESSION OF A PROHIBITED IMAGE OF A CHILD, contrary to section 62(1) of the Coroners and Justice Act 2009.

PARTICULARS OF OFFENCE

AA, on the 1st day of January 2014, had in his possession a prohibited image of a child.[19]

---

18 Ibid.
19 Ibid.

Obscene Publications Act 1959, s 2 – publication

(see Chapter 26)

STATEMENT OF OFFENCE

PUBLISHING AN OBSCENE ARTICLE, contrary to section 2(1) of the Obscene Publications Act 1959.

PARTICULARS OF OFFENCE

AA, between the 1st day of January 2014 and the 28th day of February 2014, published an obscene article, namely a book entitled 'Hardly A Scratch'.

Obscene Publications Act 1959, s 2 – having for publication for gain

(see Chapter 26)

STATEMENT OF OFFENCE

HAVING AN OBSCENE ARTICLE FOR PUBLICATION FOR GAIN, contrary to section 2(1) of the Obscene Publications Act 1959.

PARTICULARS OF OFFENCE

AA, on the 1st day of January 2014, had an obscene article, namely a magazine entitled 'Kindergarten Of Joy', for publication for gain for himself.

Customs Consolidation Act 1876, s 42

(see Chapter 26)

STATEMENT OF OFFENCE

IMPORTATION OF INDECENT [OBSCENE] GOODS, contrary to section 170(2)(b) of the Customs and Excise Management Act 1979 and section 42 of the Customs Consolidation Act 1876.

PARTICULARS OF OFFENCE

AA, on the 1st day of January 2014, was knowingly concerned in the fraudulent evasion of the prohibition of the importation into the United Kingdom of indecent [obscene] books [photographs/prints, etc].

Indecent Displays (Control) Act 1981

(see Chapter 26)

STATEMENT OF OFFENCE

MAKING [PERMITTING] AN INDECENT DISPLAY, contrary to section 1 of the Indecent Displays (Control) Act 1981.

PARTICULARS OF OFFENCE

AA, on the 1st day of January 2014, made [permitted the] public display of an indecent matter, namely a statue depicting the rape of a baby.

Safeguarding Vulnerable Groups Act 2006, s 7

(see Chapter 27)

STATEMENT OF OFFENCE

BARRED PERSON ENGAGING IN REGULATED ACTIVITY, contrary to section 7 of the Safeguarding Vulnerable Groups Act 2006.

PARTICULARS OF OFFENCE

AA, on the 1st day of January 2014, [sought to engage/offered to engage] engaged in a regulated activity, namely working with [children] vulnerable adults from which she was barred.

PART D – REPEATED OFFENCES COMMONLY ENCOUNTERED IN HISTORIC SEX CASES

NOTE – ATTEMPTS

Attempted offences dated from 27 August 1981 onwards are indicted as 'contrary to s 1(1) of the Criminal Attempts Act 1981'.

Attempts before that date are indicted as 'contrary to Common Law'.

Sexual Offences Act 1956, s 1

(see Chapter 28)

STATEMENT OF OFFENCE

RAPE, contrary to section 1(1) of the Sexual Offences Act 1956.[20]

PARTICULARS OF OFFENCE

AA, on or about the 1st day of January 2002, raped[21] BB.

---

20 If before 1 January 1957: '*contrary to Common Law*'.

21 If after 2 November 1994: '*per vaginum*' or '*per anum*' may be added to distinguish counts.

Sexual Offences Act 1956, s 5

(see Chapter 28)

STATEMENT OF OFFENCE

SEXUAL INTERCOURSE WITH A GIRL UNDER 13, contrary to section 5 of the Sexual Offences Act 1956.

PARTICULARS OF OFFENCE

AA, on or about the 1st day of January 2002, had sexual intercourse with BB, a girl under the age of 13 years.[22]

Sexual Offences Act 1956, s 12 – child

(see Chapter 28)

STATEMENT OF OFFENCE

BUGGERY, contrary to section 12 of the Sexual Offences Act 1956.

PARTICULARS OF OFFENCE

AA, on or about the 1st day of January 1992, committed buggery with BB, a child under 16.

Sexual Offences Act 1956, s 12 – non-consenting adult

(see Chapter 28)

STATEMENT OF OFFENCE

BUGGERY, contrary to section 12 of the Sexual Offences Act 1956.

PARTICULARS OF OFFENCE

AA, on or about the 1st day of January 1992, committed buggery with BB, who did not consent to it.

Sexual Offences Act 1956, s 14

(see Chapter 28)

STATEMENT OF OFFENCE

INDECENT ASSAULT ON A WOMAN, contrary to section 14 of the Sexual Offences Act 1956.

---

22 '*namely, 9 years of age*' may be added, but is not essential.

PARTICULARS OF OFFENCE

AA, on or about the 1st day of January 2002, indecently assaulted BB, a woman [girl under the age of 16/13].

Sexual Offences Act 1956, s 15

(see Chapter 28)

STATEMENT OF OFFENCE

INDECENT ASSAULT ON A MAN, contrary to section 15 of the Sexual Offences Act 1956.

PARTICULARS OF OFFENCE

AA, on or about the 1st day of January 2002, indecently assaulted BB, a man [boy under the age of 16].

Indecency with Children Act 1960, s 1 – committing

(see Chapter 29)

STATEMENT OF OFFENCE

GROSS INDECENCY WITH A CHILD, contrary to section 1 of the Indecency with Children Act 1960

PARTICULARS OF OFFENCE

AA, on or about the 1st day of January 2002, committed an act of gross indecency towards BB, a child under the age of 16.

Indecency with Children Act 1960, s 1 – inciting

(see Chapter 29)

STATEMENT OF OFFENCE

GROSS INDECENCY WITH A CHILD, contrary to section 1 of the Indecency with Children Act 1960

PARTICULARS OF OFFENCE

AA, on or about the 1st day of January 2002, incited BB, a child under the age of 16, to commit an act of gross indecency with him.

Appendix 2

Sexual Offences Act 2003: Elements of the main offences

	Rape	Pene	Asslt	Activity	Offences against >13				Child sex offences						Abuse of position of trust			
Section	1	2	3	4	5	6	7	8	9	10	11	12	14	15	16	17	18	19
Intentionally penetrates with penis	*				*													
Intentionally penetrates with part of body/item		*				*												
Absence of consent/reasonable belief in consent	*	*	*	*														
Sexual		*	*	*		*	*	*	*	*	*	*			*	*	*	*
Intentionally touches			*				*		*						*			
Intentionally causes B to engage in activity				*														
Intentionally causes or incites B to engage in activity								*		*						*		
Intentionally incites B to engage in activity																		
Penetration as feature of sentence				*				*	*	*								
Age of B – under 13					*	*	*	*	*	*	*	*			*	*	*	*
Age of B – under 16 and def knows it									*	*	*	*						
Age of B – under 18 and def knows it															*	*	*	*
Age of defendant – over 18									*	*	*	*			*	*	*	*
Intentionally engages in an activity											*						*	
For purpose of sexual gratification											*	*					*	*
'Being watched' by B											*						*	
Causes B to watch a third person/image												*						*
Position of trust															*	*	*	*
Presumption A knows B is under 18															*	*	*	*
Presumption A knows he is in posn of trust															*	*	*	*
Marriage exemption															*	*	*	*
Predating relationship exemption															*	*	*	*
	1	2	3	4	5	6	7	8	9	10	11	12	14	15	16	17	18	19

	Familial		Mental disorder/choice				Mental disorder/threats				Mental disorder/carers							
Section	25	26	30	31	32	33	34	35	36	37	38	39	40	41	64	65		
Intentionally penetrates with penis															*	*[1]		
Intentionally penetrates with part of body/item															*	*[1]		
Absence of consent/reasonable belief in consent																*[1]		
Sexual	*	*	*	*	*	*	*	*	*	*	*	*	*	*	*	*		
Intentionally touches	*		*				*				*							
Intentionally causes B to engage in activity								*[2]										
Intentionally causes or incites B to engage in activity				*								*						
Intentionally incites B to engage in activity		*																
Penetration as feature of sentence	*[3]	*[2]	*	*			*	*			*	*						
Age of B – under 13	*	*																
Age of B – under 16 and def knows it																		
Age of B – under 18 and def knows it	*	*																
Age of B – over 18															*	*		
Age of defendant – over 18																		
Age of defendant – over 16															*	*		
Intentionally engages in an activity					*				*				*					
For purpose of sexual gratification					*	*			*	*			*	*				
'Being watched' by B					*				*				*					
Causes B to watch a third person/image						*				*				*				

	Familial		Mental disorder/choice				Mental disorder/threats				Mental disorder/carers							
Section	25	26	30	31	32	33	34	35	36	37	38	39	40	41	64	65		
Position of trust																		
Presumption A knows B is under 18	*	*																
Presumption A knows he is in posn of trust																		
Marriage exemption	*	*									*	*	*	*				
Predating relationship exemption	*	*									*	*	*	*				
Familial relationship (within s 27)	*	*																
Familial relationship (within s 64(2) or s 65(2))															*	*		
Presumption A knows he is in familial relationship	*	*													*	*		
B unable to refuse because of mental disorder			*	*	*	*												
B has a mental disorder							*	*	*	*	*	*	*	*				
A knows of mental disorder			*	*	*	*	*	*	*	*	*	*	*	*				
Definition of inability to refuse			*	*	*[4]	*[3]												
Agreement obtained by inducement/threat/etc							*	*	*	*								
A is involved in B's care (within s 42)											*	*	*	*				
Presumption A knows of mental disorder											*	*	*	*				
	25	26	30	31	32	33	34	35	36	37	38	39	40	41				

1 Defendant is consenting recipient of penetration.
2 Or incites.
3 Age of defendant also a feature of sentence.
4 Slightly different definition to ss 30 and 31.

Appendix 3

Police station materials

POLICE AND CRIMINAL EVIDENCE ACT 1984, SS 62 & 63: INTIMATE AND NON-INTIMATE SAMPLES

62 Intimate samples

(1) Subject to section 63B below an intimate sample may be taken from a person in police detention only—

(a) if a police officer of at least the rank of inspector authorises it to be taken; and

(b) if the appropriate consent is given.

(1A) An intimate sample may be taken from a person who is not in police detention but from whom, in the course of the investigation of an offence, two or more non-intimate samples suitable for the same means of analysis have been taken which have proved insufficient—

(a) if a police officer of at least the rank of inspector authorises it to be taken; and

(b) if the appropriate consent is given.

(2) An officer may only give an authorisation under subsection (1) or (1A) above if he has reasonable grounds—

(a) for suspecting the involvement of the person from whom the sample is to be taken in a recordable offence; and

(b) for believing that the sample will tend to confirm or disprove his involvement.

(3) An officer may give an authorisation under subsection (1) or (1A) above orally or in writing but, if he gives it orally, he shall confirm it in writing as soon as is practicable.

(4) The appropriate consent must be given in writing.

(5) Where—

(a) an authorisation has been given; and

(b) it is proposed that an intimate sample shall be taken in pursuance of the authorisation,

an officer shall inform the person from whom the sample is to be taken—

(i) of the giving of the authorisation; and

(ii) of the grounds for giving it.

(6) The duty imposed by subsection (5)(ii) above includes a duty to state the nature of the offence in which it is suspected that the person from whom the sample is to be taken has been involved.

(7) If an intimate sample is taken from a person—

(a) the authorisation by virtue of which it was taken;

(b) the grounds for giving the authorisation; and

(c) the fact that the appropriate consent was given,

shall be recorded as soon as is practicable after the sample is taken.

(7A) If an intimate sample is taken from a person at a police station—

(a) before the sample is taken, an officer shall inform him that it may be the subject of a speculative search; and

(b) the fact that the person has been informed of this possibility shall be recorded as soon as practicable after the sample has been taken.

(8) If an intimate sample is taken from a person detained at a police station, the matters required to be recorded by subsection (7) or (7A) above shall be recorded in his custody record.

(9) In the case of an intimate sample which is a dental impression, the sample may be taken from a person only by a registered dentist.

(9A) In the case of any other form of intimate sample, except in the case of a sample of urine, the sample may be taken from a person only by—

(a) a registered medical practitioner; or

(b) a registered health care professional.

(10) Where the appropriate consent to the taking of an intimate sample from person was refused without good cause, in any proceedings against that person for an offence—

(a) the court, in determining—

(i) whether to commit that person for trial; or

(ii) whether there is a case to answer; and

(aa) a judge, in deciding whether to grant an application made by the accused under paragraph 2 of Schedule 3 to the Crime and Disorder Act 1998 (applications for dismissal); and

(b) the court or jury, in determining whether that person is guilty of the offence charged,

may draw such inferences from the refusal as appear proper

63 Other samples

(1) Except as provided by this section, a non-intimate sample may not be taken from a person without the appropriate consent.

(2) Consent to the taking of a non-intimate sample must be given in writing.

(2A) A non-intimate sample may be taken from a person without the appropriate consent if two conditions are satisfied.

(2B) The first is that the person is in police detention in consequence of his arrest for a recordable offence.

(2C) The second is that—

(a) he has not had a non-intimate sample of the same type and from the same part of the body taken in the course of the investigation of the offence by the police, or

(b) he has had such a sample taken but it proved insufficient.

(3) A non-intimate sample may be taken from a person without the appropriate consent if—

(a) he is being held in custody by the police on the authority of a court; and

(b) an officer of at least the rank of inspector authorises it to be taken without the appropriate consent.

(3A) A non-intimate sample may be taken from a person (whether or not he is in police detention or held in custody by the police on the authority of a court) without the appropriate consent if—

(a) he has been charged with a recordable offence or informed that he will be reported for such an offence; and

(b) either he has not had a non-intimate sample taken from him in the course of the investigation of the offence by the police or he has had a non-intimate sample taken from him but either it was not suitable for the same means of analysis or, though so suitable, the sample proved insufficient.

(3B) A non-intimate sample may be taken from a person without the appropriate consent if he has been convicted of a recordable offence.

(4) An officer may only give an authorisation under subsection (3) above if he has reasonable grounds—

a) for suspecting the involvement of the person from whom the sample is to be taken in a recordable offence; and

(b) for believing that the sample will tend to confirm or disprove his involvement.

(5) An officer may give an authorisation under subsection (3) above orally or in writing but, if he gives it orally, he shall confirm it in writing as soon as is practicable.

(5A) An officer shall not give an authorisation under subsection (3) above for the taking from any person of a non-intimate sample consisting of a skin impression if—

(a) a skin impression of the same part of the body has already been taken from that person in the course of the investigation of the offence; and

(b) the impression previously taken is not one that has proved insufficient.

(6) Where—

(a) authorisation has been given; and

(b) it is proposed that a non-intimate sample shall be taken in pursuance of the authorisation,

an officer shall inform the person from whom the sample is to be taken—

(i) of the giving of the authorisation; and

(ii) of the grounds for giving it.

(7) The duty imposed by subsection 6(ii) above includes a duty to state the nature of the offence in which it is suspected that the person from whom the sample is to be taken has been involved.

(8) If a non-intimate sample is taken from a person by virtue of subsection (3) above—

(a) the authorisation by virtue of which it was taken; and

(b) the grounds for giving the authorisation,

shall be recorded as soon as is practicable after the sample is taken.

(8A) In a case where by virtue of subsection (2A), (3A) or (3B) above a sample is taken from a person without the appropriate consent—

(a) he shall be told the reason before the sample is taken; and

(b) the reason shall be recorded as soon as practicable after the sample is taken.

(8B) If a non-intimate sample is taken from a person at a police station, whether with or without the appropriate consent—

(a) before the sample is taken, an officer shall inform him that it may be the subject of a speculative search; and

(b) the fact that the person has been informed of this possibility shall be recorded as soon as practicable after the sample has been taken.

(9) If a non-intimate sample is taken from a person detained at a police station, the matters required to be recorded by subsection (8) or (8A) or (8B) above shall be recorded in his custody record.

(9ZA) The power to take a non-intimate sample from a person without the appropriate consent shall be exercisable by any constable.

CRIMINAL JUSTICE AND PUBLIC ORDER ACT 1994, S 34

34 Effect of accused's failure to mention facts when questioned or charged

(1) Where, in any proceedings against a person for an offence, evidence is given that the accused—

(a) at any time before he was charged with the offence, on being questioned under caution by a constable trying to discover whether or by whom the offence had been committed, failed to mention any fact relied on in his defence in those proceedings; or

(b) on being charged with the offence or officially informed that he might be prosecuted for it, failed to mention any such fact

being a fact which in the circumstances existing at the time the accused could reasonably have been expected to mention when so questioned, charged or informed, as the case may be, subsection (2) below applies.

(2) Where this subsection applies—

(b) a judge, in deciding whether to grant an application made by the accused under paragraph 2 of Schedule 3 to the Crime and Disorder Act 1998;

(c) the court, in determining whether there is a case to answer; and

(d) the court or jury, in determining whether the accused is guilty of the offence charged,

may draw such inferences from the failure as appear proper.

(2A) Where the accused was at an authorised place of detention at the time of the failure, subsections (1) and (2) above do not apply if he had not been allowed an opportunity to consult a solicitor prior to being questioned, charged or informed as mentioned in subsection (1) above.

(3) Subject to any directions by the court, evidence tending to establish the failure may be given before or after evidence tending to establish the fact which the accused is alleged to have failed to mention.

(4) This section applies in relation to questioning by persons (other than constables) charged with the duty of investigating offences or charging offenders as it applies in relation to questioning by constables; and in subsection (1) above "officially informed" means informed by a constable or any such person.

(5) This section does not—

(a) prejudice the admissibility in evidence of the silence or other reaction of the accused in the face of anything said in his presence relating to the conduct in respect of which he is charged, in so far as evidence thereof would be admissible apart from this section; or

(b) preclude the drawing of any inference from any such silence or other reaction of the accused which could properly be drawn apart from this section.

(6) This section does not apply in relation to a failure to mention a fact if the failure occurred before the commencement of this section.

Appendix 4

Specimen Sexual Offence Prevention Order

Practitioners may find this sample useful as a template.

The format and terms have been found acceptable in several Crown Court cases.

IN THE CROWN COURT

AT XXXXXXXX

T2014XXXX

THE QUEEN

- v -

A A

SEXUAL OFFENCES PREVENTION ORDER

Pursuant to section 104 of the Sexual Offences Act 2003

BY ORDER OF THE COURT, made this day, the XX^{xx} day of April 2014,

A A, born xx January 19xx, is hereby prohibited from:

1. Residing or staying overnight in any dwelling where any girl under the age of 16 years is for the time being residing or staying overnight, without the informed consent of such girl's parent or legal guardian;
2. Being alone with any girl under the age of 16 years without the informed consent of such girl's parent or legal guardian;
3. Using any device capable of accessing the internet unless:

a. It has the capacity to retain and display the history of internet use; and

b. He makes the device available on request for inspection by a police officer;

4. Deleting, encrypting, or attempting to delete or encrypt the history of internet use on any device;

5. Using the internet to contact or attempt to contact any girl he knows or suspects to be under the age of 16;

6. Possessing any device capable of storing digital images unless he makes it available on request for inspection by a police officer.

SAVE THAT this Order does not operate to:

a) Prohibit inadvertent and unavoidable proximity such as when using public transport;

b) Restrict legitimate communication such as when responding to a request for directions.

DEFINITIONS

In this Order, the expression 'informed consent' is defined as 'express permission granted by a person who has been informed that A A has been convicted, as an adult, of sexual offences against children and that he is subject to this Order'.

In this Order, the expression 'dwelling' includes any house, flat, caravan, tent, boat or other accommodation, temporary or otherwise.

In this Order, the expression 'the internet' includes any future similar service or system.

DURATION

This Order shall remain in force UNTIL FURTHER ORDER.

Appendix 5

Serious and specified offences under the Criminal Justice Act 2003

CRIMINAL JUSTICE ACT 2003 SCHEDULE 15, PART 1 SPECIFIED VIOLENT OFFENCES

Common Law Offences	
Manslaughter	
Kidnapping	
False imprisonment	
Offences against the Person Act 1861	
Section	Description
4	Soliciting murder
16	Threats to kill
18	Wounding with intent to cause grievous bodily harm
20	Malicious wounding
21	Attempting to choke, suffocate or strangle in order to commit or assist in committing an indictable offence
22	Using chloroform etc to commit or assist in the committing of any indictable offence
23	Maliciously administering poison etc so as to endanger life or inflict grievous bodily harm
27	Abandoning children
28	Causing bodily injury by explosives
29	Using explosives etc with intent to do grievous bodily harm
30	Placing explosives with intent to do bodily injury
31	Setting spring guns etc with intent to do grievous bodily harm
32	Endangering the safety of railway passengers

35	Injuring persons by furious driving
37	Assaulting officer preserving wreck
38	Assault with intent to resist arrest
47	Assault occasioning actual bodily harm
Explosive Substances Act 1883	
Section	Description
2	Causing explosion likely to endanger life or property
3	Attempt to cause explosion or making or keeping explosive with intent to endanger life or property
Infant Life (Preservation) Act 1929	
Section	Description
1	Child destruction
Children and Young Persons Act 1933	
Section	Description
1	Cruelty to children
Infanticide Act 1938	
Section	Description
1	Infanticide
Firearms Act 1968	
Section	Description
16	Possession of firearm with intent to endanger life
16A	Possession of firearm with intent to cause fear of violence
17(1)	Use of firearm to resist arrest
17(2)	Possession of firearm at time of committing an offence
18	Carrying a firearm with criminal intent
Theft Act 1968	
Section	Description
8	Robbery or assault with intent to rob
9(1)(a)	Burglary with intent to steal, inflict grievous bodily harm or do unlawful damage

10	Aggravated burglary
12A	Aggravated vehicle-taking involving an accident which caused the death of any person
Criminal Damage Act 1971	
Section	Description
1	Arson
1(2)	Destroying or damaging property (other than an offence of arson)
Taking of Hostages Act 1982	
Section	Description
1	Hostage-taking
Aviation Security Act 1982	
Section	Description
1	Hijacking
2	Destroying, damaging or endangering safety of aircraft
3	Other acts endangering or likely to endanger safety of aircraft
4	Offences in relation to certain dangerous articles
Mental Health Act 1983	
Section	Description
127	Ill-treatment of patients
Prohibition of Female Circumcision Act 1985	
Section	Description
1	Prohibition of female circumcision
Public Order Act 1986	
Section	Description
1	Riot
2	Violent disorder
3	Affray
Criminal Justice Act 1988	
Section	Description
134	Torture

Road Traffic Act 1988	
Section	Description
1	Causing death by dangerous driving
3A	Causing death by careless driving when under influence of drinks or drugs
Aviation and Maritime Security Act 1990	
Section	Description
1	Endangering safety at aerodromes
9	Hijacking of ships
10	Seizing or exercising control of fixed platforms
11	Destroying fixed platforms or endangering their safety
12	Other acts endangering or likely to endanger safe navigation
13	Offences involving threats
Channel Tunnel (Security) Order 1994	
Section	Description
Part II	Offences relating to Channel Tunnel trains and the tunnel system
Protection from Harassment Act 1997	
Section	Description
4 or 4A	Putting people in fear of violence and stalking involving fear of violence or serious alarm or distress
Crime and Disorder Act 1998	
Section	Description
29	Racially or religiously aggravated assaults
31(a) or (b)	Racially or religiously aggravated offences under section 4 or 4A of the Public Order Act 1986
Terrorism Act 2000	
Section	Description
54	Weapons training
56	Directing terrorist organisations

57	Possession of article for terrorist purposes
59	Inciting terrorism overseas
International Criminal Court Act 2001	
Section	Description
51 or 52	Genocide, crimes against humanity, war crimes and related offences other than one involving murder
Anti-terrorism, Crime and Security Act 2001	
Section	Description
47	Use of nuclear weapons
50	Assisting or inducing certain weapons-related acts overseas
113	Use of noxious substance or thing to cause harm or intimidate
Female Genital Mutilation Act 2003	
Section	Description
1	Genital mutilation
2	Assisting a girl to mutilate her own genitalia
3	Assisting a non-UK person to mutilate overseas a girl's genitalia
Domestic Violence, Crime and Victims Act 2004	
Section	Description
5	Causing or allowing a child or vulnerable adult to die or suffer serious physical harm
Terrorism Act 2006	
Section	Description
5	Preparation of terrorist acts
6	Training for terrorism
9	Making or possession of radioactive device or material
10	Use of radioactive device or material for terrorist purposes
11	Terrorist threats relating to radioactive devices
Inchoate offences	
Aiding, abetting, counselling, procuring or inciting an offence in this Part of this Schedule	

Conspiring to commit an offence in this Part of this Schedule
Attempting to commit an offence in this Part of this Schedule
An attempt to commit murder or a conspiracy to commit murder

CRIMINAL JUSTICE ACT 2003 SCHEDULE 15, PART 2 SPECIFIED SEXUAL OFFENCES

Sexual Offences Act 1956	
Section	Description
1	Rape
2	Procurement of a woman by threats
3	Procurement of a woman by false pretences
4	Administering drugs to obtain or facilitate intercourse
5	Intercourse with girl under 13
6	Intercourse with girl under 16
7	Intercourse with a defective
9	Procurement of a defective
10	Incest by a man
11	Incest by a woman
14	Indecent assault on a woman
15	Indecent assault on a man
16	Assault with intent to commit buggery
17	Abduction of a woman by force or for the sake of her property
19	Abduction of an unmarried girl under 18 from parent or guardian
20	Abduction of an unmarried girl under 16 from parent or guardian
21	Abduction of defective from parent or guardian
22	Causing prostitution of women
23	Procuration of girl under 21
24	Detention of woman in brothel
25	Permitting girl under 13 to use premises for intercourse

26	Permitting girl under 16 to use premises for intercourse
27	Permitting defective to use premises for intercourse
28	Causing or encouraging the prostitution of, intercourse with, or indecent assault on girl under 16
29	Causing or encouraging prostitution of a defective
32	Soliciting by men
33	Keeping a brothel
Mental Health Act 1959	
Section	Description
128	Sexual intercourse with patients
Indecency with Children Act 1960	
Section	Description
1	Indecent conduct towards young child
Sexual Offences Act 1967	
Section	Description
4	Procuring others to commit homosexual acts
5	Living on earnings of male prostitution
Theft Act 1968	
Section	Description
9	Burglary with intent to commit rape
Criminal Law Act 1977	
Section	Description
54	Inciting girl under 16 to have incestuous sexual intercourse
Protection of Children Act 1978	
Section	Description
1	Indecent photographs of children
Customs and Excise Management Act 1979	
Section	Description
170	Fraudulent evasion of duty, etc in relation to goods prohibited to be imported under s 42 of the Customs Consolidation Act 1876 (indecent or obscene articles)

Criminal Justice Act 1988	
Section	Description
160	Possession of indecent photograph of a child
Sexual Offences Act 2003	
Section	Description
1	Rape
2	Assault by penetration
3	Sexual assault
4	Causing sexual activity without consent
5	Rape of a child under 13
6	Assault of a child under 13 by penetration
7	Sexual assault of a child under 13
8	Causing or inciting a child under 13 to engage in sexual activity
9	Sexual activity with a child
10	Causing or inciting a child to engage in sexual activity
11	Engaging in sexual activity in the presence of a child
12	Causing a child to watch a sexual act
14	Arranging or facilitating the commission of a child sex offence
15	Meeting a child following sexual grooming etc
16–19	Abuse of a positions of trust
25 or 26	Familial child sex offence
30–37	Offences against persons with a mental disorder impeding choice
38–41	Offences by care workers for persons with mental disorders
47	Paying for sexual services of a child
48	Causing or inciting child prostitution or pornography
49	Controlling a child prostitute or a child involved in pornography
50	Arranging or facilitating child prostitution or pornography
52	Causing or inciting prostitution for gain
53	Controlling prostitution for gain

57–59 and 59A	Trafficking for sexual exploitation
61	Administering a substance with intent
62	Committing an offence with intent to commit a sexual offence
63	Trespass with intent to commit a sexual offence
64 or 65	Sex with an adult relative
66	Exposure
67	Voyeurism
69	Intercourse with an animal
70	Sexual penetration of a corpse
Inchoate offences	
Aiding, abetting, counselling, procuring or inciting an offence in this Part of this Schedule	
Conspiring to commit an offence in this Part of this Schedule	
Attempting to commit an offence in this Part of this Schedule	

CRIMINAL JUSTICE ACT 2003 SCHEDULE 15B, PARTS 1 & 2

Common Law Offences	
Murder	
Manslaughter	
Offences against the Person Act 1861	
Section	Description
4	Soliciting murder
18	Wounding with intent to cause grievous bodily harm
Firearms Act 1968	
Section	Description
16	Possession of a firearm with intent to endanger life
17(1)	Using a firearm to resist arrest
18	Carrying a firearm with criminal intent

Theft Act 1968		
Section	Description	Conditions
8	Robbery	Where, at some time during the commission of the offence, the offender had in his possession a firearm or an imitation firearm
Protection of Children Act 1978		
Section	Description	
1	Indecent images of children	
Terrorism Act 2000		
Section	Description	Conditions
56	Directing terrorist organisation	
57	Possession of article for terrorist purposes	
59	Inciting terrorism overseas	If offender is liable on conviction for imprisonment for life
Anti-terrorism, Crime and Security Act 2001		
Section	Description	
47	Use of nuclear weapons	
50	Assisting or inducing certain weapons-related acts overseas	
113	Use of noxious substance or thing to cause harm or intimidate	
Sexual Offences Act 2003		
Section	Description	Conditions
1	Rape	
2	Assault by penetration	
4	Causing sexual activity without consent	If offender is liable on conviction on indictment to imprisonment for life
5	Rape of a child under 13	

6	Assault of a child under 13 by penetration	
7	Sexual assault of a child under 13	
8–12	Causing or inciting a child under 13 to engage in sexual activity, child sex offences committed by adults.	
14	Arranging or facilitating the commission of a child sex offence	
15	Meeting a child following sexual grooming etc	
25 or 26	Familial child sex offences	If the offender is aged 18 or over at the time of the offence
30 or 31	Sexual activity / causing sexual activity – person with mental disorder impeding choice	If offender is liable on conviction on indictment to imprisonment for life
34 or 35	Inducements / threats, etc person with mental disorder	If offender is liable on conviction on indictment to imprisonment for life
47	Paying for sexual services of a child	If the victim (or other party) was under 16
48	Causing or inciting child prostitution or pornography	
49	Controlling a child prostitute or a child involved in pornography	
50	Arranging or facilitating child prostitution or pornography	
62	Committing an offence with intent to commit a sexual offence	If offender is liable on conviction on indictment to imprisonment for life
Domestic Violence, Crime and Victims Act 2004		
Section	Description	
5	Causing or allowing the death of a child or vulnerable adult	

Terrorism Act 2006	
Section	Description
5	Preparation of terrorist acts
9	Making or possession of radioactive device or materials
10	Misuse of radioactive devices or material and misuse and damage of facilities
11	Terrorist threats relating to radioactive devices, materials or facilities
Inchoate offences	
Attempting, conspiring or incitement to commit an offence in this Schedule	
Aiding, abetting counselling or procuring the commission of an offence in this Schedule	
An offence under Part 2 of the Serious Crime Act 2007 in relation to which an offence in this Schedule is the offence (or one of the offences) which the person intended or believed would be committed	
Historic offences	
Any offence that was abolished before the coming into force of this Schedule and would, if committed on the day the offender was convicted of it, have constituted an offence specified in this Schedule	

Appendix 6

Schedules to the Sexual Offences Act 2003

SEXUAL OFFENCES ACT 2003, SCHEDULE 3

Sexual Offences Act 1956		
Section	Description	Conditions
1	Rape	
5	Intercourse with girl under 13	
6	Intercourse with girl under 16	If the offender was 20 or over
10	Incest by a man	If the victim (or other party) was under 18
12	Buggery	If the offender was 20 or over *and* the victim (or other party) was under 18.
13	Indecency between men	If the offender was 20 or over *and* the victim (or other party) was under 18.
14	Indecent assault on a woman	If: • the victim (or other party) was under 18 *or* • the offender, in respect of the offence or finding, is or has been: – sentenced to imprisonment for a term of at least 30 months *or* – admitted to a hospital subject to a restriction order.

Section	Description	Conditions
15	Indecent assault on a man	If: • the victim (or other party) was under 18 *or* • the offender, in respect of the offence or finding, is or has been: – sentenced to imprisonment for a term of at least 30 months *or* – admitted to a hospital subject to a restriction order.
16	Assault with intent to commit buggery	If the victim (or other party) was under 18.
28	Causing or encouraging the prostitution of, intercourse with, or indecent assault on girl under 16	
Indecency with Children Act 1960		
Section	Description	Conditions
1	Indecent conduct towards young child	
Criminal Law Act 1977		
Section	Description	Conditions
54	Inciting girl under 16 to have incestuous sexual intercourse	
Protection of Children Act 1978		
Section	Description	Conditions
1	Indecent photographs of children	If the indecent photographs or pseudo-photographs showed persons under 16 *and* • the conviction, finding or caution was before the commencement of this part or • the offender – was 18 or over or

Section	Description	Conditions
		– is sentenced in respect of the offence to imprisonment for a term of at least 12 months.
	Customs and Excise Management Act 1979	
Section	Description	Conditions
170	Penalty for fraudulent evasion of duty, etc in relation to goods prohibited to be imported under s 42 of the Customs Consolidation Act 1876 (indecent or obscene articles)	If the prohibited goods included indecent photographs of persons under 16 *and* • the conviction, finding or caution was before the commencement of this Part or • the offender – was 18 or over *or* – is sentenced in respect of the offence to imprisonment for a term of at least 12 months.
	Criminal Justice Act 1988	
Section	Description	Conditions
160	Possession of indecent photograph of a child	If the indecent photographs or pseudo-photographs showed persons under 16 *and* • the conviction, finding or caution was before the commencement of this part *or* • the offender – was 18 or over *or* – is sentenced in respect of the offence to imprisonment for a term of at least 12 months.

Sexual Offences (Amendment) Act 2000		
Section	Description	Conditions
3	Abuse of position of trust	
Sexual Offences Act 2003		
Section	Description	Conditions
1	Rape	
2	Assault by penetration	
3	Sexual assault	If: • Where the offender was under 18, he is or has been sentenced, in respect of the offence, to imprisonment for a term of at least 12 months • In any other case: – The victim was under 18 or – The offender, in respect of the offence or finding, is or has been • Sentenced to a term of imprisonment • Detained in a hospital or • Made the subject of a community sentence of at least 12 months.
4	Causing sexual activity without consent	
5	Rape of a child under 13	
6	Assault of a child under 13 by penetration	
7	Sexual assault of a child under 13	If: • The offender was 18 or over *or* • Is or has been sentenced in respect of the offence to imprisonment for a term of at least 12 months

Section	Description	Conditions
8–12	Causing or inciting a child under 13 to engage in sexual activity, child sex offences committed by adults.	
13	Child sex offences committed by children or young persons	If: • The offender is or has been sentenced in respect of the offence, to imprisonment for a term of at least 12 months
14	Arranging or facilitating the commission of a child sex offence	If the offender: • Was 18 or over *or* • Is or has been sentenced, in respect of that offence, to imprisonment for a term of at least 12 months.
15	Meeting a child following sexual grooming etc	
16–19	Abuse of a position of trust	If the offender, in respect of the offence, is or has been: • Sentenced to a term of imprisonment; • Detained in a hospital or • Made the subject of a community sentence of at least 12 months
25 or 26	Familial child sex offences	If the offender: • Was 18 or over; *or* • Is or has been sentenced in respect of the offence to imprisonment for a term of at least 12 months.
30–37	Offences against persons with a mental disorder impeding choice, inducements etc to persons with mental disorders	

Section	Description	Conditions
38–1	Care workers for persons with mental disorders	If: • Where the offender was under 18, he is or has been sentenced in respect o the offence to imprisonment for a term of at least 12 months • In any other case, the offender, in respect of the offence or finding, is or has been: – Sentenced to a term of imprisonment – Detained in a hospital or – Made the subject of a community sentence of at least 12 months.
47	Paying for sexual services of a child	If the victim (or other party) was under 16 and the offender • Was 18 or over or • Is or has been sentenced in respect of the offence to imprisonment for a term of at least 12 months.
48	Causing or inciting child prostitution or pornography	If the offender was 18 or over or is or has been sentenced in respect of the offence to imprisonment for a term of at least 12 months
49	Controlling a child prostitute or a child involved in pornography	If the offender was 18 or over or is or has been sentenced in respect of the offence to imprisonment for a term of at least 12 months
50	Arranging or facilitating child prostitution or pornography	If the offender was 18 or over or is or has been sentenced in respect of the offence to imprisonment for a term of at least 12 months
61	Administering substance with intent	

Section	Description	Conditions
62 or 63	Committing an offence or trespassing, with intent to commit a sexual offence	If: • Where the offender was under 18, he is or has been sentenced in respect of the offence to imprisonment for a term of at least 12 months; • In any other case: – The intended offence was an offence against a person under 18 or – The offender, in respect of the offence or finding, is or has been • Sentenced to a term of imprisonment • Detained in a hospital or • Made the subject of a community sentence of at least 12 months
64 or 65	Sex with an adult relative	If: • Where the offender was under 18, he is or has been sentenced in respect of the offence to imprisonment for a term of at least 12 months; • In any other case, the offender, in respect of the offence or finding, is or has been: – Sentenced to a term of imprisonment – Detained in a hospital

Section	Description	Conditions
66	Exposure	If: • Where the offender was under 18, he is or has been sentenced in respect of the offence to imprisonment for a term of at least 12 months; • In any other case: – The victim was under 18 or – The offender, in respect of the offence or finding, is or has been • Sentenced to a term of imprisonment • Detained in a hospital or • Made the subject of a community sentence of at least 12 months
67	Voyeurism	If: • Where the offender was under 18, he is or has been sentenced in respect of the offence to imprisonment for a term of at least 12 months; • In any other case: – The victim was under 18 or – The offender, in respect of the offence or finding, is or has been • Sentenced to a term of imprisonment • Detained in a hospital *or* • Made the subject of a community sentence of at least 12 months

Section	Description	Conditions
69 or 70	Intercourse with an animal, sexual penetration of a corpse	If: • Where the offender was under 18, he is or has been sentenced in respect of the offence to imprisonment for a term of at least 12 months; • In any other case, the offender, in respect of the offence or finding, is or has been: – Sentenced to a term of imprisonment *or* – Detained in a hospital
Criminal Justice and Immigration Act 2008		
Section	Description	Conditions
63	Possession of extreme pornographic images	If the offender was 18 or over *and* is sentenced in respect of the offence to imprisonment of a term of at least 2 years
Coroners and Justice Act 2009		
Section	Description	Conditions
62(1)	Possession of prohibited images of children	If the offender was 18 or over *and* is sentenced in respect of the offence to imprisonment of a term of at least 2 years
Inchoate offences		
Attempting, conspiring or incitement to commit an offence in this Schedule		
Aiding, abetting counselling or procuring the commission of an offence in this Schedule		

SEXUAL OFFENCES ACT 2003, SCHEDULE 5

Common Law Offences	
Murder	
Manslaughter	
Kidnapping	
False imprisonment	
Outraging public decency	
Offences against the Person Act 1861	
Section	Description
4	Soliciting murder
16	Threats to kill
18	Wounding with intent to cause grievous bodily harm
20	Malicious wounding
21	Attempting to choke, suffocate or strangle in order to commit or assist in committing an indictable offence
22	Using chloroform etc to commit or assist in the committing of any indictable offence
23	Maliciously administering poison etc so as to endanger life or inflict grievous bodily harm
27	Abandoning children
28	Causing bodily injury by explosives
29	Using explosives etc with intent to do grievous bodily harm
30	Placing explosives with intent to do bodily injury
31	Setting spring guns etc with intent to do grievous bodily harm
32	Endangering the safety of railway passengers
35	Injuring persons by furious driving
37	Assaulting officer preserving wreck
38	Assault with intent to resist arrest
47	Assault occasioning actual bodily harm

Explosive Substances Act 1883	
Section	Description
2	Causing explosion likely to endanger life or property
3	Attempt to cause explosion or making or keeping explosive with intent to endanger life or property
Infant Life (Preservation) Act 1929	
Section	Description
1	Child destruction
Children and Young Persons Act 1933	
Section	Description
1	Cruelty to children
Infanticide Act 1938	
Section	Description
1	Infanticide
Firearms Act 1968	
Section	Description
16	Possession of firearm with intent to endanger life
16A	Possession of firearm with intent to cause fear of violence
17(1)	Use of firearm to resist arrest
17(2)	Possession of firearm at time of committing or being arrested for an offence
18	Carrying a firearm with criminal intent
Theft Act 1968	
Section	Description
1	Theft
8	Robbery or assault with intent to rob
9(1)(a)	Burglary with intent to steal, inflict grievous bodily harm or do unlawful damage
10	Aggravated burglary
12A	Aggravated vehicle-taking involving an accident which caused the death of any person

Criminal Damage Act 1971	
Section	Description
1	Arson
1(2)	Destroying or damaging property (other than an offence of arson)
Taking of Hostages Act 1982	
Section	Description
1	Hostage-taking
Aviation Security Act 1982	
Section	Description
1	Hijacking
2	Destroying, damaging or endangering safety of aircraft
3	Other acts endangering or likely to endanger safety of aircraft
4	Offences in relation to certain dangerous articles
Mental Health Act 1983	
Section	Description
127	Ill-treatment of patients
Child Abduction Act 1984	
Section	Description
1	Offence of abduction of child by parent, etc
2	Offence of abduction of child by other persons
Prohibition of Female Circumcision Act 1985	
Section	Description
1	Prohibition of female circumcision
Public Order Act 1986	
Section	Description
1	Riot
2	Violent disorder
3	Affray
Criminal Justice Act 1988	
Section	Description
134	Torture

Road Traffic Act 1988	
Section	Description
1	Causing death by dangerous driving
3A	Causing death by careless driving when under influence of drinks or drugs
Aviation and Maritime Security Act 1990	
Section	Description
1	Endangering safety at aerodromes
9	Hijacking of ships
10	Seizing or exercising control of fixed platforms
11	Destroying fixed platforms or endangering their safety
12	Other acts endangering or likely to endanger safe navigation
13	Offences involving threats
Protection from Harassment Act 1997	
Section	Description
2 or 2A	Offences of harassment and stalking
4 or 4A	Putting people in fear of violence and stalking involving fear of violence or serious alarm or distress
Crime and Disorder Act 1998	
Section	Description
29	Racially or religiously aggravated assaults
31(a) or (b)	Racially or religiously aggravated offences under section 4 or 4A of the Public Order Act 1986
Channel Tunnel (Security) Order 1994	
Section	Description
Part II	Offences relating to Channel Tunnel trains and the tunnel system
Regulation of Investigatory Powers Act 2000	
Section	Description
53 or 54	Contravention of notice relating to encrypted information or tipping off in connection with such a notice

Postal Services Act 2000	
Section	Description
85(3) or (4)	Prohibition on sending certain articles by post
International Criminal Court Act 2001	
Section	Description
51 or 52	Genocide, crimes against humanity, war crimes and related offences other than one involving murder
Communications Act 2003	
Section	Description
127(1)	Improper use of public electronic communications network
Sexual Offences Act 2003	
Section	Description
47	An offence under s 47 of this Act where the victim or other party was 16 or over
51–53	Causing, inciting or controlling prostitution for gain
57–59A	Trafficking for sexual exploitation
Domestic Violence, Crime and Victims Act 2004	
Section	Description
5	Causing or allowing a child or vulnerable adult to die or suffer serious physical harm
Inchoate offences	
Attempting, conspiring or incitement to commit an offence in this Schedule	
Aiding, abetting counselling or procuring the commission of an offence in this Schedule	

Index

[All references are to paragraph number]

www.ingramcontent.com/pod-product-compliance
Ingram Content Group UK Ltd.
Pitfield, Milton Keynes, MK11 3LW, UK
UKHW021058160926
475561UK00008B/126

9 781780 43327